HUMAN RESOURCE MANAGEMENT IN RUSSIA

Contemporary Employment Relations

Series Editor: Gregor Gall

Professor of Industrial Relations and Director of the Centre for Research in Employment Studies, University of Hertfordshire, Hatfield, UK

The aim of this series is to publish monographs and edited volumes on all aspects of contemporary employment relations including human resource management, employee branding, shared services, employment regulation, the political economy of employment, and industrial relations. Topics such as mergers, corporate governance and the EU – in the context of their effect upon employment relations – also fall within the scope of the series. Aimed primarily at an academic readership this series provides a global forum for the study of employment relations.

Human Resource Management in Russia

Edited by
MICHEL E. DOMSCH AND TATJANA LIDOKHOVER
Helmut-Schmidt-University, Germany

Routledge
Taylor & Francis Group
LONDON AND NEW YORK

First published 2007 by Ashgate Publishing

Reissued 2018 by Routledge
2 Park Square, Milton Park, Abingdon, Oxon OX14 4RN
711 Third Avenue, New York, NY 10017, USA

Routledge is an imprint of the Taylor & Francis Group, an informa business

A Library of Congress record exists under LC control number: 2006031454

ISBN 13: 978-0-8153-8955-2 (hbk)
ISBN 13: 978-1-3511-5624-0 (ebk)

Contents

List of Figures

List of Tables

Preface

The present book is an investigation into Human Resource Management issues in Russia. With this publication we aim to take a look at the current state of Human Resource practices within Russian enterprises, highlighting various problems and discussing possible solutions. This is the first book to bring together international experts who have been conducting research into HRM in Russia for many years. It is also the first book in which at least one third of the contributions have been written by Russian HR experts. It is often the case that foreign experts are called on to evaluate developments taking place in Russia, resulting in a one-sided analysis of the situation. It is our aim to redress this imbalance by also presenting an insider's point of view. The book contains contributions by authors from the following countries: Russia, USA, Canada, Germany, Denmark, Finland, Sweden and the UK. The basic principle behind the book is to support and illustrate theoretical arguments and positions with practical case studies. This is the first book to be totally dedicated to the topic of HRM in Russia.

It is an HRM book primarily directed at postgraduates, researchers, and academics. The book is targeted at all those working in the fields of Human Resource Management and International Management and is concerned with the latest developments in Eastern Europe. Since the subject area of the book has not been widely researched yet, we hope our publication will inspire others to conduct further research.

In addition to this core readership, however, the book will also be of interest and use to HR practitioners such as HR managers, HR professionals, HR consultants etc. For this reason, we decided to adopt a double-barrelled approach: the more academic and theoretical chapters provide summaries of the current state of affairs in a particular field which are then fleshed out by case studies, practical examples, and the authors' own data analyses.

We published the book in English hoping to give it an international appeal. Firstly, the transition to a market-orientated economy since the beginning of the nineties has made Russia very interesting for all manner of research. Researchers from all around the world have taken an active interest in new management practices currently being implemented in Russia. Secondly, due to its vast mineral wealth and low labour costs, Russia has become very attractive for direct investors, and we hope that this publication might therefore be of interest to CEOs and consultants who are considering opening businesses in the Russian Federation.

We would like to express our gratitude to all the contributors and thank them for their readiness to work with us on this project. We also would like to thank the Palgrave Macmillan publishing house who granted us permission to reprint the article by Carl Fey and Ingmar Björkman.

We are very grateful to Ashgate Publishing for their technical support and patience. This book would not have seen the light of day without some more expert help: our special thanks go to Georg Felix Harsch, Jessica Spengler and Alexander Mirimov for very competent language assistance (editing, proofreading, translating). We are also grateful to our colleagues Natalja Press, André Roosen and Rebekka Hensen for their careful preparation of the typescript.

Opinions expressed in the individual contributions do not necessarily reflect those of the editorial board. Rather, the editors were hoping to demonstrate the plurality of voices on the issues discussed in this volume.

Michel E. Domsch and Tatjana Lidokhover
Hamburg, 2007

Introduction

The Broader Historical, Social and Economic Context of the Current Situation in Russia

Michel E. Domsch, Tatjana Lidokhover

Russia – A Riddle Wrapped in a Mystery inside an Enigma?

Winston Churchill once described the Soviet Union as 'a riddle wrapped in a mystery inside an enigma'. But will Russia be better understood now that the Soviet Union has ceased to exist and the infamous iron curtain has come down? Was it only that curtain that was blocking our view of that vast country, or does Russia have a completely unique character that makes it function differently even now that it is developing a Western-inspired market economy? Over the last decade and a half, Western scholarship amply explored the phenomenon that is Russia, and a wealth of scholarly literature on the political, social and economic situation in the country has been published. But it seems that most of this research only went to prove that Churchill's description is as valid today as it was when he first uttered it.

Purpose of the Book

Russia has undergone massive changes over the past 15 years, the most important one being the transition from a socialist centralized planned economy to a capitalist market economy.

The arrival of the market economy in Russia was sudden, and it brought huge challenges for the entire country (Kondrachuk 2004). And just as the new word 'менеджер' [manager] took up its place in the Russian lexicon during the transition period, the newly-arrived managers themselves got ready to tackle the enormous tasks they were faced with.

Over the last 15 years, they have had to take the thorny path of learning by doing, starting with management models based on gut feeling through concepts copied from the West and eventually developing models specifically geared towards the needs of the Russian economy.

It has been noted that by the mid-1990s, '… Russia's version of a market economy was [already] clearly taking shape' (Puffer 1996), and now, in the year 2006, we would like to take another look at the relatively consolidated state of the 'Russian version of the market economy'. But since a discussion of such a broad subject would inevitably require much more space, time and effort than one collection of essays could possibly offer, this publication will limit itself to discussing one particular aspect of the Russian economy: the Russian version of Human Resource Management in the market economy. This work is an attempt to bring together the main HR Management issues and discuss them in the Russian context.

Most of the research presented in this volume is empirical, and in order to set the scene for the individual contributions and introduce the theoretical background of this publication, this introductory chapter will first describe the historical, geographic, political, social and economic background of Russia and, in a second step, will then focus on HR-related issues and review existing literature. The final part of this introduction will illustrate the aims of this volume and briefly introduce the individual contributions.

The Roots of the Differences: Historical, Political and Social Background

History

The first state that ever existed on the territory occupied by today's Russian Federation was founded in the late ninth century and was called Kiev Rus. During that time, the country's population was converted to the Greek Orthodox doctrine and Christianity was made the state religion. From the early thirteenth century until 1480, Russia was subjected to almost 300 years of Mongolian rule, a very formative period for the following centuries of Russian history. During the rule of the Tartars, the industrial and cultural progress in the country was brought to a standstill and Russia was isolated from the rest of Europe for more than two centuries, while the Tartar traditions, laws and forms of government became the main influence. During that time, the seat of power was transferred from St Petersburg to Moscow, which became the centre of Moscovia, the new Russian state. In 1613 Mikhail Romanov founded the Romanov dynasty which was to rule the country as the Tsars of Russia for the following 300 years and stretch its borders across Siberia to the Pacific coast. Under Peter the Great (1689–1725) hegemony was extended to the Baltic Sea and the country was renamed the Russian Empire. Thus, Peter the Great had made Russia a major Northern European power.

During the nineteenth century, more territorial acquisitions were made in Europe and Asia. By defeating the Napoleonic armies between 1812 and 1814, Russia finally established itself as one of the Great Powers of Europe. The war against Napoleon was also very significant for Russia's home affairs: the so-called foreign campaign, which culminated in the Russian army taking Paris in March 1814, exposed large numbers of Russians to Western Europe, its culture and society, an experience which had a massive impact on the desire for reform in liberal circles. The Decabrists' Revolt of December 1825 represented a failed attempt to transfer Russia into a constitutional monarchy and to introduce the necessary reforms. This was also the starting point for the emergence of the two competing factions in Russian politics, whose controversies have shaped the way the country is run ever since: the Western-oriented reformers (who later came to be called 'Westerners') and the conservatives, who emphasized traditional Russian values (and who were later called 'Slavophiles'). Eventually, it was Tsar Alexander II (1855–81) who introduced a number of important reforms such as the abolishment of serfdom in 1861 – a measure that had been long overdue (The World Factbook 2006; Federal Research Division 2006).

After a short period of parliamentarianism and capitalism in Russia in the early twentieth century, the country was shaken by the Bolshevik (communist) Revolution of October 1917, which was to completely change the course of Russian history. The Communists outlawed private property, created a centrally-planned economy and a nationwide vertical chain of command, with the politburo at the top.

The era of the Soviet Union brought significant achievements in science, education and culture. However, the state of the economy during this period became more and more dramatic because the political system was blocking any form of free development. Changes were urgently needed. In the mid-1980s, the Soviet Union under Mikhail Gorbachev finally adopted a new course of opening itself [glasnost] and of renewal [perestroika]. The reformers were urging the government to quickly implement changes in the economic system, and thus the decline of the Communist Party and the Soviet Union began. In 1991, Boris Yeltsin became the first elected president of Russia. After an attempted coup by forces opposed to the reform process in August 1991, the Communist Party was outlawed and shortly afterwards, the Soviet Union was officially dissolved. Since then, Russia's governmental, political, economical and social structures have been undergoing a fundamental transformation process.

Geography and Environment

With its surface area of 17,075,200 square kilometres, Russia is the world's largest country. It stretches from the Norwegian border to the Pacific Ocean and from the Black Sea to the Arctic Ocean, and it lies on two continents, Europe and Asia, divided by the Ural mountains. Russia's territory includes eleven time zones with Moscow three hours ahead of Greenwich Mean Time (The World Factbook 2006; Federal Research Division 2006).

The climate in Russia ranges from the subtropical climate of the Black Sea coast to Arctic continental conditions in Northern Siberia. The largest part of the country is covered with snow for six months of the year, and general weather conditions are harsh and unpredictable. In the European part of Russia, the average temperature for the year lies at 0° C and is even lower in Siberia. Because of these harsh climatic conditions, less than 10 per cent of the country's surface provides arable land. In most cases, temperature changes are too sharp or the climate is too dry for farming. 48 per cent of Russia's surface is covered by forests and around 10 per cent is swampland (The World Factbook 2006; Federal Research Division 2006).

The land holds vast mineral and fossil resources, but mostly these are located in very remote parts of the country, and many of the deposits of fossil fuel in the European part have already been exhausted. Russia currently owns 9 per cent of the world's oil resources and around one third of the gas reserves, which makes it an important exporter of fuel (BFAI 2006). Russia's land also holds rich reserves of precious metals, diamonds and phosphorous minerals, resources of great importance for international manufacturing industries. This extraordinary wealth of resources, especially with regard to the export potential it provides, is an important, if not the most important economical trump contemporary Russia has got up its sleeve. But it also has its downsides: for years, the extractive industry, which promises quick profits, has been given preferential treatment over other branches, and the country thus failed to implement important structural reforms.

In the Soviet Union the manufacturing industry was systematically expanded without hardly any considerations of the environmental consequences. This has led to a very poor quality of drinking water in the industrial centres and a very high level of air pollution in most cities, conditions also caused by the mostly out-of-date vehicles used in Russia and the poor quality of the fuel. According to estimates (Amnesty International 2006), up to 60 per cent of Russia's air, water and land have to be considered highly polluted. Another great danger is posed by the uncontrolled disposal and storage of radioactive nuclear waste. The fact that between four and five per cent of all diseases in Russia are probably caused by pollution (Amnesty International 2006) further proves how devastating the damages are that the country's environment has had to suffer.

Population

Russia's total population is estimated at 143.4 million people, 63 per cent of whom live in the country's major cities. Eleven of these major cities have more than a million inhabitants (Rosstat 2005) and most of them lie in the European part of the country.

According to the latest figures, the demographic situation in Russia is alarming. In its annual report for 2004, the Russian Federal State Statistics Service (Rosstat) put the country's birth rate at 10.4 births per 1000 inhabitants and the death rate at 16.0 deaths per 1000 inhabitants. These figures resulted in a decline in the population of 796,000 for the year 2004. The average number of births per woman currently lies at 1.3, and the life expectancy of an average man is estimated at a disastrous 58.9 years. The reasons for these early deaths are the high level of alcoholism among men, the devastating pollution and the collapse of the state-funded public health system in the early 1990s. On average, Russian women live 13.5 years longer than their male compatriots (their average life expectancy is currently put at 72.3 years). Only in recent years has this alarming state of affairs become a subject of public debate and serious consideration on the part of the government. The government still maintains that Russia is not an immigration country, but admits that controlled immigration (especially the 're-integration' of ethnic Russians from the former Soviet republics) might be part of the solution to these problems. Also, new family policies have been introduced with the aim of increasing the birth rate throughout the country.

More than 100 different ethnic groups make up Russia's population. Around 20 per cent of the total population belong to non-Russian ethnic groups. Of this number, around 3.8 per cent are Tatars, 2 per cent Ukrainians, 1.2 per cent Bashkirs, 1.1 per cent Chuvashs and another 12.1 per cent belong to unspecified groups (2002 census, Rosstat 2005).

The official state religion in Russia is Orthodox Christianity as practiced by the Russian Orthodox Church. Around 75 million Russians are professed adherents of the Orthodox faith and around 20 million Russians are Muslims.

Educational System

One of the achievements of the Soviet System was without any doubt the high level of education it provided for its people. According to the 2002 census, 99.5 per cent of the population above age ten was literate (Rosstat 2005).

However, the country's budget for school and university education suffered dramatic cuts with the collapse of the Soviet Union. The teaching profession was hit especially hard: teachers received very little pay and the country's educational institutions severely lacked good textbooks, computers and laboratory equipment.

In the early 1990s, when the state gave up its monopoly on education, many private educational institutions were founded, but initially not all of these institutions reached the high educational levels of the Soviet era: the licences for setting up a private school or university were up for sale, there were no admission exams and the institutions sometimes charged astronomically high tuition fees.

Much of the very positive legacy of the Soviet system in the field of education was lost during the transitional period, but many new lessons were also learned. Teaching staff both in schools and in universities began to reject the traditional 'chalk and talk' approach in favour of methods that supported the involvement of students in the learning process and the development of critical thinking through more discussions and working in teams (Elkof, Holmes and Kaplan 2005). Currently, the Russian educational system is slowly recovering from the crisis it experienced in the 1990s. Broad reform measures supported by massive investment in the educational sector are being planned with the aim of bringing Russia back to the level of the other leading nations in the world and maybe even re-installing the traditional Russian leadership in certain areas of science and knowledge. According to the government, this is the only way to ensure that Russia will be able to compete permanently on a global scale. 'Education' is also the name of one of the four 'National Projects' recently initiated by Putin's government.

Policy

Structure Russia's constitution from the year 1993 distinguishes between three powers, the executive, the legislative and the judicial power, but does not invest them with equal authority. This system invests the President of the Russian Federation with a disproportionately large number of powers: he is the chairman of the Security Council and Commander-in-Chief of the army; he also has the authority to dissolve parliament at any time and call new elections. The Russian Parliament consists of two houses: the lower house (the Duma) and the upper house (the Federation Council). The President appoints the prime minister, the head of the Central Bank of Russia and the chairman of the highest judicial body, the Constitutional Court. The Duma has to ratify these nominations, but if the Duma puts in a veto against a candidate, the President has the right to dissolve the Duma (The World Factbook 2006). A variety of other top-level presidential nominations, however, require no approval from the legislative branch. Thus, the parliament's possibilities to act as an oppositional body are severely limited in light of the President's powers.

Recent Developments For some time now there has been a very serious debate, both in the West and in Russian reform circles, about the new vertical structure of power introduced by Putin. Vladimir Putin was appointed Prime Minister by Yeltsin in 1999, then became the country's acting president, was democratically elected in 2000 and re-elected in 2004. Since his ascend to power, he has been continuously trying to strengthen and secure his position by exerting more and more control over the parliament. In addition, the plurality of political parties, which had its heyday during the Yeltsin presidency (1991–2000) significantly lost its influence on Russian politics within a short time of Putin taking up office (Kuchins 2006). The United Russia Party [Partia Edinaya Rossia], founded in 2001, powerfully supports Putin and managed to gain the majority of all votes in the 2003 general elections, thus even further enhancing Putin's position.

'Putin has consistently and systematically eliminated competition among independent contending political forces and centralized … more and more political authority in the office of the Presidential Administration' (Kuchins 2006). Political scientists have often described the political model Putin has been fostering as a form of 'state-controlled democracy', an accusation to which Putin himself usually reacts by pointing to the different cultures and traditions in different countries which breed different concepts and models of democracy: 'We cannot simply copy everything. That would be counterproductive' (*The Times* 2006). According to Putin, highly centralized political authority is 'part of Russia's DNA' and most appropriate for Russia's current stage of social, economic and political development. Everything else would, in the opinion of Putin and his aides, lead to anarchy or even to the total collapse of the country (Kuchins 2006).

Two examples from recent times, which might serve to illustrate these tendencies, are the case of the Yukos group, which culminated in the de-facto nationalization of Russia's most profitable oil company and the imprisonment of its owner Mikhail Khodorkovsky, and the abolishment of direct elections for the offices of the Governors and Mayors in favour of a system of Presidential appointment similar to the process of appointment for the office of the Prime Minister.

The next Presidential elections will be held in March 2008, and already speculation is rife about whether Putin will try to run for a third term. If he did, this would raise serious legal questions, because the constitution does not allow a presidency to run for more than two terms. But, as history has shown, the laws can be changed and adapted very quickly if the need arises.

Economic Background

Economic Policies

The Kremlin's political course as described above also indicates which role is to be ascribed to the state in economic affairs in Russia. The Russian government's main emphasis in economic policy currently lies on measures to control the energy sector, the most important sector of the Russian economy in general (see next section). This raises the question of how much of a market economy the state is willing to allow in this sector. If the state's latest acquisitions are anything to go by, its influence in the oil and gas industry will be rapidly increasing in the foreseeable future. The tendency for this sector is obviously one of massive re-nationalizations. In late 2005, almost a third of the Russian oil business (Gasprom, Sibneft and Rosneft, plus the Tatneft and Bashneft groups, which are under the administration of the authorities of the Tatarstan and Bashkiria republics) as well as practically the entire gas business (Gasprom) were under state control (BFAI 2006; F.A.Z. Institut 2005).

But despite the fact that all members of the Russian government can easily agree on the 'strategic importance' of the energy sector, differences in opinion on energy policy between different factions within the government have begun to emerge. The group of the so-called 'siloviki' [literally 'the forceful' or 'the ones who believe in the use of force'], government members who mostly came from the old secret service and strongly support state intervention in economic affairs are on one end of the spectrum, while the so-called 'liberals' favour a more market-oriented approach. Both groups adhere to very different concepts and have very different goals. Recent events have shown, however, that the camp of the *siloviki* is rapidly gaining ground. The Yukos affair, which was already mentioned above, might be the most convincing proof for this tendency. In late 2005, Andrei Illarionov, Putin's chief economical advisor, resigned from his position in protest against the current tendencies in Russian economic policy, describing them as 'nashizm' ['those who are not with us are against us'] and vehemently criticizing the prevalent nepotism and the insidious nationalization of entire industrial branches.

All these governmental actions have shaken businesses' and investors' confidence and have significantly weakened the investment climate (*The Banker* 2005; F.A.Z. Institut 2005; Atradius 2005). In order to regain some trust among the business community, the government in 2005 announced a number of concrete reform measures such as a tax amnesty, shortening the statutory period of limitation for tax evasion and other white collar crimes committed during the period of privatization from ten to three years, the introduction of transparent limitations for foreign investors and further tax concessions for Russian enterprises (F.A.Z. Institut 2005).

Russia also hopes to gain more trust internationally by joining the WTO. The accession negotiations are currently being conducted at full speed but are hampered by contentious issues such as the price of gas inside Russia, the role of the state in economic affairs, Russia's farming subsidies and the country's non-compliance with international copyright regulations (F.A.Z. Institut 2005).

Composition of the GDP

In the 1990s the relative importance of the economic sectors changed significantly. Between 1991 and 2004, industrial production, which used to account for 50 per cent of the GDP, fell to a share of merely 29.2 per cent, and the share of agricultural production decreased from 14 per cent to 6.3 per cent. At the same time, the share of the service sector in the GDP grew from 36 per cent to 58.5 per cent (Rosstat 2005).

According to the latest figures from Rosstat (the Russian Statistical Authority), which since 2005 are being presented using a new detailed classification system, the Russian GDP is made up as follows (Figure I.1):

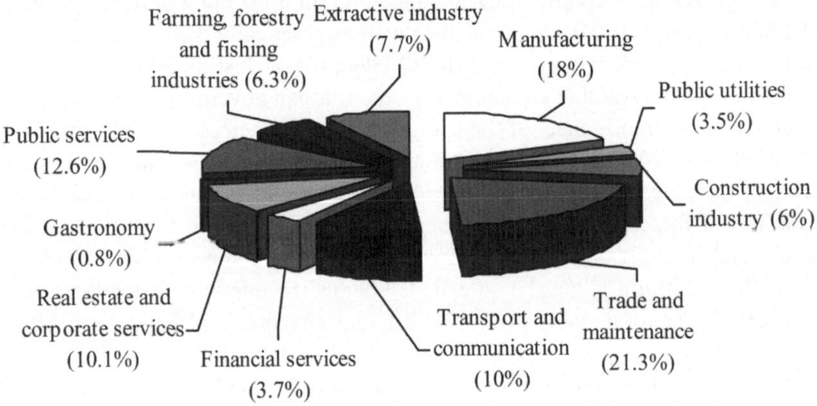

Figure I.1 Composition of the GDP (shares of the individual sectors in the GDP according to factors costs in % for the year 2004)

Source: Rosstat 2005

According to World Bank estimates, however, the figures given in these official statistics for the extractive industry (2004: 7.7 per cent) are probably too low, and the figures for trade (2004: 21.3 per cent) are probably too high. The reason for this is that Russian fuel companies often internally transfer added value generated by their extractive activities to their trade accounts in order to evade taxes. The World

Bank estimates the share of the extractive industry and the fuel business in the GDP to be actually closer to 25 per cent (World Bank 2006).

Economic Growth

The high oil price is the most important factor driving the current realities in Russia. Russia's economy achieved an average of 6.8 per cent growth between 1999 and 2004 thanks largely to rising oil prices. Compared to the leading industrial nations, Russia was still miles ahead when it came to economic growth in 2005 (Figure I.2).

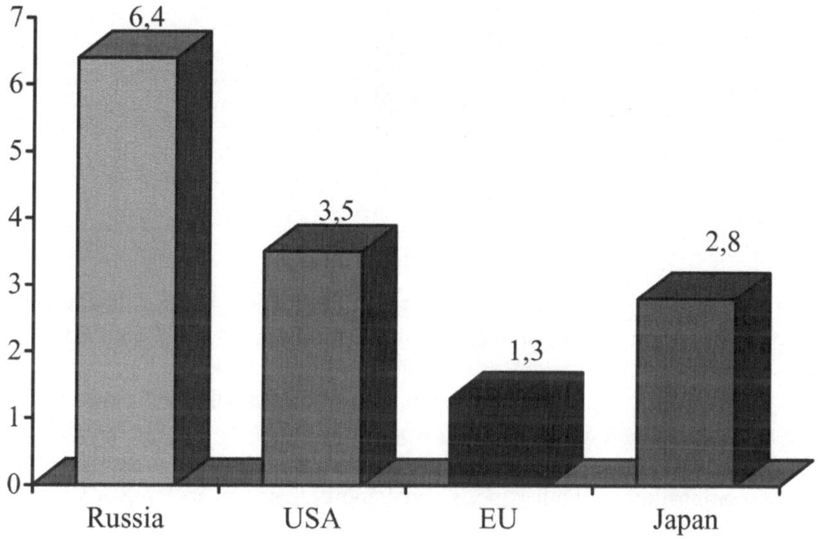

Figure I.2 Comparison of economic growth for 2005 (%)
Source: Ministry of Economic Development and Trade 2006

In 2005, the high oil prices will probably bring Russia a record surplus of 11.9 per cent of the GDP in their balance of current transactions, a huge budget surplus of 6 per cent of the GDP, hard currency reserves of 160 billion US$ and external sovereign debt of only 14.1 per cent of the GDP (Source: F.A.Z.-Institut).

GDP Growth Despite the rising oil prices, Russia's economic development lost some of its previous momentum in 2005 (see Figure I.3).

In 2005, industrial production grew by only 4.0 per cent, with the manufacturing industry being the main contributor to growth. The slight curb in growth that was noticeable from autumn 2004 affected all branches of industry with the exception of the service sector. Consumption rose not least due to the noticeable increase in income the Russian consumers experienced (see the section on the labour market).

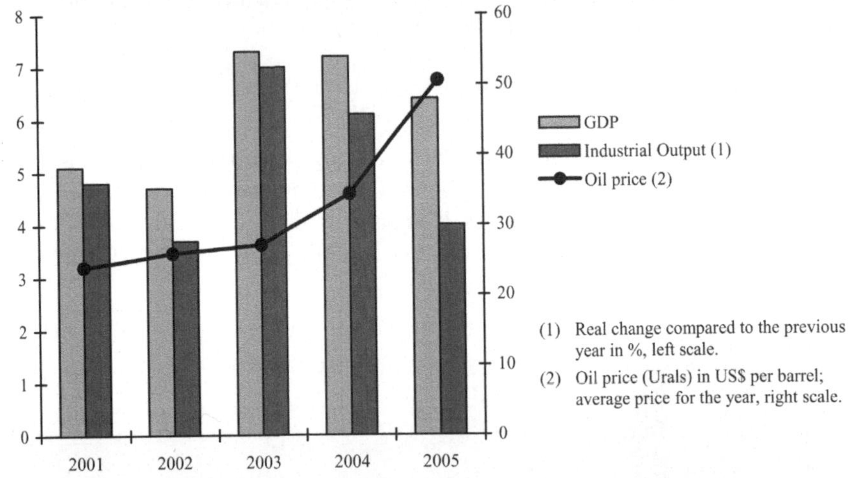

Figure I.3 GDP growth, oil prices
Source: Ministry of Economic Development and Trade 2006

Export/Import For a while now, external contribution has been slowing the economic development in Russia. This is caused in part by a slackened pace in export growth – especially concerning oil and gas (that make up 73 per cent of all exports), but also by the strong demand for imports. During the first quarter of 2005, exports increased only by 6.8 per cent, while imports rose by 15.2 per cent (Source: MEDT 2005).

The composition of both exports and imports is shown in Figures I.4 and I.5 respectively.

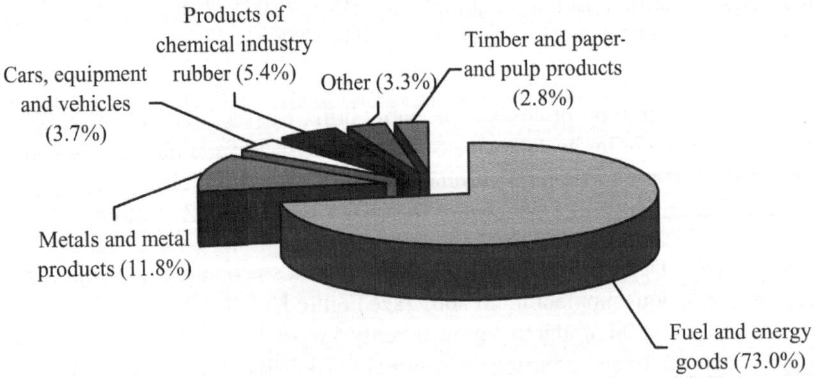

Figure I.4 Commodity structure of Russian exports in January 2006
Source: Ministry of Economic Development and Trade 2006

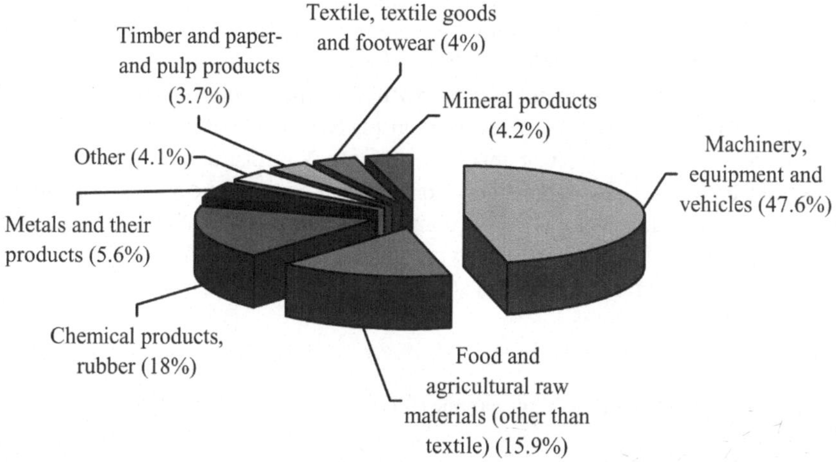

Figure I.5 Commodity structure of Russian imports in January 2006
Source: Ministry of Economic Development and Trade 2006

Prognoses and Scenarios

'Growth is strong thanks to the high oil prices but the question is: what will happen when the prices go down?' This is a question that many analysts are currently asking themselves (*The Banker* 2005). For its part, the Ministry of Economic Development and Trade of the Russian Federation (MEDT of Russia) is trying to be pragmatic, offering possible scenarios for the 2006 to 2009 period[1]:

- *The crisis scenario* (0) describes the economic situation in Russia in the case of a sharp drop in oil prices to US $27 per barrel, which is exactly the amount the oil industry needs to break even, before funds from the Stabilization Fund have to be touched. (For more information on the Stabilization Fund see next section).
- *The basic scenario* (1) reflects the current tendency of slightly weakened growth. Two versions of the basic scenario are possible, assuming that
  a. the oil price becomes stable at US $46 p/b or that
  b. the oil price falls to US $34 p/b
- *The carefully optimistic scenario* (2) works on the assumption of an increase in economic growth caused by the speedy and lasting implementation of certain 'government measures to stimulate economic growth'. This scenario, too, comes in two versions:
  c. The oil price rises and reaches US $60 p/b by the year 2009, or
  d. the oil price, like in scenario 1a, stabilizes at US $46 by the year 2009.

1 These development scenarios for the years 2005 to 2009 can be read in full on the website of the MEDT of Russia (in Russian).

According to the MEDT, the ministry is currently using scenario no. 2 for its financial planning for the years 2007 to 2009. So far, the document 'Government Measures to Stimulate Economic Growth' is only available in Russian. It mainly focuses on measures to attract investment from both Russian and foreign companies and on increasing state investment (see next section for National Projects, Investment and Stabilization Fund) in improvements to the country's infrastructure, modernization of its industry and the development of economic innovation. The central message of the document is that a change 'from a consumer-oriented form of economic growth to an investment-oriented form of growth' must be achieved (compare MEDT).

The following figures for growth according to the different scenarios could thus be predicted:

Table I.1 MEDT growth scenarios 2009

	Crisis scenario	Basic scenario		Carefully optimistic scenario	
	(0)	(1)a	(1)b	(2)a	(2)b
Oil price (Urals), US$ p/b	27	34	46	46	60
GDP % change	**4.2**	**4.8**	**5.0**	**6.0**	**6.3**
Industrial output % change	3.7	3.1	3.3	4.9	4.9
Direct investment in billion US$	–	28	30	39	41
Income growth	5.7	7.0	7.3	7.9	9.1
Inflation in %	–	4–5	4–5	4–5	4–5

Source: Ministry of Economic Development and Trade 2006

Many economical analysts, however, are sceptical about the ambitious plans of the Russian government and the MEDT and are worried that government will have to spend even larger amounts to maintain what they see as low-quality growth (*The Banker* 2005).

The Labour Market

According to Rosstat estimates, the number of the economically active population at the end of February 2006 was 73.9 million persons, or 51 per cent of the population of the country. The bulk of the employed population is concentrated in major and medium-sized business and organizations. The number of the unemployed in February 2006, estimated using the ILO method, reached 5.7 million persons or 7.7 per cent of the workforce. In February 2006 compared to February 2005, the number of the unemployed fell by 329,000 or 5.7 per cent (Source: MEDT).

The substantial upward trend of the Russian economy has obviously also had an effect on the Russian labour market. Especially the rapidly expanding service sector with is high labour requirements offers new chances of employment. The number of available jobs and the demand for labour rose by 9.7 per cent between February 2005 and February 2006, when available jobs numbered 812,000. The demand for qualified labour currently far exceeds the number of available candidates, especially in the urban areas and in the growing branches of industry. This lack of qualified candidates for available positions is one of the major factors behind the current dynamic development of paid wages and salaries. According to recently published figures, the average salary in February 2006 lay at RUR 9106 (EUR 280) and was thus 21.2 per cent higher than in the same month of the preceding year (Source: MEDT). Considering the current inflating rate, this meant an increase in income of 9 per cent for Russian employees.

Highly-qualified staff are paid considerably higher salaries in the urban centres of the country, especially in Moscow. A chief accountant, for example, might expect to earn as much as EUR 1800 a month in Moscow, and a secretary might expect to paid around EUR 800[2] (Source: FAZ-Institut).

Recent Debates

The picture we are trying to present here would not be complete without mentioning the three central projects that have been the supporting pillars of the government's new economic programme. These projects were made possible thanks to the enormous profits from the oil and gas trade.

1. The Stabilization Fund
2. The National Projects
3. The Investment Fund.

The Stabilization Fund The Stabilization Fund, set up in 2003, is supposed to protect Russia against a possible sharp drop in oil prices. The basic principle of this instrument is that all profits generated by the state through the sale of oil at a price exceeding $20 p/b ($27 p/b from 2006) are automatically put into the Fund. The legally required minimum amount in the Fund is 500 billion rubles (around EUR 15 billion), but in late 2005, the Fund already held as much as 1,500 billion rubles (around EUR 50 billion) – more than three times the minimum amount. Apart from protecting the state against a drop in oil prices, the Fund is also intended to have stabilizing effects and thus can be used in two more areas of the Russian economy: for repaying state debt and for covering the deficit in the state's pension fund (compare MEDT).

With the help of the Stabilization Fund, the Russian government did actually succeed in reaching a comparatively healthy ratio between the state's debts and the GDP. Foreign debt was successfully reduced to a minimum. The establishment of

2 More on the recent tendencies on the Russian labour market can be found in chapter eight of this book.

the Fund, of course, also led to a lively debate about how to spend the moneys in the Fund (or how not to spend them).

The Problems Year after year, Russia's state spending has been increasing, and money is urgently needed in many fields – be it for the newly set up Investment Fund (see below), the National Projects (see below), the regular allowances for the regions or for state commissions – but the state does not have access to the required sums. State-owned firms have been taking out huge loans abroad, while 50 billion euros have been deposited and thus made 'inactive' in the Stabilization Fund. The critics consider this a mistake, while the funds' supporters, among them the Minister for Economic Affairs Alexei Kudrin, see it as the only reasonable course of action. On a recent visit to Washington, Kudrin mentioned in an interview that Russia's economic growth was noticeably less affected these days by fluctuations in oil prices – thanks, in part, to the Stabilization Fund (Source: RIA 'Novosti').

The 'National Projects' On the official website of the Presidential Council for the Realization of National Projects the following statement can be found: 'It is time for the Russian population to finally profit from the economical success of recent years and the macro-economical stability that has been achieved, and thus for the economic growth to finally take a palpable shape.' Four broadly-based so-called 'National Projects' have been drawn up to help the government reach this goal. They have been named 'Education', 'Health', 'Housing' and 'Farming'.

Direct investment by the state into these projects will amount to at least 116 billion rubles (EUR 3.5 billion) in 2006, and is expected to rise to RUR 170 billion (EUR 5 billion) in 2007 (Source: official website of the Presidential Council for the Realization of National Projects). Despite the fact that these are long-term projects, Putin promised that Russia will have achieved breakthroughs in all four areas by late 2007, which means within his current term in office.

The Investment Fund The state-owned Investment Fund, financed by money from the Stabilization Fund, was set up in 2005 in order to support the state in large-scale infrastructural and innovation projects. In 2006 it had a volume of RUR 69.7 billion (around EUR 2 billion), which will be increased to RUR 76 billion (EUR 2.2 billion) by 2007 (Source: RIA 'Novosti'). The fund is mainly intended to financially support large-scale investment projects which include private financial interests, such as the long-planned and long overdue motorway connecting Moscow and St Petersburg.

Doing Business in Russia

The facts we have presented here in this broad introduction to the historical, social and political conditions and the current economic developments in Russia allow the conclusion that the country currently offers enormous possibilities for doing business. But, as has also been shown above, the situation also implies enormous challenges.

The economic and political situation in the country, despite some tendencies towards stability, is still far from stable.

But businesses must also face internal challenges (Fey 1999). All areas of business management, from financing through distribution to human resource management had to be newly defined according to market economy criteria during the transitional period. In the first years of the transitional period, businesses were gaining experience in effective production methods, financing and investment and then started to think about marketing in order to be able to effectively distribute their products. It was not until much later that human resource management as a crucial factor for a company's success became a subject for discussion in Russian business circles. As it turned out, unsurprisingly, the management of human-resources questions was a challenge that could not be taken lightly.

The individual essays in this book aim to present the various problems encountered in different areas of HR management as well as possible solutions. In order to give the reader a clearer idea of the structure of this publication, short summaries of the individual contributions will be presented in the next paragraph. But before, we will take a short look back at the research that has already been done on the topic of HRM in Russia.

Review of Research Literature

Even though a lot of research into transition economies in general and Russia in particular has been conducted over the last 15 years, the current situation and the predominant tendencies especially in personnel management in Russia have yet to be sufficiently documented.

Many of the academic publications available try to cover all countries of Eastern Europe at once. Publications especially dedicated to the subject of HRM that need to be mentioned here are Dirk Holtbrügge's book *'Personalmanagement multinationaler Unternehmungen in Osteuropa'* (1996, Wiesbaden, Gabler, in German), the book edited by Rainhart Lang, *'Personalmanagement im Transformationsprozess'* (2002, München, Rainer Hampp, in German), and *'Managing Human Resources in Central and Eastern Europe'*, edited by Michael J. Morley, Noreen Heraty and Snejina Michailova, forthcoming from Routledge in 2007. However, these publications either only contain only a few chapters dedicated exclusively to Russia or they implicitly discuss Russia as simply one part of Eastern Europe. Thus, these publications cannot exhaustively present the country's current situation. But Russia's size, its multi-ethnic population, its fast-growing economy and the increasing volume of collaborations with companies and institutions from abroad demand a much deeper and more complex analysis.

The enormous interest in business cooperation with Russia mentioned above has led to the majority of academic publications on HRM in Russia concentrating on the questions and problems of cooperation between Russian and Western companies. Some authors have discussed this subject in great depth.

Carl Fey is one of the leading authors on this topic. In his article, 'Doing Business in Russia: Effective human resource management practices for foreign firms in Russia', (with P. Engstrom und I. Björkman, *Organisational Dynamics* 28(2), 1999) he states that 'learning how to unlock the human potential of Russian employees is critical for foreign firms in order to be successful in Russia. Clearly, HRM plays a central role in achieving this goal'. His research was based on examinations of 18 foreign companies with subsidiaries or offices in Russia and was trying to point out HRM practices that worked well in the country, so that other foreign companies would be able to learn from his results.

In his essay 'Managing People in Russia: Challenges for Foreign Investors' (*European Management Journal* 12(3), 1994), Stanislav Shekshinia, another important name among HR experts in Russia, discusses the problems faced by foreign companies working in Russia.

In his article 'Can American Management Concepts Work in Russia? A cross-cultural comparative study' (*California Management Review* 40(4), 1998), Detelin Elenkov examines how far HR practices developed in the West can be transferred to the Russian context.

And what do Russian managers think of these practices? Igor Gurkov's article 'Mapping HRM in Russia: The results of Repeated Surveys of CEOs' (edited by R. Lang, München, 2002) provides some interesting answers to this question. The survey conducted among 735 CEOs showed that all managers interviewed stuck to the Russian methods of managing personnel and stressed the uniqueness of these methods but did not deny the fact that there is a need for innovative practices in the field of HRM. However, such innovations are often implemented on a trial-and-error basis without any reference to current international practices. The main question Gurkov asks is: 'How long [will] Russian CEOs [...] persist in 'inventing the bicycle' in their HRM innovations?'

Chapters 13 (the essay by Adam Smale and Vesa Suutari), 14 (the essay by Sudhir Saha) and 15 (the essay by Carl Fey and Ingmar Björkman) of this book will offer more information on this subject, examine some of the problems mentioned above and contain in-depth analyses of currently available literature.

Apart from problems of international cooperation, the adaptation of Russian enterprises to the market economy is another problematic field many researchers have dealt with. Sheila Puffer would have to be the first person to mention in this context. She is one of the leading and most prolific authors writing about HRM in Russia today. In her book *'Business and Management in Russia'* (with Associates, Cheltenham, Brookfield, 1996), she presents a whole array of very valuable research results on topics such as management education, entrepreneurship and leadership in the Russian context as well as her research on the issues of cooperation with the West mentioned above.

Another interesting study entitled 'The New Global Russian Business Leaders: lessons from a decade of transition' by M. Kets de Vries, S. Shekshnia, K. Korotov und E. Florent-Treacy (INSEAD, Fontainebleau Cedex, 2005) focuses especially on the subject of leadership. This working paper investigates leadership and entrepreneurship practices in Russia. It focuses on an emerging leadership style the authors termed 'global Russian' and provides eight lessons on leadership that could be valuable for Russian business leaders and those who seek to work with them. Chapter two in this publication (the essay by Stanislav Schekshnia, Daniel McCarthy, and Sheila Puffer) provides an in-depth analysis of currently available literature on the topic of leadership and also contributes to the existing literature by further exploring the challenges of leadership development in Russia today.

Some authors have chosen to concentrate on the Russian labour market for their research. Simon Clarke from the 'Russian Research Programme' at Warwick University in the UK has conducted large-scale empirical research on labour market issues in the course of his examination of the restructuring of employment, the formation of a labour market, new forms of employment and the development of trade unions in Russia. Chapter seven, the essay by Valery Yakubovich and Irina Kozina, also needs to be mentioned here. The authors discuss the subject of recruitment and the labour market and offer a competent analysis of the issues and problems in this field.

The names and publications (both already published and forthcoming) mentioned above should make up a rough list of the most important studies on the subject of HRM in Russia. In some cases, we have referred to individual chapters from this book, in which the authors also provide a theoretical basis for their empirical findings. These chapters also offer detailed overviews of the current state of research and available literature on their respective subjects. Overall, this book is intended to fill in many of the gaps in the academic study of HRM in Russia and answer some of the open questions on the subject.

The following section contains short summaries of the individual contributions in order to provide an overview of this volume's content.

Contents

The book is divided into three parts and consists of an introduction and 15 chapters.

The first section of the book takes a look at general HR issues. Beginning with a discussion about the influence of national politics on HR practices, it then moves on to analyze the areas of leadership, control, and trust, investigates further the particular HR-practices in virtual organizations and concludes with a case study on new HR practices implemented in a big steel plant in Russia. The second part discusses key HRM issues such as recruitment and selection, training and development, payment and compensation. Two chapters are dedicated to issues of recruitment and selection and training and development respectively. The first chapter summarizes the current knowledge on the topic and is followed by a practice-orientated chapter which provides a specific case study. The third and last section of the book consists of four chapters dealing with various HR problems encountered by multinational companies working in Russia.

Abstracts

The chapter 'Consequences of National Policy on Human Resource Management Practices in Russia' by Ruth C. May and Donna E. Ledgerwood gives an overview of the consulting experience with Russian companies from 1993 to 2005 against the backdrop of national policies:

- Putin's policies during his second term and how they are redefining competition among Russian companies
- HRM problems within organizations caused by national policy, and specific case examples of how Russian organizations are working to overcome these problems in the areas of Recruitment and Selection, Trust, Accountability/ Performance Appraisal.

In the following chapter, Stanislav Shekshnia, Daniel McCarthy and Sheila M. Puffer, will be discussing the development of leadership in Russia. Leadership development in Russia has changed dramatically since the introduction of a market-oriented economy, but especially during the last several years. The purpose of this chapter is to present the status of leadership development in Russia, with its many opportunities and challenges. The chapter discusses Russian leadership traditions and current needs. New trends in leadership development are then presented. The growth of corporate universities is covered in the next section. The many challenges facing leadership development in Russia are set out in the last section.

In their research project 'Control and Alienation in Russia' the authors Moshe Banai and William D. Reisel have looked into the relationships between 900 Russian workers' perceived control over their immediate environment and their level of alienation. More precisely, they have analyzed the relationships between the corporation's ownership type, the supervisors' leadership styles, the workers' jobs and personal characteristics, and the workers' level of alienation.

Trust and Organizational Culture is the topic of Tatiana Kovaleva's explorations. The whole system of relationships between employers and employees has changed over the last 15 years of transition. These changes have brought new understanding and new definitions of justice and fairness in the workplace and new expectations from both employers and employees of each other. The article will discuss some findings in this field.

The article 'HRM Practices in Virtual Companies in Russia' written by Sofia Kosheleva and Marina Libo contains an analysis of HRM practices in virtual companies in Russia. Quantitative analyses of HR systems at three different types of virtual organizations are presented as examples.

The case study 'Human Resource Management at a Steel Giant in Russia' written by Vera Trappmann describes the human resource policies currently being implemented at the Magnitogorsk steel plant. It also offers explanations for deviations from these policies, referring to the current nature of Russian enterprise and its determinants. The object of the analysis will be to explain the effects of economic transition in terms of employment restructuring and the labour market.

The chapter 'Recruitment in Russian Enterprises' by Valery Yakubovich and Irina Kozina discusses the recruitment practices of Russian firms. It starts with a description of the recruitment channels operating in the Russian labour market, presents estimates of their frequency from various surveys, and offers historical and international contexts in which these figures can be understood. In the next step, the authors explore how each channel is used, consider potential benefits and costs to an employer, and present the best practices. The channels discussed are: personal contacts, advertisements in the mass media, the Federal Employment Service, private recruitment agencies, educational institutions.

The aim of the essay 'Tendencies on the Russian Labour and Recruitment Markets – Employment in a Medium-sized IT company' written by Henrik Loos is to give an overview of the Moscow recruitment market (clients/candidates/service providers), highlight the situation at institutions of higher education (technical, business, MBA, linguistic) and demonstrate the HRM practices of a successful medium-sized Russian IT enterprise. The focus will be put on recruitment and integration of technical specialists, young employees and foreigners in the context of the company's organizational structure (shareholder/stakeholder structure), corporate governance principles and internal communications.

The article by Tatiana Soltitskaya and Tatiana Andreeva analyses human resource training and development practices in Russia. It discusses some of the most topical questions and problems facing Russian companies in this field. Training needs and approaches of contemporary Russian companies are structured and analyzed from several perspectives: in relation to the type of information culture dominant in the company, to the company's life cycle stage (according to the L. Greiner model), and to dominant ideas about the role of training and development in company strategy. The article is based on the authors' vast experience of training and HRM consulting for Russian companies.

The article by Lubov Ejova and Irina Olimpieva, 'Professional Training and Retraining: Challenges of Transition – the Case of the Shipbuilding Industry in St Petersburg' aims to examine the system of professional training and retraining in the shipbuilding industry. The article will start with a general overview of the employment and professional training situation in the shipbuilding industry in St Petersburg. The paper will further examine different strategies for solving the problem of professional training at various different enterprises. The authors will also analyze the attempts undertaken recently on the initiative of the shipbuilding trade unions to create a three-tiered system of continuous personnel training and retraining on a contractual basis in St Petersburg.

The article 'Pay in Russia' written by Graham Hollinshead gives an insight into pay issues in Russia. Discussed are:

- the nature of the occupation pyramid in Russia
- gender issues in income distribution

- additions to the individual pay package through work in the 'informal' economy
- the gap between 'nominal' and 'real' pay and the general problem of late payments
- the growth of a new salaried class in both the public and private sectors
- new pay expectations for 'modernized' Russian managers
- issues in expatriate pay determination
- the cross-cultural effects of status differentials between local and expatriate managers.

The chapter ends by anticipating future trends in pay and compensation.

The next chapter, 'Western-Russian Acquisition Negotiations and Post-acquisition Integration: A Case Study' by Kenneth Husted and Snejina Michailova presents the case of the Danish multinational company Rockwool, the world's largest manufacturer of stone wool. The company has acquired a part of an existing state-owned Russian manufacturer. The chapter focuses on the difficult takeover negotiations between the Western and the Russian partners and the initial steps towards managing the new relationship during the first year of post-acquisition integration. The key connection to the company was the Danish HR manager in Russia.

The principal aims of the study 'Hospitable or Hostile? Knowledge Transfer into the Russian Host Environment' by Adam Smale and Vesa Suutari are firstly, to investigate the type of knowledge that is being transferred via expatriates to the Russian host context. This not only allows for a clearer understanding of the currently perceived knowledge requirements of Russian affiliates, but also demonstrates the type of roles that Western expatriates are expected to perform in the host organization. The second aim of the study is to provide a more in-depth account of precisely what kind of roles the expatriates have to play in the transfer process in order to ensure effective implementation. The third and final aim is to identify which of the impediments to knowledge transfers are considered by expatriates to be significant obstacles in the Russian host environment.

The article 'Human Resource Management Practices in Russia and Canada: Convergence or Divergence?' written by Sudhir K. Saha presents findings from a survey of Russian and Canadian managers made up of questions about their own managerial values, the importance of certain human resource policies and practices, as well as what courses of action they would take on being confronted with certain HR problems. The article ends with a discussion of the implications of these findings for multinational corporations doing business in Russia.

This last study of the book, 'The Effect of Human Resource Management Practices on MNC Subsidiary Performance in Russia' written by Carl F. Fey and Ingmar Björkman investigates the relationship between HRM and the performance of 101 foreign-owned subsidiaries in Russia. The study's results provide support for the assertion that investments in HRM practices can substantially assist a firm in improving performance. Further, different HRM practices for managerial and non-managerial employees are found to be significantly related to firm performance.

Only limited support, however, is obtained for the hypothesized relationship between efforts at aligning HRM practices with company strategy and subsidiary performance.

Conclusion

The articles in this volume bring together a host of information on such topics as recruitment, compensation, training, leadership and other HRM-related issues in the Russian context based on a wide range of sources as well as personal experience. It was the editors' intention to present to the readers a perspective on HR in Russia built upon the experience of both the scholars who are native to the country and those who observe and study if from the outside. After more than 15 years of transition from planned to market economy, the editors felt it was time to examine the developments and the chances for reform in various areas of HRM.

References

Clarke, S. (1999), *The Formation of a Labour Market in Russia* (Cheltenham: Edward Elgar).

Clarke, S. (1999), *New Forms of Employment and Household Survival Strategies in Russia* (CCLS: Warwick and ISITO: Moscow).

Elenkov D. (1998), 'Can American Management Concepts Work in Russia? A cross-cultural comparative study', *California Management Review* 40:4.

Elkof B., Holmes L. and Kaplan V. (2005), *Educational Reform in Post-soviet Russia, Legacies and Prospects* (Oxford: Taylor & Francis Group).

F.A.Z. Institut (2005), *Länderanalyse Russland* (F.A.Z. Institut).

Fey, C. and Björkman I. (1999), 'Doing Business in Russia: Effective Human Resource Management Practices for Foreign Firms in Russia', *Organizational Dynamics*, Autumn.

Gurkov, I. (2002), 'Mapping HRM in Russia: The Results of Repeated Surveys of CEOs', in Lang, R. (ed.).

Holtbrügge, D. (1996), *Personalmanagement multinationaler Unternehmungen in Osteuropa* (Wiesbaden: Gabler).

Kets de Vries, M., Shekshnia, S., Korotov, K. and Florent-Treacy, E. (2005), 'The New Global Russian Business Leaders: Lessons from a decade of transition', (INSEAD: Fontainebleau Cedex).

Kondrachuk, V. (2004), *Vlast i Bisnes v Rossiyskoy Federacii* (Moskva: Sovremennaya Ekonomika i Pravo).

Lang, R. (2002), *Personalmanagement im Transformationsprozess* (München: Rainer Hampp).

Puffer, S. M. et al. (1996), *Business and Management in Russia* (Cheltenham, Brookfield: Edward Elgar).

Shekshinia, S. (1994), 'Managing People in Russia: Challenges for Foreign Investors', *European Management Journal* 12:3.

The Banker (2005), 'Good and Bad News', *The Banker*, Special Supplement Russia, October, 88–90.

Internet-based references

'Country Profile: Russia', *Federal Research Division*, [website], <http://lcweb2.loc.gov/frd/cs/profiles/Russia.pdf>

Kuchins A., 'Russian Democracy and Civil Society: Back to the Future', *Johnson's Russia List* [website], <http://www.cdi.org/russia/johnson/2006-39-24.cfm>

Binyon M., 'Putin Tells West not to Interfere in Ex-Soviet Republics', *Times Online* [website], (06 September 2005) <http://www.timesonline.co.uk/article/0,,135091766679,00.html>

Prioritetnye Nacionalnye Proekty, <http://www.rost.ru/> [home page]

'Protecting your credit sales in Russia', *Atradius*, March 2006, [home page] www.atradius.com>

RIA 'Novosti'– Russian Information Agency', [home page] <http://www.rian.ru/>

'Russian Economic Report – April 2006', *World Bank Moscow office* [home page] <http://ns.worldbank.org.ru/files/rer/RER_12.1_eng.pdf>

Rosstat, Federal State Statistics Service [home page] <http://www.gks.ru/wps/portal/russian>

'Russia', *CIA – The World Factbook 2006*, [website], (updated 20.04.06), <http://www.odci.gov/cia/publications/factbook/geos/rs.html>

'Russische Föderation', *Amnesty International,* Hochschulgruppe Karlsruhe 2006 [home page] <http://www.usta.de/RefAk/Amnesty/russland.html>

'Russische Föderation – Energiewirtschaft 2006', *BFAI 2006*, [home page] <www.bfai.de>.

'The Current Situation in the Russian Economy in January–February 2006', *MEDT of Russia*, [home page], < http://www.economy.gov.ru/wps/portal/

PART I
HUMAN RESOURCE MANAGEMENT ISSUES

Chapter 1

One Step Forward, Two Steps Back: Negative Consequences of National Policy on Human Resource Management Practices in Russia

Ruth C. May and Donna E. Ledgerwood

Russia's journey toward a free-market system began with the dissolution of the Soviet Union in August, 1991. Almost overnight, Russians looked to Boris Yeltsin, then President of the Russian Federation, to usher in a new era of freedom and economic growth using aggressive market reforms. History tells us that this was naïve optimism. Rather than a fast track to prosperity, Russia's efforts to adopt democratic principles and market-based economics have been marked by frenetic bursts of progress followed by periods of regression, or in the words of Vladimir Lenin, 'one step forward, two steps back' (Lenin 1904). More recently, the administrative maneuvering of Vladimir Putin has drawn criticism from global observers who claim that once again Russia is headed in a reverse direction, perhaps two steps back toward a dictatorship.

Based on our experiences as researchers and consultants inside Russian companies for more than a decade, we too are concerned with Russia's backtracking on business and political reforms. Through the insider view we are afforded in our consulting work, we can see the negative, trickle-down effect of recent national policy on human resource management (HRM) practices in Russian organizations. This effect is disheartening after seeing so much passion for progress in reforming Russian management from 2000 to 2003.

In this chapter we will discuss specific examples of the negative consequences of recent national policy on HRM practices in Russia within our client firms, and how these firms are coping (or not coping) with the unpredictability of Vladimir Putin's new authoritarian agenda. The tip of the political iceberg may be in the epicenter of Moscow, but the chilling effect of its influence stretches far and wide beneath the surface of the Russian economy, affecting regional governments and businesses across the entire country. At the organizational level, HR initiatives have regressed and achieving organizational performance has become a mosaic of inverted and subverted efforts.

Table 1.1 Russian client organizations

Organization	Industry/Sector	Location	Ownership Status
Avtovaz	Automobile	Togliatti	OJS*
Bank24.ru	Banking	Yekaterinburg	Private
BFK	Building Materials	Novosibirsk	Private
Birusa	Refrigerator Manufacturing	Krasnoyarsk	OJS
City of Togliatti	Municipal	Togliatti	State
Fosfor-Ateks	Chemical	Togliatti	OJS
Frutos	Wholesale Produce	Novosibirsk	Private
Gazprom	Gas	Moscow	OJS*
Inmarka	Dairy	Novosibirsk	Private
Joint Commercial Bank Stolichny	Banking	Moscow	OJS
Krasnoyarsk Stroitel	Construction	Krasnoyarsk	Private
Medtechnika	Medical Equipment	Novosibirsk	OJS
Mosbusiness Bank	Banking	Moscow	OJS
National Trade Bank	Banking	Togliatti	OJS
Oldam	Power Equipment	Moscow	Private
Promstroy Bank	Banking	St Petersburg	OJS
Richel	Conglomerate	Chelyabinsk	Private
Riten	Wholesale Paper	Novosibirsk	Private
Rosinka	Alcohol	Togliatti	Private
Rossibpharmatsya	Wholesale Drugs	Novosibirsk	Private
Rostselmash	Machinery	Rostov-on-Don	OJS
Russian Commercial and Industrial Bank	Banking	St Petersburg	OJS*
Severnaya Kazna Bank	Banking	Yekaterinburg	Private
Sibgigant	Supermarket Chain	Novosibirsk	Private
Smak	Fast Food	Krasnoyarsk	Private
Ural Bank of Reconstruction and Development	Banking	Yekaterinburg	OJS
Uraltransbank	Banking	Yekaterinburg	OJS
Vneshtorg Bank	Banking	Moscow	OJS*

OJS = Open Joint Stock Company
* Listed on the Russian (RTS) Stock Exchange ck Company

The Rayter Group

Our training and consulting work with Russian companies began in 1992 as a result of a partnership formed with Gregory Rachmilevich Rayter, founder of the Russian Personnel Management Association (RPMA) in Moscow. Mr Rayter was one of the first Soviet citizens allowed to travel outside the Soviet Union to receive training in Western methods of human resource management during Gorbachev's period of *perestroika* in the late 1980s. By 1990, Mr Rayter and member organizations of the RPMA were seeking to form cooperative partnerships with academicians and practitioners from the West who could assist them in importing contemporary HRM practices into Russia while drawing on their own expertise to tailor these new practices to fit the emerging business environment.

More than a dozen years have passed since our initial partnership was created with our Russian colleagues and it has been a phenomenal journey of sharing and learning on both sides. We now work together as a cross-cultural consortium under the auspices of the Rayter Group, a comprehensive consulting practice with client firms located across geographical regions and industries of Russia. For a sample list of Rayter Group clients, please see Table 1.1. All examples provided in this chapter are drawn from the companies listed in Table 1.1, but firms will not be specifically identified in most examples due to the sensitive nature of the information.

The Rayter Group's projects with Russian firms include on-site training and coaching in strategic planning and human resource management. Direct contact with a firm's executives typically spans six to nine months and includes four to six visits to the firm's principle location. Each visit lasts approximately two weeks and includes hands-on training designed to assist managers in developing strategies that capitalize on emerging opportunities in the organization's environment. Over a period of months, executives create the firm's strategies and the action plans necessary to implement the strategies. From these action plans, and their corresponding goals, job analyses (job descriptions and job specifications) are created that link the firm's overall strategy directly to its HRM practices, including recruitment and selection, training and development, performance appraisals, and compensation and benefits.

During the early to mid 1990s most of the executives in our client firms were either (1) in denial about the need to make significant changes in their operating models or (2) they had so much money that they were more interested in buying solutions than doing the hard work of creating their own. This was a period of frustration for us in our research and practice as we doubted whether there would ever be genuine reform in Russian management. Then came the economic crash of 1998 and everything changed. For nearly two years, the Russian economy teetered on the brink of implosion. After 18 months of economic stagnation, managers finally seemed willing to accept the fact that their attempts to buy pre-packaged Western plans would not work in the long run. Having failed to find simple answers to their complex problems, managers were then ready to create their own solutions that would fit the unique circumstances of the emerging free market in Russia.

Enter Putin

On New Year's Eve 2000, Boris Yeltsin handed over the presidential reigns to his handpicked successor, Vladimir Putin. Putin had entered the 'Kremlin family' in the late 1990s and served as Chief Deputy to Pavel Borodin, the Director of all the Kremlin's real estate holdings who was subsequently indicted by the Swiss government for money laundering and had a warrant issued for his arrest. Despite Borodin's difficulties, Putin advanced quickly as a Kremlin insider, building on his former career successes in St Petersburg as the mayor's liaison to Western firms' operating ventures in that region of Russia. During his days in St Petersburg, Putin earned a reputation of being 'heavy handed,' but was also known to deliver the stability and order that global investors wanted in exchange for investing in Russia. Despite his earlier career as a decorated KGB hardliner in East Germany, Putin was regarded as a savvy business player and was a welcomed improvement over Boris Yeltsin whose ill health and penchant for firing and rehiring members of his cabinet on a weekly basis had colored his last days in office. Thus, Putin easily won his first election to office in March of 2000.

As a token of gratitude for Boris Yeltsin's handing him the presidency, one of Putin's first official actions as President of Russia was to sign an executive order protecting Yeltsin and his family members from ever being prosecuted for any actions they took while Yeltsin was president. Apparently, Putin does not forget a favor and rewards those who reward him.

Putin's first presidential administration was a prosperous time for Russia as global oil prices climbed and the political climate calmed in comparison to the turbulent Yeltsin years. Although Putin raised eyebrows in 2001 when the state renationalized Russia's only independent television network, NTV, the cries of critics were outweighed by the accolades Putin received for his leadership in cutting corporate taxes and signing into law legislation which allowed for private ownership of commercial and residential property. Other key legislation supported by Putin during his first term included guaranteeing the rights of defendants and judicial control over arrests and detention which had formerly been controlled by state-appointed prosecutors. Under Putin's direction the Duma also approved legislation allowing the private sale of farmland after more than eight decades of state ownership. As a sign of support for creating a more competitive business environment, Putin also signed into law a plan for breaking up UES, the state-owned electric monopoly.

In our consulting practice during 2000 to 2003, we were encouraged by the enthusiastic commitment of Russian executives to reform their organizations. Their heightened interest was driven primarily by a growing sense of intense competition bearing down on them from domestic as well as international competitors. The business environment was becoming more legitimate and Russian companies were becoming more determined to modernize and improve their business practices, especially in the area of human resource management. Then Putin was re-elected to a second term and the rules changed again.

Putin's New Agenda

While the political and economic advances during Putin's first term gave global investors many reasons to feel optimistic about Russia's future, the president's policies during his second term have prompted a global re-examination of Russia's prospects. Growing concerns over increased political risk in the second half of 2004 led to a significant decline in economic growth in Russia despite record high oil prices. Specifically, for all of 2004 the overall deterioration in Russia's business climate cost the country 1.7 percentage points in economic growth or US $10 Billion in lost production (EIU 2005a). Moreover, worries over Putin's drift back towards authoritarianism caused domestic capital flight, which had been falling, to quadruple to $9.4 billion in 2004 from $1.9 billion in 2003 (Buckley and Gorst 2005; Weir 2005). Not surprisingly, it was mid-2004 when our consulting group began to notice a measured decline in requests for new consulting proposals from Russian companies. This is not unusual in periods of economic decline, as we well remember from 1998–99, but what makes this slowdown unique is that the primary cause of the slowdown is undeniably linked to the policies of a president who supposedly is determined to move Russia forward, not backward. So what is Putin up to and what are the implications for HRM practices in Russian firms?

The Yukos Affair – Reversal of Privatization With a March 2004 deadline for reelection looming before him, Putin's shift in priorities became apparent to all who were watching in late 2003, beginning with the arrest of Mikhail Khodorkovsky, CEO of Yukos Oil Company. Mr Putin insisted that the arrest of one of his most outspoken critics rested purely on the charges of tax evasion and criminal activity, but the world could not help but notice that Khodorkovsky had a record of 'buying' parliamentary votes on oil legislation, funding parties in opposition to Putin, and publicly criticizing government decisions. Early in his first term, Putin had reached a bargain with Russia's oligarchs that if they would stay out of politics and pay their taxes, Putin would look the other way at their sometimes questionable ways of building their business empires (Buckley and Gorst 2005). Apparently, Khordorkovsky was not very committed to that quid pro quo or he underestimated the lengths to which Putin would go to silence his critics.

Putin was soundly re-elected in March 2004, but even more importantly, his United Russia Party won a solid majority in the state Duma in December 2003 giving him full control over the executive and legislative branches of government. With control of the Duma, he could begin to reconfigure national policies according to his own agenda and he wasted no time in getting about the business of implementing repressive change.

By December 2004 Mikhail Khodorkovsky was still in jail and the bill for Yukos' back taxes had risen to US $25 billion from the original estimate of US $3.4 billion. On 15 December, Yukos' officials applied for bankruptcy protection from a US bankruptcy court in Houston, Texas with international jurisdiction and were granted a temporary suspension on the sale of any Yukos assets until management could work out a plan to pay the taxes. Ignoring the injunction issued by the Texas court, the Russian government forced an auction on December 19th of Yukos' largest oil subsidiary, Yuganskneftegaz, which was sold for US $9.3 billion to Baikal Financial Group (BFG), an unknown company with an unpublished list of officers. BFG was registered in Tver, a small city north of Moscow, at an address that turned out to be located in a building housing a mobile phone store and a café (EIU 2004a). Three days later, Rosneft, a state-owned oil company, announced that it had acquired BFG, and with it, Yuganskneftegaz, for an undisclosed sum. Igor Sechin, Chairman of Rosneft, is a close confidant of Vladimir Putin (EIU 2005b).

Within days following Rosneft's acquisition of Yuganskneftegaz, Putin finally abandoned his insistence that the case against Yukos was only about taxes, and admitted that the government's takeover of Yukos' oil subsidiary was necessary to reverse the illegal transfer of state assets into private hands which had occurred during the 1990s. Specifically, he announced, '… The state, using absolutely legal market mechanisms, is securing its interests. I consider this to be quite normal (Birch 2005, 2).' Ironically, his top economic advisor, Andrei Illarionov, did not think the seizure to be normal. In fact, Illarionov called the forced sale of Yukos' oil production subsidiary an 'expropriation of private property' which represents the 'swindle of the year'. Moreover, Illarionov claimed that the state had shifted to 'an interventionist model of economic development, with … extremely incompetent intervention in economic life by state officials (EIU 2005c).' Mr Illarionov was fired from his position with the Kremlin the week following his comments about Yukos.

With the combined production of Rosneft and Yuganskneftegaz, the government now controls output of 1.5 million barrels of oil per day (b/d), and is looking to consolidate its holdings in the Russian oil industry even further. The state's ownership of Gazprom, whose CEO is also a close ally of Putin, will be increased to 51 per cent which will give the state control of Gazpromneft, the company's oil producing subsidiary. In addition, Deutsche Bank, Gazprom's advisor, has proposed that Gazprom acquire Surgutneftegaz and Sibneft, the fourth and fifth largest oil companies in Russia. If Gazprom also adds the leftover pieces of Yukos to its holdings, Tomskneft and Samaraneftegaz, the government would then effectively control output of 4.25 million b/d which dwarfs the output of any of the global oil giants (that is, ExxonMobil, BP or Royal Dutch/Shell) and represents over 40 per cent of Russia's total oil output (EIU, 2004b). The 51 per cent stake in Gazprom would also give the state control of 20 per cent of the world's gas reserves, 16 per cent of global gas output and 25 per cent of all gas sales to Western Europe. Gazprom currently accounts for one quarter of Russia's total tax revenues (EIU 2004c).

While the government proceeded with its master plan to renationalize the oil industry, the fate of Mikhail Khodorkovsky hung in limbo until 31 May 2005 when he was formally sentenced to nine years in prison in a verdict that took 12 days to read in Moscow's Meshchansky Court. The negative implications for the Russian business climate of the Yukos affair and its final outcome for Mr Khodorkovsky cannot be overstated. Vladimir Ryzhov, an independent deputy in the Duma, stated that 'I had hoped until the very end that our leaders would put the interests of the country first, but … I fear this will lead to a similar wave of trials in the provinces.

The message (to private business) is: sell and run away' (Weir 2005, 3). In further support of Ryzhov's concerns, a report issued by the Ministry of Economics in March 2005 found that the four main deterrents to foreign investment in Russia are corruption, followed by administrative barriers, the selective application of legislation and recurring conflicts between the state and business (EIU 2005d).

Not only is Putin's policy of economic intervention bad for business investment and global relations, but the actions of Putin set a dangerous and foreboding precedent for provincial government officials. The message is clear. If you don't like the way a company is operating, go after the leaders of the company, and if you want the company's assets, take them. Almost predictably, Putin's actions are already being mimicked in outlying regions of Russia involving some of our most profitable client companies. Local and regional authorities are taking aggressive, hard-line stances toward businesses, and in effect, are redefining the competitive landscape in Russian industry. As a result, the greatest threat to a Russian company may no longer be a local competitor's product or a sudden change in customer preferences. Instead, the greatest competitive threat may be the local Mayor's deputies, the regional governor, or the Russian tax police. This growing trend in government intervention at the local and regional levels is causing many of our client firms to re-think how they will compete against other organizations and how they will practice HRM – if at all.

Centralization of Power Not only was 2004 a disappointing year for the business climate in Russia, it was equally if not more discouraging for supporters of democratic principles. While tax authorities were busy attacking Yukos in December 2004, the Russian Duma was hard at work passing Putin's legislation that abolished the direct election of regional governors. Putin claims that this new law is necessary to protect Russians against terrorism. Thus, governors will now be nominated by Putin and must be approved by regional parliaments. If one of the regional parliaments rejects Putin's nominee twice, the President has the authority to dissolve the regional assembly by a simple decree. Moreover, once a nominee is approved and takes office, the President has the right to dismiss the regional governor at any time in a case of a 'loss of trust' by the President (EIU 2005e). Before the year-end, the upper house of Russia's Federal Assembly also passed a law taking away judges' rights to elect a majority of the members of the Supreme Judicial Collegium, a body which approves judicial nominations and dismissals (Aron and Serchuk 2005).

In May 2005, the Duma passed sweeping new election laws which prohibit coalitions of small parties in the Duma. The new threshold for entry into the Duma is now five to seven percent which will make it much easier for officials to disqualify candidates from running and to ban independent observers from polling stations. Some experts believe the ultimate goal of the government is to have only one or two big, officially approved parties.

Yury Levada, head of an independent polling agency in Russia is quoted as saying, 'This is an attempt to create a one-party state. We are being pushed into the past, back to the state we previously inhabited' (Weir 2005b, 3). Putin has also proposed abandoning elections of independent candidates altogether in favor of a system where elections would be by party lists only, but as of May 2005 this measure had not been approved by the Duma (Aron 2005).

Putin's moves to re-centralize the government have important consequences for Russian firms regardless of their location. No matter how far from Moscow organizations may be located, they will be directly connected back to the national power center in Moscow via their regional governors, appointed by Putin, and their regional assembly members who are now in Putin's back pocket. Moreover, companies will be beholding to a host of other local appointees who will serve these state-appointed officials with unquestioning loyalty out of fear for their own careers if they do not 'tow the Putin line.' Simply put, Putin's recentralization of power coupled with his new authoritarian model for dealing with businesses have registered one very important lesson in the minds of Russian executives: who you know is once again becoming more important than what you do.

Blat – Competitive Weapon No. 1

During the Soviet era, personal networking and social connections were not only a preferred means of doing business, they were paramount to survival. Because government ministries often set unreasonable or even unachievable goals for industrial enterprises, managers were forced to enter into unofficial inter-organizational bartering and cooperative exchanges to reallocate limited resources and redistribute surpluses. Networking was not only important to organizational survival, but was a critical competence for moving up the career ladder within the Communist party hierarchy. This approach to gaining influence, making connections and relying on personal contacts with people in influential positions is still widely practiced in Russia and is known by the uniquely Russian term, *blat*.[1]

Blat is more than the typical Western concept of 'drawing on who you know to get things done.' Blat is more overtly mercenary and self-serving as compared to the concept of networking and being part of the 'in-group.' The in-groups in the former Soviet Union were notorious for their 'invisible hands' and covert activities. It is the revival of this Soviet type of blat that has led to explosive growth in corruption and bribery and the emergence of a full-blown counter economy run by the Mafia (Kets de Vries 2000).

Putin's recent twin policies of economic intervention and political centralization have only fueled a resurgence of the belief that personal connections with the appropriate authorities are more important to the success of a business than the price or quality of the good or service they provide (Michailova 2000). In specific cases involving two of our client firms located in the same region of Russia, plans to implement portions of their strategies based on free competitive practices have now

1 For a comprehensive discussion of blat, see Michailova, S. and Worm, V. (2003): Personal networking in Russia and China: Blat and guanxi. European Management Journal, 21:4, 509–19. See also Puffer, S. and McCarthy, D. (1995), Finding the common ground in Russian and American business ethics. California Management Review, Winter, 29–46.

been put on hold. In the case of one firm, a customer service call center which was to be launched in 2005 has been cancelled because its management has turned its attention away from improving customer service to watching attentively the actions of Putin. In the case of the other firm, a new system of performance appraisals has been delayed indefinitely until, in the words of the Director General, 'the local conditions become more predictable'.

Thus, instead of focusing on the means to increase their competitive positions purely on the basis of efficiencies, prices and services, many of our client firms have put a freeze on strategic planning initiatives and are exploring ways to redirect resources toward enhancing their blat with local and regional authorities. In fact, executives are beginning to recognize that increasing their blat with high ranking authorities is not only a smart defensive strategy, but can be a powerful offensive strategy as well. For example, top officials of one of our client firms have been able to deflect the advances of the tax police who charged them with tax evasion in late 2004 by enhancing their blat with local authorities. After hiring one of the mayor's family members, this firm convinced the tax authorities not only to leave them alone, but to attack another firm in the area that represents the only real competition they have ever had in their market. These tactics might seem unethical and shocking to most Western executives, but they are not surprising when one considers that circumventing the law and solving problems through strong rulers are long standing business practices in Russia (McCarthy and Puffer 2002; Randall 2001).

Profiling The Blatter

With blat once again emerging as a powerful competitive weapon, firms are looking to individuals whom they know can strengthen their connections to and within the government. We call these individuals who are plugged into politically correct, powerful networks *blatters*. No one in an organization has an official title as a blatter, but most people within the management hierarchy know who they are. Blatters have typically developed their powers of influence through familial connections or through long careers in industry or politics. A new class of blatters has emerged in recent years among the business elite, whom Russians call the 'new wave'. The money of the 'new wave' can buy influence, but their access to powerful politicians is often short lived due to the fact that they have the money and power that many government officials want, and thus, the budding blat relationships can turn sour rather quickly.

Not surprisingly, most blatters are part of an established executive class sometimes referred to as Red Directors. These executives are typically older, high-ranking male managers, (that is, Owners, Director Generals, Deputy Directors, or Department Heads), who held upper management positions in industry during the Soviet era and who have survived the last fifteen years of economic transition in Russia due in large part to their close ties to the 'right' government officials.

Blatters have become accustomed to positions of power and authority and they value the formal structure and prestige that come with such positions. Thus, it is important to recognize the blatters' egos and how important it is for them to be held in high regard by peers and subordinates. Blatters often receive exclusive privileges within organizations and believe that they are entitled to special treatment and benefits due to the value of the personal networks they can access on behalf of the firm. Because blatters are so powerful, they often can choose what work they wish to do or not do and delegate the rest.

The blatters' powers rest in relationships, not so much in results, so the majority of their efforts are directed at maintaining the connections with the 'right' authorities to protect the blatters' positions and their organizations' interests. Given that blatters do not have to justify their existence with typical job-related performance, they may be perceived as lazy or detached by their co-workers who don't understand their value and purpose to the organization. Yet, blatters serve a critical role within the organization, even more so today than only two or three years ago. While blatters work to protect the interests of their firms, they are above all, self-serving individuals. If pushed into a situation where they must choose between protecting their own interests or those of their firm, they will sacrifice the interests of the organization to further their own interests and ambitions.

The Consequences of Blat and Blatters for HRM

As the prospects for free and fair competition in Russia erode due to Putin's recent actions, the potential value of blatters increases exponentially. Our client firms understand this harsh reality and appear to be building up their blat resources in preparation for a vociferous battle in Russian industry driven by greed, politics and fear. As was historically the case, people are being hired primarily on the basis of who they know and not because of what they can produce or contribute to the organization. For the firms that depend on blatters to garner favor and influence with 'significant others' on their behalf, the blatters represent both a blessing and a curse. From one perspective, the firms cannot live without them. But from another perspective, blatters create such challenges for firms' HR managers that it is almost impossible to live with them. In the following sections we describe problems caused by blatters which are related to recruitment and selection, trust and accountability.

Recruitment and Selection

During the Soviet centralized era, the human resource function at the organizational level was relegated to a personnel bookkeeping operation and recruitment and selection decisions were imposed on the firm from above. Many individuals were placed in patronage jobs with or without relevant qualifications because they were related to someone of importance or they were thought to be of value to the organization or a specific manager/executive. Executive-level managers were appointed to their industry positions by the Communist Party as a means of service to the country while working up their career ladders to higher, more prestigious positions within the party apparatus.

Compensation was closely aligned with seniority and job hierarchy, and had more to do with allegiance to the party than to actual performance on the job. There was no need for job analyses, job evaluations or performance appraisals because individuals were paid by the government whatever the rate the government stated – whether they produced optimally or did nothing at all.

Since the mass reforms that began in the early 1990s, Russian companies have had to create their own systems of recruiting employees that are not dictated by the state. While there is an abundant supply of labourers in the current environment, few have the requisite knowledge, skills and abilities necessary to perform successfully on the job. There are few professional mechanisms in place (such as the International Public Management Association of Human Resources or the Society for Human Resource Management) and even fewer private executive search firms that track relevant applicant pools of qualified candidates and provide them to Russian organizations. Thus, the challenge of recruiting and selecting the right workers with the right skills and attitudes for the right job has become increasingly difficult in the Russian HRM domain.

As part of our training process with client firms, we typically request that employees within each department write their own job descriptions under the direction of their department heads who we have trained in the process of writing job analyses (job titles, job descriptions and job specifications) at an early stage of our intervention. As the cornerstone of all HR functions, job analyses should link directly to the firm's strategic initiatives and action plans.

In helping to plan for how their organization should operate, we try to get managers directly involved in the recruitment, screening and selection of candidates based on the relevant knowledge, skills and abilities (KSA's) as well as personal factors necessary to perform the job optimally. In many cases we have been successful in convincing managers that the hiring process needs to be more focused on job-related criteria than on subjective traits of the individual, but the resurgence of blat as has made this task much more difficult. Many managers see job-related decisions to be nice in theory, but no longer relevant to their Russian realities.

In one firm, the Head of the HRM Department threatened to resign because some of the recent hires did not go through any of the formal recruitment, selection and training programs that had been painstakingly created. Instead, two new blatters were brought in by the Director General and Chairman of the Board and were given jobs at the Deputy Director and Department Head levels, not because of their business knowledge and skills, but because of who they know in the regional governor's office. In fact, one of the men worked previously as a high-ranking administrator for the regional governor. In another example, plans to fire two older blatters who have been 'retired on the job' for several years have been delayed because of connections they have to the local police that could prove useful to the firm.

One cannot refute that blatters are a necessary evil for doing business in the current Russian climate. But when recruitment and selection processes are completely ignored, and when blatters are brought in through the 'back door' of an organization under an entirely different decision framework, such actions undermine HR practices and cause top management to lose credibility with employees. As one frustrated staff member in a Russian HRM department recently remarked, 'Our way of hiring in this company is still a giant theatre play'. It is indeed a frustrating dilemma for HR executives and the trainers who are trying to help Russian companies develop and utilize more objective and credible systems for recruiting workers.

The one small accomplishment we can report in this area of HRM is that in three of our client firms we have at least been able to get top-level executives to acknowledge (behind closed doors) that there is a legitimacy problem with their firms' recruitment and selection processes related to hiring blatters purely for blat sake with little or no regard given for their job-related skills or abilities. In a sense, just getting Russian executives to admit there are conflicts of interest and problems of legitimacy in their current hiring practices is a small victory. Problems cannot be fixed until there is formal recognition that problems exist. Thus, we are trying ever so delicately to encourage our Russian client firms to bring the conversations of hiring and retaining blatters 'out of the closet'.

One firm has progressed so far as to integrate the discussion of blatters into their review of environmental threats and opportunities in the strategic planning process and to discuss, in closed executive sessions, the specific threats that blatters can help to defend against and the opportunities that blatters can help to exploit. These conversations may seem rather unconventional to Western practitioners and HRM professionals, but we believe it is better to get the issues out in the open rather than to take the traditional Russian approach of pretending that the problem does not exist. Another advantage of bringing the blatter issue out in the open is to force managers to be realistic about how difficult it may be to monitor and control the blatters' actions within, and on behalf of, the firm.

Trust

Because blatters know how much their organizations need their power of influence, they have a tendency to believe that rules and expectations do not always apply to them and that they cannot be held accountable for their actions. As a result, their loyalties and trustworthiness may be called into question by their managers and co-workers.

Parallel Organizations In a representative case, the biggest blatter in one of our client firms is a Director General who is in charge of one of several large manufacturing plants that have been absorbed into a larger, private holding company. The owner of the holding company is a young, progressive businessman who has had ongoing conflicts with the Director General of the factory, particularly after discovering that the Director General was entering into contracts with suppliers that were beyond the required inputs for production, but were providing lucrative kickbacks to the Director General. The Director General is from the Red Director class and seems to be more interested in lining his own pockets than in modernizing the equipment and processes in the plant. Unfortunately, and fortunately for the young owner and his board members, the older Director General is close friends with the local Mayor and can keep local authorities from putting administrative and legal pressures on the company. As we would say in the West, the owner is between a rock and a hard place. To his credit, this owner has developed a creative solution to resolve this dilemma.

The owner understands that the plant and the parent holding company need the Director General's connections to the Mayor's office and that the Director General has a strong ego that needs to be protected and upheld in public. However, the owner cannot give the Director General free reign to operate and make decisions for fear of the negative effects it could have on the firm's profitability. To achieve his goals of protecting both the firm's interests and the blatter's interests, the owner adopted a solution that is growing increasingly common among Russian organizations, and is sometimes referred to as 'parallel organizations'.[2]

In creating a parallel organization structure, the owner of the holding company has withdrawn most of the financial resources from the plant and has placed them in accounts under the holding company. Further, the owner has placed one of his close friends in a Deputy Director position within the plant, under the Director General in the formal structure but whose sole purpose of being there is to watch what the Director General does and to report back to the owner and other board members. In some respects, the Deputy Director represents a mole or watchdog over the Director General, but the Director General is completely aware of the arrangement. In fact, the Director General knows that he cannot enter into a contract with another firm for any amount in excess of US $20,000 without the prior approval and signature of his newly appointed 'subordinate', the Deputy Director. In some respects, this solves the owner's problem of trust with the blatter because he is monitored regularly by the implanted Deputy; but it creates a whole new set of problems which we are struggling to get the owner to acknowledge.

By having one official organizational structure where the Director General is considered to have ultimate power and decision making authority, and another unofficial, yet real, structure where the Deputy Director actually has more power than the person to whom he reports, the firm is setting itself up for confusion, frustration and problems with trust among employees. This off-the-record arrangement will eventually become obvious to everyone. The owner and his board members may have successfully limited the powers of the Director General while leaving him in a position that allows him to retain face and sustain his ego, but in essence, they have further limited his accountability for results since he can now blame poor performance on his restricted abilities to act due to his 'watchdog' deputy. In turn, the Deputy Director really does not have legitimate authority, so his ability to guide the organization to success is also limited.

---

2 For an in-depth discussion of parallel organizations in Russia, see Prochorov, A. (2002), *Russian Model of Management*, Moscow, Expert Publishing House.

While using unofficial, parallel organization structures to monitor and control blatters may make sense from a more traditional Russian perspective, parallel structures destroy the legitimacy of the formal organizational structure and call into question who is really in charge. Placing a subordinate in the position of scrutinizing the actions of his or her superior is an obvious breach of the scalar chain of command. This 'band-aid' approach to managing blatters is indicative of the short-term attempts to solve longer-term problems that we see in many of our client firms.

Theft Another trust-related problem that is pandemic in Russian organizations is theft. Nearly all our client firms employ full-time security officers and many have fully staffed security departments. Ironically, the security departments in Russian organizations are not there to protect the organization's property and employees from external threats, but to protect the organization's assets from company insiders. For example, in one of our client firms, the security department has been working for more than a year to determine the whereabouts of 'lost' units of production that routinely go missing between the firm's production warehouse and the loading docks of customers' receiving stations. Management suspects that certain individuals are involved, but to date no one has been able to prove who is responsible for the numerous incidents of missing goods.

In a similar case, officers of another client firm knew that a significant portion of incoming materials was being skimmed off imported containers at the point of customs clearance, but felt they could do nothing about it. The culprit was the Deputy Chief of the Inventory Department. Although the managers knew they could not trust the Deputy Chief, they also knew they could not fire him because of his critical connections with the customs officials. Fortunately for the firm, this particular blatter was as lazy as he was greedy, so top managers created a solution that exploited the weaknesses in the blatter's own character in order to solve the problem of inventory theft.

In order to address the problem of theft at this company, we assisted the HR manager in designing a loss control system which involved training department heads and those individuals responsible for tracking supplies and inventory. In addition, a bonus system was put in place which rewarded area managers for decreases in security costs in their respective departments. To insure its ultimate success, the blatter in the inventory department, the firm's biggest thief, was put in charge of the overall program and his bonus was tied directly to the reduction in stolen merchandise for the entire firm. The plan worked because the blatter figured out that earning the bonuses by not stealing was easier than the effort of actually stealing. He also knew who was involved in the broader theft network in the firm and pressured these individuals to stop in order to positively affect his bonus. Top management was happy because they kept their blatter and reduced their losses due to theft, and the blatter was pleased because he was able to keep his position and prestige while increasing his income.

Accountability

Individual accountability (the obligation to secure desired results) is a cornerstone in individualistic Western cultures and organizations, but this has not been the case in Russia, which has a long collectivist tradition and a legacy of dodging responsibility at the organizational level. Our experience in training hundreds of Russian executives over the past twelve years has only served to confirm our earlier conclusions that a lack of accountability is one of the greatest barriers to progress in Russian management reform (May, Bormann-Young and Ledgerwood 1998). Under the Soviet centralized system, managers tended to avoid responsibility for organizational decisions and outcomes because the risks were perceived to be too high if things went wrong. There were no incentives for exceeding performance goals or expectations, but punishment was routinely administered if problems occurred in organizational operations. Thus, keeping a low profile and 'hiding' from responsibility became a means of survival during the Communist era. This mindset has carried over to present day practices and is particularly apparent in the behaviour of blatters.

Because blatters feel that they belong to a privileged class and are irreplaceable to their organizations, they are often among those executives who are the most difficult to hold accountable for organizational results. In many cases, they live out the old Russian mantra that 'if one cannot find a solution to a problem, the next best thing is finding someone to blame.' Blatters are masters at manipulating people and situations for their own gain and this makes controlling them a major challenge for HR and line managers within the firm.

In one of the most promising examples of instilling a sense of individual accountability in Russian organizations, several of our client firms have implemented a performance monitoring system known as the 'extraordinary guarantee' program. This concept was first initiated a few years ago by managers in our client firm, Riten, located in Novosibirsk. They have developed the most formal and comprehensive system of extraordinary guarantees among all our client firms. The core idea is to establish a high level of individual accountability via formal agreements between individuals whose work is highly interdependent, therefore establishing the basic protocols and setting forth parameters of expected performance. These agreements can involve people from a variety of positions or departments within the organization. The individuals participating in the extraordinary guarantees set the terms of the agreements, including the specific expectations, time limits and consequences if the terms are not fulfilled. The guarantors are also responsible for reporting on a regularly scheduled basis to a designated person in the HR department who is charged with monitoring all outstanding extraordinary guarantee agreements.

For example, at Riten an extraordinary guarantee agreement was created between the Chief Accountant and the Head of the Receiving Department. According to their agreement, the Chief Accountant must respond to requests for cash payments within 24 hours of receiving the request from the Head of the Receiving Department. Conversely, the Head of Receiving must forward official receipts to the Chief Accountant within 24 hours of paying out cash to truck drivers bringing in loads of scrap metal. If either manager violates the terms of their extraordinary guarantee agreement, the violator is reported to the HRM department and receives a cut in his monthly bonus.

While extraordinary guarantees have been used to enhance accountability and to improve working relationships, our client firms have found them to be particularly useful in controlling their blatters. As an example, the HR manager of another client firm (not Riten) was consistently being criticized because workers were being paid late. Explaining that it was not his fault, the HR manager showed the impediment to be two older blatters (Department Heads) who were not providing him with the necessary data to process the employees' time sheets by the deadline set every other week by the Chief Accountant.

To solve the problem, the HR Manager and the Chief Accountant joined forces and approached the heads of each department with a proposal to set up extraordinary guarantee agreements. The two blatters were not enthusiastic, but because the other Department Heads were willing to cooperate they agreed to participate in order to save face. Agreements were created so that each Department Head must have his or her employee data to the HR Manager no later than the day before the employee time sheets are due from the HR manager to the Chief Accountant in order for him to process payroll. If a Department Head violates his or her individual agreement with the HR Manager, or if the HR Manager violates his obligation to the Chief Accountant, the guilty executive loses one month's salary.

To make the deal more attractive and to appeal to the greed of the two blatters, each agreement was constructed so that the person reporting the violator gets the violator's pay that is withheld in the respective month. This is an important component of the contracts because it acts as a safeguard against the natural tendency of Russians to cover for one another (quid pro quo) even if the other person is guilty or has done something detrimental to the organization or group. Thus, even if a blatter has a personal networking incentive to cover for a colleague who has violated an extraordinary guarantee agreement, the blatter will have to weigh the cost of his or her silence against a monetary incentive, and one can usually count on greed winning out.

The best scenario is when two blatters enter into an extraordinary guarantee agreement with each other. Both individuals are motivated to fulfill the obligation as a matter of prestige, as well as not to lose money. The agreement is a contract in which they have set the terms that will govern their own behaviour rather than having someone else in the organization dictate rules to them. Most importantly, if they do not fulfill their obligations, they have no one to blame, or retaliate against, but themselves.

Conclusion

Putin's national policies of economic intervention and political centralization have caused firms to retreat back to blat as the primary means for competing in the marketplace. Blatters create major dilemmas for firms who need their power and influence, but who cannot always trust them to act in the best interest of their organizations. Thus, we offer four suggestions for dealing with emerging HRM challenges in Putin's Russia.

First, it is important to understand what motivates blatters and to use this knowledge to the firms' advantage. In this chapter we have provided examples of client firms that are successfully exploiting the personality characteristics of their blatters to achieve their organizational goals. The solutions are not perfect, but they are evolving – just like the Russian environment.

Second, foreigners who are trying to work within the HR domain in Russia must be realistic about the environment. We have to work with it as it is; not how we wish it to be. Westerners working in Russia need to be more aware that they are viewing Russian behaviours through their own culturally-based perspectives. For example, even though it is not accepted in the West, one could argue that in the Russian organizational context blat may actually fit into one or more categories of job specifications (knowledge, skills or abilities) which are critical for organizational success. This perspective may not match prevailing Western models, but Russia's circumstances should prompt us all to re-think how we conceptualize areas of HR practice in transitional economies.

Third, foreign firms must also realize that it is not just Russian firms that are at risk of being negatively affected by Putin's agenda of intervention and recentralization. Most recently, TNK-British Petroleum, the Russian-British oil venture, has been informed that they owe a billion dollars in back taxes. This charge points to legal and regulatory inconsistencies and raises serious questions about the relationship between the state and private businesses (EIU 2005f).

Finally, Russia will never reform without the pressure of free and fair competition and the power of democratically elected officials who can enforce a legitimate system of law and order. Russian and Western firms need to muster their collective powers to pressure Putin to shift back to policies of free markets and politics. Russia's fate depends on it.

References

Kets de Vries, M. (2000), 'A Journey into the Wild East: Leadership Styles and Organizational Practices in Russia', *Organizational Dynamics* 28:4, 67–81.

Lenin, V. (1904), 'One Step Forward, Two Steps Back', Lenin, V. (1952), *Selected Works*, English Edition 1, 1 (Moscow: Foreign Languages Publishing House).

May, R., Bormann-Young, C. and Ledgerwood, D. (1998), 'Lessons from Russian Human Resource Management Experience', *European Management Journal* 16: 4, 447–59.

McCarthy, D. and Puffer, S. (2002), 'Corporate Governance in Russia: Towards an European, U.S. or Russian Model?' *European Management Journal* 20: 6, 630–640.

Michailova, S. (2000), 'Contrasts in Culture: Russian and Western Perspectives on Organizational Change', *The Academy of Management Executive* 14:4, 99–112.

Randall, L. (2001), *Reluctant Capitalists: Russia's Journey through Market Transition* (New York: Routledge).

Internet-based references

Aron, L., 'Where is Russia Headed?', USA Today [website], (8 May 2005 edition) <www.usatoday.com/news/opinion/editorials/2005-05-08-russia-edit_x.htm>

Aron, L. and Serchuk, V., 'The Putin Presidency: Reform and Retreat', in: Foreign Policy and Defense Studies, American Enterprise Institute for Public Policy Research, USA Today [website], (8 May 2005 edition) <www.usatoday.com/news/opinion/editorials/2005-05-08-russia-edit-side_x.htm>

Birch, D., 'Russia politics: Putin Dismisses Economist Critical of Yukos Case', Baltimore Sun [website], (4 January 2005 edition) <http://www.viewswire.com>

Buckley, N. and Gorst, I. 'Oligarchs Tumble from Summit as Putin Inverts Power Pyramid', Financial Times [website], (1 June 2005 edition) <http://news.ft.com/cms/s/b808cea0-d23b-11d9-8c82-00000e2511c8.html>

Economist Intelligence Unit (EIU), (various dates as ordered in chapter): 'Russia Economy: Slipping Growth' (21 January 2005a), 'Russia Economy: Bungling the Yukos Asset Disposal' (30 December 2004a), 'Russia Politics: Yukos, Putin and the Oligarchs – Method and Madness' (3 January 2005b), 'Russia Politics: The Outspoken Silenced' (10 January 2005c), 'Russia Economy: Gazprom Eyeing an Oil Monopoly?' (1 December 2004b), 'Russia Economy: Opening Gazprom on the State's Terms' (16 September 2004c), 'Russia Economy: Report Sees Corruption as Main FDI Deterrent' (16 March 2005d), 'Russia Politics: Political Outlook' (6 January 2005e), 'Russia Economy: Tax Claim Fuelling Uncertainty' (13 April 2005f) <http://www.viewswire.com>

Weir, F., 'Russian Government sets Sights on Subversion', The Christian Science Monitor [website], (1 June 2005 edition) <www.csmonitor.com/2005/0601/p06s02-woeu.htm>

Weir, F., 'Oil booms, but Investors flee Russia', The Christian Science Monitor [website], (21 April 205a Edition) <www.csmonitor.com/2005/0412/p01s02-woeu.htm>

Chapter 2

Leadership Development in Russia

Stanislav V. Shekshnia, Daniel J. McCarthy and Sheila M. Puffer

Introduction

Leadership development in Russia has changed dramatically since the introduction of a market-oriented economy, but especially during the last several years. Under the Soviet system, managers were required to attend periodic upgrading of skills programs [Programmy povysheniia kvalifikatsii], which included topics on human resources management and leadership (Puffer 1981). Even these programs, however, disappeared during the market transition and virtually nothing emerged to facilitate leadership development appropriate for the new conditions. In recent years, however, a great deal of attention has been given to such efforts, particularly in the leading open stock companies. Many of the methods and techniques have drawn from Western management experience, but substantial aspects are adapted to the Russian environment. In spite of the substantial progress made by many large companies, other firms have lagged badly in their efforts at leadership development. This is one of many challenges in managing leadership development in Russia. Nonetheless, many progressive Russian executives recognize that leadership development programs can help improve the competitive positions and operations of their firms.

The purpose of this chapter is to present the status of leadership development in Russia, with its many opportunities and challenges. The chapter begins with an overview of leadership development globally. This is followed by findings from research, including insights from academic studies as well as interviews with company executives responsible for leadership development and participants in such programs. Russian leadership traditions and current needs are then discussed. New trends in leadership development are then presented both in Western multinationals operating in Russia and Russian companies. The growth of corporate universities is covered in the next section. The reluctance of some companies to develop these entities is discussed in the section, 'Exception That Proves the Rule?' The many challenges for leadership development to flourish in Russia are set out in the last section. The conclusion summarizes the major points of the chapter and discusses future developments.

Leadership Development in a Global World

Putting leadership development into a broad context, intellectual debate about whether leaders are born or made was launched by the Ancient Greek philosophers in the West and the Chinese classical philosophers in the East and survived well into the beginning of the twenty first century. However, while discussions continue, during the last half of the twentieth century, first American and later Western European corporations made development of future executives one of the centerpieces of their long term growth strategies. Leaders in this field such as GE, Procter & Gamble, Johnson & Johnson, and Danone have spent hundreds of millions of dollars creating in-house universities. They have directly involved senior executives and board members in the process, attracted top educators, and actively experimented with various developmental methods. They have attempted to harvest results of their work in terms of accelerating growth and sustainable profitability, higher market valuations, and strong reputation among investors, customers, and suppliers (The Economist 2003). Although companies differ somewhat in their approaches to leadership development, there is agreement among practitioners and academics about fundamentals that can make such development efforts effective in the global economy of the twenty first century.

People learn to be leaders by doing leadership work. Experience is key to leadership development. Nothing, including classroom training, self-education, study tours, and the like, can replace it. Successful organizations develop their managers by giving them challenging and relevant assignments, and providing support and feedback (Lombardo 1986; Kotter 1982; Vicino and Bass 1978).

Leadership development is an ongoing process, which should include top managers of the organization as well as those who will replace them in the future. The development of an executive is a natural progression over long period of time, which should reflect specifics of his/her current assignment, power position in the organizational hierarchy and skills and competencies acquired earlier. As the person progresses he/she acquires more complex cognitive maps, competencies and technical skills. Effective programs build on what has already been done and link development with promotions and horizontal moves (Jacobs and Jaques 1987; Bryson and Kelly 1978).

Business needs and strategy should drive development. Even though successful business executives share some common competencies, leadership development must reflect organizational specifics. Leadership theory and the most advanced companies have recognized this fact and develop specific leadership competencies, which are relevant to them rather than preparing 'leaders at large'. Being clear of what kind of leaders is needed is one of the fundamentals of successful leadership development programs (McCall, Jr. and Hollenbeck 2002; McCall, Jr. 1998).

Leadership can be learned, but natural talent is important. Development's effectiveness depends not only on getting right competencies profile and developmental tools, but also the right people. Since early experiences contribute to the making of a leader, pre-selection through various forms of assessment and evaluation has become an integral element of leadership development programs.

Leadership development is one of the core business processes of modern corporations. Having the right people go through the right experiences to develop the right competencies requires an ongoing professional approach within the organization that includes selection, job design, support, mentoring, monitoring, evaluation, and the like. To master this process, which is fundamental to long-term competitiveness, companies need to develop special expertise and make significant investments (Latham 1988).

The ultimate responsibility for development falls on the leader. Even with the most sophisticated organizational support, things do not happen without effort. Aspiring leaders have to assume ownership of the process, seek developmental opportunities, look for feedback and mentoring, and go through continuous self-reflection. Some companies encourage such behaviours by including development in their review processes and incentive schemes (Akin 1987; Bass and Vaughan 1966).

Other people play a critical role in leadership development. People become better leaders by interacting with others – followers, peers, bosses, customers, suppliers, and others. The quality of those interactions greatly influences the outcomes of a developmental process. Leading companies ensure that future leaders have positive role models among their senior executives, have sufficient time with capable mentors, and receive constructive feedback from superiors, subordinates, and peers. They create a culture of open dialogue, which greatly facilitates development (Kets de Vries 2001; Bass, Waldman, Avolio and Bebb 1987; Wood and Hertz 1982).

The complex task of leadership development warrants a variety of developmental methods enhancing learning from experience. Although leadership education should stress action rather than theory, many methods including such traditional teaching tools as lectures, group discussions, skills training, role playing, simulations, and sensitivity training have demonstrated their effectiveness as auxiliary instruments in development programs (Burke and Day 1986; Hultman 1984; Manz and Sims 1986).

Although developmental principles might be the same, different cultures require specific approaches. In all countries and companies, future leaders learn from experience and feedback, greatly benefit from targeted development, and must bear primary responsibility for their own development. But cultural specifics should not be neglected, and even within the same company, leadership development programs should reflect local nuances. Development of truly global executives requires providing international exposure at an early career stage and should include explicit cross-cultural training and experience (McCall, Jr. and Hollenbeck 2002).

In the following sections we examine the current state and trends of leadership development in Russia according to these principles, and see to what extent they apply to Russia. We will try to identify what uniquely Russian is happening there, and what has relevance beyond Russia.

Research Data

The academic literature on leadership development in Russia is scarce. Most publications describe the challenges faced by foreign multinationals launching operations in the country, local companies struggling to adapt to the emerging market economy, and educational institutions moving from teaching how to operate under the communist system to how to navigate under capitalism (Shekshnia 1998; Puffer and Associates 1996; Puffer 1992). The authors acknowledge the enormous need for leadership development at all corporate levels, and for all types of organizations, whether foreign multinationals, joint ventures, or private and state-owned Russian companies. We emphasize the need for organizations to include traditional business education, which in the West is usually seen as part of a pre-leadership development stage. Also important are personal responsibility on the part of future executives and traditional Western leadership development programs. Some interesting case studies have been written on developing Russian managers at such international companies as McDonald's and Otis Elevator and at Western business schools such as Harvard Business School, Northeastern University, and California State University at Hayworth. Political and economic changes in Russia have sparked interest in management education, which has created a wave of innovative approaches in the country. These include programs in 'civilized' entrepreneurship that combine attitude change seminars, business courses, and physical fitness, open games, assessment centers, sensitivity training, and marathon seminars.

Most of that research, however, was conducted in the 1990s. Since then, Russia, its economy, companies, and business leaders have undergone remarkable changes. The country has a relatively stable market economy that is growing faster than those of most developed nations. Many of its businesses have gone through painful restructuring programs since the 1998 financial crisis, and are expanding both in Russia and internationally. Some firms have become publicly owned and listed in New York, London, Frankfurt, or Moscow. Unlike ten years ago, it is hard to find a Russian CEO who is unfamiliar with such concepts as market capitalization, internal rate of return, project management, customer segmentation, corporate governance, or leadership development. But the situation in these areas has not become less challenging. It is the nature of the challenges that has changed over the last five years. We will examine these challenges using three principle sources of data: our academic research, consulting practice, interviews with executives of Russian companies, and Russian print and Web-based publications.

The first author of this chapter has extensive hands-on experience with leadership development in Russia, including having written the first Russian-language market-oriented human resources management book (Shekshnia 1996). Early in his executive career, he was responsible for setting up one of the first such programs at Otis Elevator in the early 1990s. Currently, he is involved as a consultant with leadership development programs in a number of Russian companies including TNK-BP (oil and gas), Ilim Pulp Enterprise (pulp and paper), SUEK (energy), RusPromAuto (automotive), KAMAZ (automotive), Megafon (telecom), Parquet

Hall (retail), News Outdoors (advertising), Multon (soft drinks), Sophia and Alexandra (food), and Sidanco (oil).

To expand our knowledge base we have conducted two types of interviews. We discussed leadership development with executives with responsibility for it in Russian companies, as well as with people who had participated in such programs. The interviewees included company owners, directors of company boards, CEOs, senior executives with line and HR responsibilities, business unit managers, training and development managers, middle managers, and high potentials. They worked at such leading companies as Troika Dialog (investment banking), Rosgosstrakh (insurance), Microsoft (software), SAP (software), Wimm-Bill-Dann (soft drinks and dairy products), Goldman Sachs (investment banking), IrkutskEnergo (energy), MTS (telecom), VimpelCom (telecom), Norilsk Nickel (metals), Otis Elevator (vertical transportation), Ilim Pulp Enterprise, TNK-BP, RusPromAuto, SUEK, News Outdoors, and Parquet Hall.

Russian Leadership Traditions and Current Needs

One cannot understand leadership development in any country without taking into account existing cultural traditions and norms. Over the centuries, Russia has developed its own distinct model of effective leadership, which has a strong impact on politics, business, and social life. The best way to briefly describe what Russians think about leaders is to present the country's most admired leader of all time – Tsar Peter the Great.

Peter, a visionary, assertive, decisive, and combative and, at the same time, protective and sensitive to rank-and-file people, remains in the Russian collective memory a role model of the effective leader. Russians recognize him as the man who created the most modern army and navy of his era, who conquered important Baltic shores, defeated Swedish King Carl XII, destroyed the old ruling class of Boyars, and put commoners into important government positions. Peter's brutality and the enormous human cost of his reforms are accepted by many Russians as the ransom of glory.

If we go one step beyond the popular image, we see Peter as a very complex and contradictory figure, but also a highly effective change leader. Opportunistic in his actions, the Russian tsar was remarkable for his ability to focus on the future and for his determination to realize his ambitions. He played a disproportionately large role in ensuring the success of his reforms. His energy, continuous personal education and development, extraordinary capacity to lead by example, his speed and decisiveness, and his creation of a new culture all provide benchmarks for change leadership. However, his mistakes were as spectacular as his achievements. He failed to develop a critical mass of change agents within the different strata of society, and he did not prepare a successor, thus placing the continued course of reform in jeopardy after his death.

Peter's followers aspired to his great deeds, but fell short of his achievements. Often effective in crisis situations, Russian leaders struggled with long-term development, comprehensive project implementation, operational effectiveness, and day-to-day management. As with Peter himself, many Russian leaders have a poor record in succession planning and development. There are few positive cases of succession at the top of Russian society. The majority of incoming leaders were not trained or prepared for their jobs, and did not even know they would be given the job. Leaders such as Alexander Nevsky, Ivan the Terrible, Lenin, and Stalin left a mess after their deaths. The only Russian monarch who devoted a significant amount of time and designed a special program to develop a successor was Catherine the Great, a former German Princess without a drop of Russian blood. Skeptical about her son's ability to rule the country, she made a great effort to develop her grandson, the future emperor Alexander I, for that role. But that exception only proved the rule. What typically prevailed were short-term thinking, unlimited desire to hold on to power, and fear of being overthrown by potential successors. These flaws prevented Russian leaders from fulfilling the role that no real leader should fail at: developing other leaders who would eventually replace them.

Peter the Great put in place what could be called the first formal system of leadership development in Russia. In his model of an all-encompassing state, all male offspring of noble families were to receive education in the Russian language, arithmetic, Orthodox religion, and good manners. They also had to serve the motherland either in the military or civilian service starting as a private or at the lowest civilian level, regardless of the family's standing in society. Peter opened the first institution to train future leaders, the Navigation School, and brought many Western professors to Russia. He even published a book to teach children from 'good' families appropriate behaviours and values. A great enthusiast for formal education, Peter nevertheless believed in life-long development, where experience played the most important role. He organized study tours to Western Europe for talented youth, and promoted promising people into challenging jobs regardless of their age or family background, the two typical cornerstones of career advancement in traditional Russian society.

After Peter's death, the system started to deteriorate within the corrupt culture of eighteenth-century Russian society. Noble families enlisted their newborn sons to the army, who by the age of 18 automatically reached an officer's rank. Later, mandatory service was abolished, the State stopped supporting study trips abroad leaving it up to families, and family ties replaced merit as the principal career driver. By the end of the nineteenth-century, the development of future leaders was left to a small circle of elite educational institutions based in the two Russian capitals – St Petersburg and Moscow – similar to the French grandes écoles. As in other countries of continental Europe of that time, training emphasized technical competency rather than people skills. The only institution that developed current leaders rather than future ones was the Russian military, which opened a few institutions of advanced education, including its famous Academy of General Staff in St Petersburg. There was no formal business education in Russia, and engineers, former military officers, and self-made entrepreneurs ran the rapidly growing factories and trading companies. With its emphasis on academic excellence, the Russian educational system of the late nineteenth and early twentieth-centuries produced many talented scientists, writers, musicians, and artists, but few capable leaders. The history of the country's industrial relations is full of violent worker riots, murders of managers and owners, contained only with the bloody intervention of the army and the police.

The October 1917 revolution changed this, and yet many traditions reemerged under different names. The State was even more centralized than under Peter the Great, and everyone, not only noblemen, had to serve it. The system of leadership development reflected the logic of centralization. There was one responsible organization, the Communist Party, which believed that the country needed only a few very capable people at the top and armies of followers each trained in a narrow skill at the bottom. Therefore, the Party selected and developed leaders of different types – super-loyal, unquestioning, and hard-working people for the lower level, Marxist intellectual apparatchiks with multidisciplinary work experience for district and regional-level jobs, and very capable bureaucrats with a broad knowledge and experience base for key political and industry positions. The Party had its own educational institutions with different levels of sophistication, thousands of professional educators, and multimillion ruble budgets, and it used such advanced tools as challenging assignments, job rotation, shadowing, mentoring, and coaching. At the same time, virtually nothing was happening at the enterprise level, where general managers were responsible for technical skills of their workers, but not for developing their successors or even direct reports.

In spite of its large scale and plentiful resources, the Soviet system of leadership development never was very effective and, in fact, failed miserably. The scale was probably one of the reasons for its ineffectiveness, since virtually no one assumed ownership nor felt emotionally involved with future leaders who could end up being transferred anywhere from Kamchatka in the east to Erevan in the south. Other reasons have more to do with Russian culture – traditional short-term thinking, fear of capable competitors, and the tendency to promote people on the basis of family ties or personal loyalty rather than merit. All these traditions worked against the well-intended system.

But as in 1917, events of 1991–92 changed everything again. The centralized system collapsed, and enterprises moved into the hands of new private owners who were left to their own devices both in managing the business and developing its future leaders. A few erratic attempts were undertaken by the Yeltsin government to provide State support for developing business leaders, such as a presidential management development program. These produced one important but disappointing result: it convinced rational people not to count on the government in this area of activity.

New Trends in Leadership Development in Russia

Western Multinationals

Western multinationals such as McDonald's, Otis Elevator, and PepsiCo, all of which entered the Russian market in the late 1980s, brought the concept of in-house leadership development into the country. The first author, at the time Director for Human Resources at Otis Elevator, Russia, remembers the initial shock that these programs produced among Russian managers as well as the enthusiasm they later generated. Since those days, multinationals in Russia have changed little of their strategic approach to developing local management talent. They use systems, methods, and tools designed in their world or European headquarters. More advanced organizations add some local flavor, but the centralized approach continues to dominate. Multinationals were, and to a large extent remain, the principal source of innovation in leadership development in Russia. They brought to the country such widely used instruments as leadership competencies profiles, assessment centers, succession planning, study tours, customized MBA programs, and secondments (temporary assignments in other positions or organizations). Recently such companies as Mars and British American Tobacco introduced their leadership development programs to the market, targeting recent graduates and young professionals. Known as the Mars Graduate Development Programmes (MGDPs) and the Challenge Initiative, respectively, the programs encourage applications from young professionals working for other companies, and provide two to three years of on-the-job training combined with leadership development training.

Although Western multinationals' leadership development programs have been present in Russia for at least 15 years, there is no hard data about their effectiveness. On the one hand, we still see expatriates managing many Russian subsidiaries of Western multinationals, and hear them speak about the shortage of leadership talent in Russia. On the other hand, such graduates of large multinationals' developmental programs as Olga Dergunova (President of Microsoft, Russia and CIS) and Alexander Izosimov (CEO, VimpelCom and ex-CEO, Mars, Central and Eastern Europe) became very successful and visible business leaders in Russia. Some people like Izosimov and Maxim Shirokov (CEO of UralKaliy, formerly of MMM) successfully moved from multinationals to Russian-owned and managed organizations. However, often Russian executives with successful track records in foreign subsidiaries fail to repeat their success in Russian companies. Ekaterina Ryasentseva, Managing Partner of Anderson Partners executive search firm explains: 'These people are used to stable organizational environments with clear rules, but in Russian companies everything is very opaque, and one needs to have a good instinct for figuring out the rules. Also, unlike in Western multinationals, business owners are very involved and senior executives fight for their attention. Many Russians experienced in Western companies do not particularly like it.'

There is certainly some truth in her words. Privately owned Russian companies put additional pressure on executives. Their founders are still around and they not only expect quick results, but also believe that they know how to achieve them. In the end, they just make decisions themselves. By way of additional contrast, for top executives of Russian subsidiaries of global companies the major challenge is to manage downward. For their colleagues in Russian companies, the major challenge is managing upward, a competency rarely developed in traditional programs.

While some Russians have done extremely well leading local operations of multinational companies, there are virtually no examples of Russian executives moving into leadership positions with global responsibilities. In part this could be a consequence of another phenomenon, the booming Russian economy that requires more and more management talent to run local businesses, and pushes the owners to rethink the whole strategy of staffing their top ranks.

While the achievements of multinationals' development programs in preparing leaders for their global operations and top jobs in privately owned Russian companies may be modest, they definitely succeeded in minting developmental experts for the latter. Russians with experience in HR departments of foreign companies, who started to move en masse to Russian enterprises in the early 2000s, brought with them not only top-notch knowledge, but also a culture of continuous development. In the process, they became a driving force in the leadership development revolution that is taking place in the country's private sector.

Russian Private Companies

In 2000, a prominent Russian businessman told one of the authors that he had no intention of spending money and time on developing future executives, since he could 'always buy the readymade ones'. By 2005, all of his companies of any significance had in-house executive development programs with multimillion-ruble budgets. The businessman had not been converted to a new religion of human development. However, he remains a shrewd opportunist but no longer sees opportunities to recruit top executives of the type he wants, with the qualities he needs, at a price he can afford.

This example demonstrates the new attitude of Russian companies toward leadership development. It is now one of the priorities, is well financed, and is driven by the business owners who have embraced the concept for their managers and themselves. Interestingly, much of the concept behind Severstal University, one of the best-known centers for management development in Russia, was initially presented in an MBA thesis written by the company's majority shareholder, Alexey Mordashov.

The combination of owners' determination, and knowledge acquired by their HR professionals and external consultants at Western multinationals, propelled leadership development into a high orbit. Better-run companies such as Severstal, Rosgosstrakh, VimpelCom, and Ilim Pulp managed to avoid traditional Russian attempts to reinvent the wheel, and instead borrowed the best global practices and adapted them to local realities. What they ended up with turned out to be very different programs. These range from the highly formalized Severstal University with hundreds of employees, its own training facilities and even a research center, to Ilim Pulp University with no permanent staff. The two, however, share some important common features.

Leadership Development Goes Beyond Training Successful Russian businesspeople are famous for quick learning. As soon as they started to think seriously about leadership development, they realized that classroom sessions would not be enough. Thus, leadership development programs in leading Russian companies normally include such elements as periodic assessment of competencies, personal mentoring, special projects, and job rotation. For example, Ilim Pulp, Russia's largest pulp and paper producer, has a program targeting employees with potential to eventually run its business units, or even the whole company. The program called 'Corporate Entrepreneur' includes all of the development components mentioned above. In 2004, the company selected 32 people to enter the program, and in 2005, 16 more joined. The selection process, which runs in stages, includes leadership competencies assessment, IQ (intellectual quotient) and EQ (emotional quotient) testing, interviews with experienced leadership consultants, and informal evaluation by senior managers and company owners. In 2004, the program consisted of five one-week in-class modules covering such themes as leadership, corporate intrapreneurship, business strategy, marketing, people management, finance, creativity, and individual business projects. The latter had to produce tangible contributions to the company's principal strategic goal, doubling its value. Projects were presented to top management, and new job assignments were given to each participant. Throughout the program, every participant worked with a mentor who was a member of the executive team. Experienced consultants evaluated his/her performance during class sessions and provided feedback. In 2005, the 2004 group met again, and was also working as mentors to the next wave of 'corporate entrepreneurs'.

Developing Values Research studies have found that successful Russian companies that emerged in the 1990s had strong and distinctive ideologies developed by their founders (Kets de Vries, Shekshnia, Korotov, and Florent-Treacy 2004a, 2004b). The 'ideological' aspect is strongly present in leadership development. According to Ivetta Kolymba, Training and Development Director at Rosgosstrakh: 'To put it simply, a training center is about training, while a corporate university (for leadership development) is about ideology.' Unlike ten years ago, companies expect their executives not only to be professionals, but also to share fundamental values. GE's Jack Welch's famous 'values/performance' matrix is becoming more and more popular among Russian companies and their owners. The essence of the matrix is that executives must demonstrate that they share company values or will be dismissed regardless of their performance.

The first author of this chapter facilitated a special session at a large Russian company in 2005 where owners, senior managers, and members of a high-potential management group debated for two days a three-page document, 'Principles of Corporate Ideology'. One of the outcomes was a decision to evaluate every executive's performance and behaviour not only in terms of key financial performance indicators, but also in terms of the spirit of the document. According to the chairman of the board, who is also the principal shareholder, the meeting was 'probably the most important part of a development program for the young guys, but it was equally important for the senior people. It refreshed their minds and underlined priorities. We don't want just to make money. We want to make money in a certain way, and people who manage this business should act in this way.'

Participation of Key Players When Russian businesspeople think something is important, they often spend money and personal time on it, and make sure their managers do the same. Business owners and senior executives participate in leadership development in many ways. They act as champions of the process like Severstal's Mordashov, or Ilim Pulp's Boris Zingarevich, who were a driving force behind their companies' programs. The latter is now spokesperson and chairman of Ilim's Corporate University board.

They follow up on the development of people participating in the program and facilitate their development by creating organizational opportunities for them. While chairman of Rosgosstrakh, Russia's largest insurance company, Ruben Vardanian personally reviewed the progress of every participant in the leadership development program. He also meets with every employee of his investment bank, Troika Dialog, who has attended a leadership course within or outside the company.

Senior executives also act as faculty at leadership development programs and as personal mentors to some of the participants. The leaders of VimpelCom, a national cellular operator, Volga-Dnepr, a cargo airline, and many other Russian companies believe that senior executives are the best instructors when it comes to teaching future leaders. While it is hard to overestimate the motivational component of such arrangements and the relevance of the material, the quality of the instruction unfortunately often destroys such benefits. Few executives have a natural talent for teaching adults, almost none of them have had special training in how to do so, and all of them have a chronic shortage of time to prepare for the job. We have witnessed on numerous occasions the poor-quality jobs performed by these very senior people, who simply read from slides prepared for them by their aides and had no idea what the audience was interested in. In Russia, where leaders play a disproportionately large role, the consequences of such mishaps could be long lasting for the young managers as well as the company.

Research shows that personal mentoring by experienced business people is one of the most powerful leadership development tools (Whitely, Dougherty and Dreher 1988; Kram 1983). Unfortunately, this instrument has not been successfully used in modern Russia. Traditionally, Russian leaders spent little or no time working individually with their successors, and this situation has not yet changed for the better. Most business leaders, who are now in their 30s and early 40s and who have never been mentored, find it hard to make a continuous effort to work with a few people on a one-to-one basis. They prefer to address larger groups or to delegate the task to professional coaches who cannot create the same effect as they might. Those who try mentoring often find that they lack specific skills to do so, and do not always know what to do with the mentees. According to one well-intentioned mentor: 'I really wanted to mentor S. and we agreed to meet every two weeks. But after two meetings, I did not know what to say and S. did not know what to ask. It was very embarrassing for both of us.' The traditional culture of high power distance does not facilitate the mentoring process, but leaders like Vardanian of Troika have become very skillful both at being mentored and mentoring others (Kets de Vries, Shekshnia, Korotov and Florent-Treacy 2004a). Such examples show that the process can become successful in Russian companies just as in many US corporations, which themselves are not low power distance organizations.

Best Expertise Sought Russian enterprises are often compared to the fortresses surrounded by the enemy, because of their desire to have everything they think they need in house. At the same time, these owners have a reputation as fast learners and early adopters when it comes to strategically important issues. With leadership development, some top Russian companies have managed to take the best from both approaches. They work with outside experts (leadership development consultants, Russian and international business schools and universities, and academics) in designing and delivering programs, but they retain the ownership of the program in their own hands.

The days of generic leadership seminars, in which local or international trainers delivered the same content to many organizations, are essentially gone. Company specifics are reflected in what these firms develop (leadership competencies profiles and corporate values), how they develop (program content), how they evaluate progress (assessment tools) and what they do later with the participants (promotion, reward, separation). Beyond the individual leaders, attention must be paid to other executives and managers who also need substantial management development in numerous areas, including an assessment of personal and corporate values (May, Puffer and McCarthy 2005). Without this broader-based leadership development, Russian companies would have a difficult time competing beyond the country's borders, and even with international competitors within Russia (McCarthy, Puffer, Vihanski and Naumov 2005). Some companies such as Yukos prefer to have the lion's share of the resources residing in house, while others such as Ilim Pulp opt for outsourcing. Yet, all of them actively seek best practices and expert help in developing and operating their systems.

Rapid growth is now occurring in the new market for leadership development consultants, and international players such as PwC, IMD, or INSEAD compete with new Russian powerhouses such as MTI or Ecopsy. Additionally, leading international experts such as Manfred Kets de Vries of INSEAD and the Netherlands work with Russian companies and individual businesspeople. Some enterprises have been building long-term partnerships with leading providers. For instance, Yukos has developed such relationships with IMD, and TNK-BP has done so with INSEAD. And Russian boutiques specializing only in leadership development have popped up in Moscow and St Petersburg to quench an increasing thirst for the best techniques and materials, and command international fees for their services. These have generally been founded by former executives with relevant experience and/or appropriate education.

Even more important, however, is that Russian companies are engaged in an ongoing dialogue about leadership development. Conferences, seminars, and roundtables such as 'Executive's Personality and its Development in Today's World' or 'The Future of Leadership Development' attract hundreds of participants including owners and senior managers of leading enterprises. In fact, the theme of corporate leadership development has spawned a vibrant informal community where ideas and best practices are shared on a regular basis and where the future of leadership development is debated.

Significant Resources Committed The breakthrough that numerous Russian companies achieved in leadership development was well funded and staffed. In organizations where business owners took interest in it, such programs helped transform the firms from underdogs into corporate stars. Companies such as Severstal, TNK-BP, MTS, VimpelCom, Rosgosstrakh, and Ilim Pulp spent millions and in some cases tens of millions of dollars on developing their future leaders, and they did everything to get the best people in the field to work with them. Another important feature is the participation of the top managers, who, as mentioned earlier, take part in the process in many roles. According to Boris Zingarevich of Ilim Pulp: 'By making most senior managers part of the development effort, we greatly reduce potential resistance and threats to our hi-pos. Yes, the direct return on a dollar spent developing a mature executive is far less compared to a talented 30-year-old manager. But when I include them, I show that it is important and mandatory for everyone.'

Talent Flight The booming Russian economy has made management talent very valuable, significantly raising executive compensation and increasing managers' mobility in the process. Participation in leadership development programs makes managers of large Russian companies even more attractive for headhunters and their clients. Retaining future leaders is becoming as challenging as developing them. Some companies try to bind them by creating sophisticated legal arrangements or long-term incentive plans. Ekaterina Ryasentseva, Managing Director of Anderson Partners executive search company, is skeptical about the effectiveness of such an approach: 'If our clients really want somebody, they will buy him out of any agreements.' Alexander Yushkevich, CEO of RusPromAuto, says: 'There is always going to be someone who offers more money to your best people, but they will stay with you as long as they are challenged on the job and feel that they are being treated fairly.'

Ruben Vardanian of Troika Dialog looks at the issue philosophically: 'I never agonize over the departure of good people. Who are they going to work for – our competitors or our clients, or our future clients? It means they will work to make our industry better in their new positions of more importance than they had with us. It's great, because we all benefit from a better and bigger investment banking industry. I do not mind developing people for others.'

Corporate Universities

Another important feature of how Russian companies manage their leadership development programs deserves a special section. The reason is that no matter what the content of the program may be, there is a strong desire to give it the name, Corporate University.

Although in-house leadership development efforts in Russia take different forms, corporate universities have become a symbol of the movement. They mushroomed at giant conglomerates with hundreds of thousands of employees such as Severstal, and at much smaller companies with less than a thousand people. The universities come in different shapes and sizes, some as the above-mentioned Severstal Corporate University are very large and important, receive international recognition, and include various programs serving different constituencies of managers. Others remain exclusive clubs where only the top people in the organization are admitted. All, however, share common characteristics, which make them an interesting and dynamic phenomenon in today's Russia.

First, they appeal to their 'students'. In-company surveys consistently demonstrate that corporate universities are among the most attractive perks organizations offer to their managers. Russians have traditionally loved to study, and the high status of a university in tsarist and Soviet societies only partially explains this attitude. At least two other aspects are equally if not more important. One is the opportunity to discuss issues of fundamental importance to the company, and another is the opportunity to interact with the most senior people in the company as well as peers from other departments. According to one graduate of Ilim Pulp University:

> The University gives you an opportunity to feel like an important part of the company, not a small piece in a large machine. There, you can talk about things you don't even think on the job – corporate vision, strategy, and the future of the company. And since the most senior people in the company participate, you have a feeling that your voice has been heard.'

It is important that many corporate universities started off with the most senior people as participants. VimpelCom University started with one group of senior management. Ilim Pulp University started with a program called DA (the first Russian letters of Directors and Shareholders), which brought together owners of the business, as well as the company CEO and most senior executives. A graduate of Sidanco University, the oil major that became part of TNK-BP, noted:

> The program was a platform for building a network, which is very helpful for me now. When I have an issue, I never go to my boss. I call on my University buddies, who do the same jobs as business unit leaders in other regions, and in 95 per cent of the cases they help me to come up with a solution.

Universities, which often have their own charters, logos, pins, T-shirts, and other attributes often develop cultures on their own and become elite clubs within corporations. In some companies their alumni constitute a compact, but powerful network that can have a strong influence on performance as well as change programs. According to Irina Gorbacheva, Training and Development Manager of Rostelecom, a long distance telephone company, their Corporate University 'serves as an information channel, which transmits corporate values, traditions, and behavioural norms to all levels of the organization.' Again, the ideological component is very pronounced here.

But participants' enthusiasm and motivation serve some other corporate goals as well. For Dmitry Afanasiev, (Director, Corporate University, Severstal): 'The University not only translates knowledge, but creates it. It follows new market and industry trends, innovates, and operates in a proactive mode.' Companies like Rosgosstrakh and Ilim Pulp, which regard their corporate universities as laboratories for new knowledge generation and development of strategic decisions, have benefited from breakthrough ideas. Most importantly, they have reaped benefits from a shared authorship of key initiatives which usually produces shared responsibility for implementation.

The word, 'university', often evokes images of brick and mortar structures with traditional classrooms, lectures, and final exams. However, the reality of many Russian corporate universities is far from that picture. They often represent islands of innovation in otherwise conservative corporate environments. Ilim Pulp, a large company often criticized for its bureaucracy, runs its IPE University as a virtual project. The university has no permanent administrative staff or faculty, nor its own premises. Yet in 2005, 250 managers were to go through seven different programs, including its core leadership development 'Corporate Entrepreneur' course. The University board, chaired by one of the owners, makes all-important decisions, including selection of the participants and their projects, curriculum, new appointments and budget. The project teams design specific programs, and consist of two company managers, two leadership development consultants, and an administrative assistant. The teams hire outside providers and manage team and program logistics. Every program has an outside consultant as a core provider responsible for the team's deliverables, participant assessments, and follow-up. The core provider designs detailed content, brings in external and internal (company managers) faculty, and supports the process. Boris Zingarevich, the University board chairman noted:

> We decided to apply a very modern approach to managing our University and we are very happy with it. Not only have we protected it from our bureaucracy, but we have also shown the rest of the company that you can realize large-scale projects with a handful of people. Now the project management approach is spreading throughout the organization.

Corporate universities try to utilize what the rest of the world has developed. Severstal has a special e-learning department within its University with programs for executives, managers, and specialists. Many other companies put their programs in electronic format and make them available to long-distance users. Projects, case studies, business games, and simulations are among the latest methods that have been actively used. After having learned what others have done, some Russian companies begin developing their own original teaching tools. Rosgosstrakh has designed an in-house simulation to train regional managers, Severstal people are writing Russia-specific cases since their students prefer them to international materials, and Ilim Pulp has experimented with mixing high-potentials with members of the executive team. Still, the general trends in Russian corporate universities are similar to those in leading international ones. They combine work and study in various ways, use company-specific materials with an outlook to the larger world, employ company managers and specialists as faculty in addition to external consultants and academics, use a variety of teaching methods in the classroom, and actively make use of technology as well as the time between sessions, and place strong emphasis on networking.

Exception That Proves the Rule?

While corporate universities are becoming a vehicle of choice for many Russian companies, some of them opt for different strategies of leadership development. A notable exception is TNK-BP, a 50:50 joint venture created in 2003 between BP and private Russian shareholders. The JV is the result of the merger between TNK, the fourth largest Russian oil company at the time, Sidanco, and BP. The company, with 100,000 employees and revenues of $12 billion, is one of the largest enterprises in the country, and is often used by other companies as a benchmark for effective management of assets, processes, and people. According to its CEO Bob Dudley, TNK-BP sees development of its future leaders as one of the foremost important strategic goals of the company for the next five years. Its HR department has assembled a very competent team of developmental specialists, but does not yet have a corporate university and does not intend to build one.

According to Paul McMorran, an executive with TNK-BP, instead of combining leadership development activities under a corporate university umbrella, TNK-BP prefers to manage assessment, training, evaluation, and promotion separately. In each of these areas, the company works actively with leading external providers. It has struck partnerships with two leading business schools – INSEAD in Europe and Thunderbird in the USA – which provide leadership development programs to two audiences – future senior executives and current senior executives.

The Thunderbird program concentrates on leadership in the global oil and gas industry and is designed to enhance participants' effectiveness in their current jobs by providing them with new strategic and competitive frameworks, reviewing trends in global energy markets, interacting with leading thinkers in the field, and reflecting on their personal leadership styles. The INSEAD program aims at broadening participants' perspective, increasing their self-awareness as future leaders, and providing them with the latest leadership tools and instruments. TNK-BP's top executives, including the CEO, board members, and other Russian shareholders, regularly participate in both programs as faculty and guest speakers. According to McMorran, the two programs launched in 2004 are very successful. INSEAD's program during 2005 was four times oversubscribed, and the company ran three consecutive sessions. Also in 2005, TNK-BP was working on developmental programs for young high potentials and first-line leaders, and both programs would most likely be delivered by an outside provider. A corporate university was not on the company's agenda. However, some of the participants in the leadership development program at INSEAD suggested that such a large organization as TNK-BP needs something in-house to develop common values and behavioural norms, since programs run by outside providers for a limited number of participants could never satisfy this need. What could the vehicle be? Why not TNK-BP University?

Challenges in Managing Leadership Development in Russia

We have described the experiences of companies that have recently taken the lead in leadership development in Russia. Their achievements are impressive, but the picture would not be complete without discussing other companies as well as the serious challenges that even these leading firms face.

No Results Yet

Massive financial and emotional investments in leadership development recently undertaken by large Russian companies have not produced any significant results, except further increasing the mobility of senior managers among Russian companies. Anecdotal evidence suggests that people who participate in developmental programs feel good about it, but the new cohort of in-house developed senior executives has not yet emerged as a phenomenon in the Russian market. This should be expected, however, since most programs are only one to three years old, and Western experience shows that it takes much longer than that to develop a fully capable executive. What is worrisome is that we do not even hear about individual cases of people being promoted into the top jobs. One of our clients who is running a serious leadership development program still prefers to go outside to the market to fill senior positions. This senior executive explained: 'The leaders we are developing will be ready in five years, but we need to make serious changes now.' Clearly this approach is somewhat contradictory to the philosophy of home-grown management and a value-driven organization that this company's leadership has proclaimed.

Thin Layer of Expertise

Although leading Russian companies have some specialists in leadership development whose skills meet global standards, their number is limited, and a new supply is constrained. As with leaders themselves, the best way to learn the trade is to practice it alongside experienced people. Historically, Western multinationals operating in the country provided such a training ground for Russian nationals, but they cannot satisfy the growing demand. Russian companies may soon face a shortage of developmental specialists unless they undertake in-house efforts to develop their own cadre of these professionals. Thus far, we are not aware of any such programs of significance.

The booming leadership development consulting sector only aggravates the problem noted above by attracting development specialists from operating companies. However, the consultants themselves experience a shortage of skills. Trying to meet increasing demand, they hire under qualified people and assign them to projects they cannot not possibly handle, thus creating tensions within the organization and in relationships with clients. Experienced people are overstretched, which drives up costs for client companies and negatively impacts consultants' performance. What is worse, since they are overloaded with assignments, consultants have little time or incentive to grow the next generation of professionals.

Lack of Specific Skills

Even the better-staffed Russian companies suffer from the lack of specific skills which come only with experience, and which also did not exist in traditional Russian organizations. The most critical of these is the mentoring ability of senior people, primarily owners and CEOs. Without it, leadership development programs will never be fully effective, and the national culture does not favour mentoring behaviour. However, the fact that a number of successful Russian business leaders have gone against the flow suggests that there is some hope (Kets de Vries, Shekshnia, Korotov and Florent-Treacy 2004a). From their example, spreading an image of the mentoring role as a critical and integral activity of successful global business leaders could help a great deal. Also, the increasing age of today's owners and CEOs should facilitate the process.

Another important but missing skill, organizational design, is related to the previous one. Although Russian organizations recognize that leaders could only be developed by doing leadership work, most are very weak in providing such opportunities. Not only are many organizations centralized with few P&L-responsibility jobs and little managerial autonomy, but their executives simply do not know how to design positions appropriate for future leaders. HR specialists, who understand job requirements, often lack a thorough knowledge of business, or have inadequate status to push the changes through. Also, many business managers have little understanding of what a 'developmental job' means and fear deterioration of the business's performance. The Russian cultural norm of intolerance of mistakes does not help the process.

Dependence on Owners

Like many other organizational initiatives such as budgeting, customer relations management, and corporate governance, leadership development took off relatively recently in Russian companies and only after business owners had realized its importance. This top-down approach has numerous advantages – high visibility for the initiative itself as well as the people developing it, speed in decision making, a green light for implementation, and serious funding. But it also has some serious risks. In organizations with no culture of leadership development or succession planning, the programs become exclusively dependent on the goodwill of one or two people. This makes these initiatives very vulnerable to such events as ownership change (not uncommon in today's Russia) or mood swings of key people. One of the authors was helping a large Russian manufacturer set up a comprehensive leadership development program, but in the course of the process, the majority stake changed hands and the new leadership canceled the program. As a consequence, a quarter of the participants left the organization, leaving the new owners to wonder what did they wrong.

This last example demonstrates what could become effective medicine against current over-dependency on owners' goodwill – external pressure. When having a development program becomes a must for attracting quality people, Russian companies will have no choice but to offer them, just as they have no choice but to pay market salaries no matter how high they become. But it will be a long road before this occurs for the majority of Russian managers and their current and prospective employees. A parallel situation exists in the area of corporate governance, which in most Russian companies is still completely dependent upon the attitudes and interests of one or more majority owners (McCarthy, Puffer and Shekshnia 2004).

Tip of the Iceberg

What we have discussed in this article so far applies primarily to large companies with sufficient size, market position, and resources to afford large-scale in-house leadership development programs. Although such companies represent a significant share of Russia's economy, hundreds of thousands of smaller enterprises face similar challenges, but lack the resources to deal with them in the same way. The founders of ParquetHall, a leading Russian retailer in floor coverings, decided as early as 2002 that they needed to replace themselves with professional managers at the helm of the company. Since then, they have had three CEOs, all of whom came from outside the company. With 400 employees operating in an extremely competitive market, the company could hardly afford its own leadership development program. ParquetHall cannot attract and keep talented HR specialists of the caliber of those at TNK-BP or Severstal. It would have a hard time paying external providers that those companies use, and its internal opportunities for creating developmental positions are limited. The founders hoped to use open-enrollment outside leadership development programs, but were disappointed with their quality. According to Andrey Linner, Chairman of the Board:

> The seminars you find in Moscow can teach a skill or two, but that's not what we want. And if you go to an executive development program at a Russian business school, you will end up in a class of 50 people, ranging from a sales girl at a Moscow jewelry store to

> a farmer from the south. All would be listening to a professor who knows as much about business as I do about teaching. I know there are some good programs abroad, but I can't send my high-potentials there since their English is pretty poor. And what can you get from one program anyway?

The situation ParquetHall faces is typical in today's Russia. Under the shining tip of the iceberg, there is a huge hole and a great need. The country does not have the people or infrastructure to help smaller companies with leadership development. There is no business school in Russia that could play the role as a center for developing and disseminating materials for leadership development. Also, there are not enough consultants who can work with smaller organizations, and there is a shortage of qualified HR professionals, even for large companies not to mention smaller ones.

We do, however, see three strategies smaller businesses could use to deal with this pressing challenge. First, they could bundle their needs and resources. Non-competing and possibly even competing companies could create consortia for jointly developing leaders, thus achieving economies of scale and competing with larger companies. Second, they could concentrate on using less expensive developmental tools such as on-the-job development and mentoring. To do that, however, leaders of the smaller companies would have to learn new skills and become mentors and coaches, which is difficult but not impossible. This could materialize since many of them are now at the stage of looking for new challenges in life. A third strategy might be to emphasize and promote self-development. The companies could make it one of their basic values and a condition for advancement, and then support and encourage aspiring leaders' initiatives. In any case, the help for smaller companies will not come from outside. Their leaders will have to rely on their own devices, but that is a competency that many of them have mastered over the last 15 years.

Conclusion

As noted in the introduction, the purpose of this chapter has been to present the status of leadership development in Russia with its many opportunities and challenges. Russian companies have drawn many leadership development tenets from Western practice, including a variety of developmental tools, innovations, and experimentations. They have embraced the reality that lasting change from leadership development programs and experiences can occur only if executives are involved by actually applying leadership development concepts to their own business decisions and situations. A major phenomenon has been the rapid growth of corporate universities within many large Russian companies which expose candidates to a wide range of experiences in house. Most of these companies, however, utilize outside professional consultants experienced in many aspects of leadership development.

Some aspects of leadership development within Russian companies are specific to the country itself. The whole idea of leadership development is presently limited to a relatively small number of very large companies, rather than being more broadly based within the Russian business community. A critical issue, given the exceedingly hands-on role of many Russian senior executives, is the need for support from such primary owners and even board members if leadership development programs are to be successful and have an impact within Russian companies. Two other issues specific to Russian companies are that there is no culture of development in Russian businesses, and the current leaders of Russian companies have little, if any, mentoring or teaching skills so critical to successful leadership development activities. On a favourable note, the government has not intruded into these activities, and this is viewed positively by most Russian executives.

Within the leadership development arena in Russia, the realization has developed among many senior executives in progressive companies that leadership development is an ongoing process and applies to all levels of management. Additionally, they understand that clarifying and shaping values are crucial components of leadership development. They understand further that leadership development must remain the responsibility of the recipients of such training and coaching. Finally, progressive executives have come to understand that leadership development in Russian companies will succeed only if strong executives and aspiring leaders insist that their companies provide them with such opportunities for personal development. Such programs should encourage them to remain with their organizations rather than leave for other opportunities.

References

Akin, G. (1987), 'Varieties of Managerial Learning', *Organizational Dynamics* 16: 2, 36–48.

Bass, B.M. and Vaughan, J.A. (1966), *Training in Industry: The Management of Learning* (Belmont, CA: Brooks/Cole).

Bass, B.M., Waldman, D.A., Avolio, B.J. and Bebb, M. (1987), 'Transformational Leadership and the Falling Dominoes Effect', *Group and Organization Studies* 12, 73–87.

Bryson, J. and Kelly, G. (1978), 'A Political Perspective on Leadership Emergence, Stability and Change in Organizational Networks', *Academy of Management Review* 3, 712–23.

— (2003), 'Coming and going', *The Economist*, 23 October 2003.

Hultman (1984), 'Managerial Work, Organizational Prospective, and the Training of Managers', *Scandinavian Journal of Educational Research* 28, 199–210.

Jacobs, T.O. and Jaques, E. (1987), 'Leadership in Complex Systems', in Zeindner, J. (ed.) *Human Productivity Enhancement* (New York: Praeger).

Kets de Vries, M.F.R. (2001), 'The Anarchist Within: Clinical Reflections on Russian Character and Leadership Style', *Human Relations* 5: 54, 585–628.

Kets de Vries, M.F.R., Shekshnia, S., Korotov, K. and Florent-Treacy, E. (2004a), *The New Russian Business Leaders* (Cheltenham, UK, and Northampton, MA: Edward Elgar).

Kets de Vries, M.F.R., Shekshnia, S., Korotov, K. and Florent-Treacy, E. (2004b), 'The New Global Russian Business Leaders: Lessons from a Decade of Transition', *European Management Journal* 6: 22, 637–48.

Kotter, J.P. (1982), *The General Managers* (New York: Free Press).

Kram, K.E. (1983), 'Phases of the Mentor Relationship', *Academy of Management Journal* 26, 608–25.

Latham, G. (1988), 'Human Resource Training and Development', *Annual Review of Psychology* 39, 545–82.

Lombardo, M.M. (1986), 'Questions about Learning from Experience', *Issues and Observations* 6: 1, 7–10.

Manz, C.C and Sims, H.P. (1986), 'Beyond Imitation: Complex Behaviour and Effective Linkages Resulting from Exposure to Leadership training Models', *Journal of Applied Psychology* 71, 571–78.

May, R.C., Puffer, S.M., and McCarthy, D.J. (2005), 'Transferring Management Knowledge to Russia: A Culturally Based Approach', *Academy of Management Executive* 19: 2, 24–35.

McCall, Jr., M.W. (1998), *High Flyers: Developing the Next Generation of Leaders* (Boston: Harvard Business School Press).

McCall, Jr., M.W. and Hollenbeck, G.P. (2002), *Developing Global Executives* (Boston: Harvard Business School Press).

McCarthy, D.J., Puffer, S.M., and Shekshnia, S.V. (eds) (2004), *Corporate Governance in Russia* (Cheltenham, UK, and Northampton, MA: Edward Elgar).

McCarthy, D.J., Puffer, S.M., Vikhanski, O.S. and Naumov, A.I. (2005), 'Russian Managers in the New Europe: Need for a New Management Style', *Organizational Dynamics* 34, 3, (forthcoming).

Puffer, S.M. (1981), 'Inside a Soviet Management Institute', *California Management Review*, 24, 90–96.

Puffer, S.M. (ed.) (1992), *The Russian Management Revolution: Preparing Managers for the Market Economy* (Armonk, NY: M.E.Sharpe).

Puffer, S.M. and Associates (1996), *Business and Management in Russia* (Cheltenham, UK and Brookfield, MA: Edward Elgar).

Shekshnia, S. (1998), 'Western Multinationals' Human Resource Practices in Russia', *European Management Journal* 12: 3, 298–305.

Shekshnia, S. (1996), *Upravlenie Personalom Sovremennoy Organizatsii* [Personnel Management in Contemporary Organization], Moscow, Russia, 1st edition 1996, 2nd edition1997, 3rd edition 1998, 4th 2000, 5th 2001, 6th 2002.

Vicino, F. and Bass, B.M. (1978), 'Life Space Variables and Managerial Success', *Journal of Applied Psychology* 63, 81–88.

Whitely, W., Dougherty, T.W. and Dreher, G. F. (1988), 'The Relationship of Mentoring and Socioeconomic Origin to Managers' and Professionals' early Career Progress, Proceedings', *Academy of Management* (Anaheim, CA), 58–62.

Wood, F.R. and Hertz, R. (1982), 'Influential Associations in Organizations. Proceedings', *Academy of Management* (New York), 399–402.

Chapter 3

Control and Alienation in Russian Enterprises

Moshe Banai and William D. Reisel

Research has shown that workers who have little control over their jobs and their immediate work environment tend to exhibit a low level of job satisfaction, disloyalty to the organization, and alienation (Banai and Weisberg 2003; Marris 1996; Mirowsky and Ross 1989).

In this study we look into the relationships between 960 Russian workers' perceived control over their immediate environment and their level of alienation. More specifically, we analyze the relationships between the corporation's ownership type, the supervisor's leadership style, the worker's job and personal characteristics and the workers' level of alienation.

Current knowledge about corporate ownership, leadership style, job and individual characteristics, and alienation is presented in the following sections, followed by a description of the methods, the findings and the conclusions.

Ownership System: Private and Public

Comparative studies of public and private organizations that have been conducted in Western societies have reached the conclusion that there are some fundamental differences between the characteristics of the two types of organizations (Allison 1979; Bozeman 1987; Perry and Porter 1982; Perry and Rainey 1988). A study by Rainey, Backoff, and Levine (1976) suggested that public sector organizations tend to have objectives of greater diversity and vagueness, weaker and more fragmented supervisory authority, greater process rigidity, and fewer performance-based incentives than private sector organizations.

Empirical studies, mostly conducted in the U.S., support these descriptions (Perry and Rainey 1988). These studies revealed that public sector organizations are required to accomplish multiple goals, which are set by various constituencies, in a relatively short time frame (Allison 1979; Whorton and Whorthley 1981). Managers in the public sector were perceived to possess lower hierarchical authority as compared with managers in the private sector (Buchanan 1974). Public sector managers were found to posses weaker, more fragmented authority over subordinates, greater reluctance to delegate decision making, and greater difficulty in devising incentives to enhance efficient performance by their employees (Rainy et al. 1976). Lawler (1981) found that rewards contingent upon performance are not widely used by public sector managers. Others (Chubb and Moe 1988; Coursey and Rainey 1990; Rainey 1979, 1983) found that public sector managers reported having less flexibility in the application of personnel procedures as compared to managers in the private sector.

Despite the fact that studies conducted in other western countries came up with similar results (Lachman 1985; Solomon 1986) it is questionable whether these findings would be observed in transitional economic countries such as Russia.

Ownership Systems in Russia

Since the Bolshevik revolution in 1917, communism was the law of the Russian state. Private property was outlawed and a centrally planned economy, based on Lenin's vision of a united Russian economic system, was established. The Politburo was at the top of the national vertical chain of command, and the individual worker at the bottom. Gosplan, the central planning committee, was the politburo's economic arm, which designed five-year plans for the entire nation. These plans dictated what product would be produced in each plant, in what quantities, and at what internal price. Industrial ministries oversaw the execution of the five-year plans. Enterprise managers were personally responsible for meeting the production plans. Managers expected their subordinates to unquestioningly execute orders in exchange for housing, health and day care, recreational centers and other fringe benefits. As a direct result of Gorbachev's Glasnost [openness] and Perestroika [change] policies, the centrally planned economic system collapsed. In 1991 the Soviet Union ceased to exist and since then the country steadily has been shifting from its previous political and economic structure into a more democratic and free market economy.

This new economic system is, however, still in its rudimentary stage. Students of the Russian transformation into a free market economy have concluded that this transformation is less successful than that of other former Soviet states (Goldman 1997; Shama 1995). Thus, although the cultural difference between Russia and Western countries may not be as great as one may intuit, the distinction between a free market economy and a transitional economy could be substantial.

Only limited information has been available concerning the results of the privatization process for the structure of corporate ownership in Russia. The State Property Committee (GKI) released data on the number of privatizations, including some of their characteristics, but little on the actual ownership results. The State Statistics Committee [Goskomstat] records about 122,000 'changes of ownership type', but the only published classification divides firms only into the very general categories of 'state', 'mixed', and 'private'. It is yet unclear whether the new ownership structure is having positive effects on enterprise performance. Private owners may be more likely to restructure and to increase profits and productivity compared to the state. Private owners who are insiders in the firm may behave differently from those who are outsiders, as might those who play different roles: for example, managers versus workers, and individuals versus various types of institutional investors. Each type of owner may have different objectives and may face different constraints, compared with the others (Earle 1999).

The next section describes control mechanisms such as leadership and job characteristics and their influence over workers alienation in state owned and private enterprises in Russia. Individual characteristics are used to control for the two samples.

Leadership

Leadership studies have shown that successful leadership style is contingent upon four major factors: Leader's personal characteristics, employees' personal characteristics, group's characteristics and job and organizational characteristics. The three models that are sometimes used to depict leadership contingencies are those of Fiedler (1967, 1996), Hersey and Blanchard (1993) and House and Mitchell (1974).

Fiedler uses three variables to explain effective leader behaviour: group atmosphere, task structure, and leader position power. Hersey and Blanchard use group maturity, which is defined as the follower willingness and ability to perform a task, as an explanatory variable for effective leader behaviour. House uses employee needs and task characteristics to explain effective leader behaviour. While each of the models comprises unique variables, all three include some factors that are part of the leader-follower-situation triangle as core elements of the model. Effective leader behaviour has been defined in those studies and others (Blake and Mouton 1985) as one that is high on both people orientation and task orientation.

This study investigates, among others, the relationships between leadership and workers' alienation in Russian enterprises. It applies a variation on Fiedler's, House's and Hersey and Blanchard's interpretation of the contingencies of effective leadership and the Blake and Mouton measure of leadership effectiveness.

Leadership in the International literature

Leadership in organizations is the ability to influence, motivate, and direct others in order to attain desired organizational objectives. Western management literature has for many years emphasized the use of democratic/participatory leadership style as the preferred and most efficient. This literature has also emphasized a combination of people-oriented and task-oriented leadership style to have the potential of achieving the best organizational results. A current study in 62 countries (GLOBE) has demonstrated that while in practice many Western managers do not resort to this style, they frequently agree about its desirability (House et al. 2004).

The GLOBE studies have identified six major leadership styles as follows:

Charismatic/value based – This style reflects the ability to inspire, to motivate and to expect high performance outcomes from others on the basis of firmly held core values. It includes sub-scales such as visionary, inspirational, self-sacrifice, integrity, decisive, and performance oriented.

Team Oriented – This style emphasizes effective team building and implementation of a common purpose among team members. It includes sub-scales such as collaborative, team integrator, diplomatic, malevolent (reversed) and administratively competent.

Participative – This style reflects the degree to which managers involve others in making and complementing decisions. It includes sub-scales such as autocratic and non-participative, which are the reverse of desired leadership qualities.

Humane oriented – This style reflects supportive, considerate, compassionate and generous leadership. It includes sub-styles such as modesty and humane oriented.

Autonomous – This style refers to independent and individualistic leadership.

Self-Protective – This style focuses on ensuring the safety and the security of the individual or group members. It includes sub-styles such as self-centered, status conscious, conflict-inducer, face-saver and procedural.

The different styles have been compared here for four countries, namely, Russia, the U.S., China and Finland, each representing a different cluster of cultures. The results are presented in Table 3.1.

Table 3.1 Culturally endorsed leadership styles in four countries

Country – Region/ Leadership Style	**Russia** Eastern Europe	**U.S.** Anglo	**China** Confucian	**Finland** Nordic Europe
Charismatic	5.66	6.12	5.56	4.95
Team Oriented	5.63	5.80	5.57	5.85
Participative	4.67	5.93	5.04	5.91
Humane	4.08	5.21	5.19	4.30
Autonomous	4.63	5.75	4.07	4.08
Self Protective	3.69	3.15	3.80	2.55

The scales range from 1 = Low to 7 = High
Source: GLOBE studies

The culturally endorsed leadership style in Russia is similar in many ways to, yet different from that in, China. The samples in both countries endorsed charismatic, team-oriented and self-protective styles. This could be a result of their similar communist political background that enhanced these leadership features. The respondents differ in their endorsement of participative, humane (Chinese scored higher than Russian) and autonomous (Russian scored higher than Chinese) leadership styles. These differences may be a consequence of cultural differences.

The Russian sample scored lower than the U.S. sample on all leadership styles except for autonomous and self-protective. The Russian sample scored lower than the Finnish sample on team oriented, participative and humane, and higher on charismatic, autonomous and self-protective. Research on learning, also suggests that it is important to have broad-based learning initiatives in Russian enterprises otherwise they will be ineffective (Czinkota 1997).

Leadership in Russia

The common Russian style of leadership could be described as paternalistic if not authoritarian. Since Russian enterprises have legally been required to follow the one-man management principle (Ivancevich, DeFrank and Gregory 1992) managers did not tend to share authority. Participative management style has yet to demonstrate an increase in Russian employees' performance (Luthans, Welsh and Rosenkrantz 1993). This may be a result of the Russian value system that is anchored in Russian history, the functional behaviour that has been dictated by real life circumstances, or the high level of uncertainty involved in the current Russian economy. Whichever is the case, the fact is that Russian managers treat their employees as if they are immature adults, continuously instructing and monitoring them. Verbal, physical, and even sexual abuses are not uncommon to this style of leadership and recommendations for ethical awareness have been expressed about Russia (Deshpande, Joseph and Maximov 2000).

Extrinsic rewards seem to be more influential in motivating Russian workers than intrinsic rewards (Welsh, Luthans and Sommer 1993). Since the power of reward and punishment is limited (Ivancevich et al. 1992), and the legitimate power is considered to be very weak in a society that generally does not abide by the legal system, managers resort to the application of expert and referent powers. Managers use their contacts in the higher echelons of government, their professional knowledge, and their clout to convince workers to comply with their instructions. In the absence of a great amount of formal extrinsic rewards, managers are engaged in a 'favor for favor' exchange process (Hermann 1994; Puffer 1994). An example observed by the lead author of this chapter is a case where the manager releases the driver early on Friday just to make sure that the same driver is available for the manager's personal use over the weekend. This barter method is probably a residual effect of the communist regime when formal rewards were supposedly equally distributed. The only way to give someone preferential treatment was by the application of the informal method of bartering. One of the common beliefs in Russia is that 'if you have friends you do not need money.'

Communication is based on a top down approach, mostly by face-to-face meetings (Lawrence and Vlachoutsicos 1993), and with very little effort to initiate horizontal communication (Ivancevich et al. 1992). Memos and other documents are reserved only for special occasions when a formal contract is being formulated. In the communist period people were afraid to commit themselves to anything that eventually would expose them to future retribution, and therefore managers prefer to communicate with other managers and employees by using a face-to-face interaction. Directives and timetables are being transmitted in a downward information channel and very little feedback is being transmitted upwards. Taking into account the confidentiality of the financial and other reports, communication might be minimized purposely. The less the managers know about the financial operations of the organization, the less can they report it to external agencies. Lateral communication is scarce since the leadership style is very centralized (Lawrence and Vlachoutsicos 1993).

Though workers are being rewarded individually they tend to see their fate as being a collective one. Whether a result of a long history of collective suffering, of communism, or of a cultural value system, Russian workers tend to define themselves as 'we' and management as 'they' (The old saying used to be that 'we pretend to work and they pretend to pay'). This social categorization is likely to result in negative norms of work behaviour rather than in positive ones, namely: the workers try to minimize performance rather than to maximize it (Hermann 1994; Ivancevich et al. 1992). Since management dictates decisions, there is limited worker autonomy. However, those few decisions made by workers tend to be group decisions rather than individual decisions. This is motivated by worker desire for risk reduction. In the absence of clear information and the severe consequences to those who made mistaken decisions in the past, it is not surprising that workers tend to share the risk involved in their decisions by consulting with colleagues and those who seems to be experts in the subject matter.

Conflicts are mostly resolved competitively or forcefully. A US businessman, renting an apartment for one month in Russia, had his water heater blown up, causing damage to the apartment below his apartment. The tenant in this apartment wanted to exploit the situation by demanding $1,000 from the businessman for redecorating the apartment, even though it was the responsibility of the landlord. The businessman's estimation was that the damage could be fixed for about $200. He had challenged the tenant to reduce her claim, and asked her to provide him with a professional estimation. She came back with a new estimation of $2,000. It seems that Russian perceive conflict situations to be win-lose situations (Graham, Evenko and Rajan 1992).

Products, components, and raw materials' prices could be slashed down by tough negotiation. However, when an agreement is reached it does not necessarily secure the deal. A seller who finds a better deal may renege on the earlier one. In the presence of a weak legal system, crude power plays resolve conflicts. It is not surprising then, that people usually cooperate and compromise in order to mutually circumvent the legal system. A Russian businessperson, who was licensed to import finished products, took advantage of an opportunity and got involved in a private business education joint venture in the US. Only after the deal was over did he find out that he did not have the appropriate local government license. Rather than paying a penalty of $2,000 he paid a government official $250 to stamp the official seal on a license that carried a pre deal date. Thus, Russians may cooperate or compromise when it comes to a conflict between 'them' and 'us'.

Leadership style of Russian managers seems to be changing from a centrally controlled style to a market oriented style. If in the past, power was centralized. Today managers are trying to shift some of the decision making power to their subordinates. Yet, in a study comparing Russian managers with US managers it was found that middle level managers in Russia enjoy less authority in decision making than their US counterparts (Puffer and McCarthy 1993). Today's Russian managers believe that with good management they can achieve most of their organization's objectives and therefore they are geared towards doing business. They have adopted the US belief that time is a scarce resource and therefore they struggle to achieve as much as possible within time constraints. While paying bribes to promote business, they still demonstrate personal trust, even though it sometimes may mean over-promising and cutting corners (Puffer 1994). By doing so, new entrepreneurs tarnish the reputation of private enterprises.

Critical abilities that may lead to the success of Russian managers are networking, socializing, and politicking, followed by motivating and rewarding subordinates (Luthans, Welsh and Rosenkrantz 1993). Puffer and Shekshnia (1994) found that the more foreign the company was, and the more privatized it was, the better was workers' compensation.

In the next sections, we present the concept of alienation and international studies about alienation.

Alienation

The philosopher Karl Marx, in his monumental work Economic-Philosophical Manuscripts of 1844 (The portable Karl Marx 1983), coined the term alienation within the field of political economy and explained that:

> … The worker is related to the product of his labour as to an alien object … the more the worker exhausts himself, the more powerful the alien world of objects which he creates over and against himself becomes, the poorer he and his inner world become, the less there is that belongs to him as his own (134).

Marx saw the worker in the industrialized world as estranged from the means of production that belong to the factory owners, and detached from the decision making process that is managed by autocratic managers, and hence deprived of intrinsically meaningful work. Marx blamed the division of labour, when 'each man has a particular, exclusive sphere of activity, which is forced upon him and from which he cannot escape' (Giddens 1971, 3) as the primary source of man's loss of creativity and man's alienation from work.

While in classical Marxism the ownership system was suggested to discriminate between alienated and involved workers, later European theories of alienation tended to emphasize workers' control over their work as the differentiating element between alienated and non-alienated workers (Feldman-Leibovitc 1995; Shlapentokh 1985).

Workers' control over their work was adopted by Blauner (Blauner 1964) to trace the way in which different social and technological conditions affect workers' attitude to their jobs and factories. In Blauner's view 'industrial powerlessness' incorporates four elements. The first element is the producer's alienation from ownership of the means of production and the finished products. The second element is the worker's inability to influence general managerial policies. The third element is the worker's lack of control over the conditions of employment. The last element is the worker's lack of control over the immediate work process. However, of significance for the American worker, Blauner contended, are the last two elements only, which directly bear upon his life. The more general and abstract aspects of powerlessness are of no concern to the worker since he has been accustomed to them. 'Today, the average worker,' Blauner commented, 'no more desires to own his machines than modern soldiers their howitzers or government clerks their filing cabinets' (1964, 15).

According to Blauner's data (1964, 29), from 75 to 90 per cent of American workers were on the whole satisfied even with routine repetitive work. But this, as Blauner himself noted, was due mainly to socialization, which encouraged the individual to rest content with little and not seek more.

The focus of Western studies of alienation has shifted in the 1960s and 1970s from a structural one to a social-psychological one (Israel, 1971). This group of studies looked into the detachment of individuals from society and from social goals. Following Durkheim's thesis that modern society lacks the common collective conscience provided by society's traditional values, Katz and Kahn (1978, 380) defined alienation as 'the negative aspect of the internalization of conventional goals in that it suggests an active rejection of them.' People feel less alienated when they belong to organizations that have some power over matters of importance for the individual such as labour unions, professional societies, and political organizations (Almond and Verba 1965; Neal and Seeman 1964; Seeman 1966). Moreover, people feel more alienated when they belong to a low socioeconomic group (Meier and Bell 1959; Bullough 1967).

Studies about the relationship between job characteristics and alienation found that, in general, workers who are engaged in monotonous, machine paced, closely supervised jobs are more likely to be alienated (Aiken and Hage 1966; Ashforth 1989; Bass 1965; Blauner 1964; Crozier 1965; Kohn 1976; Kornhauser 1965; Lawler 1973; Lawler and Hall 1970; Saleh and Hosek 1976; Shepard 1970; Weiss and Reisman 1961; Weissenberg and Gruenfeld 1968; Wilensky 1964). Korman, Wittig-Berman and Lang (1981) identified four work related factors that may contribute to social and personal alienation: disconfirmed expectations, contradictory role demands, sense of external control, and loss of affiliate satisfaction.

Korman et al. (1981) extended the focus on alienation from workers to managers and professionals. They argued that in the modern world, many employees engage their skills rather than their labour, and in most cases their output is a service rather than a tangible product, and therefore it seems that alienation is not all a result of boring jobs and non-understanding managers. They concluded that alienation is a widespread phenomenon (at least in the Western world) and better explanatory frameworks are needed to understand it.

Alienation in International Studies

Based on the literature of the 1970s, Hofstede (1980; 1983) looked into the relationships between national cultures and workers' alienation. He claims that in countries where the level of uncertainty avoidance is high (risk taking is low) people, in general, tend to feel that they have less control over the world around them, and over their own life in particular. This fact may lead these people to feel more alienated. On the one hand, organizations in countries with a high level of individualism such as the US, which tends to reinforce individualism in the work place, may lead their workers to feel more alienated. On the other hand, organizations in countries with a high level of collectivism, such as Japan, may alienate the worker if they do not take close care of the worker's family. Moreover, Hofstede (1980, 269) suggested that 'in more collectivist societies the link between individuals and their work organizations is moral by tradition … in such societies, free market capitalism with the supremacy of the profit motive, and which considers the labour contract between employer and employee as a calculative bargain, is an alien element' Interestingly enough, calculation of risk has taken over ethical principles govern by emotions in day to day interpersonal as well as business relations in Russia (Ledeneva 1998).

Investigators who compared organizational commitment of Japanese and American workers have been surprised to find out that American workers are at least equally if not more committed to their organizations than their Japanese counterparts (Lincoln 1989; Luthans, McCaul and Dodd 1985; Near 1989). These investigators are of Western background and they have used Western constructs of organizational commitment in their studies, hence, caution is called upon in the interpretation of these studies' results.

While Hofstede's sample of countries did not include Russia, a recent study by Trompenaars and Hampden-Turner (1998) found that Russians relate to organizations as a social rather than a functional system. Russians are hierarchical and more particularistic than universalistic and they tend to break system rules. Russians' locus of control is external and they may feel that state organizations influence their fate. Therefore Russian workers expect their managers to give them guidance on how to perform their job rather than to make their own decisions. However, they strongly believe in individual responsibility. They are diffused and affective in their responses, bringing their private life into the employing organizations. These sets of values and attitudes are anchored in Russians' basic perception of work as a collective rather than a private matter and as life sustaining, inescapable evil (Feldman-Lebovich 1995).

Operationalization of Alienation

Following Mills (1956) and Josephson and Josephson (1962), Korman et al. (1981) proposed that the general concept of alienation manifests both personal alienation and social alienation. Personal alienation involves a sense of separation from personal identity and it is a result of a person's high feelings of anxiety. It describes the feeling we have when we believe that our everyday actions are not reflecting our real self but something superficial to it. Social alienation is a feeling of a sense of separation from social life. This feeling is a result of high level of anxiety towards the social world that engulfs the individual. The present research tests this theory in Russia by comparing worker alienation in state and private enterprises. By empirically testing Korman's theory of alienation in state owned and private companies in the transitional economy of Russia this study makes a contribution by testing this theory outside of the US.

An extrapolation of Western theories to the Russian population may suggest that state owned companies' workers would be more alienated than private companies' workers. This view may also be supported by initial findings of research that looked into the expectations of Russian state owned companies' managers of the newly privatized business. They have prioritized the objectives of financial break even, development of employees, and self-actualization, as the most important objectives for private business (McCarthy et al. 1996). The accomplishment of such objectives, which resemble to a great extent Western management objectives, in private companies may reduce workers' alienation.

An alternative view may suggest that private companies' workers are those workers who have lost their jobs in state owned companies. Losing a job is not only a devastating personal event, but in Russia it also meant losing many of the benefits traditionally provided by the state, and for some workers, working harder for less. At the same time, state owned companies' workers maintained their old jobs and also continued to benefit from the state's compensation and benefits. Consequently, we may expect that private companies' workers would be more alienated than state owned companies' workers. While Western theory of alienation in state owned and private companies is empirically grounded, something which could not be said for European theory of alienation, it is more likely that Russian workers will develop attitudes based on their own life realities rather than on Western realities.

Job Characteristics

According to Hackman and Oldham (1974), perceptions of the task environment influence employee outcomes. Their widely studied job characteristics model (JCM) points to motivational properties in the design of jobs and the work environment. The JCM identifies five job characteristics that define the motivating potential of a job: skills variety, task identity, task significance, task autonomy, and task feedback. Skills variety is the degree to which an individual may use multiple skills in the course of performing their work. Task identity evaluates the extent to which an individual knows or participates in the completion of a whole piece of work such as a complete product rather than simply a component. Task significance evaluates the importance of the job with respect to other people. Task autonomy evaluates the extent of decision making freedom that may be exercised on the job. Task feedback describes the availability of information about performance effectiveness that is readily accessible on the job. The factor structure of the JCM is widely accepted and has been extensively supported in empirical research (Fried and Ferris 1987).

According to the JCM, a properly designed work environment can offer an employee a type of self-generated affective kick. Intrinsic work characteristics positively affect attitudes via a perceptual process. Job characteristics (for example, feedback, autonomy) lead to positive psychological states such as meaningfulness and responsibility, in turn, leading to positive attitudes such as job satisfaction. The evidence that supports the relationship between job characteristics and attitudinal and affective states is extensive. JCM is known to relate to organizational commitment, cooperation, and job satisfaction (Champoux 1991; Judge, Bono and Locke 2000).

Marxist literature also deals directly with the idea of job characteristics. Marx saw the worker in the industrialized world as estranged the decision making process that is managed by autocratic managers, and hence deprived of intrinsically meaningful work. Marx blamed the division of labour, when 'each man has a particular, exclusive sphere of activity, which is forced upon him and from which he cannot escape' (Giddens 1971, 3) as the primary source of man's lost of creativity and man's alienation from work.

Studies about the relationship between job characteristics and alienation found that, in general, workers who are engaged in monotonous, machine paced, closely supervised jobs are more likely to be alienated (Aiken and Hage 1966; Ashforth 1989; Bass 1965; Blauner 1964; Kornhauser 1965; Lawler 1973; Lawler and Hall 1970; Kohn 1976; Saleh and Hosek 1976; Shepard 1970; Weiss and Reisman 1961; Weissenberg and Gruenfeld 1968; Wilensky 1964). Korman et al. (1981) identified four work related factors that may contribute to social and personal alienation: disconfirmed expectations, contradictory role demands, sense of external control, and loss of affiliate satisfaction.

In recent studies in different nations, job significance, skills variety and autonomy were found to be related to alienation in Hungary (Banai, Reisel and Probst 2004), and skills variety, feedback and task identity were found to be related to alienation in Cuba (Banai and Reisel, 2003). In the current research, we expect that enriched, or properly designed, job characteristics such as task identity, skills variety, autonomy and feedback will be negatively related to alienation. Again, given the prominence of job characteristics in predicting employee attitudes, it is expected that job characteristics will be negatively related to alienation.

Employees' Characteristics

The literature about the relationships between individuals' characteristics and alienation has yielded mixed results. Most studies have constantly found that higher level of education creates less personal alienation (The Harris Poll, 2, 8 January 2003).

Previous studies in communist countries about the relationship between age and alienation yielded no significant results (Banai and Teng 1996; Banai and Hu 2003), yet we control for the potential effects of age in the current research.

Men were found to be more alienated than women. Banai and Teng (1996) and Banai and Hu (2003) have confirmed this observation in Russia and China, respectively, even though no theoretical explanation was provided. Therefore, we control for potential gender based differences in this research.

Methods

Setting

The study was conducted in Kazan, the capital city of Tatarstan, Russia. Kazan was selected as a location for this study because for many years it was a center of military production and as such was a closed city to foreigners until 1991. However, once the new constitution was established, much of the old military industry became redundant and was largely downsized. Many workers who were laid off from their positions in the state owned companies were searching for new jobs with the newly established private employment market (Clarke 1997). During these years, the state of Tatarstan opened its doors to foreign business people, researchers and consultants looking for solutions to the failing economy. The government was principally concerned with the challenge of how to turn the idle military factories into civilian production centers. The local university, which is considered to be one of the most prestigious in Russia, provided its support. Kazan was believed to be a suitable ground for conducting a Western style study in a place that economically and socially resembled many other parts of Russia at the time.

The sample included eight private companies and four state-owned companies. The private companies included a specialty shoe factory, wholesale trading firm, plastic consumer products manufacturer, sweets and ice cream plant, a firm that produced bath tabs, and two computer operation companies. The state owned companies included a utility company, a grain products company, an oil products company, and a gelatin company, all major employers in the city.

Local entrepreneurs created the private companies from scratch. They had to secure facilities, machinery, raw materials, labour, and financing. The management of the companies agreed to participate in the study based on blat or personal connections and exchange (Ledeneva 1998). Learning Western management methods, benefiting from free management consulting, personal favors, and socialization with foreigners were some of the motives for cooperation. The state owned companies included a major polymer production factory and a utility company. The factory was the largest in the city and the utility company had a monopoly in providing energy to the city.

The private companies were included in this convenient sample because of their availability. At this time only a handful of private companies existed in this city and even fewer could provide a sizable sample of respondents. The state owned enterprises were selected based on personal contacts. The intention was to sample the same organizations again and again over time. However, because of the turmoil in Russia this wish has proven to be unrealistic. For example, during the same period of time the president of one state owned company retired and his successor did not allow for the continuation of the research. An owner manager of one of the private companies has been assassinated. The sample employed in this study is quasi-random and we employed state-owned and private firms as proxy indicators of what might be found if one can get a representative sample of firms in Russia.

The state owned companies were large enough (between 1,600–30,000 employees) to allow for a random sampling of employees by the administration. Managers were instructed by the researchers to go through the list of workers in production and manufacturing functions in their organization and, based on the size of the company, to ask every (n) person to complete a questionnaire. To control for the type and level of the job managers and service people were omitted from the study. Due to the small size of the private companies, all employees were asked to be included. Since random sampling was supposed to accurately represent the population of the companies there was no reason to believe that the different sampling processes, that of randomly sampling in state owned companies and that of inclusion of the whole population in the private companies, would yield any inherent biases. The response rate for the various companies varies from 61 to 92 per cent.

Sample

Education. All but a few of the 960 employees received at least a high school diploma. The scale of this measure, ranging from one to five, represents the following degrees: high school, associate, bachelor, master, and Ph.D. respectively. The participants' mean for the five categories of education was 2.52, (SD=1.37).
Age. The average respondent was 42 years of age.
Gender. 51 per cent of all respondents were women; 43 per cent were male and six per cent did not respond. There was no significant difference between women's presence in the state owned and the private companies.

Procedure

The study comprised of survey questionnaires and interviews. A graduate student from Russia, under the supervision of a management professor who is bilingual, translated the questionnaire used in this study from English into Russian. A second graduate student from Russia back translated the questionnaire from Russian to English. Any resulting discrepancies between the two versions were then resolved. This back-translation technique has been advocated in cross-national studies in order to provide reliability to the questionnaire (Brislin 1980). One of the authors controlled the distribution of the questionnaires to the employees by their managers. The workers were gathered for the distribution and they completed the questionnaires without disclosing their names and were assured of confidentiality. Once completed, the questionnaires were then returned to the author and therefore there was no interference of management in the process. During the visits to the factories and the companies, one author interviewed managers and workers. Some of the interviews were conducted in English and a translator was used in the other cases. The purpose of the interviews was to get a background and more comprehensive picture of the conditions of work in companies rather than to collect organized data for content analysis.

Measures and Statistical Analyses

All participants were asked to complete a questionnaire that contained measures of leadership, job characteristics, and background information such as age, gender, and education.

Leadership Korman's (1994) 17 item leadership scale was selected to measure leadership. A sample item is 'Does the organization emphasize both performance evaluations and employees' opportunity to grow?' A five-point Likert type scale was used with anchors (1) to a very small extent and (5) to a very large extent. The instrument used here focuses on these aspects of supportive leadership style and it contains ten items. Cronbach Alpha reliability test of the internal consistency of the items is .87.

Alienation The 18-item alienation measure used in this study was developed by Korman et al. (1981) and a foreign language version was validated in Russia and the factor structure result in this research is similar (Banai and Teng, 1996). Sample items from the measure include 'Sometimes I feel all alone in the world' and 'I would prefer to live a different life than I do.' Likert-type response choices ranged from one strongly disagree to five strongly agree. Internal reliability using Cronbach coefficient alpha was .70.

Job Characteristics Hackman and Oldham's (1974) Job Diagnostic Survey (JDS) was used to assess the respondents' job characteristics. The survey consisted of 21 items, which revealed four dimensions: task identity, task variety, task autonomy, and task feedback. Cronbach Alpha reliability test of the internal consistency of task identity is .52, task variety .79, task autonomy .66, and task feedback .69.

Findings

In our evaluation of the model of work alienation in Russian state-owned and private enterprises, we performed a series of analyses that included Pearson correlation analysis, hierarchical regression analyses, and follow-up means comparisons (see Tables 3.2 and 3.3). Some differences were observable between employees in state-owned and private firms. The state-owned firms offered a significant, albeit

Table 3.2 Descriptive statistics and Pearson correlation coefficients for independent variables and alienation in public and private Russian companies[1]

Variables	Mean		S.D.								
	Public	Private	Public	Private	α^2	1	2	3	4	5	6
1. Alienation	3.16	3.11	.42	.54	.70	-	-.11**	-.11	-.04	-.08*	-.01
2. Leadership	2.99	2.53	.88	.84	.87	-.03	-	.12**	.55**	.32**	.38**
3. Task Identity	3.35	3.46	.95	1.31	.52	.06	.15*	-	.32**	.17**	.24**
4. Job Feedback	3.23	3.08	.94	1.40	.69	-.09	.32**	.18**	-	.47**	.54**
5. Job Autonomy	3.70	3.59	.88	1.00	.66	-.08	.33**	.26**	.39**	-	.56**
6. Skills Variety	3.63	3.54	.88	.86	.79	-.09	.33**	.30**	.39**	.55**	-

* $p<.05$, ** $p<.01$

[1] Above the diagonal are public companies and below the diagonal are private companies.

[2] Chronbach alpha is for entire sample.

Table 3.3 Multiple regression analysis for alienation in Russian public and private companies

Independent Variables	Public	Private
Step 1		
1. Age	.04	-.12
2. Gender	.15**	.09
3. Education	.01	.01
Adjusted R^2	.02	.00
Step 2		
4. Leadership	-.12*	.08
5. JCM Identity	-.14*	.04
6. JCM Feedback	.01	-.03
7. JCM Autonomy	-.11*	-.31*
8. JCM Variety	.06	.06
Change in Adjusted R^2	.03	.01
Change in F	4.30**	1.45
Overall Model F	4.00**	1.18
Overall Adjusted R^2	.05	.01

* $p < .05$, ** $p < .01$
Standardized regression coefficients are reported.

modestly so, explanation for work alienation in that we found that leadership, and the job characteristics of task identity and job autonomy were negatively related to work alienation. The state owned firms' model of work alienation was significant ($F = 4.00$, $p < .01$). With respect to private firms, job autonomy was the only variable that was negatively related to work alienation. The overall model in the private sample was not significant ($F = 1.18$, $p = .32$). Our follow-up means comparisons between state owned and private firms revealed a significant difference for leadership. Employees in state-owned firms rated their organizational leadership higher (mean = 2.99) than did workers in private firms (mean = 2.53; $t = -6.88$, $p < .01$).

Discussion and Conclusion

Leadership in state-owned organizations is perceived to be stronger than leadership in private organizations. Jobs in state-owned enterprises enjoy more task identity and task autonomy than jobs in the private industry. These finding contradict findings from western research where leadership was found to be more influential and jobs better enriched in the private sector rather than in the public sector.

The first independent explanatory factor that may explain differences between workers' perceptions in the private and the state owned enterprises is the perceived leadership. This factor includes items on a leadership questionnaire that refer to issues such as employees who know and understand the standards for effective job performance, existing job rules and/or performance guidelines, requirement by organization to perform unethically, employees who have a sense of control in the organization, organization that is hesitant in stating long-term goals, and organization that takes negative view of the world.

To explain this finding we resort to two possible explanations. First, leaders in the Russian state owned enterprises managed large (from a few hundreds to up to thirty thousands employees) and well established organizations that have been operating for many years. Leaders in the private sector have managed their organizations for a few years only and the organizations were comparatively small (50–300 employees). Also, the employees in the state owned enterprises have worked for their organizations for many years while those in the private businesses have worked there for only a short period of time. These facts make a major impact on the perceptions of leadership. Managers in large organizations seem to be more powerful than those in small ones. Russians, in general, appreciate power, and therefore they perceive their powerful managers to be successful (Welsh, Luthans and Sommer, 1993). Further, managerial influence can be substantial in broad-based initiatives such as quality leadership in which managers infuse quality programs into all aspects of organizational activity (McCarthy, Puffer and Naumov 1997).

Hence, it is not necessarily the ownership type that makes the difference in Russians perceptions of their managers but rather company size, number of years of employment with a company and the Russians' cultural trait of appreciation for personal power. This is particularly important given the tremendous environmental uncertainty and the need to manage in the face of poor information quality (May, Stewart and Sweo 2000). These issues were not be tested here because of the study's design and are offered as potential areas of further research.

This argument leads us to the second explanation about the type of respondents in the state owned enterprises as compared with those in the private organizations. Employees in the state owned organization were the lucky ones. They did not lose their jobs as a result of the restructuring of the economy. The employees in the private organizations were those who were the unlucky, those who were dismissed from the state owned enterprises. They also may have lost their state benefits. Research in negotiation has offered the 'endowment effect' as a possible explanation for the differences in perceptions of the two groups of employees. The endowment effect is the tendency to overvalue something you own or believe you possess (Kahenman, Knetsch and Thaler 1990). Those who had continue to possess their original jobs, and the security involved in keeping them (the endowed), have appreciated their situation, and therefore the issues associated with their jobs, such as their leadership, more than those who have lost their endowments. This is a post-factum proposition that should be tested.

The second and the third explanatory independent factors – Task Identity and Job Autonomy – involve the extent to which the employees can see the end results of their jobs, and the amount of freedom they enjoy in performing their jobs, respectively.

Workers in the state owned enterprises have more opportunities to control the nature, and to see the end results, of their jobs than workers in private enterprises. The first possible explanation is that managers in state owned enterprises structure the jobs in a way that allows workers to 'own' their jobs or complete segments of them. This could be a consequence of the sheer size of state owned enterprises where jobs could be expanded to allow workers to experience their results. Second, it is possible that there was no real difference between the jobs structures but rather a perceived difference. Workers who have worked for years in state owned enterprises have perceived their jobs to provide them with more autonomy and with some closure. At the same time, workers in private companies, who have been on their jobs for one or two years, when the economy has changed tremendously, and when their managers, who themselves started their new organizations, did not know how to delegate and how to incorporate the workers in the work processes, felt that they possessed no control over their jobs or the end results of their labour. Third, it is possible that managers in state owned enterprises had enough confidence to provide their workers with some autonomy and with knowledge of the end results of their jobs. Satisfaction survey research in Russia has confirmed that workers indeed wanted a chance to learn and grow in their firm (Linz 2003). At the same time, managers of private organizations felt insecure and intimidated, and were worried that someone would steal clients, suppliers or even the whole organization from them, and therefore they preferred to keep the cards close to their chest and did not delegate much freedom to make decisions and did not incorporate workers in the final results of their jobs.

The study is not free of limitations. First, the sample that is comprehensive and includes many organizations is still quasi-random. Second, the sampling has been conducted in one city in Russia that may not be representative of other Russian places, after all Russia is a huge country with eleven time zones. Third, despite the careful translation of the questionnaire, it is difficult to estimate its face value. Russian workers have never completed questionnaires in the past and they may find the whole experience confusing and even threatening. Despite all these limitations, the study is unique in its investigation of workers' organizational attitudes during a major economic and political transition.

From current knowledge about the transition in Russia it may be possible to infer that significant differences among workers could be better identified in certain industries and certain regions of Russia, rather than in the state owned and private enterprises. So while western dichotomy does not differentiate between public and private sectors workers in different industries and different regions of the country, this might just be the case for the new country of Russia and its transforming economy. Moreover, since Russian economic and political systems are still in transition it is possible that employees' attitudes that were measured a few years ago have changed again. It is therefore recommended to view this study's results as a snapshot that has the potential to explain current differences between state owned and private enterprises in Russia, yet the application should be carefully done by testing those attitudes again. Replication of the study may make more specific the theories used to explain the relationships between job characteristics and leadership style.

Researchers should aim to using holistic methods in analyzing transitional organizations, methods that measure and control as many organizational variables as possible. Managers should aim to improving not only their leadership style but also their employees' job characteristics as part of their improvement of the culture of their organizations.

While a profile of characteristics enables scholars and managers to look at the big picture, the study results could be used also to discuss each factor's potency in predicting ownership system. Local and foreign managers in Russia may realize that currently Russian state owned and private enterprises do not resemble public and private sectors in the west. State owned organizations seem to be more stable and less diffused in their activities, probably a consequence of seventy years of tradition. Private companies have just being created and therefore they seem to be more chaotic and less focused than the state owned enterprises, which may partly be explained by managerial opportunism (Filatotchev, Buck and Zhukov 2000). Yet, despite this tendency, it is likely that as the free market matures and managers learn how to prioritize their objectives and how to manage and measure profit, their organizations will resemble more and more western style private organization. Managers should learn how to integrate western style management into the Russia business environment to design better jobs for their employees and to exercise a desirable leadership style. This may enhance Russian organizations' culture and performance.

References

Aiken, M. and Hage, J. (1966), 'Organizational Alienation: A Comparative Analysis', *American Sociological Review* 31, 497–507.

Allison, G.T. (1979), 'Public and Private Management: Are they Fundamentally Alike in all Unimportant Respects?', *Proceedings for the Public Management Research Conference* (Washington, D.C.: Office of Personnel Management), pp. 27–38.

Almond, G.A. and Verba, S. (1965), *The Civic Culture: Political Attitudes and Democracy in Five Nations* (Boston: Little, Brown).

Ashforth, B.E. (1989), 'The Experience of Powerlessness in Organizations', *Organizational Behavior and Human Decision Processes* 43, 207–42.

Banai, M. and Teng, B.C. (1996), 'Comparing Job Characteristics, Leadership Style, and Alienation in Russian Public and Private Enterprises', *Journal of International Management* 2, 3, 201–24.

Banai, M. and Hu, J. (2003), 'Comparing Leadership Style, Job Characteristics, and Alienation, in State Owned Enterprises and International Joint Ventures in China', in Alon, I. (ed.), *Global Business in China: The Impact of Cultural Values on Management, Organizations, and Marketing Strategy* (Westport, CT: Greenwood), pp. 237–49.

Banai, M., Reisel, W.D. and Probst, T.M. (2004), 'A Managerial and Personal Control Model: Predictions of Work Alienation and Organizational Commitment in Hungary', *Journal of International Management* 10, 375–92.

Banai, M. and Reisel, W.D. (2003), 'A Test of Control – Alienation Theory among Cuban Workers', *Management Research* 1, 243–52.

Banai, M. and Weisberg, J. (2003), 'Alienation in State Owned and Private Companies in Russia', *Scandinavian Journal of Management* 19:3, 359–83.

Bass, B.M. (1965), *Organizational Psychology* (Boston, Massachusetts: Allyn and Bacon).

Birnbaum, P.H., Farh, J.L. and Wong, G.Y. (1986), 'The Job Characteristics Model in Hong Kong', *Journal of Applied Psychology* 71, 598–605.

Blake, A. and Mouton, S. (1985), *The Managerial Grid II* (Houston: Gulf Publishing).

Blauner, R. (1964), *Alienation and Freedom: The Factory Worker and his Industry* (Chicago: University of Chicago Press).

Bozeman, B. (1987), *All Organizations are Public* (San Francisco: Jossey Bass).

Brislin, R.W. (1980), 'Translation and Content Analysis of Oral and Written Materials', Triandis, H.C. and Berry, J.W. (eds), *Handbook of Cross Cultural Psychology* (Boston, MA: Allyn and Bacon), pp. 398–444.

Buchanan, B. (1974), 'Government Managers, Business Executives and Organizational Commitment', *Public Administration Review* 34, 339–47.

Bullough, B.L. (1967), 'Alienation in the Ghetto', *American Journal of Sociology* 72, 469–78.

Champoux, J.E. (1991), 'A Multivariate Test of the Job Characteristics Theory of Work Motivation', *Journal of Organizational Behavior* 12, 431–46.

Chubb, J.E. and Moe, T.M. (1988), 'Politics, Markets, and the Organization of Schools', *American Political Science Review* 82, 1065–1087.

Clarke, S. (1997), 'After Five Years of Reform, Russian Labour Management Policies are in Need of Restructuring', *Russia and Commonwealth Law Report* 7, 17.

Crozier, M. (1965), *Le Monde des Employes de Bureau* (Paris: LeSeiul).

Coursey, D. and Rainey, H.G. (1990), 'Perceptions of Personnel System Constraints in Public, Private, and Hybrid Organizations', *Review of Public Personnel Administration* 10: 2, 54–71.

Czinkota, M.R. (1997), 'Russia's Transition to a Market Economy: Learning about Business', *Journal of International Marketing* 5: 73–93.

Deshpande, S.P., Joseph, J. and Maximov, V.V. (2000), 'Perceptions of Proper Ethical Conduct of Male and Female Russian Managers', *Journal of Business Ethics* 24: 2, 179–183.

Feldman-Leibovich, A. (1995), *The Russian Concept of Work: Suffering, Drama, and Tradition in Pre- and Post-Revolutionary Russia* (Westport, Connecticut: Praeger).

Fiedler, F.E. (1967), *A Theory of Leadership* (New York: McGraw Hill).

Fiedler, F.E. (1996), 'Research on Leadership Selection and Training: One View of the Future', *Administrative Science Quarterly* 41, 241–50.

Filatotchev, I., Buck, T. and Zhukov, V. (2000), 'Downsizing in Privatized Firms in Russia, Ukraine, and Belarus' *Academy of Management Journal* 43: 3, 286–304.

Fried, Y. and Ferris, G.R. (1987), 'The Validity of the Job Characteristics Model: A Review and Meta Analysis', *Personnel Psychology* 40, 287–322.

Giddens, A. (1971), *Capitalism and Modern Social Theory: An Analysis of the Writings of Marx, Durkheim and Max Weber* (Cambridge: Cambridge University Press).

Goldman, M. (1997), The Pitfalls of Russian Privatization, Challenge, May–June, 35–49.

Graham, J.L., Evenko, L.I. and Rajan, M.N. (1992), 'An Empirical Comparison of Soviet and American Business Negotiations', *Journal of International Business Studies* Third Quarter, 387–418.

Hackman, J.R. and Oldham, G.R. (1974), *The Job Diagnostic Survey: An Instrument for the Diagnosis of Jobs and the Evaluation of Job Redesign Projects* (Springfield, VA: Department of Commerce).

Hermann, E. (1994), 'Post Soviet HR Reforms', *Personnel Journal* April, 41–9.

Hersey, P. and Blanchard, K.H. (1993), *Management of Organizational Behaviour: Utilizing Human Resources* (Englewood Cliffs, NJ: Prentice Hall).

Hofstede, G. (1983), Motivation, Leadership, and Organization: Do American Theories Applied Abroad?, *Organization Dynamics* 9, 42–63.

Hofstede, G. (1980), *Culture Consequences: International Differences in Work Related Values* (London: Sage Publications).

House, R.J., Hanges, P.J., Mansour J., Dorfman, P. and Gupta, V. (eds) (2004), *Culture, Leadership, and Organizations: The GLOBE Study of 62 Societies* (Beverly Hills, CA: Sage).

House, R.J. and Mitchell, T.R. (1974), 'Path Goal Theory of Leadership', *Journal of Contemporary Business* 3, 81–97.

Israel, J. (1971), *Alienation: From Marx to Modern Sociology* (Boston: Allyn and Bacon).

Ivancevich, J.M., DeFrank, R.S. and Gregory, P.R. (1992), 'The Soviet Enterprise Director: An Important Resource before and after the Coup', *Academy of Management Executive* 6: 1, 42–55.

Judge, T.A., Bono, J.E. and Locke, E.A. (2000), 'Personality and Job Satisfaction: The Mediating Role of Job Characteristics', *Journal of Applied Psychology* 85, 237–49.

Kahenman, D., Knetsch, J.L. and Thaler, R.H. (1990), 'Experimental Tests of the Endowment Effect and the Coase Theorem', *Journal of Political Economy* 98, 1325–48.

Katz , D. and Kahn, R.L. (1978), *The Social Psychology of Organizations*, 2nd Edition (New York: John Wiley and Sons).

Kohn, M. L. (1976), 'Occupational Structure and Alienation', *American Journal of Sociology* 82, 111–130.

Korman, A.K., Wittig-Berman, U. and Lang, D. (1981), 'Career Success and Personal Failure: Alienation among Professionals and Managers', *Academy of Management Journal* 24, 342–60.

Korman, A. (1994), 'A Measure of Organizational Leadership Style', Unpublished manuscript, (New York: Baruch College, The City University of New York).

Kornhauser, A. (1965), *Mental Health of the Industrial Worker* (New York: Wiley).

Lachman, R. (1985), 'Public and Private Sector Differences: CEO's Perceptions of their Role Environments', *Academy of Management Journal* 28, 671–79.

Lawler, E.E. III (1973), *Motivation in Work Organizations, Monterey* (California: Brooks and Cole).

Lawler, E.E. III and Hall, D.T. (1970), 'Relationship of Job Characteristics to Job Involvement, Satisfaction, and Intrinsic Motivation', *Journal of Applied Psychology* 54, 4, 305–12.

Lawrence, P. and Vlachoutsicos, C. (1993), 'Joint Ventures in Russia: Put the Locals in Charge', *Harvard Business Review* January–February, 44–54.

Ledeneva, A.V. (1998), *Russia's Economy of Favours: Blat, Networking and Informal Exchange* (Cambridge: Cambridge University Press).

Lincoln, J.R. (1989), 'Employee Work Attitudes and Management Practice in the US and Japan: Evidence from a Large Comparative Study', *California Management Review* 32, 89–106.

Linz, S.J. (2003), 'Job Satisfaction among Russian Workers', *International Journal of Manpower* 24: 6, 626–52.

Luthans, F., McCaul, H.S. and Dodd, N.G. (1985), 'Organizational Commitment: A Comparison of American, Japanese, and Korean Employees', *Academy of Management Journal* 28, 213–9.

Luthans, F., Welsh, D.H.B. and Rosenkrantz, S.A. (1993), 'What do Russian Managers Really Do? An Observational Study with Comparison to US Managers', *Journal of International Business Studies* 24: 4, 741–61.

Marris, P. (1996), *The Politics of Uncertainty: Attachment in Private and Public life* (London: Routledge).

May, R.C., Stewart, W.H. and Sweo, R. (2000), 'Environmental Scanning in a Transitional Economy: Evidence from Russia', *Academy of Management Journal* 43: 3, 403–27.

McCarthy, D.J., Puffer, S. and Shekshnia, S.V. (1993), 'The Resurgence of an Entrepreneurial Class in Russia', *Journal of Management Inquiry* 2: 2, 125–137.

McCarthy, D.J., Puffer, S. and Naumov, A.I. (1997), 'Olga Kirova: A Russian Entrepreneur's Quality Leadership', *International Journal of Organizational Analysis* 5: 3, 267–90.

Meier, D.L. and Bell, W. (1959), 'Anomia and Differential Access to the Achievement of Life Goals', *American Sociological Review* 24, 189-202.

Mills, C.W. (1956), *The Power Elite* (New York: Oxford University Press).

Mirowsky, J. and Ross, C.E. (1989), *Social Causes of Psychological Distress* (Hawthorne, New York: Aldine de Gruyter).

Neal, A.G. and Seeman, M. (1964), 'Organizations and Powerlessness: A Test of the Mediation Hypothesis', *American Sociological Review* 29, 216–26.

Perry, J.L. and Porter, L.W. (1982), 'Factors Affecting the Context for Motivation in Public Organizations', *Academy of Management Review* 7, 89–98.

Perry, J.L. and Rainey, H.G. (1988), 'The Public-Private Distinction in Organization Theory: A Critique and Research Strategy', *Academy of Management Review* 13, 182–201.

The Portable Karl Marx (1983), (Harmondsworth: Penguin Books).

Puffer, S.M. (1994), 'A Portrait of Russian Business Leaders', *Academy of Management Executive* 8: 1, 41–54.

Puffer, S.M. and McCarthy, D.J. (1993), 'Decision Making Authority of Former Soviet and American Managers', *The International Executive* 35: 6, 497–512.

Puffer, S.M. and Shekshnia S.V. (1994), 'Compensating Local Employees in Post Communist Russia', *Compensation and Benefits Review*, September-October, 35–43.

Rainey, H.G. (1983), 'Public Agencies and Private Firms: Incentive Structures, Goals, and Individuals Roles', *Administration and Society* 15, 207–42.

Rainey, H.G. (1979), 'Perceptions of Incentives in Business and Government: Implications for Civil Service Reform', *Public Administration Review* 39, 440–448.

Rainey, H.G., Backoff, R.W. and Levine, C.H. (1976), 'Comparing Public and Private Organizations', *Public Administration Review*, March-April, 233–244.

Rosenthal, R. and Rosnow, R. (1991), *Essentials of Behavioural Research: Methods and Data Analysis*, 2nd edition (New York: McGraw Hill).

Saleh, S.D. and Hosek, J. (1976), 'Job Involvement: Concepts and Measurements', *Academy of Management Journal* 19: 2, 213–24.

Shama, A. (1995), 'From Exploiting to Investing: An Empirical Study of Entry Strategies of US Firms to the Former Soviet Bloc', Paper presented at the annual meeting of the Academy of Management (Vancouver, Canada).

Seeman, M. (1966), 'Alienation, Membership and Political Knowledge: A Comparative Study', *Public Opinion Quarterly* 30, 353–67.

Shepard, J. M. (1970), 'Functional Specialization, Alienation, and Job Satisfaction', *Industrial and Labor Relations* 23, 207–19.

Shlapentokh V. (1989), *Public and Private Life of the Soviet People: Changing Values in Post-Stalin Russia* (New York: Oxford University Press).

Solomon, E.E. (1986), 'Private and Public Sector Managers: An Empirical Investigation of Job Characteristics and Organizational Climate', *Journal of Applied Psychology* 71, 247–59.

Trompenaars, F. and Hampden-Turner, C. (1998), *Riding the Waves of Culture: Understanding Cultural Diversity in Global Business*, 2nd edition (New York: McGraw Hill).

Weiss, R.S. and Riesman, D. (1961), 'Social Problems and Disorganization in the World of Work', in Merton, R.K. and Nisbet, R.L. (eds) *Contemporary social problems* (New York, Harcourt, Brace, Jovanovich), pp. 459–514.

Weissenberg, P. and Gruenfeld, L.W. (1968), 'Relationship between Job Satisfaction and Job Involvement', *Journal of Applied Psychology* 52, 469–73.

Welsh, D.H.B.; Luthans, F. and Sommer, S.M. (1993), 'Managing Russian Factory Workers: The Impact of US-based Behavioural and Participative Techniques', *Academy of Management Journal* 36: 1, 58–79.

Whorton, J.W. and Worthley, J.A. (1981), 'A Perspective on the Challenge of Public Management: Environmental Paradox and Organizational Culture', *Academy of Management Review* 6, 357–61.

Wilensky, H. (1964), 'The Professionalization of Everyone?' *American Journal of Sociology* 70, 37–138.

Internet-based references

Earle, J. S., Economic Reform Today: Privatization in the Digital Age, Number 2 [website], (1999) <http://www.cipe.org/publications/fs/ert/e32/e32_08.htm>

The Harris Poll (2003), Substantial Increase in Alienation as '9/11 Effect' Wears Off [website], (8 January 2003) <http://www.harrisinteractive.com/harris_poll/index.asp?PID=349 #2>

Chapter 4

Trust and Organizational Culture

Tatiana Kovaleva

Introduction

Organizational culture is a hard-to-define concept for Russian companies. Usually the culture of a group is discussed in terms of the values and norms that influence the behaviour of the people working in a company. The organizational culture is the result of the group's accumulated understanding of how to resolve issues of external adaptation and internal integration (Schein 2004). Due to the transition period in Russia, the environment in which companies operate has changed dramatically and the new market requirements have come into conflict with the way things were done before. The whole system of work and social values has had to change. The values of a safe workplace and a predictable future have had to be exchanged for the opportunities to do business, make money and build a career. The whole system of the relationship between employer and employees has had to change. These changes have brought a new understanding and a new definition of justice and fairness in the workplace and new expectations from both employer and employees as to each other's behaviour. It has introduced anxiety into companies and shown how rigid and difficult to change issues of organizational culture are because they are a product of the human needs for stability, consistency and meaning.

At the same time, many foreign companies have entered the Russian market in a large number of sectors because they see great opportunities and a huge potential market. This tendency is expected to increase even more in the future. The foreign companies have brought not only a new understanding of competitiveness but have also pushed Russian companies to new levels of competitiveness. They have brought their own basic work assumptions and cultural paradigms which are taken for granted in their national business practices. Together with the process of reduction of state ownership and the development of private business, the process of forming a new culture started under the strong influence of or was often directly initiated by foreign management and NGOs. The role of the latter in the process of establishing business and organizational culture in Russia has so far not been investigated. The NGOs have provided technical aid to Russian management through training and internships at industry-related companies outside Russia. In the 1990s USAID invested millions of dollars into internship programmes for Russian managers at companies in the USA. After such training and internships Russian managers acquired not only an understanding of the new market and of American management systems but also the patterns, norms of behaviour, models of relationships and expectations of employees. The internships and special training started a process of socialization of new Russian managers into the American style of doing business. The economic crisis, doubts about the validity of national norms and values and the general dismay created a perfect atmosphere for the transfer of some aspects of organizational culture. As organizational theory suggests, bringing new business culture norms and models into national businesses might cause problems and dysfunctions.

National differences are closely related to a diversity of views on values, moral foundations and ethical systems in a society. These national differences and unique patterns of managing business opportunities have been determined by different preconditions for effectiveness which stem from the national culture, social values and the employment system.

This article aims to discuss some issues of trust and their influence on organizational culture in general and the individual motivation and relationship between owners and top managers in the context of new challenges to management in a new global economy.

Trust and Organizational Culture

Issues of trust play a very important role in Russian social and business life. The unlawful character of the Russian state and of management (Prokhorov 2002) in historical perspective resulted in the cluster nature of Russian management. The informal structure of national companies has a tendency to consist of small groups of people who have a high level of trust among each other in the group and a very low level of trust between the groups. Inside a group, people usually help each other and try to resolve not only work problems but also private problems. Outside the group another set of norms and rules exists and its application depends on how hard the respective groups compete for the limited resources. The cluster nature of management helped the Russian nation survive through difficult times and should be perceived as an important influencing factor and an important part of the organizational culture, even more so in the new economic system. If this culture can be defined as a pattern of shared basic assumptions learned by a group through solving problems of external adaptation and internal integration that have worked well enough to be considered valid (Schein 2004), the basic underlying assumptions need to be examined. Taking into consideration the focus of cultural aspects on the trust issue, two sets of assumption emerge as especially important:

1. Assumptions about authority and law
2. Assumptions about appropriate behaviour.

Assumptions about Authority and Law

In every culture there are shared beliefs about what is appropriate behaviour towards authority and law as well as shared instincts in those areas. At one extreme, one can identify strict obedience to law and submission to the power of authority. This pattern of obedience correlates closely with (1) the assumption that law is developed to defend human rights in general and loyal citizenship in particular; (2) a belief in the fairness of laws (the law remains the same and equally applies to everybody); (3) a pragmatic orientation towards legal techniques to defend people's rights and (4) the assumption that the law will not change during its application.

When speaking about corporate or organizational cultures, internal law is usually considered in terms of (1) rules and procedures, (2) policy, (3) working instructions, etc. The 'obedience' orientation is the predominant orientation in Germany and a key assumption of US managers and of managers from some other European countries. This orientation has its roots in a long democratic history of the business environment on the one hand and in the activities of trades unions on the other hand. The 'obedience' orientation became more effective in those countries where procedures to resolve difficult labour issues were developed. The author has set up the hypothesis that the very strong tendency for Germans to abide by rules and procedures correlates with German corporate governance structures. Within the German corporate governance system, the top authority level consists of two tiers: the management board, which manages and represents the company, and the supervisory board, which supervises the management's decisions and actions. Depending on various factors such as the size and the activity of the company, up to 50 per cent of the members of the supervisory board can be staff delegates. The long collective history of success of such structure led to the underlying assumption that following rules and procedures is the best individual and collective way to survive and to prosper in organizational and national surroundings.

Closely connected to this mindset is a certain level of trust between the company's boards, the management and the workers. A high level of trust in organizational cultures with 'obedience' orientation relies on procedural justice and on result justice more than on relationship justice. The climate of a certain level of trust is created by the fact that there is a working legal system in place and the possibility of activating this system in defence of one's rights. A long common history and the employees' accumulated knowledge have led to the underlying assumption and belief that following procedures, rules and laws will lead to survival and prosperity.

At the other extreme from the 'obedience' orientation is the 'avoidance orientation', which correlates closely with the assumptions that (1) the law is created to only defend the important people of the world; (2) the law is applied differently to different people, depending on the level of importance of the person in a hierarchy; (3) other people must develop their own defence methods and procedures to survive in such a hierarchy and an authority system; (4) apart from abiding by the law, there are always alternative ways of reaching one's goals. In short, this orientation is based on taking for granted the assumption that the law is a means of control of one part of the people over another in the interest of one group of people. The consequence of this assumption leads to a very simple rule: if following a law can be avoided, it is better to do that and to follow one's own understanding of what is right and what is wrong.

The 'avoidance orientation' is the dominant orientation in Russia. This attitude is deeply rooted in Russian management history: 'The whole nation from groom to monarch, from porter to general director has the same tendency not to keep within the law and to avoid observing the law with all their ability.' Law in Russia was usually developed to instil fear in parts of the population and not for the common good, which gave rise to notable inconsistencies between individual codes of law and many double meanings. Application of the law always depended on the social status of the person concerned and on the specific situation. The Russian collective historical experience of survival led to another mechanism of protection and cultural norms: (1) a relationship is more important than a law; (2) for protection a person has to be a part of a group; (3) do not trust people who do not belong to your group and especially those who belong to a more powerful group.

At the corporate and organization culture level this has several applications. First, the informal relationship structure of the company has almost the same power on a company's decisions as the formal organizational structure. Second, the main criterion for a person to be a part of the managing team is his personal devotion to a senior manager. Third, there is a lack of trust between different levels of a hierarchy. Fourth, having written procedures and rules will never mean that people will follow them.

The interaction between two management orientations during the transition period gave birth to very strange forms of organizational culture especially in small and medium-sized companies. The peculiarity of the current period of market development in Russia is that it is characterized by relative economic stability and slow growth. And if, during an unstable period and in an atmosphere of anxiety about the future and new orientation, people are more open to new ideas, values and patterns, then the more stable a period, the more people are inclined to adhere to basic values and beliefs.

Some researchers argue that the cost of management in Russia should be higher compared with West European and American companies. Some business processes in West European and American business practices might be built on the culture of those countries and management can rely on staff following procedures and technology. In Russia there is a need for more personal control and more visible management. The basic distrust of all instructions which flow from top to bottom necessitates extra control efforts from the management. The issue of distrust cannot be resolved by any formal procedures and documents. Recognizing this we can conclude that, in an atmosphere of trust, the cost of management of an organization should be less than in an atmosphere of distrust. This is called management profit: profit which results when one organization spends less on management than another.

Assumptions about Appropriate Human Behaviour

At the core of every culture are assumptions about the proper way for individuals to behave in relation to their environment. One extreme is identified as the 'result' orientation which correlates closely with (1) the assumption that nature can be controlled and manipulated, (2) a belief in human perfectibility, (3) a pragmatic orientation toward the nature of reality. In other words, it is taken for granted that people can control their fate and can earn wealth if they work hard. At the other extreme from the 'result' orientation is the 'process' orientation which correlates closely with the assumption that there is a very powerful force behind people and that people are subservient to it.

The 'result' orientation is the dominant orientation in the USA and is reflected in the popular term 'self-made man'. The key assumption is that if someone works hard and focuses on the task and manages to overcome difficulties etc, he or she will eventually succeed. This mindset implies taking an active role in what is going on.

The 'process' orientation is the dominant orientation in Russia. It is based on the basic assumption that even if somebody works hard and spends all his or her life at work, it does not guarantee that he or she will have a better and more prosperous life. The assumption is that in Russia wealth is not a matter of work but a matter of distribution (Ezzy 2001). The whole of Russian history is a history of stable and unstable periods and the peculiarities of the Russian management system made the long-term accumulation of wealth impossible for a family. Therefore, according to deeply rooted national belief, work is not a way to improve one's private life. And if that is the case, then why bother to work hard? It is much better, then, to focus more on the here and now, on individual enjoyment and on the acceptance of whatever happens. This national belief is based on a deep distrust of the entire management system of the country and makes the issue of employees' motivation a very complicated task.

Trust and Loyalty to the Company

In the section above it was shown how the issue of trust based on national cultural assumptions influences the formation of organizational culture and group behaviour at the deepest level. On a personal level, an individual's work experience, the personality and the expectations of an individual combined with significant events form the precise level of individual (personal) trust in a company and determine the level of loyalty to it. The author has observed the following four levels of loyalty within a company.

First level: *Insignificant*. At this level trust in a company is minimal. The employees do not trust the company and as a consequence are unwilling to allow the company any influence over their lives. They will try to keep their relationships with company staff as formal as possible. These employees consider the company merely as a means to making a living and/or to achieving personal goals. All social contacts with staff are reduced to the minimum level necessary for business contacts and personal needs and goals. The employees do not intend to stay for a long time with the organization and are inclined to keep their personal efforts during working time to a minimum if they are not working for their own goals. Because the connection with the company is very weak, these employees will leave the company very readily and they are not prepared to work intensively on the company's goals. The moment management puts more requirements on the work place and work conditions deteriorate, these employees will leave the company.

In many small and medium-sized companies in Russia there are positions with 35 to 70 per cent employee turnover. According to the author's estimate, about 30 per cent of employees in small and medium-sized businesses have only recently taken up their positions.

Second: *Group trust*. At this level employees become part of a small group which usually is a group of people working together. The level of trust in the group is very high. The group does not merely consist of some people who happen to work together, but its members are almost friends or in fact real friends. They usually have set up a system within the group to help each other with their work and with certain personal problems. At this level a group becomes a self-organizing cluster and in most cases meets all work requirements, reorganizing and redistributing work among members according to group needs. At this level loyalty of the individual to the company depends on average group loyalty and the history of the person's attitude towards the company. If the history of the relationship between the group and the company has been smooth, the entire group and each individual in it is dedicated to the company's goals and is very loyal to the company.

However, if a company takes some significant action such as dismissing some members of the group who are respected by other members of the group, then it might destroy the trust relationship between the group and the company. The individual members of the group will feel anxiety and in an attempt to come to terms with the situation will rally around a leader. Thus the group will become less transparent and less controllable by company management. This phenomenon was very clearly observed by the author during a consulting project with a medium-sized company. A new strategy for the company was developed and a plan for organizational changes was being developed. At this stage the consultants started interviewing staff of the company in different departments with the purpose of involving them in the process of developing the plan. Each time the consultants received the same answer: 'Yes, I understand, but my colleagues think … .' Finally, the consultants had to discuss the issue first with the leaders of the groups and then with all the groups together. People did not want to take personal responsibility for the decision before the whole group and the leader had agreed. As this story illustrates, at this level of trust one part of the task of the management is to find a way to manage the relationships between the individual groups (clusters) and the company itself.

Third: *Company Trust*. At this level of trust employees trust the company and perceive it as a kind of home, intending to stay with the company for as many years as possible. Work becomes an important part of personal life. People consider themselves as part of a company, a big group. Often, such a level of trust and an attitude like this are based on a long work history with a company and are associated with a feeling of belonging and often with personal devotion to the company's chief executive or to the idea (mission) of the company, and on some very positive and significant events such as bonus payments, top-management appreciation, and so on.

At this stage, employees trust the company's statements and devote themselves to the pursuit of the company's goals. A high level of confidence in the company and its management is often combined with a high level of motivation. If such employees have the necessary qualifications, some business processes might be organized around staff commitment and some part of the control system can be removed.

At this level management costs become less, and a company might really get some management profit. The high motivation of such employees guarantees the full commitment of employees, an atmosphere of trust motivates staff to maximize their productivity and find fulfillment at the same time. However, full commitment from employees requires proper responsibility from the company. Trust is closely related with a relationship history between the person and the company and implies an informal mutual agreement. An agreement here means that employees believe that the company will keep its promises and the company trusts that its employees will do their best to achieve the company's goals. If within the framework of such a psychological agreement the company treats its employees with no respect and breaks its promises, this will have much deeper consequences for the employees. They will feel they were tricked and manipulated. There are two scenarios which may result from such a situation. People may start playing the game of a simulated commitment to pursue their own interests (Ezzy 2001) or feel depressed and unmotivated. The transition period in Russia was characterized by the very different expectations of 'new' companies (or owners of the companies to be more precise) and employees. Most of the hired employees expected fair treatment and a guarantee of salary payments if the company had the money based on previous employment experience. On the other hand, the owners of companies viewed workers as instruments for earning money for themselves and paid salaries depending on their financial situation. That period had very interesting consequences: on the one hand there is a certain percentage of employees among the staff of most private companies who do not trust any employer. They show very average productivity and it is not easy to motivate them to do more. Their level of trust in the company could be characterized as 'insignificant'. The workplace for them is no more than a source of income. All their interests are outside of the company and they try to make some extra money outside the company as well. They meet the minimum requirements, and that is their personal approach to external adaptation issues.

A second scenario became usual for ambitious people who found out and understood the 'rules of the game' in the market environment. They have ambitious personal goals in their lives and the company becomes an instrument for achieving these goals. Often their strategy in that case is to get better qualifications at the company and then to sell themselves to another company for more money. The third scenario observed applies to people who are very sensitive to an atmosphere of distrust and manipulation. If they cannot or do not want to accept double standards, they leave the company and try to find a more comfortable place to spend their lives. Eventually, owners and top management of small and medium-sized companies choose and follow a certain trust strategy without even realizing that they choose a motivational structure for the staff.

Forth: *Identification*. This is the level of full trust and full commitment to the company's goals. At this level a person does not consider other job alternatives and often mixes personal life and work life. The full confidence in the company's owners and top management becomes the driving force behind the high expectations from both sides. An employee has a feeling of belonging to the 'family' and the management (owners) expect efforts above the norm. This level of identification has strong consequences for the employee. All work problems are taken to heart and work success is considered personal success and work failure considered personal failure. Identification causes strong dependence on the company, including emotional dependence. Destruction of this trust might lead to depression and even the destruction of personal values. The author has observed a management tendency in small and medium-sized businesses in Russia: understanding that a high level of identification gives big business advantages due to high staff motivation and management profit, some companies started to use certain methods of influence on the staff (mostly taken over from Japanese management practices). While the Japanese model of management expects two-party responsibilities, from both sides (such as life-long employment and life-long training of the employees), the management of Russian companies in some cases does not want to take on extra responsibilities. The labour market in Russia is filling up with unmotivated, disappointed and distrustful employees.

Trust and the Relationship between Owners and Hired Top Managers

In the section above the influence of trust on organizational culture and individual employee motivation was discussed. In every company there is one employee with the greatest influence on the company's effectiveness and success. In Russia this person is usually called the general director – a person who is hired by the owners directly and who makes the decisions or has a direct influence on a company's strategy. It is natural to suppose that the level of trust between the owners and the top manager hired by them has an impact on the decisions and results of the company and that these issues might have even stronger implication, taking into consideration some of the peculiarities of ownership in Russia. According to empirical analysis, company ownership and control in Russia are heavily concentrated and this often means that personal relationships with a degree of emotional trust play a much more important part in operating and strategy decisions. The structure of ownership, together with the history of entrepreneurship in Russia, causes some peculiarities in ownership-management relationships.

The first peculiarity is the attitude towards ownership. Many researchers argue that there is no respect for another person's ownership rights in Russia. The cultural assumption that wealth in Russia can only be captured and not earned is deeply rooted in Russian history and several centuries old. Part of the history is that government changes usually resulted in the redistribution of wealth. A strong and educated general director who finds him or herself working for an owner without any education and any understanding of how to manage business sooner or later is bound to ask the question: 'Who has the right to the increase in value of the property: the owner or the top manager? The owner who invested some money in the start-up period of the business and after that did not put any extra investment into it or the top manager who created extra value for the company?' Western compensation systems for top-managers usually provide options or shares for talented top managers. Concentrated ownership and distrust of hired managers has usually prevented owners in Russia from giving a share to even very talented general directors. This lack of compensation mechanisms results in a lack of motivation. As one general director said: 'I know what to do to make the business grow, but I do not know why I should do it: my salary, even a big salary and bonus payments are not a sufficient motivation for me.'

The second peculiarity is a peculiarity of the Russian market. The market is still very changeable and unstable. The nature of business in Russia has a very individual character. Its success and failure very much depend on individuals who work for the company. This dependence is much greater than on the Western markets with their strong rules and formalized procedures. In Russia, too much relevant and important information is held in the heads of the employees, not in procedures, documents or information systems. In Russia, the success of the company depends more on the intellectual capital of employees in small and medium-sized businesses than in Western markets. But tacit knowledge is very difficult to share and transfer to other people, and it very much depends on attitudes and trust between people.

The third peculiarity is the lack of corporate governance. Around the world the question of management activity and behaviour and protection of the owners' interests (the agency problem) is resolved through a proper corporate governance structure and policy. In spite of the fact that the corporate governance structure is under revision after a number of recent corporate scandals, it is still left up to the companies themselves whether they want to apply corporate governance codes or not. This idea is very hard to understand in Russia. There is no evidence that proper corporate governance has brought any advantages even to large companies. For small and medium-sized businesses with concentrated ownership there is a limit to the benefits of corporate governance anyway. Lack of corporate governance practice leads to the only attitude owners often have towards top managers: loyalty first. Trust has become the main governing factor in owner-manager relationships.

Competitiveness in the New Economy

In the preceding section we discussed how the issue of trust influences organizational culture and the motivation of employees, but how much influence on business success do these factors really have? Many years have passed and still many companies see their success only in terms in obtaining access to unique resources such as strategic raw materials, land and real estate, special customs deals, low-interest loans etc. Getting access to resources becomes a real competitive advantage and a defence against competitors. However, some authors have argued that there is a world-wide shift towards the conditions and competitive rules of the new economy.

In the old economy resources were distributed among firms irregularly and this fact caused competitive advantages for some firms and market vulnerability for others. However, times are changing and if the assets or services which belong to a certain company can be bought or sold in one or several markets, then those assets become available for other players in the market and, as long as the market continues to increase and become a global one, fewer and fewer possibilities for competitive advantages will remain. Teece (2004) argues that Russia's opportunities upon entering the global market were no worse than those of its competitors.

Modern companies should examine the resources they employ very carefully and pay attention to those which provide and guarantee long-term competitive advantages.

Companies' resources can be divided into three main groups (Bobrushev):

1. Fixed assets are the resources which can be bought on the open market. Examples: real estate, machinery, equipment, and so on
2. Intangible assets are the assets which are developed only by means of direct investment and accumulation, Examples: patents, trade marks, information system algorithms, any codified knowledge of the company
3. Abilities: the companies' combined knowledge how to work in the market and the combination of the individual skills of the companies' employees. In other words, a company's competencies.

The difference between assets and abilities is that assets are what a company owns and abilities are the concrete applications of what a company owns. On the global open market fixed assets and even intangible assets become easy objects for trading and only abilities are still very difficult to copy, to sell and to buy. Even buying manpower does not guarantee that the buyer will be able to reproduce all the abilities the vendor has. One of the reasons why abilities or in a broader sense competences of companies are difficult to copy is their social nature. Personal relationships between all stakeholders of the company are very difficult to copy and to reproduce. It means that competence becomes the only means of distinguishing themselves on the market for most companies and in the new economy they should base their sustainable competitive advantage on competence rather than on other resources.

Figure 4.1 shows another factor for sustainable competitive advantage besides competency: dynamic capabilities. Teece, Pisano and Shuen (1997) have developed a concept of higher-order capabilities: 'we define dynamic capabilities as the firm's ability to integrate, build, and reconfigure internal and external competencies to address rapidly changing environments. Dynamic capabilities thus reflect an organization's ability to achieve new and innovative forms of competitive advantage given path dependences and market positions.'

Thus, in the new economy, included in modern market requirements for companies are the development of both (1) abilities – the companies' combined

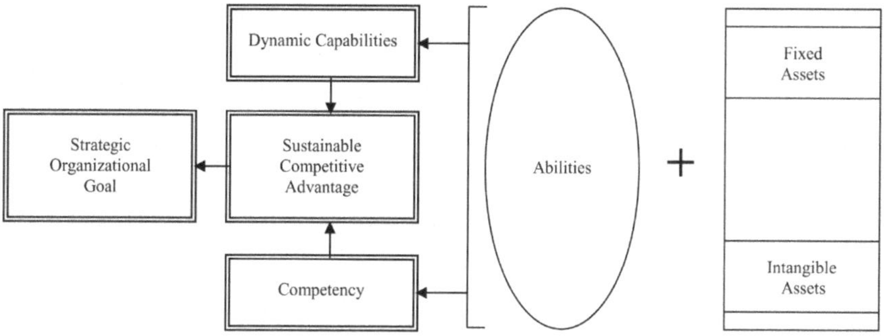

Figure 4.1 Factors for sustainable competitive advantage in the new economy

knowledge of how to work in the market and (2) dynamic capabilities – the capability to recognize and utilize new market opportunities. Dynamic capabilities provide companies with new possibilities for potential and rapid growth in their own or other areas. Competency is a crucial factor for retaining competitive advantages. The interrelation between dynamic capabilities and competency of the company

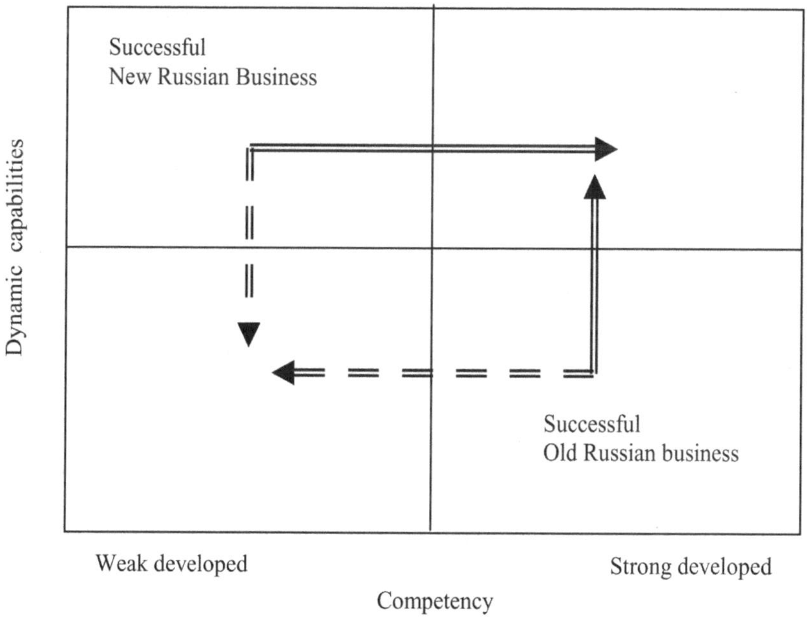

Figure 4.2 New challenges for successful Russian companies

should be investigated separately and, of course, strong dynamic capabilities have an entrepreneurial element and perception of risk which is shaped by past experience.

The author's consulting experience of over 10 years with successful new Russian businesses and with old Russian businesses leads to the assumption that both successful categories of Russian business have faced (or will do so in the immediate future) challenges with both elements of competitive advantage but in different ways.

Successful old Russian businesses (businesses which have survived since Soviet times) usually have strongly developed competencies in both the technical and social sphere, and they were usually supported by an appropriately strong organizational culture. Gaz Prom, for instance, had a very well developed scientific base and proper technical training for most employees. An organizational culture based on unconditional discipline and diligence of the employees since Soviet times plus huge social and networking capital in the form of political and administrative support plus good intangible assets sustained the business during the upheavals of the Perestroika period. However, most companies, even natural monopolies, cannot afford to only use old competencies any more. The market is changing and they need to look for new market opportunities to survive in an increasingly competitive environment. The development of dynamic capabilities has become a central challenge for such businesses in the current situation.

Successful new Russian businesses appeared and became successful in most cases due to good dynamic capabilities of their owners' or management's teams. In addition, the profits they made on the high potential, almost free market compensated for the lack of competency. However, step by step almost the entire market became shared and a strategy for increasing effectiveness and retaining market share came to take the place of the 'Just Go' strategy. To find ways to accumulate organizational knowledge, to create barriers for new competitors and to defend themselves against current ones is a challenge for most successful Russian businesses.

The Dangerous Nature of Competitive Advantage in the New Economy

The cumulative knowledge of the company has becomes a central competitive advantage for most companies these days. There are two types of knowledge a company can employ. The first one is codified knowledge, knowledge which can exist independently from a particular individual. Organizations keep this knowledge in data bases, in information systems, in documents, in other papers and in electronic devices.

The second type is tacit knowledge which is limited to an individual or a group of people. It is not certified knowledge, has many aspects and nuances, it is invisible and it can only be partly observed in applications. Not every successful manager can clearly explain why he or she made a certain decision. Only by observing the result of some specialists' work can we say that one person is more qualified than another.

Very often the process is the same for the external observer and only invisible details and small things make a difference.

Market globalization has changed the world. It generated a need for fast changing product lines and services and for technically complicated types of work. It has created new challenges for corporate management. The management cannot formalize every task and control every process any more in such a rapidly changing environment, and cannot use formalization and codification alone in order to coordinate employees' work, to control it and to guarantee quality of work. It becomes too expensive. Procedures are changing too quickly. It is more advisable to train employees to recognize what a result means and motivate them to achieve it. Thus, a company able to create a system of external employee competency control and internal work quality control has a huge advantage. But, in that case, management needs to rely on very elusive, invisible and poorly controlled aspects of its human resources: attitude, culture and trust.

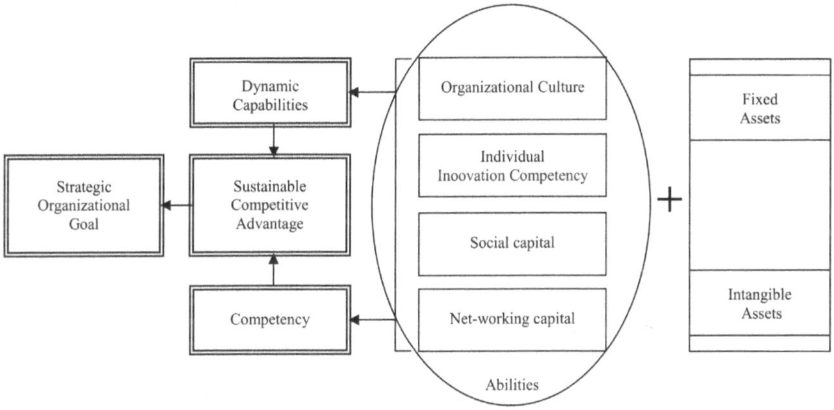

Figure 4.3 Structure of a company's abilities in the new economy

Figure 4.3 shows the structure of a company's ability to create sustainable competitive advantages through raising competency and dynamic capabilities.

The basis of a company's ability to recognize market possibilities and to use its assets effectively is its individual innovation competency. Competency in this case means enough knowledge, skills and motivation to achieve an established goal. On the other hand, business organization is group work and, more importantly, competitive group work. A permanent struggle between departments and teams for limited resources in a company leaves little room for any good idea to survive and to be accepted. To organize a mechanism of 'natural idea selection', companies should create and control the social capital of the company: a private trust relationship between employees from different departments and different levels of management. Proper social capital helps an idea to become a real project.

However, social capital without proper management can lead to political games between groups and result in domination of one group's interests over the company's interests. Organizational culture as an accepted standard of employee behaviour might be and should be the deterrent factor against political games. Proper organizational culture allows companies to create networking capital on the market in the form of trust relationships with clients, suppliers and stakeholders. Networking capital gives a company a huge advantage in times of uncertainty and risky products and projects. It decreases the cost of changes and facilitates the acceptance of new products and projects.

Therefore, a company's ability to create sustainable competitive advantages in the new economy involves more risks than the creation of competitive advantages in the old economy. In the old economy, having a competitive product, access to finances and good promotion could guarantee a company's success. All factors of market success were obvious and controlled. In the new economy social factors play a significant role. External market factors cannot defend a company from competitors any more. Vague internal factors like individual innovation competency, social capital and corporate culture become the main factors in competitive advantages. However, all factors have a very strong relationship with issues of trust and its role in a company's effectiveness.

Conclusion

Competitive advantage in the new information economy involves many risks. The most important part of a company's resources for ensuring success in the global market is the company's abilities: combined knowledge of how to work in the market and the combination of its employees' individual skills.

During the transition period, many traditional attitudes in the relationship between employers and employees were changed, but still the work culture and organizational culture in many companies is a concept which is very hard to define. Russian companies are facing a huge challenge: they need to develop a practice of procedural trust to increase management profit and to survive in a global market.

References

Avner, B.-N. and Putterman, L. (2002), 'Trust in the New Economy', June.

Teece, D. (2004),'Capturing Value from Knowledge Assets', *Russian Management Magazine* 1.

Teece, D., Pisano and Schuen (1997), *Dynamic Capabilities and Strategic Management*.

Rauterberg, G., 'The New Economy: E-commerce, Intellectual Property Rights, Trust and other Dangerous Things', (TU/e Eindhoven).

Prokhorov, A. (2002), *The Russian Model of Management* (Moscow).

Kotter, J. and Cohen, D. (2004), *The Heart of Change* (Moscow).

Ezzy, D. (2001), 'A Simulacrum of a Workplace Community: Individualism and Engineered Culture', *Sociology* 35: 3.
Schein, E. (2004), *Organizational Culture and Leadership*, 3rd edition (Jossey-Bass).

Internet-based references

Bobrushev, S., 'Knowledge Management as a Strategic Asset', <www.cfin.ru.>
<http://db.socionet.nw.ru>

Chapter 5

HRM Practices in Virtual Companies in Russia[1]

Sofia Kosheleva and Marina Libo

Preface

This article discusses telecommuting as a phenomenon where two of the most important fields of the contemporary management – Human Resources (HR) and Information Technology (IT) intersect. This phenomenon presents both a new work paradigm and a new form of personnel management in virtual organizations. We have undertaken a quantitative analysis of HR systems at three different types of virtual organizations.

In this article we have set the following as our goals:

- To demonstrate the transformation of key elements in the structure of the workplace: the workplace environment itself and working time, the period and character of employment, employers and compensation of labour
- To do a SWOT-Analysis of how telecommuting relates to the individual, organization and the public
- To describe (make an inventory) of the cross-cultural aspects of telework in Russia
- To distinguish and characterize the types of virtual companies in Russia
- To analyze the peculiarities of HRM in virtual companies in Russia
- To provide a comparative analysis of the main HR practices in virtual companies involving: Selection, Training, Evaluation, Promotion, Compensation, Communications, Adaptation and Workplace conditions
- To describe the various HRM instruments used in different types of virtual companies.

Our research was based on an analysis of 40 virtual companies operating in Russia during the years 2000 to 2003. Our methodology includes:

1. On-line and traditional interviews with top managers (CEOs and HR

1 The authors would like to express their thanks to Dr Carl Fey, Stockholm School of Economics in Russia, for the important role he played in this project. This project is part of a larger research project on HRM co-ordinated by Dr Carl Fey.

managers) from 40 virtual companies
2. In-depth interviews with CEOs and teleworkers from different types of virtual companies
3. Case-analysis (description and analysis) of HR systems and HR practices in different types of virtual companies
4. Cross-cultural interviews with CEOs of Chinese virtual companies and Russian 'telecenters'
5. Focus-groups and professional discussions concerning telework problems.

Introduction

The development of information technologies and their breadth of application are leading to considerable changes, not only in the economy, but also in culture, politics and all the spheres of social life. One can argue that modern society is characterized by a qualitatively different type of socio-economic order which has come to be known as the information economy.

The technological changes taking place in society have led to the transformation of traditional business forms and the appearance of virtual ('shell') companies, that is, individuals, groups and organizational units dispersed in space and interacting by means of information technologies to achieve a common goal.

Table 5.1 Transformation of the key elements in the structure of the workplace paradigm

Elements	Traditional paradigm	Distant paradigm
Time	Fixed, same for everyone	Optimal for each teleworker
Place	Constant, determined by labour legislation	At home, mobile workplace, optimal for each teleworker
Period	Mainly long-term	Mainly short-term, project-oriented
Employment	Full-time	Mainly part-time, by many organisations
Employer	Single	Multiple employers
Compensation of labour	Mainly based on working time and behaviour	Based on results

New Workplace Paradigm

With the appearance of flexible and mobile communications facilities, a fixed workplace and working time are losing their original meaning.

In connection with the changes that have been observed, one can speak of the appearance and development of a new, 'distant' working paradigm based on the 'teleworking' concept, which implies 'working in the optimal place, at the optimal time'.

As can be seen in Table 5.1, the key elements in the structure of the workplace paradigm – workplace and working time, employment period and employment character, employer, and compensation of labour – are being transformed.

Based on the HRM positions, the following can be regarded as the general theses of the new work paradigm:

- global expansion of the spatio-temporal characteristics of the notion of the workplace
- transformation of the management concept into a co-ordination concept
- determining role of competencies and information technologies
- concentration of priority concerning decision-making and responsibility placed on the worker rather than the employer.

Under these conditions, the value of (and therefore, demand for) qualified specialists who are highly adaptable, who work in different professional spheres and who determine the content and form of their employment on their own is growing.

This tendency makes it possible to supplement the existing working categories of 'white collar', 'grey collar' and 'blue collar' with a new category: 'virtual collar' (employees doing intellectual work who are able to carry out their professional activity at any place and any time).

Strengths (Opportunities) and Weaknesses (Threats) of Telework

The problem of the positive and negative effects (consequences) generated by telework – the so-called 'externalities' of telework – is one of the most important and widely discussed issues connected with the phenomenon of telework.

An analysis and understanding of the possible strengths, weaknesses, opportunities and threats caused by telework is deemed significant for the broad and active implementation of telework in a company, for the effective use of teleworkers already employed by a company, and for the process of making a decision about recruiting additional distant personnel.

In order to simplify the external approach to the analysis of the telework phenomenon, we have singled out three levels of such analysis:

1. Organizational level – describes the strengths (opportunities) and weaknesses (threats) which companies can face as a result of the implementation and/or use of telework.

A preliminary and current situation analysis at this level allows for general (generalized, non-specific) diagnostics and a general (generalized) forecast of the benefits and losses connected with the implementation and/or use of telework. It also makes it possible to draw a general conclusion about the possible scale of its use in a company and to make a decision aimed at extending or limiting the use of telework or completely rejecting telework.

2. Individual level – describes the strengths (convenience, benefits) and weaknesses (inconvenience, difficulties, costs) involved in organizing one's labour activity which an employee can face when working distantly or planning to switch to a distant form of work.

A preliminary or current situation analysis on the individual level allows one to recognize and evaluate the scale and significance of the strengths and weaknesses involved in using the distant form of work for a certain employee.

The specific character of this level of analysis is that it allows one to take into account not only the economic and organizational aspects and factors connected with recruiting a specific employee for telework, but also social aspects and factors of their life and life plans (programs), as well as psychological aspects and factors connected with their individual peculiarities and preferences concerning their way of living, the organization of their employment, labour procedures and labour conditions, habits and needs affecting the organization, and the efficiency of performing their professional activity.

3. Public (social) level – describes the influence of the expansion of telework as a form of population employment upon the social and economic aspects of societal life, connected with the change in working conditions, migration, the employment rate, the standard of living, informatization, legal support, and so on.

A preliminary or current situation analysis at this level allows one to evaluate the objective and unmanageable possibilities and restrictions of using telework in society (including a specific country), forecast the scale and speed of its expansion, and describe the possible consequences of specific actions planned or taken by public administrations and companies concerning the possibilities of implementing telework widely.

Let us concretize the basic strengths (opportunities) and weaknesses (threats) of using telework in relation to the different analysis levels – the organizational and individual levels – taking into account their influence on the practice of managing the personnel of companies.

Strengths of Telework at the Organizational Level:

Reduction of production premises costs and office costs. Premises costs are one of the main fixed costs in the majority of companies. Therefore, production premises costs and office costs are minimized when employees are transferred to a distant form of work; only a minimal office remains, or no office at all.

Flexibility of organization. Employees work within temporary project groups consisting of specialists who are most suitable for the aims of the project or for meeting the production target. If restructuring or reorganization takes place, people can go on working without any serious problems for them personally, because they are not constrained by the rigid assignment to administrative and production positions in the organizational structure.

Absence of time restrictions on professional activity. Geographical positions and time zones do not influence the periodicity and frequency of contact or work effectiveness. A 'time compression' effect takes place and an 'immediacy culture' is formed. Companies with broad geographic coverage actually work 24 hours a day because the work continues, 'passing' from one employee to another following the movement of the sun.

Flexible staff. For activity categories with variable activity, time cyclicity, and alternating rises and declines (for example, cycles of advertising activity), telework makes it possible to increase or decrease staff quickly depending on the necessary level of activity and thus to support the required level of company efficiency during periods of instability or abrupt changes to significant environmental factors.

Rise in employee productivity. Employee productivity during the transition to a distant form of work rises due to the reduction (or absence) of non-productive time losses arising as a result of interruptions to the work process (such as coffee or cigarette breaks, which are inevitable under office conditions). Productivity also rises due to the saving of a considerable amount of time which was previously spent by the employees travelling to and from the office.

Lack of absenteeism and late arrival to work. The problems connected with violations of labour discipline and the working schedule are absent. There is a reduction in the loss of working time due to absenteeism because of personal reasons connected with illness, having to help one's relatives, or unforeseen family circumstances. All time losses are filled by the employees themselves owing to flexible, independent labour time planning.

Retention and development of skills and competencies. Telework allows the employees to retain their professional skills and competencies, keep them in the relevant condition, and perfect them constantly even during drastic life changes such as moving to a new place, giving birth to and caring for a baby, health problems or other significant events. Employees can choose their period of work and degree of employment (from part-time or temporary to full-time employment) at their own discretion in accordance with their personal situation, but they will still be sought-after specialists who have the possibility of being involved in company activities. This allows the employees to retain and maintain their professional skills and qualifications.

Increasing motivation. The distant form of work is accompanied by a decrease in or total absence of the monitoring of employee working activity, an increase in trust towards employees on the part of managers and employers, mutual trust between the interacting colleagues, and an increase in employee independence and responsibility for their work. It also contributes to self-expression and the realization of the employees' best professional qualities. All of this produces a positive motivating effect and contributes to maintaining devotion to the company.

Increasing the efficiency of HR practices. Introducing telework in a company helps increase the efficiency of traditional HR practices towards distant personnel: the possibilities of attracting previously unavailable personnel become broader, the quality of recruiting the most competent specialists gets higher, the conditions for retaining specialists in the company improve, the conflict level in the groups of employees and between the company subdivisions is reduced, the opportunity appears to individualize the motivation instruments and the employees' compensation structure, and the appraisal system is more result-oriented and takes on a complex and objective character.

Service improvement. Moving employees closer to clients, broadening the range of services provided, extending service beyond the limits of the working day or working week without having to pay for overtime.

Weaknesses of Telework at the Organizational Level

High cost of setting up a workplace. Individual distant-working employees require additional expenses from the organization for equipping their mobile workplace (office). It must be noted that the availability of qualified administrative and/or technical personnel is very significant to the establishment of telework activities. The absence of such personnel can completely paralyze the tele-employees' work. Connected with this is the need to provide non-stop technical support for the teleworkers' workplaces and telecommunication processes 24 hours a day, seven days a week.

The creation and equipping of a telecenter for the employees' collective work in a convenient place which is relatively easy to reach by public transportation makes it possible to decrease the expenses for technical equipment to a certain degree, but this is associated with increasing expenses for the transportation of the employees to the workplace.

Losses connected with the costs of effective equipment use. Expensive office equipment necessary for effective office activities in a modern company is of great value. However, when this kind of equipment is spread over independent distant workplaces, its servicing costs increase considerably.

Absence of clear assessment criteria and of direct monitoring (control) of employee activity. Managers lose the opportunity for direct visual control over their employees' activity, which makes it harder to influence the process of their work. The focus of the appraisal of the employees and of their efficiency is shifted from monitoring their activity to monitoring their results, which also restricts the opportunities for the managers to exert a correcting influence on the working process.

Absence of visible promotion. Vertical promotion as a stimulation instrument ceases to exist. The disappearance of status, of formal symbols of authority, and of the existing regulatory powers is one of the main organizational changes during the transition to a virtual organization. This is not always welcomed by the management of a company and by its employees who are aimed at an administrative career path.

Possibility of working for competitors. The intangibility and intellectual character of a product contribute to the appearance of opportunities for its use by partners and competitors equally. The situation is aggravated by a low level of information protection.

Low level of professional communication with colleagues. The predominantly individual, solitary character of the teleworkers' activity creates the threat of an abrupt decrease (sometimes leading to the complete disappearance) of professional communication with colleagues. For a number of professions where the exchange of information and individual experience is critical (for example, journalists, consultants), this can have a negative effect on the professional growth and development of the specialists. Under these conditions, the problem of finding ways and creating conditions for the support of broad and rich professional communication among teleworkers is quite acute.

Weak organizational culture. In a virtual organization, there is a great likelihood of a weak or even non-existent organizational culture. To maintain an organizational atmosphere which would unite the employees within a virtual organization, it is necessary to develop both the internal structures and the visual components of an organizational culture. This is important because of the possible threat of the 'indistinguishability' or similarity of most virtual organizations as perceived by teleworkers, which has a negative effect on their devotion to the company, their loyalty to their employer, and their length of co-operation.

Difficulty of effectively combining traditional and distant personnel within one company. The presence of this threat is characteristic for companies using both traditional and distant personnel in their activities. The existence of a mixed labour collective gives rise to problems connected with the varying efficiency of using traditional HR practices for managing different categories of employees. There are some difficulties with combining strategic principles of HR management and specific instruments of personnel management at the level of decision-making concerning specific employees who belong to different personnel categories but are dealing with the same problems.

Traditional psychology of the employer. Among the managers of different companies, many people are unsure of their capabilities and of their ability to exercise effective 'distant management'. Additionally, a large number of managers do not believe in the ability of the company personnel to work honestly and effectively without having their activity monitored, and they feel that most employees will be inclined to underperform when working distantly.

Strengths of Telework at the Individual Level

Working in the optimal place at the optimal time. Distant teleworkers can choose their place and time of work, which enables them to optimize their time and the physical and intellectual effort expended in fulfilling their professional activity, to equip their working place according to their needs and habits, and to optimize the use of the workplace in accordance with their personal (individual) circumstances.

Continuity of work process. A decrease in the temporal and structural 'disruption' of the work process, concentration and focusing the attention on the fulfilment of the professional activity according to the complexity of the task, and the consolidation of working operations.

Flexible operating schedule. The distant form of work allows one to successfully apply a flexible approach to the organization and use of working time which is oriented both on the external factors, conditions and requirements of the activity and on the internal psychological and biological (physiological) peculiarities of a working individual. The possibility of a flexible working day can increase work efficiency since the employee can use his most active periods to carry out the work.

Self-organization and self-control. Responsibility for the organization, implementation and results of the work is focused on the teleworker, and the absence of any regulation of the work elements or working process as a whole leads teleworkers to feel greater independence and an increase in personal responsibility for their professional career. This gives rise to the aspiration for more conscientious, effective and productive activity on the part of the teleworker, and their active focus on the results of their work makes these teleworkers more effective than traditional employees.

Improving the work/life balance. Distant work allows teleworkers to optimize their work/life balance, taking into account the individual inclinations, preferences and conditions of family life of specific employees, and to devote the necessary time to family relations in order to support both the integrity of the family and the favourable psychological state of the employees.

Decrease in time and effort expended on transportation to and from work. One of the most obvious advantages of telework for the employees is a considerable decrease in (or the complete elimination of) the time and money spent on transportation to and from work. In megalopolises, the traffic problem is quite pressing.

Improvement of working conditions for people with health restrictions. In most developed countries, people with physical disabilities who have a certain level of professional education and possess the relevant professional competencies are regarded as an efficient labour resource. However, due to health restrictions, it is not always possible to enlist their services under traditional conditions. For this population group, the distant form of work offers the opportunity to be included in active (actual) labour activity, to enhance their sphere of professional and personal communication, and to benefit from full-fledged social self-realization.

Weaknesses of Telework at the Individual Level

Feeling of isolation. As practice proves, some level of direct social interaction with managers, colleagues and subordinate employees is absolutely necessary for workers, no matter how interesting, rich and varied their work is. Without such interaction, or when its level is low, teleworkers lose their sense of identity with the organization and the social and emotional links essential for maintaining the psychological comfort of the working place.

Lack of trust. One of the key prerequisites for successful virtual companies is a feeling of trust between the distant workers and the company managers. A high level of independence and the autonomy of the teleworkers presupposes the presence of trust towards them. However, in reality, most teleworkers experience a lack of trust on the part of managers and, in turn, do not trust the managers completely either. This is more of a psychological effect than an organizational one, and it is caused by the lack of direct communication and the depleted emotional constituent of the professional interaction.

Personal peculiarities of teleworkers. Despite all the strengths and advantages of telework, it is not a suitable form of labour organization for all people without exception. A large number of qualified specialists need external control on the part of managers and colleagues. There is one more essential psychological aspect: for some people, the need to 'go to work' is an important part of their lives, and the existence of a 'working place' which is common to all (or to the majority) of the company employees presents the opportunity to enhance and improve their social skills and contacts. The creation of 'telecenters' can help in some of these cases.

Teleworker's position. A home-based workplace might not always be sufficiently well-equipped for certain kinds of telework. Technical equipment is not always the question. For example, even well-motivated teleworkers can frequently have problems focusing their attention, and the quality of work may suffer if the distant workplace is in a small apartment which the employee shares with small children or ill (feeble) elderly people.

Work task. Not all tasks can be performed well in a dispersed, self-governing environment. There are a large number of tasks which yield a considerably better result if performed in close interaction within a group of employees. This can be exemplified by certain kinds of creative work where joint discovery of the best solution is an important part of the creative process. Team spirit and internal motivation generated in the best way possible by leaders and managers during direct personal contact with their employees also play an important role in some kinds of activity.

Strengths of Telework at the Public (Social) Level

Decrease in urgency of transport problem. This occurs due to the decrease in the total number of travelling employees and the lightening of traffic at the beginning, in the middle and at the end of a working day. This is particularly prominent in megalopolises.

Better opportunities for work and employment in the population. Telework can potentially allow people in regions with a high unemployment rate to gain access to vacancies anywhere in the country or the world. However, in order to use this opportunity, there are two requirements to be met: the potential teleworkers must possess professional qualifications which are in keen demand, and they must also have well-developed personal skills for using electronic networks (skill with working in such networks) which will allow them to be seen by potential employers.

Economic revival. Many modern programs of economic revival regard telework and teletrade as key aspects of developing future opportunities for trade and work. This is because the experts believe that they will intensify these megaspheres both in view of attracting more customers and in view of including a large number of teleworkers in these processes.

Ecological improvement. Modern trends in the fight against environmental pollution view the broad introduction of telework into existing traditional companies and the transfer of some traditional personnel to teleworking conditions as part of a wide-ranging ecological program which will, in particular, make it possible to reduce the harmful emissions in the atmosphere which are connected with the intensive use of transportation.

Weaknesses of Telework at the Public (Social) Level.

The difficulties facing the expansion of telework can be of an objective and insurmountable nature if caused by processes and phenomena at the social level, for example:

1. Existence of stable clichés in the public conscience
2. Influence of specific national peculiarities connected with cultural traditions
3. Absence of relevant legal basis
4. Low level of informational infrastructure development
5. Absence of conceptual support for telework on the part of the public administration.

The strengths (opportunities) and weaknesses (threats) of telework which manifest themselves on the organizational, individual and public (social) levels have thus been pinpointed and described as a result of analyzing the telework phenomenon. This analysis is supplemented with a brief description of the cross-cultural peculiarities of telework development in Russia.

Cross-Cultural Aspects of Telework Development in Russia

An examination of the telework phenomenon in view of cross-cultural peculiarities allows one to distinguish not only the internal features inherent in it but also the external features determined by the environment and producing a positive and negative effect on its development.

The following factors can be regarded as cross-cultural, for instance:

1. Demographic factors, such as the density of population and the percentage of urban and rural population
2. The urbanization level and the associated problem of managing traffic flows
3. Technological factors, such as household appliances (including phones, computers, Internet access) in the possession of the population
4. Economic factors, such as the per capita income, national workforce structure, and level of unemployment
5. Institutional factors, such as the presence of telework legislation and the attitude towards telework in society
6. Cultural factors caused by the national peculiarities of the way of life, as well as behaviour and relation models.

Let us single out some essential peculiarities of the conditions for introducing telework which are typical of modern Russia:

1. The sizeable territory of Russia and the presence of several time zones can be an obstacle to doing business effectively by traditional companies, but it can contribute to a more active implementation of telework, at least for some of the employees in traditional companies
2. A relatively low level of transport infrastructure development and a large territory mean that a significant part of the rural population has practically no opportunity to gain access to the comforts of civilization, but the establishment of telecenters and the computerization of the population will enable the activation of an additional part of the labour force capable of working
3. Because a large share of the population has gone through higher education and has received a high level of technical education in general, this has formed favourable conditions for the effective implementation of virtual organizations in Russian businesses
4. Personal communication and relations between company employees are highly significant, and the boundary between work and personal life is fuzzy
5. There are strong traditions of sole power and dominant behaviour models among managerial staff
6. There has been an increase in the number and proportion of employees in non-traditional employment situations: part-time, temporary employment,

off-hour jobs, freelance work, project work, informal employment.

Virtual Company Typology in Russia

Telework constitutes a heterogeneous phenomenon and presupposes different organizational forms. The following criteria are often used to characterize the phenomenon of telework: location, the time of working distantly, the employee's status and significance, saturation with knowledge, the intensity of IT usage, the character of the work and sphere of activity, the period of employment, and external and intra-organizational co-operation.

A comparison and analysis of three basic scenarios is deemed essential in the context of effective HRM objectives:

1. The company's degree of virtuality as determined by the percentage of teleworkers compared to the total number of company employees
2. The teleworkers' significance in achieving the company goals, which is determined by the importance of their sphere of activity and a subjective assessment of their significance on the part of managers
3. The amount of time in which work is carried out distantly as determined by the percentage of time spent on distant work compared to the total amount of working time.

According to the above-mentioned criteria, it is possible to single out three types of virtual companies.

Type 1 – fully virtual companies, a 'network of professionals', mainly characterized by:

- the vast majority of employees working virtually
- the high degree of work saturation with knowledge
- the fact that, most of the time, the employees work out of the office.

These are virtual companies to the utmost extent. They are mainly represented by networked companies with a horizontal structure in which the majority of personnel are virtual employees or people doing intellectual work distantly. The significance of these employees for the company and their share and input in the overall results of the company activity are very high: they create the main company values, and the productiveness and efficiency of their work directly influences the company's efficiency. Examples of Type 1 companies are consulting companies represented by networks of professionals, legal advice companies incorporating distant lawyers, psychological associations, information portals, translation bureaus, and so on.

Type 2 – partly virtual companies, 'key workers', chiefly characterized by:

- a smaller percentage of company employees working distantly

- the notion that the telecommuters are the key personnel and that their significance in achieving the company's goals is quite high; these are mainly professionals with highly tailored responsibilities within the company
- telecommuters working distantly most of the time but having access to the real office space.

This type of company is rather numerous and heterogeneous. In companies of this type, the majority of the employees are traditional staff, and traditional management methods are used towards them, whereas a smaller proportion of the most significant workers (about 24 per cent) are virtual staff doing intellectual jobs. This situation requires a combination of traditional and distant HR management methods and results in a mix of these methods peculiar to each company.

Type 2 – companies are exemplified by insurance companies and real estate agencies where some members of staff work distantly, IT companies in which the programmers work outside the office, electronic and traditional media companies, and so on.

Type 3 – partly virtual companies, 'rational companies', characterized by:

- the low significance of telecommuters for the company
- telecommuters being used on a part-time basis
- the telecommuters' low degree of responsibility for the results of their activity and their low psychological contract.

These companies are characterized by the small number and low significance of distantly working employees as opposed to the qualitative and quantitative prevalence of traditional staff, and also a variety of types of teleworkers: employed on a part-time, contract, temporary, project, or freelance basis.

The main reason for using teleworkers is the reduction of company expenses connected with the fact that the employees work away from the office (on their own territory) and use their own equipment, and the company is not accountable for their social and medical support and does not provide paid leave. Distant-working personnel do the work which is secondary to the company and which can be done via outsourcing. Type 3 companies function mainly in innovational fields such as high-tech, IT and communications.

In Russia, companies of the third type are the most numerous representatives of virtual companies. However, it is this type that can be viewed as the most problematic with respect to human resource management because of low motivation, a low degree of loyalty and trust, the limited responsibility of the telecommuting personnel, weak social security on the part of the company, and the low level of psychological contract.

To change the situation for the better, it is important to understand the distinctive peculiarities of human resource management in different types of companies and to choose the most effective practices to be used.

Peculiarities of HRM in Virtual Companies in Russia

The comparative examination of 40 virtual companies operating in Russia revealed differences in using the main HRM instruments.

Table 5.2 Significance of the main HR-practices in virtual companies

HR practices	**Significance** (rating)
Workplace conditions	1
Communications	2
Promotion	3
Compensation	4
Selection	5
Adaptation	6
Training	7
Evaluation	8

One can conclude from Table 5.2 that the most important and efficient instruments of HR management in virtual companies are placed differently: workplace conditions, communications, promotion, compensation, selection, whereas adaptation, training and evaluation are less significant. The specific character of HRM in virtual companies of different types based on the breadth and intensity of the main HR practices' usage is shown below in Table 5.3:

Table 5.3 Usage of the main HR-practices in virtual companies of different types

HR practices	**Type 1** 'Network of professionals'	**Type 2** 'Key workers'	**Type 3** 'Rational companies'
Selection	Average	Delicate	Average
Adaptation	Delicate	Average	Average
Training	Delicate	Delicate	Delicate
Evaluation	Delicate	Delicate	Delicate
Promotion	Average	Prevailing	Average
Compensation	Prevailing	Prevailing	Average
Communications	Prevailing	Prevailing	Prevailing
Workplace conditions	Average	Average	Prevailing

As indicated by the table, the companies of the first type are characterized by the most developed and multi-level HRM system as compared to the other types. The most important instruments are: compensation and communications. The second place is occupied by selection, promotion and workplace conditions and the other instruments play a supporting role.

HR practices in companies of the second type are characterized by the combination of elements of traditional and distant HRM elements. The most important instruments are: promotion, compensation and communications. Adaptation and workplace conditions are used somewhat less extensively.

Reluctance to use various HR practices and an absence of attempts to perfect the system of managing teleworkers is characteristic for companies of the third type. Communications and workplace conditions are used most intensively.

Table 5.4 gives a comparative analysis of the main psychological characteristics of personnel management influencing the teleworkers' efficiency in different types of virtual companies.

Table 5.4 Comparative analysis of the main psychological characteristics of distant personnel management in different types of virtual companies

HRM Psychological characteristics	**Type 1** 'Network of professionals'	**Type 2** 'Key workers'	**Type 3** 'Rational companies'
Motivation	Based on internal professional interest and the employee's values	Uniqueness of working for the company and importance of results for the company are special motivators	Based on financial results, shifting the emphasis to internal contensive motivators is necessary
Trust	Presents the foundation for efficient activity, based on professionalism, responsibility and trust towards colleagues	Exists between teleworkers and managers, weak between teleworkers and traditional employees	Has low significance, important role is played by the manager's personality and the company image
Social efficiency	High social efficiency, high satisfaction with labour, high quality of life	Low social efficiency, personal and professional isolation	Lowest level of social efficiency

Description of HRM Instruments in Virtual Companies of Different Types

Virtual Companies of the First Type – 'Network of professionals'

Selection Selection is given a high priority because personnel are the main resource of the company. These companies attract the most professionally competent employees who are recognized experts in their fields of activity. In view of the fact that the geographical area for seeking and attracting potential employees is quite broad, selection is mainly made through electronic communication facilities. However, there is an argument to be made that due to the importance of trust, psychological contract and devotion to the company, virtual employees should be hired using traditional methods (especially interviews), while electronic selection should be used to a greater extent to hire traditional employees.

Adaptation The employees of Type 1 companies have already experienced distant work for the most part and do not need to adapt to this form of work. There is, however, a call for adaptation to the company – its organizational structure, psychological atmosphere, and peculiarities of activity. Successful adaptation requires the maximum awareness of the employees regarding the company goals, objectives and lines of activity, its main values, requirements towards personnel, and so on. Electronic tutorship can be quite effective in establishing informal horizontal links with colleagues.

Training In most cases, the virtual employees of Type 1 companies are highly qualified in their field of activity and, at first glance, do not require advanced training. The information economy, however, is based on a continuously renewed body of knowledge and the concept of continuous training as the basis for maintaining company competitiveness. This is why it is important to provide these virtual employees with the opportunity to continuously build up and expand their professional competencies. It must be noted that self-education is the most widespread and effective form of education for such specialists. It not only contributes to keeping professional competence at the relevant level, it also has a motivating function.

In order to increase the employees' loyalty and their feeling of devotion, some companies formalize this process and encourage their employees by taking into account the time spent on self-education in the working process. It is also quite useful to provide distant-working personnel with 'non-professional' training to develop their personality potential, which enables complex personal development and more effective professional realization.

Appraisal The ongoing appraisal of virtual employees in Type 1 companies is hampered due to the nature and form of their labour: the employees are not directly supervised and it is impossible to control the amount of effort applied by them, the time expended on work, and the quality and quantity of resources used. Their activity has a clearly defined intellectual character and is largely deprived of algorithmization.

Therefore, appraisal is not based on ongoing control but on the obtained results, clearly defined objectives and scheduled indicators. The presence of stable feedback and a high degree of trust between the employee and the company are important factors for adequate appraisal.

Promotion In Type 1 companies, horizontal structures are predominant. Promotion in its traditional sense is hampered. Virtual employees are more interested in horizontal promotion connected with broadening their authority and responsibility, enriching their labour, and raising their status based on the high level and exclusiveness of their competencies.

It is interesting to note that the value of external promotion is lower with teleworkers in this company type, which gives way to internal motives, such as professional and personal self-realization. This indicates the particular importance and significance of psychological, personally oriented factors in managing virtual employees.

Compensation The virtual employees of Type 1 companies are in great demand on the market owing to their high level of competence, professionalism and productivity. This determines the high level of compensation for their labour. It goes without saying that compensation is one of the most significant motivating factors for these employees, but not the main one.

It is important for the system of compensation to be based on the principles of managing intellectual employees, to take into account qualitative indicators of their labour and to be directed at stimulating creative self-realization in the professional sphere. Forms of non-material compensation connected with trust and the freedom to choose ways of achieving a result are of considerable significance.

Communications The employees of Type 1 virtual companies, being high-level professionals, form a network for the more efficient application of their abilities and to exchange professional knowledge and experience. At the same time, they are individual proprietors of their own internal intellectual resources, skills and experience, and they always have an alternative for independent activity which can present certain risks for the company.

This is exactly why a system of communications is the most important instrument for personnel management in these companies. It plays the role of a mechanism for the extraction, accumulation, preservation and transfer of knowledge and experience, which represent the most valuable company resources.

It is important to enhance the range of communication technologies, to use not only electronic means of communication but also personal meetings in order to maintain team spirit and personal affection for and devotion to the company.

Workplace Conditions For the virtual employees in Type 1 companies, workplace conditions have a high priority. Working in the best possible place, at the best time, under the best conditions is critically important for the efficiency and productivity of the teleworkers. It is necessary to provide constant/periodical monitoring of the home or mobile workplaces of the employees, to improve these workplaces and provide additional equipment, and to control and maintain the optimal working conditions.

The psychological comfort of the workplace is very important.

Motivation The motivational instruments are aimed at the motivational principles of intellectual (non-manual) employees. The motivation of teleworkers is based on their professional interests and takes into account their goals in life and their values. It is also important to reveal, value, stimulate and actively use those personal qualities of the employees which they themselves regard as the most important.

This characteristic of building a system of motivation for virtual employees is highly valued by these employees, and it contributes to reinforcing their devotion to the company and yields high results.

Trust The efficiency of Type 1 companies is largely determined by the efficiency (ability to produce high results) of the virtual employees working in them who 'measure' their participation in the business processes on their own, depending on their attitude to the company.

A positive attitude is based on the level of mutual trust between the company and the employees. Trust contributes to the accumulation and transfer of knowledge and experience, the co-ordination of efforts to achieve common goals, increased devotion to work, and the preservation of confidentiality regarding insider information.

This is particularly important in connection with the problem of retaining teleworkers in a company, because the periods of time in which employees work for one organization are rapidly decreasing, and it is possible to work for several companies at the same time.

Trust is based on a high level of professionalism, responsibility and respect towards one's colleagues. Trust cannot be impersonal; to maintain it, it is necessary to create personal interaction and psychological tolerance between employees and managers.

Social efficiency Type 1 companies are characterized not only by economic efficiency, but also by social efficiency characterized by a high level of labour satisfaction, professional and personal self-realization, trust towards colleagues and the management of the company, and also devotion to the company, which allows employees to co-operate with it for a long time.

Virtual Companies of the Second Type – 'Key Workers'

Selection The selection of distant-working personnel for Type 2 companies takes place mainly in electronic form. The new virtual form of selecting distant-working personnel contributes to a more dynamic implementation of new, effective HRM instruments in the company on the one hand, while on the other hand it is characterized by a certain degree of risk connected with the veracity (adequacy) of the information submitted by the applicants. An employee's professionalism, image and reputation, which cannot be risked, guarantee conscientious relations with the employee.

In companies of this type, a distinctive feature and, at the same time, problem is presented by the opportunity and the need to combine the most effective methods of managing traditional and distant workers. A more dynamic (compared to other company types) transition of key specialists from the traditional form of employment to telework is registered in companies of this type.

Thus, the origin of distant-working personnel in companies of this type can have a dual nature connected with external or internal selection.

Adaptation One of the interesting results of this study is that the factor of adaptation is more important in companies of the second type than in the other types of virtual companies. In our opinion, this is connected with the need to organize the adaptation process for profoundly different personnel groups (categories) – that is, distant and traditional workers – which requires that managers make the additional effort to enhance and modify the complex of adaptation instruments and forms which are in use.

The complexity of this task lies in the fact that, for the traditional personnel, there is an approved and efficient system of professional, socio-psychological and organizational adaptation in management practice which is not adequate and efficient for the distant-working personnel.

It must be noted that the number of teleworkers in companies of the second type is relatively small, but these workers occupy an exclusive position and are most valuable for the company, and their role and input in achieving company efficiency are quite high. This is why, in most companies of the second type, individual adaptation programs are developed and realized for each key employee working distantly.

Training In this type of partially virtual company, the factor of training is more significant than in fully virtual companies. In most cases, this is connected with the fact that virtual employees appeared in the companies a relatively short time ago, and the companies already have a training system for traditional personnel, so the basic principles and approaches of this system are applied to virtual personnel as well. However, this approach is not always appropriate for the distinctive features and needs of teleworkers.

Additionally, considering the fact that teleworkers are key employees in companies of the second type, that the tasks accomplished by them are critical for the company, and that they contribute most to the results achieved by the company, it is necessary to create conditions for individual professional self-perfection specifically for them. This requires that the company apply a personalized approach to the maintenance and development of the virtual employees' professional level.

Appraisal The appraisal of teleworkers is of moderate significance in companies of the second type. The specific character of this appraisal is that it is mostly based on trust, not on control. Most often, appraisal is not carried out regularly but rather upon completion of a project/task. Teleworkers can experience a lack of ongoing appraisal and attention, a lack of interest in the results of their activity on the part of the company, and impaired/insufficient feedback.

Due to the fact that the teleworkers' labour in companies of the second type is primarily individual, the appraisal system must be flexible and provide for stable feedback. An additional positive effect of such an appraisal system will be to sustain the feeling of devotion among the teleworkers.

Different appraisal systems applied to traditional and virtual employees can give rise to the negative effect of the stratification and opposition of these personnel categories. To overcome these risks, both appraisal systems must be based on the principles of comparability and justice. It is also necessary to link the appraisal system for virtual employees with the efficiency of traditional personnel groups and the company as a whole and to embed it in the general system of efficiency appraisal for the company personnel.

Promotion The factor of promotion is more significant in companies of the second type than in the other company types. In our opinion, this is caused by two factors: firstly, due to the specific character of their situation, distant-working employees – being key personnel – still have limited opportunities for vertical promotion compared to traditional employees; secondly, these companies have developed a system of horizontal promotion in the form of work enrichment, the enhancement of the sphere of responsibility, an increase in the level of significance of the decisions taken, the enhancement of regulatory powers, and the recognition of individual input towards the efficiency of the company and the status of being a key specialist.

In companies of the second type, the key specialists (distant-working employees) are frequently paid more than their managers, have a better social benefits package and more flexible contract conditions. The use of these instruments is evidence of the importance of distant-working personnel for the company, and it plays the same role as traditional vertical promotion.

Compensation The significance of compensation for the virtual employees in Type 2 companies is very high. This is apparently connected with the recognition of the significance of these employees for the company and the appraisal of their role and input into the achievements (results) of the company.

As stated above, the compensation level of key distant-working employees can be higher than that of the top company managers, but it is necessary to base this compensation on the results of their work. It must be noted that the non-material compensation component acquires additional value for the employees in this type of company because it is connected with the appraisal of their significance, has an individual character and is aimed at professional and personal self-development and self-realization.

An important, though ambiguous, role is played by the inclusion of components connected with the results of the work performed by the groups/subdivisions of traditional employees and the company as a whole in the structure of the teleworkers' material compensation. On the one hand, this can be an effective motivating and rallying factor, while on the other hand, it can harbour a certain risk for the distant-working personnel due to the possible ineffective use of their ability to participate in group/organizational processes.

Communications The factor of communication is very significant in companies of the second type. This is due to the fact that, for the key specialists working distantly and exerting considerable influence on the business processes and efficiency of the company, it is critical to have a complete and stable connection with the company, its subdivisions, groups and individual employees. This is why such companies use a wide range of modern communication facilities which are necessary for effective management.

Effective communication within companies is based on bilateral, clear and efficient connections. At the same time, there is a problem with the disproportionate use of direct (personal) and distant (electronic) communication by virtual and traditional employees, which leads to the formalization of relations between these two personnel categories and psychological estrangement, and which can have a negative effect on the effectiveness of the common activity.

One of the solutions to this problem can be found in the creation of project teams which include traditional and distant-working employees. Teamwork intensifies communication processes, contributes to the manifestation and strengthening of informal (interpersonal) relations, and reduces the psychological distance between different personnel categories.

Workplace conditions The significance of workplace conditions for companies of the second type is quite high, as demonstrated by the view that teleworkers are more efficient (productive) because they work under the optimal conditions during the optimal periods of time.

Optimizing the equipment in distant workplaces for their key employees is an important task for the management of these companies. However, in companies of the second type, there is a problem with observing the principle of justice in equipping the workplaces for traditional and distant-working personnel.

A solution to this problem can be found by providing IT support and combining and co-ordinating the work schedules of both personnel categories.

Motivation The motivation of distant personnel in companies of the second type has its own specific character which lies in the unique position and role of these employees in the company, and also in the significance of the results of their work for overall company efficiency.

The exclusiveness and value of the knowledge and experience of these employees for the company, along with the high expenses for their recruitment and retention in the company, are the main factors defining the special attitude of the company management towards the motivation of this personnel category.

To retain and stimulate teleworkers, these companies use a flexible, individual approach oriented on the individual life values and professional values of the specialists, and also on the satisfaction of the requirements significant to them. When company resources are scarce, one of the solutions can be the 'shared' use of a distant employee by several companies at the same time.

Trust Trust in Type 2 companies has a very high level of significance and must be established thoroughly in order to play a uniting role between the traditional and distant-working personnel. To strengthen trust, it is very important to organize the transfer of knowledge in the company.

One of the problem areas is horizontal knowledge dissemination based on the effective bilateral exchange of information and experience between virtual and traditional employees of the company, database and corporate resources, fairness for all personnel categories, and the destruction of any barriers (both administrative and psychological) between distant-working and traditional personnel.

A higher level of trust between teleworkers and company managers compared to the level of trust between teleworkers and traditional personnel is a problem specific to companies of the second type. One possible solution is for these companies to introduce elements of telework into the labour activity of traditional employees, to engage them in 'teleprograms' or 'teleschemes'.

Social Efficiency A low level of social efficiency in the companies of the second type is determined by the following factors: insufficient attention of the company management to the optimization of communication systems and the transfer of knowledge; the limited nature of professional communication both between different personnel categories and between distant-working employees; exceptionally functional communication between distant-working employees; their professional isolation and 'locking' with the managers only; weak devotion to the company on the part of distant-working personnel.

Virtual Companies of the Third Type – 'Rational Companies'

Selection In companies of the third type, the electronic methods of distant personnel selection are prevalent. Selection takes place within short periods of time and is based on formalized standard criteria.

The intentional narrowing of the information about a potential candidate which is taken into consideration in order to make a decision about employment is a characteristic feature of the selection of teleworkers in companies of the third type. A teleworker is regarded only as a source and bearer of competencies in a specific professional area. As a matter of fact, the company is oriented on using only the employee's informational (professional) 'shell'.

This has a number of effects which lower the efficiency of using this personnel category: the psychological distancing of teleworkers from the company, weak devotion and low loyalty, and the limited use of their professional and personal resources to achieve organizational goals and results.

Due to the low significance of teleworkers for companies of the third type, this approach to the selection of distant-working personnel may not have considerable negative consequences for the company, but it hinders the employees from being included more fully in the organizational conditions and processes, which lowers their efficiency.

Adaptation In most cases, the teleworkers in Type 3 companies have considerable experience of distant work and do not need to adapt to this form of work. The company orientation on the short-term use of teleworkers and the standardization of their activity also restricts the potential variety of instruments and technologies of professional activity used by them. This minimizes the company's expenses on the teleworkers' adaptation.

At the same time, standardization and the ability to process the professional competence of this employee category increases their high level of universalism and puts them in great demand on the labour market. This is why in companies of the third type, there is a problem with the effective organizational and psychological adaptation of distant-working personnel to the original company atmosphere and its corporate culture in order to form not only an attractive company image in the teleworkers' opinion, but also a unique and competitive image compared to other virtual companies.

Training The factor of training for distant-working personnel in companies of the third type is not of great significance. Teleworker training is generally not provided. This is a result of both the sufficient competence level of this personnel category and the efforts of these companies to minimize capital and extra expenses on personnel.

As the teleworkers' work is mostly of an individual nature, the most effective form of education is self-education, which is not provided and not financed by the company according to the conditions of the contract.

One of the most commonly used forms of training is e-coaching, which strengthens the bilateral links between a teleworker and a traditional mentor.

Our research has demonstrated that in virtual companies of the third type, training and development programs for distant-working personnel should be introduced only in cases when the periods of co-operation allow one to see the results of the training and to use them in order to achieve the company's goals.

Appraisal The appraisal of teleworkers in companies of the third type is based on control and achieved results. The appraisal has a dual nature oriented on different levels of work complexity, the significance of the work for the company, and the employees' responsibility for the results.

When the work is highly complex, specific and significant and teleworkers bear a high level of responsibility for the results of their work, ongoing control is not usually exercised and only the actual results of the work are evaluated.

At the same time, the appraisal process is accompanied by stable bilateral feedback between the teleworker and the managers, during which the distant worker personally informs the manager and receives correcting instructions from him or her.

When the teleworker performs routine, single-type work, tight ongoing control is exercised, which includes establishing a system of clear activity criteria (standards), terms and zones of responsibility, and a system of fines and incentives which come into action when the established parameters and the results of the work are observed/violated.

In technical terms, the appraisal mechanism in companies of the third type is realized by using a database to visually provide information on and illustrate the progress and current results of an activity, which emphasizes the intention to comply with the expected standards and results, and which stimulates competitive spirit in employee relations and activities.

Promotion The significance of promotion in companies of the third type is considerably less pronounced compared to other types of virtual companies. The model of personnel management in companies of the third type regards the life cycle of a teleworker in the organization as a brief one which is limited to three stages: selection – fulfilment of the project – departure.

Therefore, promotion is actually non-existent. However, when a company has to resort to the services of a certain category of distant employee repeatedly, it can use elements of horizontal promotion, enhancing the responsibility zone and increasing the complexity of the job performed by them.

Compensation The compensation of teleworkers in companies of the third type is directly connected with the results of their activity and is strictly material (financial). This results in a considerable extension of the actual working week among teleworkers in Type 3 companies, as stated in the research, from 40 hours (according to the Labour Code of the Russian Federation) to 70 hours, which allows them to maximize their compensation by achieving results in a shorter period of time.

The overwhelming majority of teleworkers regard this 'time-concentrated' working style as temporary and are ready (agree) to mobilize their internal forces (intellectual and physical efforts) temporarily. It must be noted that this fact largely corresponds to widespread notions about the Russian mentality.

Communications Communications in companies of the third type are relatively important but problematic. One can distinguish several aspects of establishing communication in companies of the third type.

The first aspect is connected with the primary use of electronic communication and the prevalence of formal communication between teleworkers and the personnel and managers of the companies over informal communication, which limits (waters down) the quality of the communication, does not help overcome the psychological barriers and distances between different personnel categories, and lowers the level of satisfaction with the communication.

The second aspect is the considerable prevalence of vertical communications over horizontal, with 'ascending' communications (directed from the teleworkers to the managers) being the most developed. 'Descending' communications between distant-working personnel and the management of a company, especially communications taking place at the managers' initiative, are considerably less developed.

Communications between teleworkers and traditional employees are the least developed. It must be noted that these communications are practically non-existent in a number of companies, which has a negative influence on the efficiency of the interaction between different personnel categories (especially in project work), the organizational atmosphere, and the unity and devotion of the personnel. This also lowers the overall level of manageability of the company personnel.

To increase the efficiency of managing distant personnel, the managers of Type 3 companies must pay special attention to establishing communications, taking into account the above-mentioned problems.

Workplace Conditions Workplace conditions are quite significant for the teleworkers in Type 3 companies. Despite the low significance of the distant-working personnel themselves for the company and the mainly routine and/or standard character of the work done by them, the opportunity to work at the optimal time in the optimal place determines the speed and quality of their professional activity. However, in most companies, managers pay little attention to the optimization of and equipment in the teleworkers' workplace, assuming that the workers must take care of this themselves.

At the same time, depending on the place and value of human resources in the corporate culture of the company, there can be another attitude towards the organization of the distant employees' workplaces: the company may supply them with basic equipment and consumables and pay their telecommunication expenses.

Our research has demonstrated that, in most cases, teleworkers need their employers' assistance in equipping their workplaces.

Motivation The significance of the motivation of teleworkers in companies of the third type is not high. This is connected with the absence of the necessity to retain this category of employees in the company for a long period of time, and also with the standardization of their professional activity.

Motivation in these companies has a clearly pronounced financial character and is based on the results achieved by the employee. On the one hand, this simplifies the system of employee motivation and stimulation, while on the other hand, it conceals a real threat to company stability if the teleworker receives higher compensation in another (alternative) company for a similar job.

Due to the standard nature of their work, the switching expenses for tele-employees working in companies of the third type are minimal; they can usually leave one company and transfer to another quite quickly and smoothly. To reduce this threat, it is necessary to direct one's attention to the teleworkers' internal motivators as well and to involve them in building the motivation system for the company personnel.

Trust In companies of the third type, the atmosphere of trust is largely influenced by the unique nature of the interaction and relations between managers, distant and traditional employees. The lowest level of trust is detected between teleworkers and traditional employees, which impedes the formation of a climate of solidarity and a strong corporate culture.

Our research has demonstrated that it is most important for teleworkers to establish trusting relations with the managers controlling their work. A positive company image, which primarily influences the more or less trusting attitude of the teleworkers to the company, its managers and personnel, is also essential.

The organization of the knowledge transfer process is quite significant for creating and maintaining trust in a company. Since a high staff turnover rate among distant personnel is characteristic of partially virtual companies of the third type, the company managers should pay particular attention to such basic elements of the knowledge transfer system as the formalization of the knowledge and experience of arriving employees, the exchange of knowledge among teleworkers, the maintenance and formalization of the current experience of the company personnel, and the passing on of formalized knowledge to followers and/or newly recruited employees.

Social Efficiency A critically low level of social efficiency among distant personnel is registered in companies of the third type compared to other types of virtual companies.

Teleworkers actually feel distanced, or to be more exact, 'torn away' from the company, which demonstrates an absence of interest in the personality of the teleworkers and a disinclination to invest in their training, development and the organization of their labour with all the HR instruments available.

This causes a feeling of personal and professional isolation and dissatisfaction with working in this company. However, due to the fact that teleworkers are not the main productive force and do not create the key values of Type 3 companies, companies remain economically efficient even if their teleworkers are inefficient.

Conclusions

As a result of a comparative study of 40 virtual companies operating in Russia, three types of companies were singled out which differ in their degree of virtuality, the significance of telecoworkers, and the amount of time in which telework is carried out.

Our research showed that the traditional set of HR practices has a different structure (fullness) and efficiency for different types of virtual companies.

Thus, for companies of the first type, 'Networks of professionals', the most effective HR instruments are selection, communications, compensation and workplace conditions; the most important (critical) conditions for efficient work by telecommuters are trust and internal professional motivation, taking into account their personal values.

For the second type of company, 'Key workers', the most effective HR instruments are horizontal promotion, communications and compensation; the most important conditions for efficient work by telecommuters are the uniqueness of the operations performed and the importance of the results for the company, mutual trust with the management, and overcoming personal and professional isolation.

For companies of the third type, 'Rational companies', the most effective HR instruments are communications and workplace conditions; the most important conditions for efficient work by teleworkers are financial effectiveness, company image, and the manager's personality.

Regarding the importance of teleworkers for achieving a company's goals, we consider their economic input in the effectiveness of a company's activity to be the professional and personal potential possessed by the distant-working personnel who have fundamental competencies and skills.

References

Daniels, K., Lamond, D. and Standen, P. (2000), *Managing Telework, Perspectives from Human Resources Management and Work Psychology* (NY).

Delantey, J.T. and Huselid, M.A. (1996), 'The Impact of Human Resource Management Practices on Perceptions of Organizational Performance', *Academy of Management Journal* 39: 4, 949–69.

Delery, J. and Doty, D. (1996), 'Models of Theorizing in Strategic Human Resource Management: Tests of Universalistic, Contingency, and Configurational Performance Predictions', *Academy of Management Journal* 39: 4, 802–35.

Fisher, K. and Fisher, M. (2001), *The Distance Manager, A Hands-On Guide to Managing Off-Site Employees and Virtual Teams* (Boston).

Korte, W.B. and Wynne, R. (1996), *Telework – Penetration and Practice in Europe* (Amsterdam).

Lipnack, J. and Stamps, J. (2000), *Virtual Teams: People Working Across Boundaries with Technology* (NY).

Nilles, J. (1999), *Managing Telework, Strategies for Managing the Virtual Workforce* (NY).

Pratt, J. (1997), 'Why Aren't More People Telecommuting? Explanations from Four Studies', *Transportation Research Record* 1607, 196–203.

Toffler, A. (1980), *The Third Wave* (London).

Westfalls, R.D. (1997), 'Does Telecommuting Really Increase Productivity? Fifteen Rival Hypothesis', Proceeding of the AIS Americas Conference.

Internet-based references

Huws, U., Korte, W. and Robinson, S., 'Telework – Towards then Elusive Office. Chichester', JALA International, Inc [website], (1990)<http://www.jala.com>

Malone, M.S., 'The Virtual Corporation', (NY), (1994) <http://www.virtualorganizations.net>

Chapter 6

Human Resource Management at a Steel Giant in Russia[1]

Vera Trappmann

Human resource management in Russian industrial companies seems to be organized in a very different way than in most capitalist economies. The main reason is its origin in the Soviet economy. However, one could argue that after 15 years of economic transformation, and many years of company restructuring, it should have adapted to market conditions, implying the use of instruments known and used in Western economies. Yet, the examination of the human resource management at one major steel producer in Russia, with about 66, 000 workers, reveals that this is only partly the case.

Human resource management in Russia is still different compared to its Western counterparts. The following contribution tries to seek out why this is the case as it describes the actual human resource policy at the Russian steel plant. It offers an explanation for the noted aberration by examining the determinants of the actual nature of the Russian enterprise. Object of analysis is the effect of economic transition in terms of employment restructuring and its consequences for the labour market.

This article is based on qualitative interviews with human resource managers at a major steel company in the Ural region. The study was exploratory in nature. The structure of the article is as follows. First, the article explores the restructuring of the company and then it presents the company's practice of human resource management. The last part of the paper discusses the characteristics of the Russian labour market. It might help to understand the current practice of human resource management at the company level.

1 This field research was carried out in December 2003, and has been generously financed by the Hans Böckler Foundation, as part of a project on social industrial dialogue between Russia and Germany at the Federal State Institute Sozialforschungsstelle Dortmund. I am grateful to Lubov Ejova from the Centre of Independent Social Research in St Petersburg who helped to enter the field and carry out the research. I am even more grateful to the higher management at MMK who enabled this case study in sharing their views, knowledge and experience with me.

The Industrial Complex

The Magnitogorsk Iron and Steel Works Open Joint Stock Company (Magnitogorskiy Metallurgiskiy Kombinat, or, Magnitogorsk Metallurgical Complex, MMK) was founded in 1932, close to a large iron ore deposit, a mountain called 'Magnetic Mountain', which is the supplier of the name of the company, and the surrounding town. The company and the town have been founded by Stalin as one of his first industrialization projects building socialism. At the beginning, in this area there was nothing: no people, no machines, no supplies, no trees, and no energy. Recruitment of people was from all over the country, construction took place in very difficult conditions, and training of staff, mainly peasants, was on-the-job. It was built up to one the world's leading steel companies during the 1930s, a fact that was a source of great pride among the workers of Magnitogorsk. The sentiment persists even today, almost 90 years after the socialist revolution. Magnitogorsk stood as a 'symbol of achievement and the newfound power of the Soviet Union, Magnitogorsk was the October revolution itself' (Kotkin 1997, 70). Moreover, steel was one of the highly valued products, most needed for Soviet industrialization and later on became the pillar of the military-industrial complex. Since the 1930s, the production of steel climbed from 2.5 tons to 20 million tons in the late 1980s, falling dramatically as a consequence of the collapse of the Soviet Union in the early 1990s. With privatization in the mid-nineties, the production recovered, and today the plant' utilization rate is at 95 per cent.

Privatization, Restructuring and Modernization

The plant was privatized in 1992. As part of the so-called second model of the Russian privatization program[2], the company was transformed into a shareholding company. The employees, provided with vouchers (distributed by the state and serving as a currency with which to purchase assets of the state-owned industry), were offered 51 per cent of the company's shares for face value. At the time, the company had a market capitalization of 40 million dollars; the most recent value estimation of 2005 is about 5,854 billion dollars (MMK 2006; ATON 2003; Black et. al. 2000). Today, the company is management-owned up to 96 per cent. It was in the late 1990s that the management came out on top as the controlling group of shareholders, divided into different subsidies and groups (Krischer and Holzhinrich-Scherler 2001). Only, in 2004, the state auctioned off its last bit of shares, amounting to 23.8 per cent. These were sold for 790 million dollars to the general director. Soon afterwards, the general director resigned, a new one was appointed, and the former director was elected in April 2005 as the chairman of the board of directors (*Die Welt*, 2005).[3]

2 For an overview of Russian privatisation, see Trappmann 2001.

3 The directors of MMK relate to the most influential men of Russia's industry (World Bank 2005b).

Since the mid '90s the company started a large modernization program, mainly investing in new state-of-the-art technology: replacing open-hearth furnaces, which inflicted the greatest environment damage, by oxygen converters; creating a complex for flat products, including continuous casters; and modernizing coke-making facilities (Krischer and Holzhinrich-Scherler 2001). Having already invested more than 1.1 billion dollars (Vremia Novosti 2003), it seems that the main aim of the management is the consolidation and competitiveness of the company.[4] Investments are part of long-term company restructuring (Estrin 1998). Critics see positive microeconomic behaviour resulting from privatization when control is in the hands of only a few individuals (Djankov and Murell 2000).[5]

Among the Russian steel producers, the MMK has the most diversified production. Instead of making profit only by selling raw steel on the world market, the management introduced a new market orientation: concentrating on product development, product refinement, and answering the rising demands of the local market for construction and automotive industry. MMK is Russia's leading steel maker of rolled products with a market share of about 20 per cent. This competitive advantage on the world market results mainly from three factors: low cost supplies of iron ore and coal, in-house electric generation, and low labour costs.[6]

Given this structural adjustment in products and markets, it is astonishing that little employment restructuring has taken place. Today, the company, including its subsidiaries, has about 66,000 employees out of which 27,000 are employed in the core steel production. What is striking, this number did not change much during transition.

Human Resource Management at MMK

One important part of the company's strategy in becoming or sustaining its position as a world leader is the renewal of management. Therefore, the main objective of human resource management at MMK is the formation and training of the core management. As the average age of the leadership is between 50 and 60 years and even older, and as the turnover of management has been high during the last years due to the creation of subsidiaries, the company pays special attention to the formation of a new generation of management and leaders.

---

4 The general director states that investments are the best cure for the Russian industry (Website MMK), he was awarded the most professional director in 2003 by the Russian association of employers' (*Delowoy Peterburg* 2003), and the company was awarded the winner of All-Russian context for the 'organisation with highest social efficiency' in 2005, and 'personnel qualification and training and re-training system' in 2004 (MMK website).

5 The World Bank for long neglected the aspect of microeconomic restructuring in favour of macroeconomic liberalisation, and privatisation, and only recently corrected its assessment (Nellis 2002, and Wyplosz 2000).

6 However, rising prices of raw material and ongoing restrictions on Russian steel imports do put a challenge on Russian steel producers (Lisin 2004).

This chapter will discuss the following aspects of human resource management at MMK: restructuring of employment, recruitment of young professionals, formation of the core personnel and the maintenance of a management reserve, personnel assessment, and personnel development.

Recruitment of New Employees

The company starts its recruitment at colleges and universities. Searching for candidates, it opens a kind of grapevine or a contact pool. Students are invited for a traineeship at the company site during summertime. The most promising ones are encouraged to apply for a position at the complex. Applicants have to pass traditional tests on their craftsmanship, knowledge, and social or psychological constitution. In recent times, the knowledge of a foreign language has had to be proven as well. Applicants are divided into three groups, their members characterized according to: technical intelligence and expertise, organizational skills, or comprising both technical intelligence and leadership qualities. This sets up at an early stage a division that is typical at the industrial site: a division between specialists or experts and managers. A particular training program is designed for each group. It prepares the group's members for leadership positions in the company. Every group formation starts with a seminar at which the shop level managers present the different shops of the company.[7] The participants form a labour pool from which the company's leaders will choose those that will form the so-called reserve of core or *kadrovy* personnel.[8]

Formation of a Personnel Reserve of Young Leadership

Building the personnel reserve is a long-lasting process. During the first year at the company, the new specialists are assigned to a mentor [*nastavnik*] who supervises and promotes the development of the new employees with respect to their professionalism, their social adaptation, and to their mastery of the technological process at the shop level. In the second year, they are sent to a so-called school of adaptation where after that year the young professionals will be divided into two groups: those who will become technical specialists and those who will become

7 Just for the sake of completion: If other than young specialists are needed, they are employed after a consultation with the personnel department and the shop that seeks new workers or specialists. From this consultation, the qualification of the employee is categorized according to an internal system of classification of competence. According to this classification of grades, the pay is defined.

8 Clarke calls these core workers and line managers the 'labour aristocracy' whose efforts kept the system going. Soviet production was organized around that crucial stratum, they were better paid than all but the senior managers and often had access through party membership or trade union activity to decisionmaking processes at the company level (Clarke 1996).

leaders in classical terms. In the third year, special training is provided for these two groups at the so-called school for young specialists.

Among the young specialists, a competition is organized carrying out psychological, and practical tests to identify the best specialist and best manager. Participants have to have at least one year of working experience in a leading position, and be under 30 years of age. The winners are rewarded with better pay for the next year, a recommendation for the nomination to a higher *kadrovy* reserve position and with the right to further higher education financed by the company.

The reserve is divided into three categories: operational personnel reserve, perspective personnel reserve, and key personnel reserve. Once the reserve is established, it gets special training. Special programs are designed according to the level of leadership that a new professional is designated for. Additionally, traineeships as deputies in these positions have to be mastered.

A particular feature linked to the reserve system is the internal stratification and especially the vertical organization of the Russian industrial enterprises.[9] Formal hierarchies were and are very strong; authority traditionally passes from the general director, through the chief engineer to the shop chiefs, chiefs of sections, then foremen and brigadiers. Even in leading positions you have several levels of expertise, specialists are graded into 'only specialist', 'specialist of second grade', 'specialist of first grade' up to 'leading specialist'. The grading of specialists determines their status and their pay. It is a common practice in traditional Russian enterprises to have the level of expertise regularly assessed. This is done at MMK every four years.

Assessment of Employees

An important pillar of human resource management is the labour assessment of workers, specialists and executives. In front of a committee, which consists of a representative of the human resource department, a professional expert (such as a professor of the Higher Institute for Metallurgy), and the shop chief, the workers, specialists or managers have to prove their competences. The consultation is recorded and signed by all participants. The leadership qualities of management are also the object of consultations with subordinates, superiors, and colleagues. Then, the committee decides upon the grading of the employees. They can be upgraded or downgraded. Alone, among the executives, which are the group mostly important to the human resource department, 6,000 executives are assessed every year.

9 Simon Clarke identifies three key features of the internal stratification: 1. the distinction between production and auxiliary workers, 2. status hierarchy based on age and experience, and 3. status based on individual's personal qualities (Clarke 1995a). Most of the exiting sociological literature on Russian enterprise is written by a group around Simon Clarke at Warwick University. However, most of the work is carried out during the 90s, so in some cases, the situation might have changed a bit since then. But currently, there is no more recent research or literature available.

Following the assessment, individual personnel development plans are designed. Every specialist is bound by tariff agreement to undertake this training.[10]

Case studies show that in most industrial complexes, the power of control related to the pay set by the human resource management department was somewhat limited by informal practices at the shop level: line managers possessed substantial informal power by payment of bonuses or the bestowal or withholding of favours and benefits. They could penalize and reward individual employees in selective distribution of a wide variety of non-monetary benefits provided through the enterprise and the trade union (Clarke 1996).

Maintenance of High Qualifications of Personnel

Competence-building, and increasing the qualification level of the management, are the main objectives of the personnel development department. Instruments of qualification upgrading for the core personnel are seminars, trainings, role-playing games, business and simulation games, traineeships (also abroad) and higher education. A novelty is the so-called 'leader-clubs' where managers meet in an informal style for exchange and discussion. Experts are invited to give lectures, also on topics with relevance to managerial practice in broader social terms, like health protection or time management. Among the top leaders, these seminars are highly frequented and enjoy a good reputation.

The whole process of training and re-training is highly formalized, which might not be astonishing given how many executives have to be trained each year. At MMK, comprising the subsidiaries, there are about 5,000 to 6,000 specialists and managers. The methods and the amount of training have increased, however, the structure seems to resemble the practice during Soviet times. As one respondent stated during an interview: 'In principle, it is all as it was. We didn't change much, maybe we introduced some English names, but we do the same stuff.'

Manual Workers and Human Resource Management at MMK

Manual workers play a minor role for the human resource management department at MMK. This is because much did not change for the MMK workers due to transition. Therefore, training policy did not change much either. Workers get trained on the job, and given the fact that job positions for workers in the Soviet production system were very specialized, workers tend to hold on a job position until they retire. In most cases, where technology did not change, workers do the same operations for many years. The longer they work on one job position, the more experience they have, the better they perform their job, the better they get to know the technology and master the often peculiar equipment. This is due to the Soviet style of equipping companies in times of shortages. Often, machinery was very old, or designed for one particular

10 This practice of obligatory upgrading of qualifications is widespread in Russian industry (see also Berger, Earle and Sabirianova 2001).

shop and its specific needs, constructed at the site itself. If foreign equipment was bought, it was adjusted to suit local conditions, often looted, and then parts had to be remade, and not always fitted perfectly. As a result every piece of machinery became unique (Alasheev 1995). Workers developed a specialized, often tacit knowledge about how to make best production with this machinery. Their job requirements became unique, which, as a consequence, made them both specialists who do not need to acquire further qualifications and who are difficult to replace. Production workers experienced therefore a high degree of autonomy (Clarke 1996).

While it is still seniority that offers workers job security in Russia, in Western (steel) industry constant standardized technological change requires adaptational qualification from workers. For the workers in the West, job security is replaced by the gain of employability, the capability 'to take up job opportunities in a fast-changing world' (European Commission 1999). Therefore, workers seek to build up their employability by participating in lifelong learning processes, and human resource departments are keen on developing training programs for workers, in many countries in cooperation with trade union representatives and works councils.[11] However, the traditional seniority approach towards workers at MMK, does not hold for all Russian steel complexes. At the Tulachermet Kontsern in Central Russia, the management intends further education and training of the entire workforce. Workers are offered training that is not only firm-related but covers a broad range of topics intending to make workers more motivated, more flexible, and committed to work. The training is part of the survival strategy of the company, which intended to regard workers no longer only as a low-cost factor. According to this logic, productivity and product quality are based on flexibilization of the productive workforce. The new strategy resulted in a diversification of products (including consumer products) and in the expansion of employment by about 30 per cent (Baglione and Clark 1997).

Recruitment of Workers Workers are recruited after finishing secondary school. They start working at a shop under the auspices of a foreman who takes care of the adaptation of the worker. After a qualifying period, it is decided at what level or qualification grade the worker will be employed. There exist six grades according to which the workers' pay is defined. In Soviet reality, the pay was often distributed among the shops and the foreman of a shop decided upon the pay. Using a special fund of bonuses, most workers were paid according to the norm and not to their individual grading. Given the fact that line managers were dependent on the workers to get their shop plan fulfilled, a higher pay was part of the informal agreement between workers and line managers (Vedeneeva 1995).

11 This approach towards lifelong learning can first be found in the Russian shipbuilding industry (Ejova, Olimpieva and Trappmann 2004; Olimpieva and Ejova in this volume).

Organizational Restructuring of Human Resource Management Department

At MMK, the qualification and training is offered by an independent organization, formed by the former vocational training department of MMK, the library of MMK, the computer centre formerly owned by the trade union at MMK, and a local branch of the Institute of Economy and Management in Moscow. The former head of MMK's personnel management department is the director of this new centre.

It proposes training for executives and managers and vocational training for the workers. Besides, it designs new educational programs. It offers its services to the employees of MMK, its subsidiaries, as well as to the city's economy.

A particular problem of the centre is the lack of good teachers. The centre employs 150 people, however, a lot of the teaching is achieved in cooperation with other institutions of higher education. Here, the concentration of academies and scientific institutions in Moscow is a clear disadvantage for a distant region. The new training institution tries to amend that problem through both, bolstering the local expertise and designing long-distance programs of education.

Restructuring Employment at MMK

The number of employees didn't drop much over the course of transition, and the cutback that occurred was realized without any redundancies, nor any voluntary separations. Part of restructuring strategies was: reducing recruitment, internal placement, and active reduction of personnel by various means, like voluntary separations, lay-offs, and a strict retirement policy.

Lower Recruitment Rates The number of employees was mainly reduced by reducing recruitment. If in the 1980s the company recruited about 800 employees every month, the current monthly recruitment stands at the level of 300 employees.

Separations The fact there were no voluntary separations is easy to explain: the status of work in the steel industry and the pay compared to local incomes is quite high. At MMK, the average salary is 180 per cent higher relative to the regional average income (ATON 2003). This low rate of voluntary separations of workers is documented for the whole steel and metal industry, which has the lowest rate of voluntary separations of all industrial sectors (Russian Labour Ministry, in Broadman and Recantini 2001). The workers in core branches of production – heavy industry, energy, and military-industrial sector – were most privileged, and workers closest to production of the final product enjoyed the highest status (Clarke 1996). Separations occurred only in the case of low labour discipline. This reflects the overall situation in the Russian steel industry (Baglione and Clark 1997). Problems with labour discipline were widespread in Soviet enterprises due to the enterprises' welfare functions and the individual obligation to work. The enterprises were forced to employ also those people who were restricted in their ability to work due to criminal backgrounds, disability or sickness. In a market economy, these people would have been removed from the labour market by social insurance systems or benefit systems (Clarke 1998, 24).

Retirement Policy A big problem for the MMK is the high employment of pensioners. The human resource management would like to de-allocate the positions to younger employees, especially in management positions. Therefore it offers lump sums to its employees if they reach statutory retirement age. However, most pensioners decide to continue working because it is hard to make a living only on pension. If the average income of a production steel worker at MMK is 12000 Rubles, the average pension is 2,000 Rubles.

Internal Placement If in the process of company restructuring a production site was closed (like the open-hearth furnace), workers were trained to work at another shop, often equipped with modern technology, like the converter or hot rolling mill. During Soviet times, internal shop mobility was high, however, it was low between shops. Workers perceived the placement at a different shop like placement at another company (Clarke and Donova 1999). It will be an interesting next step to analyze the process of internal mobility at the MMK in greater detail.

Other case studies also document that rapid restructuring of employment took place without redundancies. Moreover, in the near future, no further redundancies are planned at MMK. This is, as was told in an interview, due 'to big politics, to industrial politics which means that nothing is decided at company level'. It might astonish that there are no redundancies planned. If in future, the company plans to invest further in modernization and to increase productivity, lower numbers of employees will be needed.[12] There exist several alternative explanations why no redundancies occur. These will be discussed in the following section.

Employment in Russia

Labour Hoarding

Traditionally, due to labour shortage at the macro level, Soviet enterprises tended to hold a surplus of labour force at the micro level (Kornai 1992). While this seems to be a reasonable strategy, case studies in Russian enterprises reveal that this labour surplus could not always be mobilized for production. A large part of the labour surplus consisted of auxiliary workers who were required during Soviet times to meet the demands imposed on the enterprises by the local community or the Party authorities. These demands included services like agricultural work, maintenance and repair, and social and welfare tasks. In order not to lose anyone from the core production personnel for these unexpected tasks, the companies 'hoarded' auxiliary workers (Clarke 1996). Auxiliary workers were often low-paid, unskilled, engaged in very labour intensive,

---

12 MMK employs 5091 people for every ton of steel produced, while in the West comparable integrated mills employ only half or third of that number (ATON 2003).

low productivity tasks and during transition they might have become the first ones to be laid-off. Nevertheless, the general directors assume that they still employ a labour surplus of about 15 per cent (Broadman and Recantini 2001). A strategy among the workers, particular among the female workers, to prevent redundancies, is self-downgrading. Women, especially highly educated women who were more easily fired then men, tended to de-qualify in order to keep a lower paid, but maybe more secure job (Clarke 1999; Clark and Sacks 2004). In general, even today, it does not seem an unreasonable strategy for an enterprise to keep a high level of employment. The fact that production implies a high level of firm-specific skills induces the enterprises, even in times of lower production, to keep employees trained for special equipment. Considering the modernization program at MMK, this reason becomes less an argument for labour hoarding in the future.

Hidden Forms of Unemployment

One theory about the low level of redundancies in Russian core production industry and a correlating rather low level of unemployment assumes that redundancies take place but in hidden forms as temporary lay-offs, administrative leave, and short-time works, and last but not least as forced separations which are officially recorded as voluntary. Administrative leave means that workers are told that they do not have to go to work for a couple of months. For some workers there might have been little chance to get re-employed, others were re-employed if the number of orders increased.[13] Administrative leaves are often unpaid, or with a minimal amount of money. Short-time work means reducing working hours due to economic reasons, however this has never been the applied in the steel industry. Nonetheless, in the Russian context, a distinction between employment and unemployment becomes difficult and one is dealing more with the phenomenon of dis-employment (Standing 1998).

Coping Strategies To survive these times of dis-employment, people have developed a number of strategies to cope with the unexpected fluctuations in household income. One that has already been widespread in Soviet times is second employment. Others, which developed during transition, are increase in home production, subsistence economy, change in place of residence, renting out an apartment, ceasing living with relatives, or moving in with relatives (Loshkin and Yemtsov 2001). This is true for the industrial, urban, as well as rural areas (Pickup and White 2003). Individual management of risks predominates in transition economies like Russia, due to the erosion of state provision of insurance and the lack of new collective institutions (Müller 2005). Most vulnerable in times of individual risk management is the rural population, and employees in sectors where the average income is under the subsistence level, such as in education and health care. Approximately 25 per cent

13 The author has carried out biographical interviews with Russian ship workers in 2003, which confirm this situation.

of the Russian population, according to the World Bank, live under subsistence level (World Bank 2005).

Second Employment

Interestingly, there has been no dramatic growth of secondary employment since the Soviet period (Clarke 2002). People on administrative leave, for example, take a long time to start searching for second employment. Rather, they take time to get used to the new situation, rest, and take care of household tasks before they decide, in the face of shortage of money and falling stocks of food, that they will have to find second jobs. In most cases, second employment is a source of additional income and many employees with different qualification levels and occupations carry it out. The following forms of secondary employment exist: a registered regular second job, *kalym*, work on short-term contract, self-employment, or trading. Formalized supplementary work [*po sovmestitel'stvu*] arose already in the Soviet times as a result of labour shortage. People from all occupational groups were used to take up secondary employment occasionally. It was taken up as much inside the home company as in other companies. *Kalym* was additional work carried out during a regular working day using the company's equipment and raw materials for personal income. It also happened that orders were carried out on behalf of other sections of the home enterprise. These days, short-term contracting becomes more popular, as it frees the employer from all liabilities, like taxation, and social security payments.

Second employment, in a way, is an equivalent of overtime work, part-time, and casual primary employment in other countries. Paid legal overtime was less common in Russia and with the new Labour Code from 2002, overtime must be paid at increased rates. This is not the case for second jobs, so employers tend to register workers for a second job or to sign a short-term contract.

One assumption is that second employment would increase labour mobility. However, this is not the case. First, as second employment primarily serves to upgrade the workers income, it rarely offers any opportunity of upgrading skills or mastering a new profession. Second, the recruitment to and acquisition of second employment often depends on right connections and personal contacts (Clarke 2002).

Russian Enterprise as a Welfare Institution

A rival theory posits that Russian enterprises function as welfare institutions. Their services in providing housing, health care, holiday trips, and retirement provisions, and the lack of a welfare state, make redundancies politically impossible (Layard and Richter 1995, Jackman 1998). Additionally, unemployment benefits are very low, oriented to the minimum wage and, given inflation, they are under the subsistence level. As an alternative to redundancy, companies get state subsidies to prevent lay-offs. Western critics argue that this policy of hidden unemployment undermines the generation of a functional labour market and argue for open unemployment (Jackman 1998). However, this argument ignores how the Russian labour market works.

Workers are not recruited from the pool of unemployed, but from other enterprises (Clarke 1998; Yakubovich and Kozina in this volume).

Labour Mobility

While there was almost no labour mobility in the Soviet times, in the initial period of liberal economic reforms, statistically, the whole labour force turned over, out of which 90 per cent were job-to-job transitions. Moreover, most of labour mobility was internal, with significant effects on the labour market: intensification of labour, de-skilling, and the closure of an anyhow almost non-existent external labour market (Clarke and Donova 1999). Especially in the case of successful companies, external mobility was and still is very low. Senior management intends to hold highly skilled employees while lower-skilled workers do not leave a prosperous company. Therefore, a common recruitment strategy, besides the internal labour mobility (redeploying personnel), is the informal search. Most people find jobs through personal networks and this tendency is reinforced during transition. (Clarke, Kabalina, Kozina, Donova and Karelina 1998). The personal degree of labour mobility depends on the density and extent of social capital. The initial contact of an employee with a new company always occurs with the help of relatives. The change of a company depends on the recommendation of family members and colleagues. If a company enjoys a very good reputation, a recommendation alone is often not sufficient. The prospective employee would need a direct contact or, even better, a direct bond, with the new employer.[14] In recent time, the role of families and relatives is diminishing in favour of professional ties (Clark and Sacks 2004). Only those jobs that do not require high qualifications are easily gotten without personal contacts.[15] The main motivation for people to look for new jobs is the wage level and the security of regular payments. Work increasingly becomes a source of income (for survival)[16] (VTsIOM 1998). The high level of informality in recruitment results from characteristics of the transition economy. The external accreditation system has broken down, so that relying on a recommendation helps to make employment decisions. Moreover, trust plays a crucial role in the transition economy. It has become a hard currency of the economy especially in situations when not always all transactions take place within legal frameworks. Third, a personal relationship or bond based on gratefulness is a good way of bolstering individual power of management. This is important, as the struggle for control has divided competing sections of the management. The support of workers is often a way of deciding who controls the company. Another reason for

14 Ledeneva provides an account of how the whole Soviet and Russian economy is pervaded with an 'economy of favours', the so-called *blat* system (Ledeneva 1998).

15 This affects mostly elderly women applying for low-paid jobs as cleaners or deskmen.

16 This is particularly interesting as traditionally, Socialist Soviet production, was ideologically seen as a means to increase cultural, educational and material well-being of the labour collective. A system of authoritarian paternalism ruled Soviet enterprise, including the guarantee of employment and minimum subsistence (Clarke 1995a).

the informal labour acquisition is the backwardness of the labour market institutions (Clarke 1999).

Labour Market Institutions

In the Soviet times, formal labour market institutions only existed for placement of young people and particular categories of the population, like invalids or those released from prison. Unemployment is officially registered since 1991, when the Employment Law first acknowledged and permitted unemployment.

In the same year, the so-called Federal Employment Service[17] was established to deal with redundancies. The Employment Service reports figures of the number of people applying for assistance in search for work, not necessarily unemployed. It also registers unemployment, and pays the newly created unemployment benefits. Besides, it provides services like training and retraining, financing of job creation, employment subsidies and public work. For job seekers, the Employment Service offers two functions: first, information about vacancies, and second, placement services such as counselling, psychological testing, and various trainings. People have few expectations of the Employment Service, as companies tend to announce only worst paid and lowest skilled vacancies through the Service. As a rule, the unemployed would turn to the Service only as a last resort. As a result, the Employment Service serves only the most vulnerable strata of the population. Another problem/obstacle is the budget of the organization: it derives from payroll tax at the regional level. So the harder a region is affected, the more people get unemployed, the smaller is the budget of the Employment Service, and the fewer means are available for urgently needed active labour market measures (Clarke 1999). After paying the unemployment benefits, money is first spent on subsidies for existing jobs, a lesser amount on job creation by small business, and the least is spent on training (Clarke 1998).

In general, active labour market policy is still in its kinder shoes in Russia. Overall, there is little funded job creation and little availability of financing for setting up a business. A notable exception has been the case of the restructuring of the mining industry. Closures of mines led to more than 600,000 redundancies from 1992 until 2001. To absorb this massive unemployment, Russia experienced support from the international community. The European Commission tried to facilitate the formation of active labour market instruments. Funds were spent on job creation programs and on the creation of new small and medium enterprises or on the expansion of existing enterprises in the coal sector. However, the effect of spending these financial resources was minimal, the number of new jobs created was low in comparison with

17 The Employment Service replaced the so-called Labour Recruitment Bureaux, which enjoyed a really bad reputation of being badly staffed and underfinanced, having to place individuals with little chance to get employment, including people with poor disciplinary records. This bad reputation has been transmitted to the new institution of Employment Service.

those destroyed. And the most astonishing is that no retraining of workers occurred (Haney and Shkaratan 2003). There exists a theory that the degree to which training is dominated by retraining for new types of jobs is an indicator of the restructuring of the labour force. If the theory is true, it leads to the conclusion that the amount of external labour restructuring is small and that the employed receive more training than the unemployed, self-employed or people out of the labour force (Berger, Earle and Sabirianova 2001).

Conclusion

The restructuring of Russian steel industry is dominated by management decisions. Restructuring at MMK meant modernization, market exploration, and product innovation. To a far lesser extent, it implied employment restructuring. MMK's success on the Russian and the world market does not expose the company to further restructuring of labour. The current low wage level, by world standards, does not demand further rationalization of employment. From the workers' perspective, the threat of unemployment might foster the acceptance of low wages. And as long as labour mobility is not regulated by an external market, but relies on informal good relations with companies, workers are even more dependent on their job positions. The trade union representatives at MMK also do not request higher wages; they are more or less in line with the course of the company's management.[18] As long as trade unions and workers prefer job security to higher wages[19], there won't be sufficient pressure for employment restructuring at the company level. With high profit rates, the management does not recognize labour restructuring as a challenge.[20] The main challenge is the recruitment and maintenance of a new young generation of managers, and in this respect, MMK has become very active, while relying on traditional recruitment strategies as well as introducing new instruments.

18 This concordance of trade union and management is typical for the industrial relations in Russia. It represents a legacy from Soviet times when trade unions were part of the management responsible for securing labour productivity and motivation in distributing social benefits to the employees. The system dominating the industrial relations in Russia is the so-called social partnership. It is a system that has reduced the right for strike, and which mainly looks for social peace (Ashwin and Clarke 2002; Trappmann 2003).

19 Another aspect, compared with the Western experience, is the lack of institutional support for mass redundancies. The EU steel industry has received financing for redundancy packages, early retirement packages and retraining, so that labour adjustment happened without social tragedies.

20 And maybe it is really a minor problem, which only has been exaggerated by Western observers (Brown et al. 1994).

References

Alasheev, S. (1995), 'On a Particular Kind of Love and the Specifity of Soviet Production', in Simon Clarke (ed.), *Management and Industry in Russia, Formal and Informal Relations in the Period of Transition* (Brookfield: Edward Elgar), pp. 69–98.

Ashwin, S. and Clarke, S. (2002), *Russian Trade Unions and Industrial Relations in Transition* (Basingstoke and New York: Palgrave).

ATON capital (2003), 'The Russian Steel Industry: Russia, The Saudi Arabia of Steel'.

Baglione, L.A. and Clark, C.L. (1997), 'A Tale of Two Metallurgical Enterprises, Marketization and the Social Contract, in Russian Industry', *Communist and Post-Communist Studies* 30: 2, 153–80.

Berger, M.C., Earle, J.S. and Sabirianova, K.Z. (2001), 'Worker Training in a Restructuring Economy: Evidence from the Russian Transition', IZA Discussion Paper No 361.

Black, B., Kraakman, R. and Tarassova, A. (2000), 'Russian Privatization and Corporate Governance: What Went Wrong?', *Stanford Law Review 52,* 1731–808

Broadman, H.G. and Recanatini, F. (2001), 'Is Russia Restructuring? New Evidence on Job Creation and Destruction', World Bank Policy Research Working Paper, Juli.

Brown, A.N., Ickes, B.W. and Ryterman, R. (1994), 'The Myth of Monopoly, A New View of Industrial Structures in Russia', World Bank Policy Research Working Paper, 1331, August.

Clark, C.L. and Baglione, L.A. (1998), 'Men of Steel Meet the Market: Interpreting Firm Behaviour in Russia's Metallurgy Industry', *Journal of Economic Issues* 4, 925–63.

Clark, C.L. and Sacks, M.P. (2004), 'A View from Below: Industrial Restructuring and Women's Employment at Four Russian Enterprises', *Communist and Post-Communist Studies* 37, 524–45.

Clarke, S. (1995a), 'Formal and Informal Relations in Soviet Industrial Production', *Management and Industry in Russia: Formal and Informal Relations in the Period of Transition* (Brookfield: Edward Elgar), pp. 1–28.

Clarke, S. (ed.) (1995b), *Management and Industry in Russia: Formal and Informal Relations in the Period of Transition* (Brookfield: Edward Elgar).

Clarke, S. (ed.) (1995c), *Conflict and Change in the Russian Industrial Enterprise* (Cheltenham: Edward Elgar).

Clarke, S. (1996), 'The Russian Enterprise in the Era of Transition', in Clarke, S. (ed.) *The Russian Enterprise in Transition. Case Studies* (Cheltenham: Edward Elgar), pp.1–61.

Clarke, S. (ed.) (1998), *Structural Adjustment without Mass Employment? Lessons from Russia* (Cheltenham: Edward Elgar).

Clarke, S. (1999), 'Labour Market Behaviours and Institutions in the Transition to a Market Economy in Russia', Manuscript (Warwick University).

Clarke, S. (2002), *Making Ends Meet in Contemporary Russia: Secondary Employment, Subsidiary Agriculture and Social Networks* (Cheltenham: Eward Elgar)

Clarke, S.; Kabalina, V.; Kozina, I.; Donovy, I. and Karelina, M. (1998), 'The Restructuring of Employment and the Formation of a Labour Market in Russia', in Clarke, S. (ed.), *Structural Adjustment without Mass Employment? Lessons from Russia* (Cheltenham: Edward Elgar), pp. 87–146.

Clarke, S. and Donova, I. (1999), 'Internal Mobility and Labour Market Flexibility in Russia', *Europe-Asia Studies* 51: 2, 213–43.

Die Welt, 8. April 2005.

Die Welt, 15. Februar 2005.

Djankov, S. and Murrell, P. (2002), 'Enterprise Restructuring in Transition. A Quantitative Survey', *Journal of Economic Literature*, April.

Earle, J.S. and Estrin, S. (1998), 'Privatisation, Competition and Budget Constraints, Disciplining Enterprises in Russia', Manuscript.

Ejova, L., Olimpieva, I. and Trappmann, V. (2004), 'Social Partnership in Shipbuilding Industry: a Comparative Analysis of the Situation in Germany and Russia', Manuscript, (St Petersburg).

Estrin, S. (1998), 'Privatization and Restructuring in Central and Eastern Europe', in Boone, P.; Gomulka, S.; Layard, R. (eds), *Emerging from Communism: Lessons from Russia, China, and Eastern Europe* (Cambridge, Massachusetts/London, England: MIT Press), pp. 73–97.

European Commission (1999), 'The European Employment Strategy, Investing in people – More and better jobs'.

Haney, M. and Shkaratan, M. (2003), 'Mine Closure and its Impact on the Community, Five Years after Mine Closure in Romania, Russia and the Ukraine', World Bank Policy Research Working Paper, 3083.

Jackman, R. (1998), 'Unemployment and Restructuring', in Boone, P.; Gomulka, S.; Layard, R. (eds), *Emerging from Communism: Lessons from Russia, China and Eastern Europe* (Cambridge: MIT Press), pp. 123–152.

Kornai, J. (2002), *The Political Economy of Communism* (Princeton: Princeton University Press).

Kotkin, S. (1997), *Magnetic Mountain. Stalinism as a Civilisation* (University of California Press).

Krischer, B. and Holzhinrich-Scherler, A. (2001), 'Die wirtschaftliche Situation der russischen Stahlindustrie am Beispiel dreier Stahlwerke', *Stahl und Eisen* 121: 11, 113–119.

Layard, R. and Richter, A. (1995), 'How much Unemployment is Needed for Restructuring', *Economics of Transition* 3: 1, 39–58.

Ledeneva, A.V. (1999), *Russia's Economy of Favours: Blat, Networking and Informal Exchange* (Cambridge: University Press).

Lisin, V. (2004), 'Russia-EU Economic reactions: Abandoning the Stereotypes of the Past', Speech at the 6th General Meeting of the EU-Russia, Industrialists Round Table, The Hagues.

Loshkin, M.M. and Yemtsov, R. (2001), 'Household Strategies for Coping with Poverty and Social Exclusion in Post-Crisis Russia', World Bank Policy Research Working Paper.

Müller, K. (2005), 'Der Sozialstaat in den Transformationsländern. Erbe, Rahmenbedingungen und aktuelle Entwicklungen', Beitrag zum GfP Workshop Sozialraum Europa, (Berlin).

Nellis, J. (2002), 'The World Bank, Privatization and Enterprise Reform in Transition Economies: A Retrospective Analysis', The World Bank.

Pickup, F. and White, A. (2003), 'Livelihood in Post Communist Russia: Urban/Rural Comparisons', *Work, Employment and Society* 17: 3, 419–34.

Standing, G. (1998), 'Reviving Dead Souls: Russian Unemployment and Enterprise Restructuring', in Clarke, S. (ed.), *Structural Adjustment without Mass Employment? Lessons From Russia* (Cheltenham: Edward Elgar), pp. 147–185.

Trappmann, V. (2003), 'Die Fesseln der Vergangenheit: Lokale Bedingungen für transnationale Gewerkschaftskooperation in Osteuropa am Beispiel Polens und Russlands', in Croucher et al. (eds), *International Trade Union Co-Operation Experience and Research Issues*, Workshop Documents, (Dortmund).

Vedeneeva, V. (1995), 'Payment Systems and the Restructuring of Production Relations in Russia', Simon Clarke (ed.), *Management and Industry in Russia. Formal and Informal Relations in the Period of Transition* (Aldershot: Edward Elgar), pp. 224–39.

World Bank, Russian Federation (2005), *Reducing Poverty Through Growth and Social Policy Reform* (Washington).

World Bank (2005b), 'From Transition to Development. A Country Economic Memorandum for the Russian Federation', Draft version.

Wyplosz, C. (2000), 'Ten Years of Transformation. Macroeconomic Lessons', World Bank Policy Research Working Paper, 2288.

Internet-based references

Deutsche Bank AG London, Deutsche Bank Report [website], (2001) <http://research.gm.db.com>

MMK, Consolidated Financial Statements [website], (2006) <http://www.mmk.ru/eng/financial/2005/index.wbp>

Trappmann, V., 'Ausverkauft?! Privatisierung in Russland' [website], (Januar 2002) <http://www.weltpolitik.net/regionen/russland/article/1141.html>

PART II
KEY HRM ISSUES

Chapter 7

Recruitment at Russian Enterprises

Valery Yakubovich and Irina Kozina

Introduction

While contemplating recruitment strategies, a typical Russian firm sees its pool of potential job candidates organized into three concentric circles. The inner circle is the internal labour market (ILM) comprised of the firm's current workers who are always the first candidates considered for any vacancy. The outer ring is the external labour market (ELM) which contains the people who have no affiliation with the firm either directly or through social ties. Finally, the area between is the extended internal labour market (EILM) usually defined as the social networks of the firm's current workers (Manwaring 1984).

Although the triad ILM – EILM – ELM is a conventional way to think about the structure of the labour market (Doeringer and Piore 1971; Manwaring 1984), its application to the Russian case eliminates a few interesting institutional features that have implications for recruitment methods. First, former workers often maintain direct ties to the firm and return there after a stint of employment at other places (Clarke 1999; Earle and Sabirianova 2002; Yakubovich 2006). Therefore, they should be treated as an integral part of the EILM (Yakubovich 2006). Second, while most modern firms strongly prefer to hire from the internal labour market rather than the external one (Doeringer and Piore 1971), Russian firms go further by clearly expressing a preference for the EILM over the ELM. In other words, they turn the triad ILM – EILM – ELM into a surprisingly robust hierarchy which survived through the economic turmoil of the 1990s and the recovery of the early 2000s. Each component of the triad is shaped and maintained by a distinctive mix of labour market institutions and recruitment practices inherited from the command economy of state socialism, adopted from Western management and developed 'in-house' in response to idiosyncratic circumstances of the post-socialist economic, political, and social environments. These institutions and practices gradually evolve through the actions and inactions of key constituencies such as the state, owners and managers, HR professionals, trade unions, and the workers themselves. Change is slow and uneven, and the outcome of the process is far from obvious. Nevertheless, the major tension is evident: that between the traditional paternalistic organization of recruitment under state socialism and the rational bureaucratic organization typical for a modern market economy (compare, Weber (1922) 1978). Personal relationships govern paternalistic recruitment and loyalty to the boss is one of the main selection criteria. In contrast, formal rules and procedures govern rational bureaucratic recruitment and the selection criteria are primarily meritocratic. Our goal in this chapter is to carefully document how and to what degree the existing labour market institutions and recruitment practices resolve this tension, in order that scholars can understand the dynamics behind the observed phenomena while human resources practitioners are able to effectively align their recruitment methods with the environment in which they operate.

We start with a brief description of the context in which recruitment practices have been developing since the economic liberalization of 1992. Next, we outline the general approach to recruitment in Russian firms and proceed with a detailed discussion of recruitment practices in each of the three sectors of the labour market introduced above, drawing on almost ten years of our own research as well as the literature. To explore the latest developments, we utilize the rich data being collected in the ongoing project 'Management and Labour Relations: Management Practices of Modern Russian Enterprises' that includes 55 case studies of large, medium-size, and small firms from a variety of economic branches located in seven Russian regions.[1] We conclude the chapter with a speculative discussion of the direction in which Russian recruitment practices are headed and the actors that shape them.

The Russian Labour Market as a Context for the Transformation of Recruitment Practices

The Russian socialist state's control over labour was undermined already in the late 1980s when Gorbachev's reforms legitimized unemployment, freed wages, and allowed private economic activities (Ohtsu 1992 (1988); Oxenstierna 1990). However, the deep economic decline and political crisis that followed put Russia's state, enterprises, and citizens in survival mode. Major structural reforms of the economy proceeded very slowly and controversially or were put on hold altogether. Enterprises mobilized their limited financial and administrative resources towards maintaining the infrastructure, employment, and minimal production level. The metaphor 'adaptation without restructuring' (Kapelyushnikov 2001) most tellingly characterizes the state of the labour market in that period.

Under such circumstances, those few firms that could offer well paid jobs virtually closed their doors to outsiders, hiring exclusively from the internal labour market or through personal connections (Clarke 1999; Yakubovich and Kozina 2000). Exceptions to this rule were allowed only when a worker with rare skills had to be found. At the same time, failing firms' most valuable workers were most likely to leave first to pursue other opportunities, and the firms had no resources

1 The project covers the four-year period from April 2002 until March 2006 and is carried out by the Inter-Regional Institute for Comparative Analysis of Labour Relations (ISITO) in collaboration with the Center for Comparative Labour Research at the University of Warwick, United Kingdom. It is directed by Simon Clarke, Tony Elgar, and Veronika Kabalina and funded by the British Economic and Social Research Council (ESRC).

to attract equivalent replacements. As a result, neither successful nor failing firms were particularly interested in overhauling their recruitment practices. Numerous new labour market intermediaries which mushroomed at the time had no choice but to limit their role to providing unskilled and low-skilled workers who could fill low-paid high-turnover jobs.

As the economy started to improve in the aftermath of the financial crisis of August 1998, previously failing enterprises faced the challenge of renewing their dilapidated labour force while more successful ones experienced strengthening competition for skilled labour. The aging of the labour force, decreasing life expectancy and low birth rate further aggravated the shortage of skilled workers. The collapse of the Soviet system of vocational training and the low quality of education available in new market-oriented fields did not help address it either. The task of identifying and attracting qualified candidates on a large scale became critical. Firms approached this task with a variety of managerial tools which are discussed in detail below.

General Approaches to Recruitment

To place recruitment into the overall strategy and structure of a Russian firm, we have to understand first the managerial model by which a typical Russian firm is governed. By and large, the management of Russian enterprises is highly centralized in the hands of the CEO. To maintain the centralization, the CEO tightly controls financial flows and human resources. The control over human resources is often justified by the CEO's 'unalienable right' to assemble his own management team. By the same token, the members of the CEO's team form the teams of their immediate subordinates, and so the process is replicated on each level of the organizational hierarchy. Since 'personal chemistry' is believed to be the key to a managerial team's success, informal selection criteria dominate formal ones and, accordingly, the role of human resources departments is reduced to handling paperwork. Even the background check, a staple of a Soviet Personnel Department, is often taken over by security departments, post-reform structures mushroomed in response to the inability of the state to enforce contracts and protect businesses from criminals.

At the same time, there are countervailing factors that bring departments of human resources to the frontline of recruitment. First, as a line manager's span of control increases, the effort required to fill a growing number of vacancies increases, too. The demand on the manager's time becomes unbearable when the firm grows rapidly. Second, striving to increase efficiency and productivity, firms resort to Western managerial and organizational know-how. The carriers of such knowledge are foreign consultants as well as a new generation of Russian HR professionals who speak foreign languages, hold professional certificates and degrees from Western educational institutions, and often have some work experience at Western companies. They offer prepackaged sets of templates for training, evaluation and promotion, compensation systems, job analysis, and other HR functions. Expecting in return a high pay as well as high status, they are not satisfied by the traditional secondary role of HR departments and struggle for control over the labour force, in general, and recruitment, in particular. In that struggle, they often find allies in the firm's outside owners and Western partners. The former want some additional leverage over executives, the latter expect to see familiar transparent management practices.

The distribution of control over the labour force between a firm's line management and human resources management is highly contingent on intra-firm factors and we have very little evidence to make far-reaching generalizations. It is clear, however, that it is a crucial determinate of the firm's recruitment practices.

Where Do Job Candidates Come From?

The Internal Labour Market

For the majority of Russian firms, the current labour force is the primary pool of candidates to fill emerging vacancies. Managers justify this practice by low costs of internal search and deep knowledge of current workers' skills and potential. Likewise, current workers better understand the characteristics and requirements of the jobs and employer. Better information leads to a better match with minimal costs.

The logic appears entirely consistent with the concept of the internal labour market developed in labour economics. ILMs are a rational and efficient response to turnover and training costs; they preserve firm-specific human capital and ensure that senior workers will train junior personnel (Doeringer and Piore 1971). However, the similarities end here. While the textbook ILM operates according to bureaucratic rules and classificatory logic, the ILM of a typical Russian firm is structured by informal ties among workers and between workers and managers (compare, Stark 1986). A candidate's social fit with the collective and loyalty to the supervisor become leading selection criteria. The HR department often learns about a vacancy after a candidate has been found by the immediate supervisor of the position, when processing the paperwork remains the only function to be completed.

The literature defines the ILM at the level of an establishment rather than a firm as a whole which is rather restrictive for some categories of employees. This is particularly true for large holding companies and business groups which dominate the modern Russian economic landscape. Managerial career ladders in such organizations are not confined to one establishment. A manager or whole management team that built reputation at one establishment is often assigned to run another. The exposure to a diverse set of business units becomes a prerequisite for the advance to a top position at the firm as a whole. The practice appears particularly common among rapidly growing businesses which set up new units through Greenfield investments or acquisitions. In our study, it has been observed at a number of companies in construction materials, petrochemicals, and telecommunications. Managers responsible for financial and macro-economic policies are more likely to be recruited this way than those responsible for production.

The Extended Internal Labour Market

If an internal candidate is not found, the position becomes available in the extended internal labour market (EILM) which by definition encompasses the social networks of the firm's current workers (Manwaring 1984). There is nothing unique about Russian managers' preference for personal contacts. At the most general level, the reasons are quite similar to the ones emphasized by their Western counterparts. First and foremost, personal contacts help employers and job candidates learn about each other and thereby improve the fit between them (Fernandez et al. 2000; Rees and Shultz 1970; Simon and Warner 1992). However, in the Russian context, such information benefits are often specific to the economy in transition. For example, because a widely accepted vocabulary that could be used to specify job requirements is still lacking, firms often cannot articulate the qualifications and skills they are looking for. Only those who have intuitive knowledge of the firm's operation can identify appropriate candidates.

When the employer can explain his job requirements, he often distrusts the formal signals that are supposed to indicate them. Mushrooming new universities and institutes do not have established reputation. A labour book, the legal document issued by a person's first employer and used to trace her work history, can be easily altered and even purchased in the black market. Generic job titles, often listed in labour books, say little about the duties and responsibilities the person may have had in previous jobs.

In addition to solving information problems, hiring through personal contacts ensures that newcomers are faster socialized into the firm and therefore have an easier time acquiring tacit knowledge which is deeply embedded in the social context (Bailey and Waldinger 1991; Fernandez et al. 2000; Manwaring 1984, Reichers 1987, Sutton and Louis 1987). In the Russian case, socialization also implies the personal loyalty of a worker to the boss which can be valued higher than skills and experience. There is a very pragmatic reason for the high value of personal loyalty in the context of emerging markets: any Russian enterprise operates in the shadow economy at least to some degree; disloyal employees may expose the firm's questionable business practices to the state or to criminals and thereby make it vulnerable to legitimate demands as well as blackmail.

There is some evidence that job candidates referred by personal contacts are similar to their referrers, at least, in terms of observable formal characteristics (Fernandez et al. 2000; Rees and Shultz 1970). Thus, if the firm is happy with its current workforce, it can reproduce it by hiring through social networks. Finally, recruitment through the EILM is a 'fringe benefit' which is used by management as recognition of workers' influence and can be withdrawn as a disciplinary measure (Manwaring 1984, 168).

A long tradition of research equates the recruitment through social networks with labour market closure, because vacancies become unavailable to outsiders, that is, to those who do not have personal ties to the enterprise (Granovetter 1995; Grieco 1977; Manwaring 1984; Petersen et al. 2000; Waldinger 1996). Contacts act in the best interests of their relatives and friends, trying to shield them from competition. This is exactly what happened in Russia in the 1990s. Relatively good vacancies did not appear in the external market and by various estimates between 60–75 per cent of all the vacancies were filled through personal networks which were mobilized to exert influence on employers rather than to find job information (Clarke 1999, Gerber 2003, Kozina 1999, Yakubovich 2005). For employers, labour market closure is a double-edged sword. On one hand, employers recognize the importance of social cohesion for the economic wellbeing of their enterprises and therefore do not resist workers' promotion of their relatives and friends. On the other hand, market competition forces employers to pay attention to candidates' technical qualifications. Innovative recruitment practices often emerge under these conflicting pressures.

For example, personnel departments at Russian firms maintain lists of relatives and friends of their workers interested in being hired. The lists usually contain detailed information about candidates' qualifications but a personal relationship to a current employer is a prerequisite for getting in line. Such 'hybrid' methods appear first in foreign-owned firms, whose owners push for more rationalization and transparency in business processes, and then are adopted by others through diffusion. Among firms in our study, a metallurgical plant in the Ural Mountains lists about 1,600 relatives and friends of its workers who hope to get a job with the company. A producer of electric equipment in Siberia modifies this practice by allowing retiring workers to suggest a relative as a replacement. This helps rejuvenate the labour force, mitigates inter-generational tensions, and creates an additional control mechanism:

> It makes it easier for them [pensioners] to retire, and the family maintains a breadwinner. And it is convenient for us that someone looks after the youth – if something happens, we can call and complain .... [from an interview with a shop's deputy chief].

The conventional concept of the EILM is too narrow, though, because it ignores the fact that in addition to personal networks, the ties between workers and their places of previous employment are common recruitment channels. A few studies of the Russian labour market document the phenomenon of return mobility when workers who left the firm voluntarily or were fired come back.[2] The scope of this phenomenon is still debated. In Clarke's study of 16 manufacturers in four Russian cities, the extent of return mobility varies from 0 to 34 per cent (Clarke 1999, 235). Brown and Earle (2002) analyze a nationally representative sample of 530 industrial

2 Clarke (1999, 234–5) traces the origins of repeated hiring to idiosyncrasies of the Soviet welfare system. Under that system, distribution of the most valuable goods such as housing and cars was accomplished primarily through workplaces and organizations, which varied widely in their ability to actually deliver them. Accordingly, workers would take a job in a more promising firm to obtain housing and then would switch back to the previous employment. Surveys carried out in industrial enterprises in 19 cities in the Soviet period estimate the level of return mobility at 15 per cent of all inter-factory transfers and 20–27 per cent of all separations for particular enterprises. Overall, 12 per cent of quitters later returned to their former place of work (Otsu 1992, 281).

firms and estimate the rate of rehiring at not more than 10.5 per cent of accessions in any year between 1990 and 1999. A representative study of the Samara labour market reports the extent of return mobility at 21.4 per cent (Yakubovich 2006).

Clarke (1999, 236–7) offers a number of reasons for return mobility: general economic uncertainty distorts employers' and workers' expectations regarding their labour market opportunities; employment at new private enterprises turns out to not be as attractive as it appeared from outside, forcing workers to return to their origins; workers' firm-specific skills make them unemployable at other places; newly employed workers quickly discover that in a time of crisis newcomers are laid off first, their return to the place of previous employment restores their insider status and thereby provides some security.

On the demand side, return mobility can be seen as a substitute for the Western practice of temporary layoffs when a worker is dismissed because of slack business but is then invited back as soon as the firm recovers. A similar practice of Russian firms is known as 'unpaid leave'. The limited data available suggests that between 11–16 per cent of employees experienced, on average, eight weeks of unpaid leave within any given year between 1996–98 (Earle and Sabirianova 2002). However, the practice stands on a weak legal and institutional foundation since it violates labour contracts (Earle and Sabirianova 2002). Return mobility addresses this problem while working exactly the same way. For instance, when demand for its product increased in the fall of 1994, the Samara Chocolate Factory took back almost all the pensioners it had dismissed a couple of months earlier (Clarke 1999, 237). These days, the practice becomes indispensable for the former Soviet firms that manage to grow on their old equipment. They address the shortage of skilled workers by bringing back middle-aged and retired former employees who left in the downturn of the 1990s:

> We started pursuing retirees, so they would stay or come back while before we motivated them to quit [from an interview with the head of a trade union, Samara Machine Building Plant].

Our ethnographic fieldwork in various Russian regions documents mid-level managers' extensive knowledge of the whereabouts and well-being of their former employees which keeps the latter in the extended internal labour market.

A referral program, when a worker is paid a bonus for bringing qualified candidates, is a well-established practice of motivating workers to mobilize their networks for the benefit of the employer (Halcrow 1988). The bonus is supposed to realign the employer's interest in finding a qualified worker with the interests of the referrer who otherwise would worry much more about helping his friends than solving the employer's problem (Neckerman and Fernandez 2003). In Russia, referral programs are pretty rare and used primarily by most successful firms who seek candidates of rare qualifications and skills for high-paid positions. Our study of 55 firms offers only one example of a Machine-Building Plant whose management introduced RUR 1,000 ($35) for referring a skilled worker who would be hired and survive a probation period.

Paradoxically, the proliferation of referral programs leads to formalization of informal channels and transforms networks from being workers' tool for labour market closure to being employers' tool for market opening (Yakubovich 2006). Indeed, the literature traditionally contrasts formal recruitment which 'occurs when firms take deliberate steps to generate applicants' with informal methods which 'involve little expenditure of effort or resources; thus they are often described as passive' (Waldinger and Lichter 2003, 94–5). Manwaring's EILM owes its existence to the inaction of the employer who postpones announcing new vacancies to give contacts of present employees a head start, or avoid notifying certain agencies altogether even when he is obliged to do so (Manwaring 1984, 163). Networks take care of vacancies without employers' apparent intervention and, left to their own devices, close the market to strangers.

On the contrary, with the advent of referral programs, social networks become a means for screening for talent and reaching out to potential job candidates who otherwise would not apply (Breaugh and Mann 1984; Fernandez et al. 2000). Management textbooks present such an outreach effort towards a larger more diverse pool of applicants as an economically sound strategy of managing human resources (for example, Baron and Kreps 1999, 339–40). The proactive use of network ties by an employer alters the incentives of the workers who become more motivated to represent the interests of their employers than to do favors to their social contacts. Going beyond the immediate circle of family and friends, they assist in opening the labour market rather than closing it. In this regard, social networks complement formal channels such as government-run employment centers, private employment agencies, and mass media which we discuss in the following section. Most importantly, hiring through networks becomes another function of HR departments and, by extension, a component of bureaucratic recruitment. This trend barely takes shape in Russia but the direction appears clear. The competition between line managers and HR professionals will determine its long term outcome.

The External Labour Market

A Russian firm's strict preference for hiring internally and in the EILM implies that there are two reasons for jobs to remain vacant after passing those stages: either no one among potential candidates wanted the job or no one was qualified to get it. The very same two factors determine a vacancy's future in the ELM.

Internally undesirable vacancies belong to the secondary sector of low-skill, poor pay, high-turnover jobs. The technological backwardness and mass deskilling at old Soviet enterprises still generate them in large numbers. The formal requirements to seekers of such positions are very basic: the existence of a Labour Book,[3] no

3 The labour book is the main document that confirms a person's work history. The Russian Labour Code requires that an employer makes a record in a worker's Labour Book if the person held the job for more than five days. The requirement that a worker has it simply means that the employer wants to verify his work history.

predisposition to alcoholism and other 'harmful' habits, and conscientiousness. The Federal Employment Service, private employment agencies, and job ads in mass media are the main channels through which such positions are filled.

The Federal Employment Service (FES) is supposed to play the dual role of the distributor of unemployment benefits and an employment agency. It was established in 1991 and, according to the Labour Code of that period, all enterprises were required to submit their vacancies to the FES' database. Never enforced, the provision is absent from the new Labour Code of 2001. Thus, the FES' current legal status is consistent with what the FES is in reality – the last resort for the most disadvantaged workers (Clarke 1999; Kabalina and Kozina 2000). Non-surprisingly, only a small percentage of secondary sector jobs are actually filled through it. According to rough estimates of the HR professionals from the firms we surveyed, about 90 per cent of unskilled jobs are filled through ads in mass media. For attractive jobs with no internal candidates, ads in mass media are low-cost but ineffective a method; about 90 per cent of those who respond to job ads are deemed unqualified and only one person out of 100 is found to be a good fit. Thus, the high cost of screening makes low cost of attracting candidates irrelevant. Only a firm with a full-fledged personnel department may consistently benefit from job ads.

Private recruitment agencies seek candidates for both skilled and unskilled jobs. In fact, in the Russian business literature, the term recruitment is often transliterated as *рекрутинг* [recruiting] and refers exclusively to the business conducted by specialized private recruitment agencies. The first agencies appeared in Russia in the early 1990s, signifying the collapse of the state monopoly on labour allocation. A number of them were set up or run by entrepreneurs who gave up or lost their increasingly unattractive jobs in the state sector, ended up in the labour market for that reason, and saw an opportunity in becoming a labour market intermediary herself. Initially, recruitment agencies offered their services to foreign firms but gradually reached out to joint ventures, Russian distributors of foreign products, and finally to Russian private firms. Their proliferation at the early stage was slow in part because of the closure of the Russian labour market described above, and in part because of the dominance of the Soviet norms and practices which stigmatize commoditization of labour. As of 2004, up to one thousand agencies operated in Russia, including about 350 in Moscow, 100 in St Petersburg, 35–40 in each of the ten largest regional centers with population over one million, and several agencies (up to eight) in other 20–25 cities. Not more than 30 agencies are foreign owned. They generate about $100–140 millions in revenues annually, most of it from Moscow (70 per cent) and St Petersburg (10 per cent). The market is growing at a rate of 20–25 per cent a year since 2000 (Alliance Media 2004). Established in 1996, the Association of Personnel Search Consultants [*Ассоциация консультантов по подбору персонала*] fosters the maturation and professionalization of the recruitment industry.

Recruitment agencies can be classified into three categories: executive search, cadre agencies [*кадровые агенства*], and employment agencies [*агенства по найму*]. Members of the first category 'headhunt' for candidates to fill top positions in major corporations. By some estimates, they comprise less than 10 per cent of the agencies' total pool (Melnikova 2005). Cadre agencies focus on the middle-level management and specialists; employment agencies fill standard white- and blue-collar positions. Some combinations of these functions are possible. Although almost all the firms in our study have experience with private recruitment agencies, the assessment they give them is rather low in terms of the quality of the service in comparison with the price paid. In response, recruitment agencies blame the immaturity of the Russian labour market where widely understood job descriptions and requirements are still wanting. As a result, their clients cannot clearly articulate their expectations. This is particularly true for the small business which often needs workers with rather unusual combinations of skills. It is a simplification to treat recruitment agencies as pure formal labour market channels. Their ultimate success depends on recruiters' embeddedness in the relevant networks of employers, on one side, and job candidates, on the other.

The emergence of the Internet as an alternative labour market intermediary is threatening both traditional ads in mass media and low-end recruitment agencies. Both employers and workers actively engage the Internet in search for each other. Firms advertise jobs on their websites; workers post their resumes on their personal pages; 'virtual' agencies and their 'real' predecessors, which expand into the cyberspace, do both. Kuhn and Skuterud (2004) find that between 1998 and 2000 regular Internet job search in the US grew from 6 to 9 per cent in the population at large, from 7 to 11 per cent for employed workers, and from 15 to 26 per cent for unemployed job seekers. Observers of this spur of activity claim that the Internet opens new channels of communication between workers and firms, reduces the problem of imperfect and asymmetric information pervasive in labour markets as well as costs of search. At the same time, it heightens the problem of adverse self-selection: less able candidates, who in the past would not bother to apply, find it very easy to do electronically (for review, see Autor 2001).

Empirical evidence of the effectiveness of the Internet as a matching channel is limited. Even among Internet users surveyed in 1999, only 4 per cent found their most recent job over the Internet compared with 40 per cent via referral (Li et al. 2000). Those who search on the Internet do not abandon conventional methods but, on the contrary, engage them more. According to the US Current Population Survey, unemployed workers who look for work on line use 'on average of 2.17 conventional search methods, compared to 1.67 for other unemployed workers' (Kuhn and Skuterud 2004, 221). Kuhn's and Skuterud's analysis shows that durations of unemployment are not shorter and can even be longer among Internet searchers and the adverse selection is the most likely explanation for this. The unemployed may be forced to search on the Internet because their social networks are poor (Kuhn and Skuterud 2004). Observing the use of Internet technologies at an employment fair in France, Neuville (2001) finds widespread mismatches which force fair participants to fall back on social networks and face-to-face contacts.

Internet users in Russia are still a pretty exclusive segment of the population with relatively high education and skills. Since the late 1990s, when computer specialists monopolized the channel, there emerged a tendency towards a much wider representation. In 2002, 11.8 per cent of résumés at www.rabota.ru were posted by students, 9.4 per cent by administrative personnel, 7.6 per cent by workers in the finance industry, and only 6.4 per cent by programmers (The Career Forum 2002). Recruitment agencies pay for the right to access this and similar sites and to browse through the résumés. There is no evidence to judge how agencies use that information or how effective the Internet channel is in general. We expect that over time the problem of adverse selection will challenge the Russian virtual labour market, too. To address it, the market will have to develop new institutional arrangements which are at this point impossible to foresee (Autor 2001).

Educational institutions are important players in any labour market. Under state socialism, they personified the state system of distribution of labour, which centrally assigned graduates of vocational and higher schools to state enterprises. Market reforms freed enterprises from the obligation to unconditionally accept such graduates, which led to the system collapse. Educational establishments can no longer rely on the state to secure employment for their graduates; instead, they have to act as market intermediaries matching the graduates with jobs. Those are old enough to have become accustomed to guaranteed employment for their graduates under state socialism attempt to capitalize on preexisting relationships with employers. Under the distribution system, educational establishments tended to deal with the same pool of employers from year to year and therefore often built quite stable relationships with them. Such relationships did not disappear overnight after the compulsory requirements of distribution were abandoned. Some researchers argue that enterprises feel committed to their schools and try to accommodate the graduates even if this is economically unsound (Gimpelson and Lippoldt 1999). An alternative explanation refers to the long-term character of the placement contracts between enterprises and educational establishments which were signed at the end of the 1980s. Researchers believe that contractual obligations force enterprises to hire graduates; as soon as such contracts expire they are very unlikely to be renewed (Kapelyushnikov 2001).

Such arguments would be sufficient if the relationships between employers and educational institutions were frozen in time. Our research shows that they are undergoing substantial transformation resulting in new organizational forms. Universities and institutes organize job fairs, sign agreements with the enterprises to secure the status of a young specialist for those graduates who launch their careers there, create associations of employers which pursue collaborative projects with potential employers and thereby put to productive uses its intellectual potential and raise funds for its primary educational activities. The projects usually involve some students who get a chance to demonstrate their abilities to prospective employers and, if successful, to receive attractive job offers.

Overall, the external labour market has been growing together with the economy as a whole. According to various sources, between 32–55 per cent of managers use and recognize as effective ads in mass media and between 20–38 per cent think the same about recruitment agencies, despite the fact that in the late 1990s only 8 per cent of hires were made in the ELM (Kozina 1999). At the same time, for some categories of workers the role if the ELM remains minor. In particular, according to the survey carried out within our study, only 5 per cent of current managers passed through open competitive selection while 31 per cent were recruited through personal ties and 51 per cent were promoted internally. Interestingly, for personnel and marketing managers open recruitment is sufficiently common, about 15 per cent for each group (see Figure 7.1).

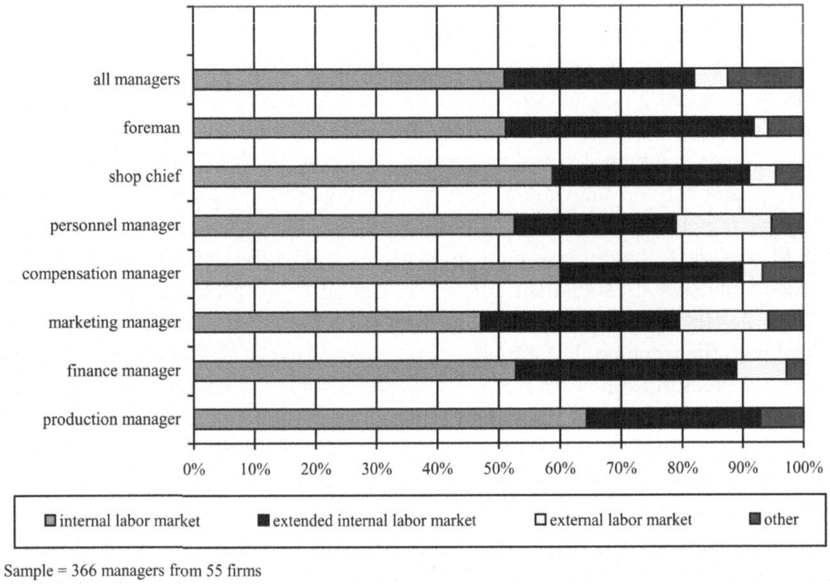

Figure 7.1 The distribution of managers by recruitment channel

The Institutional Dynamics of Recruitment

Some exceptions notwithstanding, the description of the recruitment practices and channels presented above is rather static. In this last section we would like to discuss the direction in which they are developing and the forces that shape that direction. Our emphasis is on both similarities with and differences from developed labour markets. Overall, our presentation suggests that the Russian institution of recruitment is not qualitatively different from its counterparts in any developed market economy. It is populated by similar actors who do similar things. The closure of the Russian market may be higher but it is a matter of quantity rather than quality and can be explained by the severe shortage of attractive jobs during the economic downturn of the 1990s. Some evidence presented earlier clearly indicates that market openness is greater in booming sectors of the economy. Can we conclude that there is nothing at all qualitatively distinct about the Russian case?

To start answering this question, let us engage some historical evidence from a developed economy. In response to job shortages related to the conversion to a peacetime economy in the US after the World War II, firms did not restrict access to their jobs to insiders, as happened in Russia in the 1990s after the collapse of the Soviet economy and state. On the contrary, personnel departments in the US implemented formal selection and evaluation procedures for choosing qualified individuals from a large pool of candidates. Personnel professionals succeeded in defending their turf because by then the profession had been firmly institutionalized (Baron et al. 1986).

In Russia, the institutionalization process is accelerating. Numerous formal organizations and informal communities of HR workers set standards and norms that mold recruitment as a profession. To appreciate the intellectual and organizational vibrancy of HR workers, it is enough to visit one of their communities on the Web. For example, the site www.e-xectuve.ru is full of hot debates on a variety of theoretically and practically important topics, such as the value of recruitment agencies, professional ethics, kickbacks in hiring, headhunting by HR departments, and so on. There is a clear generational shift among HR personnel. While the typical Chair of a Soviet Personnel Department is a retired senior military officer, young HR professionals are highly educated, speak foreign languages, and know modern human resources methods. They seek compensation commensurate with their knowledge and skills and strive to change the status of personnel departments within organizations by asserting that human resources management has a strategic component and therefore deserve representation in the executive suite. As we discuss above, line managers treat claims like these with suspicion and attempt to preserve their prerogative in making personnel decisions. The outcome of this struggle is firm-specific. However, our study shows, that by and large, top and line management so far preserve their position by routinely circumventing formal procedures and delegating to HR departments the routine paperwork associated with making a hire.

Although the Russian case may still prove to be idiosyncratic, the literature suggests that HR professionals alone are unlikely to achieve formalization of recruitment practices. In particular, the state's actions and inactions are crucial. Going back to the example of personnel departments in the US in the 1940–50s, it is worthwhile to mention that the state enhanced their role in recruitment by introducing veteran preference policies (Baron et al. 1986). An example of the Russian state's effort is the abovementioned provision of the Russian Labour Code circa 1990s which required firms to submit all their vacancies to the Federal Employment Service. However, the requirement was never enforced and completely disappeared from the new Labour Code introduced in 2001.

In fact, neither the current Labour Code nor other labour legislation says anything about recruitment. Article three of the Labour Code explicitly forbids any kind of discrimination in the labour market (The Labour Code of the Russian Federation 2001). In practice, however, discrimination is open and rampant. Russian employers routinely indicate age, gender, health, physical appearance, and other ascriptive characteristics in job ads. From the content analysis of employment ads published in Samara newspapers in June and December 1998, Alasheev (1998) finds that 18.6 per cent of the ads published in June and 23.8 per cent in December contained an explicit gender requirement. To confirm that the situation has not changed much since then, it is enough to look at job ads on Russian websites. There is nothing extremely unusual about such requirements. Even in developed labour markets, employers often expect applicants to satisfy them (Barber 1998, 21; Rees 1966, 562; Waldinger and Lichter 2003, 150–53). The difference is that in such markets they are typically illegal. Firms have no choice but to formalize their recruitment and promotion practices which gives a boost to HR departments even if discriminatory attitudes survive covertly or even subconsciously. The 1964 Equal Opportunity Law in the US had such an unintended effect (Dobbin et al. 1993). However, the state's effort has to be strong and consistent, since proving in court any discrimination in recruitment is extremely difficult. Alternatively, bureaucratization of personnel practices can happen in response to the pressure from trade unions (Baron et al. 1986), although recruitment is not their first priority either. Moreover, such a development is unlikely in Russia where trade unions are in an extremely weak position and very poorly represented at private firms (Ashwin and Clarke 2003).

The evolution of the Russian labour market is far from over and its outcome is far from clear. Unavoidably, our presentation is just a snapshot of this process, albeit the one which we believe provides a valuable framework for scholars and practitioners interested in understanding and increasing the effectiveness of Russian recruitment practices.

References

Alasheev, S. (1998), 'Content-Analysis of Job Ads in Samara Newspapers', Report.

Ashwin, S. and Clarke, S. (2003), *Russian Trade Unions and Industrial Relations in Transition* (Basingstoke: Palgrave).

Autor, D. (2001), 'Wiring the Labor Market', *Journal of Economic Perspectives* 15: 1, 25–40.

Bailey, T. and Waldinger, R. (1991), 'Primary, Secondary, and Enclave Labor Markets: A Training System Approach', *American Sociological Review* 56: 4, 432–45.

Barber, A.E. (1998), *Recruiting Employees. Individual and Organizational Perspectives* (CA: Sage Publications).

Baron, J.N., Dobbin, F.R. and Jennings, P.D. (1986), 'War and Peace: The Evolution of Modern Personnel Administration in US Industry', *American Journal of Sociology* 92: 2, 350–383.

Baron, J.N. and Kreps, D.M. (1999), *Strategic Human Resources: Frameworks for General Managers* (New York, NY: John Wiley & Sons, Inc.).

Breaugh, J.A. and Mann, R.B. (1984), 'Recruiting Source Effects: A Test of Two Alternative Explanations', *Journal of Occupational Psychology* 57, 261–7.

Clarke, S. (1999), *The Formation of a Labour Market in Russia* (Cheltenham, UK: Edward Elgar).

Dobbin, F., Sutton, J.R., Meyer, J.W. and Scott, W.R. (1993), 'Equal Opportunity Law and the Construction of Internal Labor Markets', *American Journal of Sociology* 99: 2, 396–427.

Earle, J.S. and Sabirianova, K.Z. (2002), 'Understanding Employment: Level, Composition, and Flows', in Mansoora Rashid (ed.), *The Russian Labor Market: Moving from Crisis to Recovery* (Washington, DC: World Bank).

Fernandez, R.M., Castilla, E. and Moore, P. (2000), 'Social Capital at Work: Networks and Employment at a Phone Center', *American Journal of Sociology* 105: 5, 1288–1356.

Gerber, T. (2003), *Getting Personal: The Use of Networks for Successful Job Searches in Russia: 1985–2001*, Working paper.

Gimpelson, V. and Lippoldt, D. (1999), 'Private Sector Employment in Russia', *Economics of Transition* 7: 2, 505–33.

Granovetter, M. (1995), *Getting a Job: A Study of Contacts and Careers*, 2nd edition (Chicago: University of Chicago Press).

Grieco, M. (1987), *Keeping It in the Family: Social Networks and Employment Chance* (London: Tavistock).

Kabalina, V. and Kozina, I. (eds) (2000), *State and Private Employment Services in the Labor Market* [In Russian: Государственные и частные службы занятости на рынке труда], (Moscow: ROSSPEN).

Kapelyushnikov, R. (2001), *Rossiyskiy Rynok Truda: Adaptatsiya bez Restructurizatsii* [Russian: *The Russian Labor Market: Adaptation without Restructuring*], (Moscow: Higher School of Economics).

Kozina, I. (1999), 'Restructurirovanie rynka truda i kanaly mobilnosti', (Russian: Restructuring of the labour market and mobility channels.), *Employment and Households' Behavior. Adaptation to Conditions of the Russian Transitional Economy*, Kabalina, V. and Clarke, S. (eds.), (Russian, Moscow: ROSSPEN), pp. 172–200.

Kuhn, P. and Skuterud, M. (2004) 'Internet Job Search and Unemployment Durations', *American Economic Review* 94: 1, 218–32.

The Labour Code of the Russian Federation (2001).

Neckerman, K. and Fernandez, R. (2003), 'Keeping a Job: Network Hiring and Turnover in a Retail Bank' *Research in the Sociology of Organizations* 20, 299–318.

Halcrow, A. (1988), 'Employees are your best recruiters', *Personnel Journal* 67, 42–9.

Neuville, J.-P. (2001), 'Good "Tips" in the Labor Market. Can the Internet Make an "Economy of Quality" a Market?', *Sociologie du Travail* 43: 3, 349–68.

Ohtsu, S. (1988, 1992), *Sovetskiy Rynok Truda* [Russian: The Soviet Labor Market, a translation from Japanese] (Moskow: Mysl).

Oxenstierna, S. (1990), *From Labour Shortage to Unemployment: Soviet Labour Market in the 1980's* (Stockholm: Swedish Institute for Social Research).

Petersen, T., Saporta, I. and Seidel, M.L. (2000), 'Offering a Job: Meritocracy and Social Networks', *American Journal of Sociology* 106: 3, 763–816.

Rees, A. (1966), 'Information Networks in Labor Markets', *American Economic Review* 56: 1/2, 559–66.

Rees, A. and Shultz, G.P. (1970), *Workers and Wages in an Urban Labor Market* (Chicago: University of Chicago Press).

Reichers, A.E. (1987), 'An Interactionist Perspective on Newcomer Socialization Rates' *Academy of Management Review* 12: 2, 278–87.

Simon, C.J. and Warner, J.T. (1992), 'Matchmaker, Matchmaker: The Effect of Old Boy Networks on Job Match Quality, Earnings, and Tenure', *Journal of Labor Economics* 10: 3, 306–29.

Sutton, R.I. and Louis, M.R. (1987), 'How Selecting and Socializing Newcomers Influence Insiders' *Human Resources Management* 26: 347–61.

Stark, D. (1986), 'Rethinking Internal Labor Markets: New Insights from a Comparative Perspective' *American Sociological Review* 51: 4, 492–504.

Waldinger, R. (1996), *Still the Promised City? New Immigrants and African-Americans in Post-Industrial New York* (Cambridge, MA: Harvard University Press).

Waldinger, R. and Lichter, M.I. (2003), *How the Other Half Works*, (Berkeley, CA: University of California Press).

Weber, M. (1922, 1978), *Economy and Society: An Outline of Interpretive Sociology* (Berkeley: University of California Press).

Yakubovich, V. (2005), 'Weak Ties, Information, and Influence: How Workers Find Jobs in a Local Russian Labor Market', *American Sociological Review* 70: 3, 408–21.

Yakubovich, V. (2006), 'Passive Recruitment in the Russian Urban Labor Market', *Work and Occupations*, (forthcoming).

Yakubovich, V. and Kozina, I. (2000), 'The Changing Significance of Ties. An Exploration of the Hiring Channels in the Russian Transitional Labor Market', *International Sociology* 15: 3, 479–500.

Internet-based references

Alliance Media, 'Maly bizness dlya podbora personala ne polzuetsya uslugami kadrovykh agenstv' [Russian: To Hire Personnel, Small Buisnesses Do Not Use Recruitment Agencies], (2004) <http://www.allmedia.ru/newsitem.asp?id=728026>

The Career Forum [website], *Elektronny Recruting: Moda ili Vyzov Vremeni?* [Russian: Virtual Recruitment: A Fashion or Challenge of Times?], (2002) <www.careerforum.ru
/data/articles/atc_detail_arch.php?sec=1&id=665.>

Li, C.; Charron, C. and Dash, A., *The Career Networks*, (Cambridge, MA: Forrester Research), (2004) <http://www.forrester.com>

Melnikova, T.L., *Kadrovye i Rekrutingovye Agenstva. Tipologiya i Analiz Raboty*, (Russian: Cadre and Recruitment Agencies. Typology and Performance Analysis.), Rabota and Zarplata, (2005) www.zarplata.ru/workman/print_id~304.asp

Chapter 8

Tendencies of the Russian Labour and Recruitment Markets – Employment in a Medium-sized IT Company

Henrik Loos

Introduction

This paper contains an overview of current tendencies in the Moscow recruitment industry before the backdrop of recent developments on the Russian labour market and gives an example of human resource management practices in a medium-sized Russian IT company from the point of view of an employee undergoing the full employment cycle from recruitment to resignation.

The first part is a summary of the author's work experience as a recruiter for a Western recruitment firm over the course of 2005, while the second part draws on the author's notes from his time of employment at an IT company in 2004. At the time, the author was teaching Intercultural Management in an MBA programme and collecting field data on organizational behaviour within Russian enterprises.

Tendencies on the Labour Market(s)

The Russian Economy and its Labour Market(s)

Recent political, social and economic developments in the Russian Federation have had a great impact on the national labour market. These economic changes, which affected organizations to various degrees in respect to their *size*, *industry*, *location* and *ownership*, have also altered the labour market and the society as a whole. For the purpose of this paper, these four parameters will be used to reveal how the economy's structure has led to a fragmentation of the labour market and what consequences this development had for the recruitment industry.

Top 400 Enterprises by Revenue Although the predominance of Russia's big business ['krupny biznes'] has been continually reduced over recent years, which resulted in an increase in the overall share of SMB, large enterprises still account for over 90 per cent of Russia's GNP (Source: Russian Union of Industrialists and Entrepreneurs – RSPP: 2005). The dispersion of revenue amongst the top 400 companies gives us an even clearer idea of the economic concentration at hand, as nearly 70 per cent of total revenue can be attributed to the 40 largest companies listed in the rating (Table 8.1).

Table 8.1 Dispersion of revenue amongst Russia's top 400 enterprises

	2004 in %	**2005** in %
1–40	71	68
41–80	8	9
81–120	5	6
121–160	5	5
161–240	3	4
241–280	4	4
281–320	2	2
321–360	1	1
361–400	1	1

Source: Expert 38/2005

Top 400 Enterprises by Industry The rating of the top 400 companies by industry reveals the concentration of economic activity in a handful of industries (Table 8.2).

Table 8.2 Russia's dominant industries

Industries	**in %**	**Industries**	**in %**
Oil and Gas	34	Wholesale	3
Transport	9	Food and Drink	3
Black Metallurgy	9	Chemicals	3
Engineering	7	Insurance	2
Energy	7	Building and Construction	2
Non-ferrous Metallurgy	4	Coal	1
Telecommunications	4	Others	4
Banking	4		
Retail	4		

Source: Expert 38/2005

However, the most dynamically developing companies do not belong to the leading industries. In the rating, 123 companies (compared to 56 in 2004) of the 400 belong to a group called the 'New Business Generation', and emerged in the mid-nineties. Their revenue currently amounts to 12 per cent of total revenue, of which the retail sector makes up the largest share (28 per cent), followed by telecommunications (22 per cent), banks (15 per cent), wholesale (13 per cent) and IT (11 per cent) (Source: Expert, 38/2005).

Top 400 by Geography According to the study, 103 holdings of the top 400 enterprises are registered as interregional holdings, 116 companies are registered in the Russian capital, 23 in St Petersburg and 19 in the Moscow Oblast. The locations of the individual branches of the largest interregional holdings reveal their impact on economically developed Federal Subjects and give an idea of the unequal distribution of wealth amongst the population of the Russian Federation. By the same token, the majority of large regional companies represent an indispensable economic factor for their Federal Subjects, such as OAO AvtoVAZ for the Samara Oblast, OAO Magnitogorsky Metallurgichesky Kombinat for the Chelyabinsk Oblast or OAO Novolipetzky Metallurgichesky Kombinat for the Lipetzk Oblast.

Four Federal Subjects A comparison of four selected Federal Subjects in terms of wealth shows to what extent Moscow and the Moscow Oblast have become detached from the rest of the country, and how certain Federal Subjects like the Yamalo-Nenezky Avtonomny Okrug have emerged as relatively prosperous regions (here, mainly due to OAO Gazprom). One main indicator is the average monthly net salary and its comparison to the local subsistence wage [*prozhitochny minimum*] (Table 8.3). The official national minimum wage [*minimalny razmer oplaty truda – MROT*] of US $28 (800RUR) a month introduced on 1 September 2005 can not be used as a guideline for actual wages paid, as it is lower than the subsistence wage and mainly used for administrative purposes.

Table 8.3 Subsistence wage and average monthly salary (August 2005 in US$)

	Subsistence (living) wage	Average monthly net salary
National Average	100	245
Moscow City	150	465
Moscow Oblast	115	320
Vladimirskaya Oblast	90	215
Yamalo-Nenezky Avtonomny Okrug	185	930

Source: Rosstat 2005

By the same token, the Vladimirskaya Oblast, burdened with outdated enterprises from Soviet times, is already considered economically less developed than the average Federal Subject (despite its close proximity to the Moscow Oblast). A comparison of monthly income per capita (Table 8.4) highlights the differences and explains why most companies oriented towards the consumer market initially target Moscow and the Moscow Oblast. Here they find a market of approx. 20 million easily accessible consumers with sufficient purchasing power (for example 100 per cent market exploitation of mobile phone ownership per capita).

Table 8.4 Monthly income per capita (August 2005 in US$)

	Monthly income per capita
Moscow City	820
Moscow Oblast	250
Vladimirskaya Oblast	145
Yamalo-Nenezky Avtonomny Okrug	625

Source: Rosstat 2005

The relatively high figure for Moscow has many reasons, one being the extraordinary high rental prices for apartments. Many Muscovites see this as an essential source of income given the average rental price, for example, for a so-called one-room flat on Leninsky Prospect currently at between US $450 and 550 per month.

It is important to bear in mind that the registration of a company as a legal entity does not have to coincide with its physical location. For example, the subsidiaries of Roman Abramovich's OAO Sibneft, have brought immense funds to the Chukotka Independent Okrug budget and have turned the once impoverished Federal Subject into one of the leading Subjects in terms of average monthly salary (US $730).

> According to the administration of the Chukotka Independent Okrug, profit tax from Slavneft-Trading and Sibneft-Chukotka make up 60 per cent of the region's budget. … Eventually, Roman Abramovich was registered as a resident there and now pays one billion RUR [US $35.7 million] in income tax into the budget (Proskurina 2005).

Ownership of Companies A large percentage of Russian companies are still state-owned (Table 8.5).

Although the figures clearly show the tendency towards privatization of state-owned organizations, in recent months there has been a tendency towards renationalization of companies from industry sectors considered strategically significant by the government, recent acquisitions in the oil and gas industry (for example, OAO 'Rosneft' – 'Yukos' and OAO 'Gazprom' – OAO 'Sibneft').

Table 8.5 Employment according to company ownership (August 2005)

Company ownership	1992 in %	2004 in %
State-owned	68.9	36.0
Privately held	19.5	50.7
Mixed Russian	10.5	8.9
Foreign and joint ventures	0.3	3.7
NGOs and religious organizations	0.8	0.7

Source: Rosstat 2005

Salaries according to Industries The rating of average monthly salaries according to industry (Table 8.6) more or less mirrors the rating of the most important industries (Table 8.2).

Table 8.6 Average monthly net salaries in US$ according to industries

Industries	monthly net salary in $US	Industries	monthly net salary in $US
Gas	1205	Building and construction	285
Oil drilling	850	Chemical and petrochemical industry	260
Fuel industry	690	Mechanical engineering	240
Finance and insurance	610	Food and drink industry	235
Oil-refining	500	Construction materials industry	225
Non-ferrous metallurgy	480	Municipal service	210
Electric energy	390	Timber	190
Coal	370	Retail and wholesale	175
Transport	345	Health care, sports and social work	170
IT	340	Culture and arts	155
Black metallurgy	335	Education	150
Telecommunication	325	Agriculture	100
Science	305		

Source: Rosstat 2005

However, one has to bear in mind that the interpretation of macroeconomic data (particularly from Rosstat) is usually met with doubts concerning its validity and consistency. As we shall see below, the data presented here is primarily to be judged not by its nominal, but by its relative value, which will reveal tendencies on the labour market and strategies for recruitment companies.

Labour Market(s) The figures above represent a quantitative approach to showing the disparate distribution of wealth in the country by comparing the different salary levels per capita. This development has reached a stage where it seems appropriate to break up the national labour market into several markets according to the *size* of organizations in these markets, their affiliation to a certain *industry*, their *geographical* location and their *ownership*. Furthermore, these markets now often exist independently from each other, making it at times impossible for individuals to migrate from one market to another.

A few exemplary characteristics (necessarily disregarding a complex matrix of parameters) of middle and top management executives found in these markets will give a rough idea of how the markets have shaped the careers of these individuals (and vice versa) since the downfall of the Soviet Union. Many recruitment companies in Russia use this data as landmarks when setting out strategies for business development, determining roles and profiles for recruitment projects or setting up candidate databases.

Labour Markets and their Population

Size of the Enterprise As in any economy, the size of a company influences the organizational behaviour of its employees and demands distinct management styles. From a Western point of view, large Russian enterprises are still characterized by a great degree of bureaucracy, strong hierarchies and a centralization of power reminiscent of Soviet times. On the other hand, companies from the SMB sector, which were generally founded in the mid-nineties, are very much shaped by the individual members of the management team. In both cases it is crucial to remember how certain traits of the Russian management style will have different effects on an organization, depending on its size.

> At any point in time, the Russian management model always remains in either one of two possible modes – either in the stable, calm mode, or it changes into the unstable, emergency or crisis mode of management. In the unstable mode, management is conducted with non-competitive, administrative-distributive measures. In moving towards the unstable mode, the style of behaviour radically changes on all managerial levels. The management system becomes aggressively competitive (Prokhorov 2003).

Both modes of management (entailing different management styles, for example, behaviour control vs. result control) can be found in both large and SMB companies. However, in small enterprises the change from one mode into another happens more frequently, as the companies are under more pressure to respond to changes in the market. Also, changes in mode are sometimes difficult to anticipate, because business processes have not been properly implemented and sometimes not even formulated. It is therefore difficult to integrate a manager from a large into a small enterprise, and whenever such a transfer does happen, he or she is hired for a senior position in order to conduct radical changes, implement business processes and eventually lead the company towards growth. Traditionally, this is accompanied by a marked change in the company's staff, as the new managers often swiftly replace large numbers of employees with new recruits of his choice. This procedure is referred to as 'arriving with your team' – [*prikhod s kommandoy*].

On the other hand, the change from an SMB firm to a large corporation can be more attractive, particularly if the company represents a well-known brand and can offer a higher salary with a better benefit structure. This may outweigh the loss in influence and freedom to make decisions, but integration into a large company in many ways depends on how well a new staff member is able to integrate into the micro-group of colleagues who generally form a department. This can be difficult at times, as departments in Russian companies are known to form a cluster structure within the Russian management model:

> In the majority of Russian commercial organizations, power is built like a bunch of grapes, that is firstly from top to bottom and secondly by clusters, entirely enclosed groups shaped like the biological cells in the grapes' peels – and although some sort of information ties [and others] may exist between them, the seclusion of every group is predominant (Prokhorov 2003).

Differences in size are mirrored by an increasing polarization of salary levels in large organizations. The need to recruit executives who have gained experience in managing enterprises within a transformational economy means searching for a very rare breed. Unfortunately, internal recruitment does not usually supply a sufficient number of candidates, as companies have only recently begun to pursue a fundamental policy of benchbuilding [*kadrovy rezerv*] and succession planning aligned with corporate strategies. Recruitment departments are forced to either 'poach' candidates from their competitors (which is generally not considered unethical) or to use the services of recruitment firms. In any case, this raises both overall attrition rates and salary levels, rendering many SMB companies unable to compete.

Industry In Western economies, industries form their own labour markets primarily by uniting professionals with certain capabilities. General management skills supersede specific knowledge and skills as the employee progresses towards the top of the organizational hierarchy. Due to political, economical and sociological changes at the beginning of the nineties, the majority of Russian managers were neither educated nor trained to work in various, suddenly emerging roles, or to adapt to substantial changes in their tasks. Since then, it has not been unusual to see engineers working in the banking business, doctors working in law firms or nuclear physicists selling cars. For some, this has become a major trait of corporate Russia in general:

> The analysis of actual managerial decisions taken in organizations shows that the manager's former experience, his subconscious mechanisms of perceiving reality, the evaluation of oneself and the environment have a far greater impact on management practices than knowledge acquired in institutions of higher education. It is this cultural difference, which is totally incomprehensible to foreigners, evokes their bewilderment and leads to spreading myths, pinning labels and raising prejudice (Krol et al 2004).

Although practical experience in any profession still overrides knowledge obtained in an institution of higher education, times are beginning to change and more attention is being paid to professional education. A maturing economy is faced with growing competition and therefore demands a more competitive edge, which only professionally educated and trained staff can provide. As we shall see, this has also raised the importance of a well-founded human resources management approach within HR departments. The oil industry (regardless of its peculiarities) is considered to have been the forerunner in this respect, having combined local expertise and Western management savvy three to five years prior to other industries. Today, the fast developing industries with Western management styles are catching up and go to great lengths in hiring professionals. Thus it does not come as a surprise that the oil industry as well as the retail, banking, real estate, communications and IT industries are employing a growing number of foreigners in middle and top management positions.

Geography If migration from the regions to the capital(s) has always been a strong trend since Soviet times, movement in the opposite direction has remained the exception.

Today as much as then professionally experienced specialists or independent high potentials move to Northern regions for well-paid jobs, save up some money and return after some years to central Russia to settle down. On the other hand, some of these professionals are beginning to consider staying on, as some of the less accessible towns in Russia's North have become increasingly attractive due to the rise in living standards and a better infrastructure (for example, Khanty-Mansysk, Nizhnevatorsk).

By far more significant in numbers are professionals who move within a Federal Subject to its capital or from a regional capital to Moscow, St Petersburg, Yekaterinburg or Novosibirsk, currently the most important hubs of the labour markets. Professionally experienced specialists and middle to top management executives usually leave their families behind when moving to these centres. Mostly, the family also moves to the capital after a year or two. Another group are young and mobile graduates, who actively look for jobs in the capitals as they are faced with unemployment in their small home towns or villages.

The geographic factor is most striking when it comes to salary levels. If a Moscow taxi driver today earns over US $1,000/month, a car salesman over US

$3,000 and a computer programmer (C++, ABAP, JAVA, Visual C, SQL) over US $4,000, it becomes obious that the average salary levels listed by Rosstat in Table 8.6 have little nominal significance for the Russian capital. As a rule of thumb, St Petersburg reaches 80 per cent of the Moscow salary level, Ekaterinburg 60 per cent and Novosibirsk 50 per cent.

Ownership One of the most influential parameters for forming labour markets has become the question of ownership. Here, the biggest rift runs between the state and the private sector. The gap is still growing, as privately held enterprises are being successfully modernized and most organizations from the state sector are disintegrating because of continuous underfunding. It is no secret that HR managers generally consider most candidates from the state sector to be of low motivation, inadequately educated and hopelessly corrupt. And if migration to the private sector has become nearly impossible for civil servants (exceptions are cases where top officials, for example, become board members), employees from the private sector hardly see any incitement (including financial) to move to the state sector. Enterprises with the state as the majority shareholder take up an intermediate position. The five main variations of company ownership are listed below.

1. Enterprises foreign shareholder / joint venture
2. Enterprises major shareholder private/public & western management style
3. Enterprises major shareholder private/public & Russian management style
4. Enterprises major shareholder state
5. Organizations from state sector

Increasingly, the gaps between privately held Russian companies with a Russian management style, privately held Russian companies with a Western management style and Western/joint venture companies are becoming wider. For certain roles, many Western companies reject all applications from candidates over 35 who have never worked in a Western management environment before. These candidates are considered unable to integrate into Western business processes, adopt best practices and feel comfortable in a Western corporate culture, or the process of achieving these goals seems too costly.

The above-mentioned ranking reflects salary levels only to a certain degree. If the overall salary levels of employees in Western companies are still higher compared to Russian companies, the salaries of top executives in large Russian companies by far exceed the levels paid in Western companies (particularly if they are competitors). The leap from mid to top management in a Western company generally signifies breaking the US $200k/a salary barrier. In Russian companies executives can expect up to three times this remuneration and the proportion remains the same for Russian specialists and foreigners with skills rarely found on the Russian labour market (for example, risk management, investment banking and so on).

In Moscow, the overall salary levels for certain profiles are beginning to reach inflationary levels that have forced many Western companies to adjust their pay levels in order to keep attrition rates low. On the other hand, Western companies are still considered attractive employers because of motivators such as corporate education and training and the practical experience to be gained working there. Even now, this still outweighs a Russian university degree in Economics or an MBA.

A striking example here is the auditing profession, where the 'Big Four' have successfully recruited and developed young talents from prestigious institutions of higher education. Today, many Russian companies are looking for controllers, internal auditors or CFOs who have gained experience in working with various Western accounting standards. Many of the young 'senior consultants' from the 'Big Four' (who have not finished their ACCA or CPA) are 'poached' by Russian companies, which offer them two to three times their current remuneration and sometimes promote a senior consultant to the position of CFO overnight.

Middle and Top Management Stereotypes Although a new generation of professionals who witnessed the collapse of the Soviet Union at a very young age has now emerged, most of the middle to top management executives were educated and received their first professional experience during Soviet times. Based on this assumption, A. P. Prokhorov (Prokhorov 2003) distinguishes four main groups of managers whose mentality was on the one hand formed in the Communist past and on the other has undergone great changes since Russia's turn towards a market economy. One thing that has not changed according to Prokhorov is the fact that these groups socially hardly ever mingle and whenever they are obliged to interact professionally, this always leads to almost insurmountable conflict.

The first group, *otstavniki* [the ones who resigned] represents middle to top level managers of former production plants who were educated in a strictly administrative style of management with its harsh and tough military ways, which results in their granting very few rights to employees and eliminating their independent thinking. Their strong sides are a hands-on approach to business, discipline, and organizational talent. Today, these managers can be found in large Russian-owned enterprises throughout the country's dominant industries, where they still adhere to the described Russian management style.

The second group, *byvshiye spekulyanty* [the former speculators] tend to be found in the trade sector. Their strongest trait is an intuitive understanding of money and the ability to work under difficult conditions with maximum mobility. They know how to make use of networks and make profit on the fringes of legality by setting up financial schemes in order to evade taxes. Their weakness is the fact that they mostly lack any professional or academic training.

The third group, highly educated professionals, *biznesmeny-intelektualy* [the businessmen-intellectuals] are usually former teachers, medics, lawyers, psychologists and civil servants with a higher education. Their main strength is professional savvy but they generally lack business acumen and leadership skills. They are often found in industries such as insurance, pharmaceuticals, business advisory and IT.

The fourth and smallest group comprises former functionaries of the Komsomol and the Communist Party. They never really learned how to earn or save money, but were great in administering state budgets, allocating funds and conducting large-scale projects. Their negative sides are well known: cronyism, red tape and bribery. The biggest damage done to the state during privatization can usually be traced to people from this group. Today, they can be found at the executive level in private companies with state ownership or in organizations from the state sector.

Tendencies on the Moscow Recruitment Market

The Market

HR Deficit In general, the chief strategy for most Russian companies during the privatization process of the nineties was to acquire a maximum of assets, followed by the goal to secure maximum market share. Today, the focus has moved towards human resources as overall growth and the maturity of some markets have led to an unprecedented demand in professionals. Unfortunately, the labour markets have turned out to be unprepared for such a demand, which is currently felt when searching for specialists and qualified executives for middle to top management positions. Broadly discussed in the Russian press under the term '*kadrovy golod*' [human resources famine], this development came as a surprise to most employers, who hardly ever paid much attention to acquiring and developing their human resources.

> A few years ago only the very progressive leaders thought about how to select the best candidates, integrate them properly into the company and how to motivate and manage them in order to achieve best results (Ivanova 2005).

The HR deficit also came as a surprise to many employees, who are now increasingly assessing their professional value on the labour markets independent of their organizations. Consequently, attrition rates have soared in all the industries, prompting an increase in overall salary levels. Nowadays, many employers complain about the lack of corporate loyalty at all levels of organizational hierarchies. In 2005, these were the main tendencies to influence the recruitment market, increasing both the importance of HR departments in organizations and the role of recruitment firms.

Given the demographic development, these tendencies will intensify rather than abate, if the overall population is to drop by one third by 2050. As early as 2013, the number of graduates from institutions of higher education in Russia will begin to drop significantly due to the very low birth rates of the early nineties. But the drop in numbers is exacerbated by a lack of professional education facilities providing graduates with the knowledge and skills to match role profiles in enterprises. According to L. Evenko (Evenko 2005), only 20,000 graduates receive an MBA every year. He estimates the current demand at between 3.5 and 4 million trained economists with various specializations.

Compensation The dynamic developments on the labour markets are also reflected in a fifth parameter in addition to *size*, *industry*, *geography* and *ownership* of enterprises. It concerns the *legality of compensation*. Again, the tendency is clear: many companies are striving to consolidate their accounts according to Western standards and are forced to pay taxes and an official 'white' salary [*belaya zarplata*] without any underhand additional payments 'in the envelope' [*v konverte*]. Unfortunately, the majority of Russian companies still only pay their employees small nominal salaries and the remaining sum 'in the envelope'.

The low salary figures delivered by Rosstat in Table 8.6 can be partly attributed to the low salaries paid officially. At the same time, the official salary has become an important motivator for employees and candidates. Here, the all-clean policy of Western companies is beginning to pay off, as a 'white salary' has become a competitive advantage for recruiting professionals. With consumer loans and mortgages gaining in popularity, the attractiveness of a legal 'white' salary is substantial for service providers who demand legal proof of income like anywhere else in the world. In 2005 according to various sources, employees receiving 'white salaries' in privately/publicly held companies with a Western management style and in companies with foreign shareholders saw a salary increase of a little over 11 per cent. Interestingly, most of the RUR based salaries in foreign companies/joint ventures rose higher than US $-based salaries.

Some companies have recently introduced flexible compensation packages, which allow employees to choose benefits from a modular system. On top of the list are medical insurance, gym memberships, company cars and luncheon vouchers, followed by corporate mobile phones and laptops. Corporate pension schemes remain the exception (little over 13 per cent), but corporate loans have become widespread among privately owned enterprises.

Companies The Association of Recruitment Consultants [*Assotsyatsya Konsultantov po Podbory Personala – AKPP*] comprises around 1,500 executive search and recruitment agencies in Russia, with 150 member agencies based in Moscow alone. The overall revenue of the Russian market is estimated at US $100 million (US $60 million for Moscow).

As opposed to a Western understanding, the term executive search in Russian has partially undergone a change in semantics. While Western executive search companies exclusively fill positions paying more than US $150k/a, most Russian executive search firms start to operate at much lower levels and use the term mostly for advertising purposes. Furthermore, many Russian companies offer both traditional recruitment and executive search services and substantiate the difference with higher fees for the latter. Only very few companies in Moscow can be considered genuine executive search agencies. The majority are foreign brands, whereby some of the international companies have transformed their subsidiaries into licensed representative offices in which the licensee pays most operational costs and a fee to the headquarters abroad: This is the case with Adjuvare (Whitehead Mann Group), Amrop Hever Group, Boyden, Egon Zehnder, IIC Partners, Morgan

Hunt, Neumann International, Preng and Co, Ray and Berndtson, RosExpert (Korn/Ferry International) and Ward Howell.

Like Western executive search companies, many of the Western recruitment companies have only gradually come back to Russia after the crisis of 1998. On this market, there is fierce competition with the many Russian companies, which have been successfully operating since the mid-nineties. In most Russian ratings, companies are classified by their fee structure. Leaving aside the agencies charging fees of more than 20 per cent of annual compensation, the most important players on the Moscow market are: Agentstvo Kontakt, Ancor, Antal, Avenir, BLM-Consort, Coleman Services, CVO Group, Evropersonal, Go Getter, Imikor, Kelly Services, Imperia Kadrov, KPG Resources, Manpower CIS, Metropolis, Norman DL, Penny Lane Consulting, Russian Connection and Staffwell.

Instruments The print media still play a major role for publicizing vacancies. Openings in the blue-collar and junior executive market are placed in *Rabota dlya Vas*, *Priglashayem na Rabotu*, *Est Rabota*, *Rabota i Zarplata*, *Rabota Segodnya* and the popular *Iz Ruk v Ruki*. More senior and specialist vacancies are advertised in *Exclusive Personnel* and *Elitny Personal*. The latter publishes articles on HR issues and has become a forum for HR managers. Adverts for more senior positions are to be found in *Vedomosti*, and Western companies tend to advertise in *The Moscow Times*.

Job boards [*dzhob bordy*] on the Internet are also very popular. Unfortunately, most of these sites are not very well hosted and offer little additional services to employers. On the other hand, they represent large data bases which can be easily searched by selecting parameters. Examples of such websites are 'job.ru', 'jobcenter.ru', 'rabota.ru', 'jobtoday.ru', 'kdm.ru', 'rdw.ru', 'izrukvruki.ru', and 'rezume-bank.ru'. A more advanced tool in this respect is the job site 'headhunter.ru', used by HR departments as well as recruitment agencies. Free of charge to candidates, it offers additional services to employers and agencies, such as standard candidate invitation letters and SMS notification. Another interesting project is 'e-xecutive.ru', an Internet portal created by Ward Howell, which unites the 'professional community' composed of middle to top management executives. Access is only gained upon recommendation from a member. The site provides articles on management issues, education, vacancies, business news, discussions, chats, and so on.

Tendencies

Many of the tendencies listed below are due to a Muscovite perspective on the market and may therefore not affect the majority of recruitment companies. The tendencies for HR departments listed here are applicable to companies with a Western management style.

HR departments:

- Management sees HR as a strategic business unit
- HR departments introduce human capital management
- Emergence of recruitment groups in HR departments (active search)
- New compensation and motivation systems (flexible benefits, corporate pensions and loans)
- Corporate training and education management (not provision!)
- Emergence of close ties between HR departments and educational institutions (career fairs, partnerships).

Recruitment companies:

- Greater overall demand in executive search and recruitment services
- Greater differentiation between executive search and recruitment services
- Greater differentiation of firms according to industries
- Greater integration of services (selection, search, assessment, coaching, consulting, Internet-based services)
- Expansion into hubs (St Petersburg, Yekaterinburg, Novosibirsk, Kazan)
- Greater demand in outstaffing and outplacement services
- Greater demand in HR consulting combined with IT consulting
- Focus on high-quality rather than high-quantity databases (regular updates, categorized candidates)
- Demand in boutique agencies due to industry specialization and higher confidentiality
- Long-term client relationships
- Partnerships with local agencies
- Partnerships with international agencies.

Field Data: Employment in a Medium-sized Russian IT Company

> The IT sector is the most civilized type of business in Russia [by the standard of its interior structures]. (Prokhorov 2003)

The Company

Introduction The company discussed here would be classified as a 'New Economy' enterprise, a medium-sized IT company based in Moscow and founded in 1997 as a privately/publicly held enterprise by four shareholders (the current CEO and three leading specialists employed in various departments of the company). According to the Civil Code of the Russian Federation, the legal entity is a closed joint stock company [*zakrytoe aktsyonernoye obshestvo – ZAO*] and is consequently not obliged to publish annual reports. The founders of the company all have degrees in technical professions; while other key management positions are held by qualified economists from Russia and abroad.

Brief History In many ways, the history of this company epitomizes the development of medium-sized Russian organizations over the last ten years. Its shareholders clearly belong to the third group of Russian management stereotypes, the 'businessmen-intellectuals' (see above). In Soviet times, these extremely gifted individuals would probably have become scientists at a research centre, but the economic development of the country left them with no choice but to start a company and embark upon a career in business. On a personal level, this intensified the ties amongst them and created a specific start-up atmosphere in which team spirit, dedication and product knowledge were more important than business acumen.

Table 8.7 Key data for 2002 and 2003

		2002	2003
Sales (in US$ Mill.)	Sales volume	11.2	15.5
	Target sales volume	-	20.7
Sales according to geographical markets (in %)	CIS	51	50
	Europe	31	32
	Overseas	18	18
Personnel		300	345
Expenditure on personnel of overall expenditure (in %)		34	32
Distribution of expenditure on personnel (in %)	Administration	27	21
	Russian Sales	11	10
	International Sales	10	9
	Marketing	8	12
	Service	6	6
	Development	38	42

The difficulties began when the organization started to grow and the gap between ownership and managerial positions within the hierarchy of the organization led to confusion concerning the distribution of power, responsibilities and authorities. Some reached the peaks of their careers rather early in time and others (like the CEO) took up the more responsible roles.

At this stage of the company's development the individual traits of the company leaders became evident and the weaknesses of the 'businessmen-intellectuals', their lack of leadership skills and inability to build organizations, were increasingly felt. The influx of new personnel from the other three groups aggravated the situation and created the need for more refined business processes and more formalized information flow. The highly educated and talented management team (in particular the CEO) realized that the organization was only going to survive if it overcame the start-up atmosphere and implemented changes for further growth.

When the author was hired at the end of 2003, many of the processes and practices had been implemented, but they either turned out not to be functional or had led to results that were completely different from what had originally been intended.

In 2003, the company was audited by KPMG according to IFRS, which revealed a net loss for the year 2002 of US $35,000. In 2003 the net loss had already been turned into net profit and the company became the market leader in its segment on the Russian market. During 2004 the company was struggling with a handful of competitors for the fourth position in the global market ranking. The company in third position was generating 30 times the revenues of the Russian company, the one in second position 60 times and the global leader 120 times.

At the time, the company was structured into departments according to functional responsibilities: CEO and Administration, Technical Department, Sales Department, Marketing Department, Russian Office, Client Service Department, HR Department and Local Offices abroad.

According to internal figures the company's labour productivity in 2003 was 20 per cent that of the industry leader. At the beginning of 2002, the CEO recognized the increasing difficulties within the company and issued a strategy paper containing a SWOT analysis, which was distributed to all employees.

Strengths: Expert knowledge
Weaknesses: Leap from small to large company, business process, documentation, low product quality, low customer focused functionality of product, long product to market cycles, low quality of after sales services
Opportunities: New markets abroad, OEM sales
Threats: New strategic partnership between competitors and global IT players, acquisition by competitor

Additionally, the CEO gave the order [*prikaz*] to implement an HR policy intended to make the company more competitive. This was presented to the staff and published on the Intranet:

- Key targets were:
  - Higher professional standards
  - Higher professional capabilities
  - Better work environment
  - Better employee development
- Key fields were:
  - Effectiveness of training
  - Knowledge management
  - Self-learning organization
  - Integration (adaptation) program

- Instruments were:
  - New job descriptions (general regulations, work conditions, main responsibilities, rights and work conditions, planning and control)
  - Assessment in hiring process
  - Search among friends
  - New bonus system (years, sales, projects)
  - Optional elements of compensation package
- Corporate culture was defined through:
  - Tradition
  - Team spirit
  - Common values

As a result, the attrition rate in 2002 remained unchanged compared to the year before, 34 people were dismissed and 79 people were hired, including professionals for key positions such as Head of Technical Department, Head of Sales and Head of Russian Office. But while the attrition rate was not unexceptional on the middle to low levels of management, the situation was very different on the top management level. In 2003, the company hired and dismissed two sales directors (but eventually filled the position permanently). A year later, the author witnessed how two marketing directors from abroad were hired and dismissed again before they had finished their trial period. This position then remained vacant for some time and was eventually also filled with an internal candidate.

Obviously, employment as a content editor in a marketing department did not give the author insight into the reasoning behind many management decisions. On the other hand, being the target of the HR policy and witnessing its results amongst peers left the author with only one conclusion: not one of the goals listed above was actually being reached. At the same time, and this is important to stress, some of the business targets were still met and the company continued to grow.

The Position

Search and Hiring I was hired for the role of content manager in the marketing department after responding to an advert in *The Moscow Times* in English. After a very brief conversation on the phone with an HR manager in Russian in order to verify details given in the advert, I sent off my CV and received and invitation for an interview within three days.

As the company's office was located in a formerly secret research facility, the admission permit system for the premises was even stricter than is usually the case with ordinary office centres. At the admission office my pass [*propusk*] had not been prepared in time, and I was told to wait until the manager who had invited me could be identified. After several phone calls to the HR department and my passport being photocopied, I was escorted to the HR department by a young employee from the admission office 'making sure I wouldn't go astray, as this building is still a top secret object'.

The HR manager received me with politeness and asked me how to print out the CV I had sent, because she was not familiar with pdf files. After a joint effort we succeeded in not just printing out my own CV, but also other candidates' CVs, some of whom were to be interviewed for the same position on the same day. A white board next to the entrance stated existing vacancies with the number of candidates who had applied and the last names of successful candidates recently hired.

I was introduced to the line manager (my future boss) who turned out to be a Russian-speaking expatriate, conducting the interview in English and Russian with familiar Western content. This did not resemble a structured interview, but touched professional, educational and personal moments of my biography. I was given the chance to ask frank questions and received exhaustive answers. The HR manager would sometimes ask a few questions on topics that had already been discussed in English, but the line manager would always ease the situation. On leaving I was told to wait for an answer within the next days and I left the building again escorted by the young employee from the admission department making sure I would not go astray among the stray cats and some elderly women selling raw meat, sausages and other produce on the ground floor next to the main exit.

A week later I called the HR manager and was told that they were still in the process of interviewing candidates but apparently my chances of getting hired were very high as the majority of other candidates 'were of terrible quality'. Another two weeks later I was told I was to start my job at the beginning of the following month.

My first day at work consisted of dropping by at the HR department to have my photograph taken for the Intranet and to sign two documents:

1. 'A Service Agreement (in English) continuing for the period of three months governed by and construed in accordance with the laws of England.' It stated the monthly remuneration which was to be paid out every month, additional remuneration in compliance with the company's internal regulations, the payment of mobile telephone bills according to the company's mobile communications payment policy and the opportunity to study foreign languages with a personal tutor. My duties were stated as follows (given here with all the grammatical mistakes of the original):
   - 'Translation and adaptation of information materials of the company (news, advertising brochures, catalogues and so on.) on the German language
   - On special inquiries – translation of the German texts into Russian
   - Monitoring of group of the German-speaking news sites determined by the head
   - Update of corporate Web-sites
   - Qualitative development of the corporate site'
2. 'Confidentiality Agreement (in English) governed by and construed in accordance with the laws of the Russian Federation.'

When I mentioned the medical insurance and gym discount promised in the interview, I was told that this would only apply after the three month trial period.

Integration For the rest of my first day I was introduced to my colleagues in my future department and was shown my workplace. The content management department consisted of six editors (four expatriates, two Russians) and one department head (another expatriate), all working together in a room of approx. four by five meters. Since we were part of the marketing department it seemed a little strange not to be introduced to the whole team, but the fact that they were working in different rooms did not make anyone feel awkward. On the other hand, I was introduced to the IT department responsible for website management.

My colleagues showed me how to operate the content management system and took me to the lunchroom, where a three-course daily meal was served free of charge. I was told that the expatriates were generally not too enthusiastic about the quality of the food, and when I witnessed a few cases of food poisoning a few months later (which, of course, only affected expatriates), I was convinced of staying away from the cafeteria. Eventually, only the Russian members of our department used to have lunch there.

Because I was employed as a lecturer, the company did not have to register me like other expatriates. It must be said that the HR department went to great lengths to supply non-residents with the proper registration stamps in their passports [propiska] and on their migration cards. Additionally, all foreigners were given full visa support for multiple-entry one-year visas and a work permit.

Work Once the trial period was over, I never got to sign any further documents concerning my employment, although I was offered medical insurance and the opportunity to visit the local gym.

Very soon interdepartmental problems started to arise, very much in line with the cluster theory of Prokhorov's Russian management model. It seems noteworthy that the first clashes occurred with staff from departments I initially had not been introduced to. The PR manager and the Head of Market Communications (who was engaged to one of the shareholders) formed one cluster, which was trying to gain influence over another cluster, our content management department. Gradually, misunderstandings escalated into an overt struggle, in which all tools of office warfare were used (holding back information, setting each other up, overtly insulting each other trough e-mails and so on.) Unfortunately, the situation couldn't be defused and was only resolved when the CEO moved the most notorious brawlers into different departments.

The second main trait of the Russian management model, its change of modes from *zastoy* [calm mode] to *avral* [emergency mode] soon became the chief characteristic of all work processes. Whenever a project was started across departments, every department would wait until one of the other departments would start to act. As soon as it became clear that the deadline would not be met everyone spent most of their time and energy finding the culprit. Once the culprit had been determined (and for bigger projects that would mean being fired) everyone changed into the *avral* mode, doing extra hours even at weekends. Those who would sacrifice most of their free time and managed to convey this to the top management would then be rewarded like heroes.

Anticipating the changes in mode became one of the main challenges. Soon I realized that reading the face of our head of department after a meeting with the CEO, getting the latest informal info from the smokers' corner [*kurilka*] or knowing who had lunch together was more important than any e-mails or meetings. Fortunately, I didn't suffer the fate of the two marketing directors who had come to Russia from large Western corporations without any knowledge of the language and culture. Their fate is best demonstrated by three e-mails the CEO sent to the employees of the company upon engagement and dismissal of John West (name changed):

> We searched for an appropriate candidate for this opening for a long time, the future of the company depends on professional management. We are pleased to welcome John to our team and are sure that his experience and knowledge will further our position in the global marketplace, as well as supporting our on-going product development and the successful promotion of our products throughout the world.

One day before Christmas (John had already sent out his Christmas and New Year's wishes in an upbeat e-mail) we all received an e-mail (marked 'urgent!') as soon as the paramedics had left the building and John had recovered from a light heart attack:

> I regret to inform you that today we have cancelled our contract with marketing director Mr West as he did not pass the trial period. I feel sorry for this happens, but it was our first experience of hiring a person from abroad and we learnt a lot from it. I hope in future recruitment we will avoid the mistakes we did now.

The Russian version of the email, which was sent out nearly simultaneously sounded a little different (translated by the author):

> Working with John meant giving him a list of tasks, as he did not come up with any ideas of his own concerning the development of his department. I therefore had to set tasks for him – something I don't usually do with my top managers. He completed these tasks by using other people's ideas (sometimes even without making any amendments or corrections), putting his name under these ideas and pretending to be the author. I believe that the marketing department has a sufficient number of professionals who do not need an extra layer of management. Although I personally liked John, I believe that I have made myself clear. The company doesn't need lazy-bones and part-timers who conceal their lack of results behind fancy words. Sooner or later these people will be brought to light and expelled from our company!

The lack of formalized communication soon became disturbing. The Marketing Department would meet once a week on Mondays, when the Head of Product Marketing would give a speech and ask everyone for a report on past results and coming targets. These reports were often presented with trembling voices as the boss would openly scold members of the department for insufficient performance. An 'I want you in my office' would then be a final sentence and would always leave people guessing whether the person summoned would come back to work the next day. At the same time it became clear that this kind of management style was either conducted intentionally or intuitively, deeply engrained in the manager's mentality.

Compensation Monthly salaries were always paid in US $ cash ('black salary'). The employees were usually informed by e-mail to drop by at the accountancy department and receive payment. In the course of 2004, the company evidently tried to consolidate its accounts. As a consequence, monthly payments for Russian employees were processed through a cash dispenser, which appeared on the premises of the company. Bonus payments always came as a surprise. They were issued after the successful completion of a project such as the launch of a new corporate website. Additionally, people were given t-shirts and cups bearing the company's logo sometime after the project had finished. This would happen randomly, as nobody ever really knew the point in time, when a project had actually been finished.

Dissolution of the HR Department Leaving the company implied receiving signatures from a list of people [*obkhodnoy list*], including the HR director, whom I thus finally had a chance to meet. I was surprised to find her in a nearly empty office but soon learned that she was also just about to leave the company, because the CEO had decided to dissolve the HR department altogether. One HR manager (the woman who had conducted my initial interview together with my future boss) was to stay on as part of the accounting department to administer HR documentation, while all other responsibilities from hiring to HR development were to be handed over to the line managers. The leaving head of HR was pleased with the decision since she had been in constant conflict with the CEO over the performance of leading managers.

Conclusion The liquidation of the HR department was met with shock by the staff. Line managers were suddenly faced with tasks they had never been trained for. On the other hand, I never had the impression that the HR department was taken seriously by the management, a fact the HR director would eventually confirm. Apart from organizing corporate parties, holidays and visa support and improving compensations schemes, the department was never consulted on strategic decisions.

Throughout my time at this IT company, I was fascinated to see the Russian management model in action as it emerged from the basis of an imposed Western business model through the individual traits of the management team.

Thus, Western management concepts remained abstract notions and Western terminology underwent semantic changes, for example 'customer focus' here meant designing a product only specialists knew how to operate and setting up an after-sales hotline with a US phone number, 'internal communication' meant conversing with people next door through e-mail or informally in the smokers' corner, and 'performance assessment' amounted to scolding staff in public or dismissing executives whenever the CEO felt like it. Disappointed with many of the Western concepts, the 'buzinesmeny-intellectuals' intuitively resorted to the Russian management model. The changes from *zastoy* [stagnation] to *avral* [emergency] mode were compelling to observe but very annoying to endure and it took some time to understand how to anticipate the change from one mode into another.

In the end, I learned that one of the secrets of Russian management is to know when the time has come to implement the '*avral'* mode. Knowing that only in this mode staff will work effectively, Russian executives understand when to put extreme pressure on staff, lash into people verbally or simply fire key members of staff in order to create this mode – in words of one executive: '*Inogda nado, shtoby narod ne rasslablyalsya!* [Sometimes you have to so the people don't relax!]'.

References

Evenko, L. (2005), 'Rynok MBA v Rossii Zhdyot Bum', *Izvestia* (14.10.2005).

Expert (2005), '400 Krupneyshykh kompaniy Rossiy', *Expert* (16.10.2005).

Ivanova, S.V. (2005), *Kandidat, Novichok, Sotrudnik. Instrumenty Upravlenya Personalom, Kotorye Realno Rabotayut na Praktike.*

Krol, L.M. et al. (2004), 'Upravlencheskaya Kultura Organizatsy'.

Prokhorov, A.P. (2003), 'Russkaya Model Upravlenya'.

Proskurnina, O. (2005), 'Grazhdanin Chukotki', *Vedomosti*, (24.10.2005).

Internet-based references

Federal State Statistics Service – ROSSTAT [website], (2005) <http://www.gks.ru>

Russian Union of Industrialists and Entrepreneurs – RSPP [website], (2005) <http://www.rspp.biz>

Chapter 9

Training and Development of Personnel in Russian Companies

Tatiana Soltitskaya and Tatiana Andreeva

Identifying the Problem

The competition for quality and new standards of doing business in a globalized world call for the creation of knowledge centres and efficient information policies and the continuous training and development of personnel in contemporary companies. According to J. Kay's model of the foundations of corporate success (Kay 1993), one of three strategic sources of competitive advantages is an organizational architecture that provides for the efficient usage of corporate knowledge. Therefore, every company striving to expand beyond the limits of local business faces the challenge of building a training and development system.

Let us start by specifying some definitions. The term 'training' has a double meaning – knowledge acquisition and skills development. Knowledge is an ability to answer questions about the reasons, characteristics, mechanisms, or dynamics of a phenomenon, process, or event. Skills are the ability to apply this knowledge in practice. Organizational life surely requires both knowledge and skills.

The problem of the efficient usage and development of organizational knowledge is undoubtedly a pressing issue for contemporary Russian companies. They face a difficult struggle with international competitors on many domestic markets, and they are losing their traditional price advantage as the cost of resources gradually evens out. Organizational skills and knowledge, management systems, and other internal factors turn into key sources of competitiveness in such a situation, with training and development systems among them. In this article, we tried to analyze the vast experience of St Petersburg University School of Management in the organization of corporate training programs.

Before starting our discussion of various trends in corporate training, we would like to highlight several factors that, in our opinion, influence the formation of training and development policies in Russian companies.

1. *Stage of life cycle.* Due to the specifics of the development of the domestic market economy, most Russian companies find themselves in one of the first three life-cycle stages in the L. Greiner model (Greiner 1972, 2002). Its position on the life-cycle curve largely defines a company's attitude towards

its internal resources in general and in particular towards its training policy, its most popular training topics, and so on. We will discuss this influence in detail later on.

2. *Peculiarities of education system.* The classical Russian system of education is mainly oriented on the general professional development of an individual, which influences the Russian managers' view of training tasks and results.

Another factor often mentioned in the mass media is the frequent discrepancy between basic education and the factual field of activities, both among managers and rank and file personnel. For the elder generations, this can be explained by the state policy for the preferential development of a technical education which existed a few decades ago. When the development of the market economy led to the formation of a realistic demand for various professions, thousands of highly qualified engineers found themselves unclaimed on the labour market as a result of this policy, and they started to look for employment in totally different fields. Interestingly, the variance between education and field of work often occurs among the younger generations as well. This happens because higher education is often seen mostly as a way to develop intellectual faculties, and therefore formal professions are chosen out of interest and/or the accessibility of education, while factual work is chosen by market demand or by chance. Overall, this leads to an intensive need for functional training in many Russian companies.

C. Fey, A. Pavlovskaya and N. Tang (Fey, Pavlovskaya and Tang 2004) identified this factor in their comparative study of training systems in Russian, Chinese and Finnish companies. They discovered that functional training is more relevant and necessary for Russian and Chinese than for Finnish employees. This is explained by the fact that the former often do not have a professional education and work in a field different from the one stated in their higher education diploma.

3. *Peculiarities of national business culture.* Russian business culture is widely discussed in the literature, but within the framework of this article we would like to draw attention to one particular trend: the rigid system of information secrecy developed in many Russian companies, first influenced by decades of functioning in a 'closed' bureaucratic system, and later as a result of a lack of knowledge of principles of efficient management. Such companies restrict and strictly regulate the exchange of information between departments and, to an even greater extent, between different management levels. The guiding principle of such systems amounts to 'employees need not know anything except their direct duties' (which are already quite narrowly defined).

We will discuss the influence of this factor later in this text, but let us make an important remark here. From the point of view of many western specialists, such as P. Senge (Senge 1996) and C. Argyris (Argyris and Schon 199), the knowledge possessed by an organization is much greater than just the sum of the knowledge of its employees. Individual training is an important but insufficient condition for the formation of organizational intelligence and the development of internal competitive advantages. D. Kim (Kim 1993) believes that organizational learning starts only at the moment when employees share their knowledge and/or skills.

Let us now analyze the training and development practices in Russian companies from the standpoint of contemporary theoretical concepts.

Stage of Life Cycle and Approach to Personnel Training and Development.

In our opinion, the features of the training and development policies in Russian companies can be correlated with key ideas from the Larry Greiner life-cycle concept (Greiner 1972, 2002). As one may recall, Greiner's concept presupposes that a company passes through particular stages in its process of growth and development. These stages are growth through 1) creativity, 2) direction, 3) delegation, 4) coordination, and 5) collaboration. Key management tasks and problems, as well as key success factors, are predetermined for each life-cycle stage, as they are influenced by the company's developmental path.

Key Training Needs

Our experience shows that companies in the first stage of their life cycle – growth through creativity – usually do not have a clear training and development policy. Training programs in these companies often follow 'fashionable' trends and are mostly oriented on the development of personnel loyalty and team spirit. The outcomes of such training programs are rarely followed up and assessed. The key factors of company development in this stage explain this trend.

In rare cases, companies in this stage may train their employees so that they develop some functional skills, but then they concentrate on the skills that are crucial for the company's survival (for example, knowledge of taxation regulations). These companies usually use external training companies to provide training.

More active training takes place in this stage only if a business is connected with fast-developing and high-tech services. In this case, raising the level of the employees' skills (mostly that of technicians and engineers) becomes the main physiological need of a company. An organization that deals with continuously renewed equipment, changing services, and so on, cannot function successfully until this need is satisfied.

Individual and organizational training are two different things, as we mentioned earlier. However, in the first stage of the life cycle of an organization, these two types of training are equivalent because employees tend to exchange knowledge and skills when socializing informally.

Here are some examples of the typical demands for training from companies in this stage. Several years ago, sales training was 'fashionable', and many famous companies ordered such training, though sales growth in this stage of development is usually caused by other factors. A new product – extreme training – has recently appeared on the market, and it is becoming more and more popular among companies because they regard it mainly as a form of corporate entertainment which increases loyalty.

In companies that are in a stage of growth, though, priorities in training become more structured. As a company grows, maintaining order becomes more important, and the management takes steps to organize training. It introduces regulations and formally describes work tasks, makes written correspondence and reports necessary, and so on. These are the first measures to maintain the same level of skills and knowledge in an organization, that is, to separate organizational and individual knowledge and training. It is at this stage that an elementary system of internal personnel training is formed. As regards the prior subjects of training, at this stage companies mostly focus on functional training in fields where they lack the competence for further development. For this group, sales training is very popular.

In the next stage – growth through delegation – companies tend to show an active interest in various types of training. Among the most popular topics here are:

- management training for middle management (the most typical demand for the last two years: 'Teach a manager to be a manager and to manage personnel')
- building an organizational structure
- forming/strengthening the corporate culture.

Companies in this group start to use training as a diagnostic instrument to evaluate and develop personnel, and they gradually develop corporate training centres. In their further development, training centres that function successfully start to offer their services to other companies, sharing their experience with clients, for example. Many Russian distributor companies have such experience, and they train both their employees and their partners during technical and management training courses, conferences, schools, and dealer schools.

As regards the programs for top managers, interest in strategic management training has arisen in the last two years in capitals and other large cities (this is apparently connected with a certain stage of growth). At the same time, significant changes in the demands on and expectations from such training have also taken place. Such training was previously often viewed as a strategy development session, in essence – a brainstorming session, with the trainer's main aim being to facilitate the process. Neurolinguistic specialists were often involved. Recently, demands have changed from this type of training to a more academic education, and within these limits, top managers are introduced to the theoretical problems of strategic management and the experience of successful companies in strategy development.

We would also like to mention the situation of knowledge management in Russian companies. These days, this topic is often discussed in countries with developed economies. In our opinion, and according to the Greiner model, this problem becomes immediately relevant to companies which are in the fifth stage of growth, which most Russian companies have not yet reached. The key problems of co-ordination and collaboration appear only in companies that work in intellectual fields or in huge holdings. And for most Russian companies, in our opinion, solving this problem is important only on the level of organizing the circulation of information within a company.

Assessing Results of Training

According to the Greiner classification, and in our opinion, the problem of a more effective and clear assessment of training results most often arises in companies that are between the second and the third stages of development. In our view, there are two main groups of such companies: those which have a result-oriented culture, and those whose culture is mainly oriented on personnel motivation. Let us examine their characteristics.

Companies with a result-orientated culture expect to get immediate results from training, and they want more from training programs than they can give. They want these programs to solve two problems: 'to gain more money' or 'to save time'. This is why such companies are often disappointed with their training results. Even if the expected changes take place after training in the company, they usually develop more slowly than the manager wants, and often he or she simply does not notice them. In such cases, we believe satisfaction with the training results can be increased in several ways:

- by using only the type of training that provides an immediate and guaranteed result (of course, the range of such training services is not very wide)
- by introducing an internal training manager in such companies so that he or she can carry out a combined assessment of the training results; this is difficult for a normal personnel manager or external trainer to do
- by explaining to a client the difference between knowledge and skills (and the speed of their development), and by introducing a strict system of knowledge control at the end of the training (tests, and so on).

For companies whose culture is oriented towards personnel motivation, the main result of training is that the employees want to continue working in the company and improve their working skills. In these companies, detailed analyses of the training needs are carried out before ordering a training program. Another characteristic of these companies is that they are ready to realize long-lasting training programs, as they see a connection between the employees' development and the successful development of the company as a whole.

It is also interesting to see what Russian managers expect from strategy training (and, therefore, how they assess the training results), which, as we mentioned earlier, is becoming more and more popular. Usually, companies want to learn about modern strategy terminology and to develop a common language for their top management team during the training so that it can facilitate strategy discussions and the posing of problems. For some companies, this is the main result expected from strategy training. Beyond terminology, other companies want either:

- to agree on a development strategy for the near future (that is, to add practical training – brainstorming – to theoretical training) – in which case, the trainer needs good facilitating skills plus a knowledge of strategy theories
- or to get concrete 'hints' from a trainer about how to develop a company further – in which case, they want a trainer to be an industry expert or an authoritative consultant.

We would like to note that here we are mostly referring to companies based on Russian capital. Foreign companies in Russia usually order functional training, as they are mostly interested in acquiring specialized knowledge.

Influence of Organizational Culture on Personnel Training Policy

Let us analyze another aspect of training policy in Russian companies: the aspect of the organizational culture. The organizational culture in many ways determines a company's orientation towards personnel training and also the peculiarities of its training policy. E. Schein defines an organizational culture as 'accumulating training results on the basis of previous success' (Mumford 1980).

Schein thinks that these days, only a few companies have a training culture. Describing the culture of a training-oriented organization, the researcher formulated the characteristics of an organizational culture which contributes to the development of training processes in a company and of a culture which hinders the development of employee motivation for training (see Table 9.1).

In modern companies, according to J. Boyette and J. Boyette (2002), the organizational culture is far from the ideal one described by E. Schein and other researchers. Unfortunately, our experience proves that in many Russian companies, the organizational culture hinders training.

For training to take place, Schein (Mumford 1980) suggests creating 'parallel systems' in an organization that would guarantee a psychologically safe atmosphere for training and the practicing of skills, as well as the establishment of norms for rewarding creative thinking and experimentation. An example of such a parallel organization is offered by corporate universities that function in collaboration with consultants, business schools and research centres.

Informational Culture and Personnel Training Policy

The attitude towards information in an organization is a component of the organizational culture and is determined by its values and aims. This component is one of the definitive ones for a training system. Donald A. Marshand (1999) describes four types of informational culture which can be found in modern companies (see Table 9.2). Let us view this classification and its variants in Russian companies in detail.

Table 9.1 Cultures contributing to training in an organization or hindering training

Culture contributing to training	Culture hindering training
1. Brings interests of all sides into balance (no single groups – consumers, hired managers, providers, stockholders, local authorities and so on – is the most important to managers, because managers understand that each of these groups, if they were allowed to dominate, could delay the development of the company or destroy it)	**1. Distinguishes between 'strict' and 'soft' problems** (problems connected with fulfilling tasks have priority over problems connected with relationships among people)
2. Is focused on people and not on systems (managers think that people can learn and will learn, and that they appreciate training and changes)	**2. Is focused on systems and not on people** (rational technocratic approach to organizing, with managers busy creating and maintaining systems)
3. Makes people believe that they can change their environment (people hold the common belief that they manage themselves and influence an organization. 'If we are sure that changing the world is impossible, what is training for?' E. Schein)	**3. Lets people change only if it is necessary** (people in these organizations are conservative, they concentrate on solving problems, not on innovations)
4. Provides time for training	**4. The main principle for employees is – 'to work all the time without rest'**
5. Chooses a holistic approach to problems (systematic thinking)	**5. Divides problems and makes employees solve separate problems and sub-problems** (analytical thinking)
6. Encourages open communications	**6. Limits information** (only necessary work and organizational information)
7. Is based on belief in group and team work	**7. Is based on belief in individual work and competition between employees**
8. Leaders are available for communicating (trainer)	**8. Authoritarian leaders** (chief)

Source: Schein 1994

Table 9.2 Classification of types of informational culture and training policy

Type of informational culture	Main characteristics of informational culture	Type of personnel training policy	Main characteristics of training policy
Functional	Information is used to control and influence employees	Functional	Specialists acquire highly specialized knowledge
Interaction	Atmosphere of confidence, active information exchange for preventing problems and adapting to changing environment	Problem-oriented training	Problem-oriented training for interfunctional groups
Research	Foresight is dominant informational activity	Perspective-oriented (anticipatory) training	Everyone, including top-managers, is in active training, emphasis on studying external experience
Openness	Employees and managers are open to new insights into nature of crises and to radical changes	Creative training	Non-traditional forms of training

Current Training Needs

The most typical informational activity in a functional informational culture is control. In the context of this culture, a functional policy of personnel training is formed. Firstly, the system aims at training specialists. The subject of the training is the concrete knowledge and skills that are necessary for a specialist's work: accounting standards, norms of personnel record keeping, changes in legislation for a company's lawyer, information system skills, and so on. The preferred training forms are tuition, training at the workplace, narrowly specialized workshops, and consultations with experts. The trainers are usually tutors, experienced specialists, or experts from legal, auditing and other consulting organizations. Secondly, the system is aimed at training department managers who usually are specialized in their fields, have received a specialized education and have no foundation in management. Often during the structuring stage of an organization, the top management realizes that the management competency level of the middle managers is low. The training program thus includes management courses and training practice where managers can learn about management functions, the procedure of delegating authority and planning department work, the informational instruments of management (from managing meetings to feedback procedures), and so on. Thus the main principle of a functional training system is 'to train every employee according to his or her duties'.

In a functional personnel training system, the need for training for each employee is diagnosed from the point of view of the organization's interests. Diagnosing the need for training for new employees includes analyzing the work tasks that will be given to the employees and the corresponding competencies necessary (special and management skills). Assessing a new employee in the stage of selection or adaptation, the HR department and training manager can diagnose key competencies by offering fragments of tasks and can then suggest the optimal training program for a candidate. The assessment of the training needs for all other employees is based on an analysis of the fulfilment of current work duties, which includes an evaluation of the work results of the employees with the aim of finding training options that could help solve problems such as low productivity.

On the one hand, in the context of this culture we find some tendencies that are characteristic, as we said earlier, of companies at the stage of growth through direction (in the L. Greiner model). However, in our opinion, in full measure this culture can be found in Russian companies with a strict hierarchy and a complex bureaucracy system (in large holdings and governmental bodies), irrespective of the particular stage of growth.

In an *interaction culture,* specialists and managers trust each other, and thus they can exchange information which is important for improving processes and increasing effectiveness. A direct information exchange about possible failures is necessary for solving problems and adapting to changes. In an information interaction culture, a *problem-oriented personnel training* policy is usually formed. Refusing to use traditional passive methods of training (lectures, seminars) means forming a system of problem-oriented training and conferences in which representatives of different functional departments take part. The training topics will depend on the problems that are currently important, initially those of the interfunctional interaction between departments and employees. For example, a workshop for the sales and procurement departments of a distributor could be devoted to the development of a sales strategy in the context of changes in the market demand for the company's products. Such training could be led by an invited trainer, a sales management expert, or a distribution manager. Workshop training consists of informational and analytical sections and involves working out a program of action. Recalling Greiner's model, our experience shows that such a training policy is widespread among Russian companies which are at the stage of growth through delegation – when interfunctional interaction is emphasized.

In a research culture, managers and employees try to understand future tendencies and find the best way to ward off possible danger. Everyone in the company – from the general director to the rank and file staff – should be 'alert'. An informational research culture, which makes the principle of foresight the basis of company success, does its best to orientate employees towards a perspective. In this case, a perspective-orientated personnel training policy is formed (so called 'anticipatory training'). In such companies, top managers and primary specialists who determine the direction of the development of the organization are trained first. They study the experiences of leading companies in different branches and regions, often invite marketing and management gurus to their company, and carry out conferences and symposiums for their employees to learn how to foresee and predict the future. Small companies that have an informational research culture often send their managers and employees to business training programs at leading universities and business schools; they primarily send them to learn new ways of thinking and to acquire new management techniques. In our opinion, this type of culture and training policy is seldom found in Russian companies; when it is found, it is mostly in entrepreneurial companies or in those which work in the fields of high-tech and intellectual services, as well as in companies where the key manager (usually the owner) feels a 'thirst for the new'.

The last type of culture is an openness culture. Such companies follow old business methods and deliberately refuse to free themselves to search for new perspectives and ideas that can contribute to changes in competition conditions beyond the bounds of industries and markets. A lot of companies have enclaves of an openness culture where they bring information together and process it, create new products and business development scenarios, and develop partnerships with consumers and providers.

An informational openness culture creates the necessary prerequisites for developing a creative policy of personnel training. In this case, a company is apt to create learning work groups and teams for a continual process of training. Creative training projects are supported which destroy stereotypes of organizational behaviour and let the company see itself and its external environment in a new way. Such an organization is interested in new products on the training market and often orders non-standard training programs, such as creativity training for top managers, extreme leadership training and team-creation training, finance and management account training in the form of business simulation games, and cross-cultural training in mixed groups (managers and employees, employees and clients, specialists from different professional spheres, and so on). According to our research, there are few such companies in Russia.

Diagnosing the need for training in a whole organization is typical of organizations where a perspective-oriented and creative training policy dominates. Comparing strategic intentions and aims with the real capacities of a company reveals the best prospects of development for an organization and provides direction in creating training programs.

Effectiveness Evaluation

The way to evaluate the effectiveness of training naturally depends on the chosen training policy and informational culture. A functional policy of personnel training is aimed at results such as quantitative growth in fulfilling a certain function. Sales training is expected to result in sales growth. Management training programs are expected to result in profit growth.

In the case of a problem-oriented training policy in a company, the criterion for evaluating the effectiveness of a training program is clear: solving a certain problem or creating a method of solving problems of a certain type. Sales training is intended to teach sellers to make a decision (to follow a standard) when communicating with a conflicting client, for example, and to stimulate a company to work out a corresponding standard of behaviour and order of interaction between departments in a situation of that kind in the future. A management training program will be created to solve a certain management problem.

A company which is perspective-oriented in its personnel training will evaluate the effectiveness of its training programs by creating an information pool after every training session and training course and by remaining well-informed about the latest trends in the development of the market, branch, business, or region. Sales training is effective if sellers learn about new sales technologies because of it. In management training courses, a company's managers can learn about new management methods, such as the balanced scorecard, for example, or about the theory of talent management in a company.

The result of training in a company where a creative policy of personnel training dominates is often unpredictable. In Russian companies, this result is equated with the appearance of a new project or the creation of a new business branch in a company. However, the absence of an immediate training result is also considered to be a result. The very act of thinking and communicating about important topics is considered valuable.

We have thus seen what influence the informational culture has on creating a personnel training policy and what types of culture and policy are most widespread in Russian companies.

Analyzing the Training and Development Experience of Russian Policies

The experience of the School of Management of St Petersburg University in organizing corporate training programs shows that these days, Russian companies can be divided into three groups by the degree of development of their personnel training system and by the role this system plays in the strategy of the company's development.

Group 1: Companies Which do not View Training as an Independent and Significant Activity

There is no deliberate training policy or structure in such a company and no evident prerequisites for developing a system of personnel training. Employees can enter educational institutions if they like or can attend training courses in educational or consulting companies. The results of this training can be assessed only on an individual level: 'What has this training given to me?' Training in an institute of higher education or attending seminars often stimulates an employee to leave his or her company, because communication in an educational environment and involvement in a professional network prompts the circulation of information about the internal environment in different organizations, stimulates comparison, and contributes to a successful career. Spontaneous training programs may appear from time to time, mostly as a result of accidental factors. Spontaneous contact between a company and a training organization, without any preliminary diagnosis of training needs and without concrete training aims, leads either to the dissatisfaction both of the employees who are forced into training and the managers who must pay for an odd and unwanted product, or to momentary emotional satisfaction and interest in training (mostly due to the competence and personality of a trainer) without long-lasting results which can be used in a company's everyday activity.

Example 1. A company with 25 employees has worked for three years in the field of buying and selling industrial building materials. It has several permanent clients and is being managed by a proprietor. Suddenly, its sales decline. The manager requests that a consulting training company analyze the current situation and train the employees. The company has a primary (undeveloped) information interaction culture. The employees are trained according to the anti-crisis training program and the sales training program for field agents. During the anti-crisis training, a new work program is developed and put into practice successfully. The manager is satisfied with the results, but he still decides to stop collaborating with the training organization because he thinks that the aim has been achieved and the problem is eliminated. The situation repeats itself a year and a half later, but the company cannot use the right methods to solve this problem on its own because the acquired knowledge was not preserved by being put into practice every day, and thus it did not develop into experience and skills regarding sales management and anti-crisis activity. The manager therefore has to turn to the training organization for help again.

Example 2. A wholesale buyer has worked for seven years in the food industry and has 600 employees. When a new general director is hired by the proprietors, sales training begins with the objective of introducing the general director to the group and developing a common approach to sales management. The company has a strict hierarchy and a functional information culture. A hired trainer organizes intense interaction between the employees, which is typical of other kinds of information culture and which results in criticism of the situation in the company, dissatisfaction with the proprietors' management style, and a conflict between the new general director and the most active elements of the group. The post-training life of the company is characterized by long-lasting confrontation in the group and low business effectiveness. During the following two years, those employees who had been trained in business programs conceal this fact from the management because of its negative attitude to training.

Group 2: Companies Where Personnel Training is One of the Functions of the Personnel Manager

In these companies, training functions are a part of the personnel department. Training policy and personnel development policy are being developed in such companies. This is the duty of the personnel manager or the director of human resources. His or her function is to organize training and to hire trainers from outside a company. This policy can be called a 'testing policy'. A company tests different forms and methods of training, different trainers, and partnerships with different training organizations, thus learning about different concepts and methodologies behind the personnel training process.

Example 1. A network of restaurants and cafes has been active for seven years on the Russian market. There is a central office in St Petersburg and several regional sub-units in other Russian cities. There are 1,250 members of staff. The company has a mixed type of information culture – a functional information research culture. The functional information culture is more typical of the service departments, and the research culture is more typical of the top management.

During the last two years, the personnel department has created a system of continuous training for service personnel on its own. Now training has become important in order for the middle management to acquire management skills and for the top management to learn strategy management. The personnel department organized a call for tenders to carry out management skills training. Five training companies from St Petersburg, three training companies from Moscow and two institutions took part in this call for tenders. The company chose a St Petersburg-based company to put its training program into practice and ordered that a strategy management training course take place in one of the colleges. The training was successful, but later on the problem of a difference in terminology and management theory arose as a result of different training methods. The company subsequently ordered an additional training course to form a common management outlook and a common management vocabulary for its managers. According to employees of the personnel department, the greatest difficulty in organising the training process was the problem of choosing a methodology in accordance with the company's strategy of personnel development. Ultimately, they asked the institution specialists to solve this problem.

Group 3: Companies Where Training is a Strategic Problem of the Management

A certain level of training need has been reached in this type of company. There is a functional guarantee of this process – internal, external or mixed. The main principles and values of the training are formulated and declared. The top management is involved in organizing and carrying out training in companies of this group. Managers lead several corporate training courses. Top managers themselves learn both inside a company and outside of it, bringing the results of their individual training back into their organization.

Example 1. A polygraphic publishing company has existed on the market for nine years and is one of the leading organizations in its market niche. 150 employees work in the production, sales and support departments of the company. The company has an information interaction culture with enclaves of an openness culture.

For the last four years, the company has regularly ordered different training courses for its personnel. The top managers of the company are studying in an MBA program. After attending a course on human resources management in an organization, the top managers created the new position of 'training manager' and charged this new employee with forming a training concept. The training manager formulates a personnel training concept in collaboration with one of the leading business schools in Russia. The main principles of personnel training in the company are formulated and declared. Entry training is obligatory for all new employees. A program of sales training is being used continuously. Developmental training becomes a bonus for employees and part of their compensation package.

In our opinion, a company's membership in any of the groups described above depends on a number of facts: the information culture which was formed in the company, the stage of growth of the organization, certain characteristics of the business environment, the type of industry, and the current situation on the labour market in the region.

Important Problems on the Market for Corporate Training

In conclusion, we would like to note several important problems which hinder the effective development of the market for corporate training.

We have to accept that one of the sources of problems for training effectiveness is the companies themselves. This is mainly because the companies have difficulties with setting training aims and with describing the problems which they want to solve with the training. This problem is partly the result of the status of personnel managers in Russian companies, and it arises in companies where a personnel specialist fulfils the functions of a coordinator/administrator only and does not influence personnel management policy very much. In such cases, the personnel manager does not really understand why top managers initiate this or that training program, which he must organize. As a result, the personnel manager can be an ineffective 'link' in organizing this process, both when this training is realized by the inner strength of a company or when it is realized by its outer strength.

On the other hand, a problem of equal importance is that of dissatisfaction with the training results, which is caused by the great variety of training service providers. On the whole, this problem can be defined as 'the lack of client orientation' of many

Russian trainers, or as a lack of qualified specialists who are ready to work with the concrete problems of concrete companies/clients. On the one hand, this is due to the lack of experience in training in many fields. However, as our experience shows, even if a trainer has been educated and has worked abroad, it unfortunately does not solve the problem because the domestic audience has particular traits, and foreign methods do not always seem adequate to it.

In this article, we tried to pinpoint and analyze the main tendencies in personnel training and development in modern Russian companies. We also saw that the training policies in Russian companies are formed under the influence of a complex of factors, such as the specific characteristics of the national environment, the stage of life cycle, the information culture of a company, and the role of personnel training in the strategy of the company's development

References

Argyris, C. and Schon, D. (1996), *Organisational Learning. Reading*, (Mass.: Addison-Wesley).

Boyette, J. and Boyette, J. (2002), *Guide through the Wisdom Kingdom: Best Ideas of Management Gurus.*

Fey, C.F., Pavlovskaya, A.G. and Tang, N. (2004), 'Are Human Resources Management Practices Universal? Comparison of Russian, Chinese and Finnish Practices', *Russian Journal of Management* 1.

Greiner, L. (1972), 'Evolution and Revolution as Organisations Grow', *Harvard Business Review* 37–46, (Translated by: Klemina, T.N. (2002), 'Evolution and Revolution as Organisations Grow', in Greiner, L.E. (eds), (St Petersburg State University bulletin), *Management* 4, 76–94.

Ivanova, E. (2002), 'Personnel Training: No Alternative' *Personnel Elite* 34, 268.

Kapustin, S.N. and Krasnova, N.L. (2000), 'Marketing Approach to Corporate Training, *Marketing in Russia and Abroad* 4.

Kay, J.A. (1993), *Foundations of Corporate Success: How Business Strategies add Value* (Oxford, Oxford University Press).

Kim, D.H. (1993), 'The Link between Individual and Organisational Learning', *Sloan Management Review* Fall, 37–50.

Marshand, D.A. (1999), *The Art of Management.*

Mumford, A. (1980), *Making experience pay* (McGraw Hill).

Schein, E. H. (1994), 'Organisational and Managerial Culture as a Facilitator or Inhibitor of Organisational Learning', Working Paper for the MIT Organisational Learning Network, 19 May1994.

Senge, P. (1996), 'Leading Learning Organisation' *Training and Development*, December, 36–8.

Chapter 10

Professional Training and Retraining: Challenges of Transition (The Case of the Shipbuilding Industry in St Petersburg, Russia)

Lubov Ejova and Irina Olimpieva

Introduction

Transformation processes in Russia of the late 80s have affected the institutional bases of the staff professional training system in the industrial sphere of the economy. Over the last decade and a half, the most serious shocks have been experienced by industries where the role of centralized regulation and the state order was the most significant in Soviet times. Shipbuilding is one such industry. Peculiarities of training and raising the skill level in the shipbuilding industry are connected with the following factors:

1. Shipbuilding is considered to be in the sphere of high-technological production, where higher demands have always been made of staff skill level.
2. This branch was referred to as the Military Industrial complex (henceforth VPK), and accordingly, had all the privileges for priority state financing. This, in turn, had an effect on the system of staff training and retraining.
3. The inclusion of shipbuilding in the VPK predetermined the existence of a particular corporate culture typical for all shipbuilding enterprises: patriotism, military discipline and rigid system of hierarchical submission in everything, including matters connected with training and retraining personnel.
4. In Soviet times, shipbuilding was one of the industries which exported its production. This also was a reason for referring it to the category of special branches, which implied special attention and priorities in financing. Although the production of Soviet shipbuilding was mainly exported to the COMECON market (Council for Mutual Economic Assistance among socialist countries) and was therefore sheltered from the pressure of market competition from developed capitalist countries, the very fact of producing things for export placed shipbuilding in special conditions, in comparison with many other industries.

Thus, the task of training and retraining the staff in the shipbuilding industry has always been a priority. The existing centralized system of training and raising professional skills of the staff was well integrated in the planned economy. On the whole, this system, despite certain imperfections, met the requirements of large-scale shipbuilding enterprises. Changes in socio-economic and legal conditions and the crisis in the shipbuilding industry in the early 90s and some years later have resulted in breaking down the existing system. The problems of economic survival of enterprises at that time changed the very task of recruiting, which for those days was one of retaining the available potential of personnel, rather than perfecting and increasing that potential. Recent years have been connected with a gradual improvement of the economic situation in the shipbuilding industry. Enterprises began to feel a lack of qualified specialists; and the task of professional training and retraining personnel has become more acute.

In this article, we will examine how the system of professional training shipbuilding industry of St Petersburg was changing, and what attempts are currently being undertaken to solve the problem. The shipbuilding industry remains one of the leading industrial branches in St Petersburg. In terms of the industrial potential of the city, shipbuilding's share makes up 12 per cent; in total volume of export production it has reached 25 per cent. These indices support ranking shipbuilding among town-forming industrial branches. The majority of Russian shipbuilding enterprises – 27 industrial plants as well as 30 research institutes and design bureaus as well as a great number of small and medium sized enterprises – are located in St Petersburg and the Leningradskaya region. About 30 per cent of the whole production of Russian shipbuilding and 75 per cent of works in R&D are concentrated here; over 55 thousand people are employed in the shipbuilding industry of St Petersburg and the Leningradskaya region. The situation that has developed around training and retraining personnel in St Petersburg's shipbuilding industry reflects general trends in the branch. We argue, therefore, that the tendencies described in the article and conclusions concerning relevant changes are not limited to St Petersburg's industry.

The article will start with a general overview of the situation in professional training and retraining in the shipbuilding industry during Soviet times. Then we will identify the problems of professional education and the retraining of personnel that typify the current situation in shipbuilding and are consequences of socio-economic reforms. In the article, we intend to pay special attention to the new trends which have arisen in recent years in the system of professional education and in particular, to the new forms of interactions at institutional level between the state (city authorities), employers (shipbuilding enterprises) and trade unions.

The article will use the data obtained from the comparative study of social partnership systems in shipbuilding industries of Russia and Germany conducted by authors in 2003–04, and information obtained from the long-term collaboration between CISR researchers and representatives of Territorial Organization of Trade Unions of Shipbuilding Industry in St Petersburg.

Soviet System of Professional Training and Raising Professional Skill

In Soviet times, the system of personnel training and retraining was organized based on educational-level gradation and close ties with enterprises. Peculiarities of professional training in shipbuilding, as a branch of VPK, were determined by the fact that many of large-scale enterprises had as a base the technical training colleges, specialized educational centers, technical schools and institutes which were financed – either partially, or in full – by the enterprise's budget. Working in compliance with the state educational standards, such educational institutions were structural divisions of large-scale enterprises and were referred to as being part of the so-called social sphere, along with departmental housing, hostels and medical institutions, which also belonged to the enterprises. Similar to other aspects of the social sphere, the system of professional training was aimed at attaching employees to a certain enterprise from the very beginning of the education process. In the course of training, students were engaged in practical work at workplaces at the enterprise, became acquainted with equipment and technological processes, and entered into the social environment of the enterprise. Trainees had to work off three years after graduation from the educational institution. That was an obligatory condition. In general, this order of things was characteristic for the Soviet system of professional education at large. In shipbuilding, however, they are most evident.

There were also some peculiarities in training of technical specialists that distinguished higher educational organizations in shipbuilding industry from other educational establishments. A number of institutions of higher education in the sphere of shipbuilding used a so-called 'mixed' (combined) system of training which envisaged that senior students attended day classes during one semester, and evening ones during another. The 'evening' students would work in the daytime at the enterprise. The idea was as follows: future specialists had to start their labour career by becoming acquainted with working professions in practice and to develop gradually their specialization. For example, technologists gained work experience as machine operators. As a result of this experience, they were able not only to understand design drawings, but also to conceive the specificity of technological process through their own practice.

The negative aspect of this system is connected with a surplus of young specialists in shipbuilding as a result of the economic stagnation in the middle of the 70s. As a result, graduates from higher schools who dealt with 'mixed' system of training were for a long time compelled to fill working positions. This did not correspond to their level of qualification. Such problems were characteristic of minor small mono-industrial cities in the Northwest, as well as so-called 'closed' cities which had developed around enterprises belonging to the military shipbuilding industry. In a large city as Leningrad, with its developed industry, a young specialist had a greater chance of finding in other enterprises a job which would correspond to his/her qualifications.

Enterprise Level

Departments for personnel technical training (OTOK) coordinated all the work aimed at training and retraining the enterprise's staff. The directions of this work were common for all enterprises:

- the coordination of work with educational institutions (specialized schools, training centres, technical secondary schools, technical institutes, postgraduate study)
- raising the professional skill level of the staff at the enterprise
- retraining personnel (subsidiary professional training).

OTOKs at enterprises had a wide range of connections and contacts with various educational organizations engaged in professional training for the shipbuilding industry. Without going into great detail regarding the general principles of interaction between enterprises and educational institutions which were standard in point of fact, we should note that the special position of the branch in the VPK (see above) resulted in a high level of financing of those educational institutions which trained specialists for the shipbuilding industry. Above all, this concerned special professional training for the shipbuilding industry. A number of large-scale enterprises had special training (rooms) equipped with advanced (for those days) and rather expensive training equipment for future specialists in key professions. Great amounts of money were spent for these purposes. Let us reiterate that this money was allocated from the state budget. Accordingly, the wages of teachers dealing with this branch were also much higher than those that were average for the city.

In addition, OTOK mediated between enterprises and the sectoral system of raising the personnel's professional skill. The system encompassed training canters that were located not only in Leningrad, but also in other cities of the country. The most convincing examples are the centre 'Temp' located in Nikolaev (Ukraine) which ceased to exist for Russia after the disintegration of the USSR, and also the training centre of enterprises belonging to shipbuilding industry in St Petersburg.

OTOK coordinated the work on determining enterprises' demand in specialists of every description (both non-production personnel, and working staff) and sent applications to appropriate educational institutions. In addition to recruiting new personnel, OTOK coordinated the work on retraining and raising the level of the staff's professional skill. Once a year, all industrial subdivisions of the enterprise (technical and administrative departments, and industrial shops) had to submit applications to OTOK with details substantiating their need for raising the professional skill level of the staff – which included workers, technical specialists, and managers. On the basis of these applications and the information about available vacancies obtained from the personnel department, the annual plan of training and retraining personnel at the enterprise was drawn up.

OTOK's work aimed at training and retraining workers followed three directions:

- Raising the level of professional skill – training for promotion to higher qualification within the same profession: for example, the welder of the II category would like to be trained for obtaining the III category qualification. Since the shift to higher professional category was connected with the increase in wages, and for the worker was often the only way to increase his earnings, this proved to be the most significant factor in the formation power relations within the workshop at the enterprise. A nomination for promotion to a higher category was, to a considerable extent, conditioned by a worker's informal relations with the brigade-leader, foreman, or superintendent of the workshop.
- Mastering contiguous professions was very popular in Soviet times, and was characteristic of the shipbuilding industry as well. Such forms of professional training were stimulated by additional payment for 'combining professions'. Such practices promoted reduction in the number of workplaces, though resulted in latent increase of work intensity.
- Professional retraining. Whereas the first two directions were somehow connected with the worker's needs and wishes, this third form was often imposed 'from the top'. The workers were compelled to agree with mastering a new profession, in order to hold onto their workplaces and to maintain good relations with the heads.

The engineering staff dealt with other conditions in getting nominated for a higher qualification category. Technical officers had to go through a certification procedure. As a rule, the staff departments of the enterprise conducted the attestation of the personnel. The documentation (attestation forms, regulations for certification procedure, and so on.) was sent from the ministries.

The enterprise had no right to change standards and requirements at their own discretion. The results of certification, held once every 4–5 years, were reported and also sent to the ministries. Based on the results of interviewing, the certification commission gave recommendations which could advise either to reserve the (current) post for the employee, promote or demote him. It was only after certification that specialists had an opportunity to promote their category and hence their salary. That was why certification was always perceived by specialists as examination and caused nervousness and a lot of emotions. As regards the heads of the enterprise, their promotion did not depend on certification procedures. It was executed by the director's orders and was indisputable.

Raising the level of professional skill of the managerial personnel was also connected with findings of invited sociologists and psychologists who conducted different trainings, psychological testing, and so on. Involving specialists of such kind into solving the organizational problems of industrial enterprises has become very popular since the late 70s. These actions were not regular; they were undertaken, as a rule, only at large-scale enterprises under the decision made by either the directorate or the heads of large divisions (Ejova 1996; Shmonin 1999). However, the experience of such actions has played a certain role in the further development of training managerial personnel. As the methods were developed and perfected, the personnel became used to these procedures. By the end of the 90s, this had resulted in creating a base for the development of staff management services and educational centers in the shipbuilding industry.

To sum up, in Soviet times the shipbuilding industry had a centralized system of education, and of training and retraining personnel, perfectly incorporated into the centralized planned economy. Educational centers within this system were well-provided for, with equipment and a guaranteed high quality of education. As it was mentioned above, priority financing of shipbuilding as an important branch of VPK became the main condition for the existence of a developed system of professional training. This can in many respects explain those nostalgic moods which were obviously prevalent in interviews with representatives of trade unions and employees of enterprises who shared their views of the former system. Big money was spent, but whether it be direct investments (to the very educational establishments) or indirect ones (through enterprises), these means were allocated from the state budget.

However paradoxical it is, the impressive scope of shipbuilding's system of training and raising the level of staff's professional skill partially resulted from an imperfection of planning measures, and also from the necessity to 'fulfill and over fulfill the plan' stipulated by these items. Planned figures of every next year were formed based on those of the previous one. They had to show, if only slightly, a positive trend. This provoked overstating demands and resulted in inefficient use of assets, which was of no great concern to enterprise employees since the funds were allotted from the state budget.

Similar to the former systems of housing and social welfare, the systems of training staff and material stimulation played an important role in the process of attaching employees to certain enterprises. Along with the obligatory three-year work-off after graduating from an educational institution, the work at particular enterprises became a condition for further professional promotion. At the same time, the opportunity to receive any bonuses or to get any benefit from the so-called social sphere of the enterprise (including getting a place in a waiting list for dwelling, having the possibility to place children in a kindergarten, or being able to go to a rest-home and so on) directly depended on the employee's affiliation with this enterprise.

The Current Situation in Managing and Retraining Personnel in the Shipbuilding Industry

Transformation processes and the crisis in the shipbuilding industry that took place in the early 1990s have totally ruined the system described above. Some of the shipbuilding enterprises were privatized, others remained under state ownership. Despite all efforts to the contrary, none of enterprises could avoid the deep crisis: in the mid-90s all enterprises, regardless of the form of ownership, met with the same problems. There were neither orders, nor working capital; employees did not receive wages for months; and workplaces were being curtailed. For this period, the volume of the Russian State's orders for the VPK reduced by 20 times, the level of production capacity at shipbuilding enterprises fell by 25–45 per cent.

The social sphere (dwellings, educational and pre-school institutions, hostels, sports clubs, medical and sanitary stations, recreation centers, and so on) were either passed over to municipal ownership or privatized, as the means for their maintenance from the state budget were no longer allotted. It was a very painful process, and many analytical articles have been devoted to its analysis (Kabalina, Fedorina 1999; Zhuravskaya and others 2003, Gaidar 2003; Desyatiletie ekonomicheskikh reform v Sankt-Peterbyrge 2001; Dakhin 1999; Predpriyatie i Rynok 1997).

The article will not dwell upon this period. We will only mention briefly the problem of competitiveness which shipbuilding enterprises were faced with in market conditions. There was a need to search for quite new orders and to reconstruct enterprises. This meant that in the conditions of significant financial deficit, a reorganization in the spheres of engineering, technology, management, and recruiting was necessary Moreover, this new system of management at the enterprise should be based upon modern information technologies.

After the suspension of state financing, the task of personnel training and retraining fell entirely to the enterprise. In the situation of crisis, the main task of enterprises lay in desperate attempts to retain current staff potential, rather than in its build-up and development. In solving this task some of enterprises were rather successful, others were not. However, one can assert that the crisis period has brought essential losses in staff potential of the industry, and its resumption will take a long time.

At the moment the situation with regard to workforce demand in shipbuilding is ambiguous: on the one hand, long-term production decline has caused mass redundancies of workers, creating highly qualified 'washed out' workers. On the other hand, recent positive economic changes have sharpened the need for a high-skilled working force. In recent times, the situation with bookings at shipbuilding enterprises and R&D institutions in shipbuilding industry has changed for the better. Large-scale enterprises have obtained a series of orders for the next five years, including export orders for the Navies of China and India. Also it is expected that in the very near future Russia will need over 100 ships intended for North and arctic navigation. It is also supposed to develop further the civil navy and inland water transport.

At the moment almost all of the enterprises in the shipbuilding industrial complex have a need for workers and specialists with different levels of professional skills. According to the data of the Ministry of Education of the Russian Federation, the demand for specialists by industrial shipbuilding enterprises in St Petersburg exceeds by 2.5 to 2.7 times the number of specialists provided by state budget forms of professional education. The general problem is reinforced by some general factors and by those specific to St Petersburg, and for shipbuilding as a branch of industry.

First, it should be pointed out that there has been a sharp decrease in the *inflow of young people* into shipbuilding industry and, as a consequence, an aging of the working force. In Soviet times, the overwhelming majority of young workers were recruited by shipbuilding industry of St Petersburg from peripheral areas. The main attraction for these young people was the possibility to receive housing in St Petersburg that would be provided by the social welfare system of the industrial plant. The absence of this main attraction nowadays has been a substantial obstacle to recruiting young people to industrial enterprises. In addition to the degradation and destruction of professional education system in shipbuilding industry, a general loss of prestige of working specialties has become a significant negative factor. As of the early 90s, the number of specialized and technical schools had sharply decreased, most highly qualified teachers had left work, capital assets were used up to the highest degree, and affiliation with enterprises was lost. Technical schools could no longer graduate specialists whose qualifications would correspond to the demands of modern industrial technologies. The re-profiling of specialized and technical schools began to take place. They introduced training programs in various professions which, while desirable on the labour market, had nothing to do with shipbuilding.

To lease premises to others has become another strategy of economic survival for many establishments and institutions, among them, specialized technical schools. Granting on lease their own quarters allows them to have a stable, informal source of income (Ejova, Olimpieva 2002). Indirect evidence of this is the following: although over the decade of reforms the number of institutions for primary professional education in Russia decreased insignificantly – from 4,196 in 1985 to 4,166 in 1995, the quantity of graduates fell 3,5 times for the period from 1990 to 1995, totalling 428,4 and 128,8 thousand persons, respectively. For the same period, the quantity of graduates in engineering and metalworking industries, including shipbuilding, fell 7,5 times – from 225,3 to 31,1 thousand (*Socialnaya Sfera Rossii* 1996, 176–77). Thus, having kept their formal status – that of educational establishment – technical schools focused on activities which did not correspond to their basic training specialization.

At the moment, the prestige of specialized technical schools in the shipbuilding industry is extremely low. They have the reputation of being 'social gutters' because the level of drug and alcohol addiction among their students is very high. In fact, the graduates themselves do not aspire to work in shipbuilding because of the difficult and harmful work conditions, often inadequate wages. Instead they look for labour market vacancies in more attractive workplaces in the commercial sphere or in customer services. As a result, only about 30 per cent of graduates decide to work in industrial enterprises. According to the head of the personnel department at 'Severnaya Verf' open stock-company ['Northern Shipyard'], in 2004, only six of 120 students undergoing practical training at this plant stayed to work there.

A considerable part of graduates from specialized technical schools do not come to work at the enterprise because of compulsory military service, after which only a few can recall their initial profession. Officers of personnel departments at shipbuilding enterprises advocate either to respite senior students subjected to call-up, or count the fixed term of their professional work as an alternative to military service. However, the state has not taken any decision so far.

The need for innovations has sharpened the need for highly qualified technical specialists. During the years of stagnation many enterprises lost innovative potential. This problem refers in particular to the situation with the lack of specialists in project and design bureaus. The need of competitiveness requires introduction of innovative technologies, and therefore specialists possessing advanced knowledge (according to the prognoses of Ministry of Education, the need for technical specialists in shipbuilding in St Petersburg constitutes 80 per cent of overall need in specialists in shipbuilding in Russia). At the same time, due to the poor economic situation, the bureaus and enterprises are not able to recruit the necessary number of young well-trained graduates of high educational establishments with professional skills corresponding to the demands of advanced high-tech production.

Another feature typical to the shipbuilding industry is a *high level of manpower mobility,* several types of which, as regards specialists, can be listed as follows:

- The lack of highly skilled workers is partially compensated by the shuttle migration of workers from military shipyards in other cities of the North-Western region, which are characterized by extremely high level of unemployment. These 'closed' cities – urban settlements created around military enterprises – have almost no employment opportunities except for shipbuilding plants. With the destruction of the Military Industrial complex and suspension of military orders the population of these cities found themselves without work and salaries and had to look for jobs in other cities. The situation is aggravated by the narrow specialization of workers who have been employed at military shipyards for many years. That is, the enterprise in need of certain category of specialists or workers has to 'rent' personnel of other enterprises. For example, welders and assemblers from the A-Shipbuilding Centre located in the town of Severodvinsk, come to St Petersburg and work at Severnaya Verf on contractual basis. The shuttle migration of workers is not always of centralized character, it is often a result of the personal initiative of individuals.
- Migrants from neighboring NIS countries – Byelorussia, Ukraine, and so on – provide another source of temporary employment covering mainly the lack of low-qualified workers. There is not any official data on the number of migrants employed in shipbuilding industry because of the semi-formal character of hiring.
- There is also an intensive migration of specialists within the city. This happens because shipbuilding enterprises entice personnel from each other. The flows are caused by high diversity of working conditions at different enterprises, and especially by differences in salaries at economically successful and unsuccessful enterprises.
- One more tendency is a shift of highly qualified personnel to other branches. The most complicated problem is a transition of specialists aged 30–35 to privately owned structures where salaries are often twice as high. The employees get experience, become highly qualified specialists and leave for another enterprise.

In this way, shipbuilding's branch system of training and raising the level of qualification of the personnel was practically ruined (with the exception of some successful enterprises which found resources for the organization of professional education – we will dwell upon them below). On the other hand, this system experiences a growing need in highly qualified staff, connected with the beginning of economic stabilization and further development of the shipbuilding industry in St Petersburg.

The problem of staff training has become more acute because of Russia's expected entrance into the WTO (World Trade Organization). This will present international standards and new challenges. The situation is aggravated by 'cheap' manpower in the form of migrants from enterprises of the Northwest and the near abroad.

New Trends

Currently, one can assert that all enterprises, regardless of their economic situation, recognize the necessity of shifting their strategy from one of merely retaining personnel to personnel development. Since the budgetary financing is a thing of the past, and the development of the personnel is currently financed from profits, the distinctions in strategies of professional training are stipulated, first of all, by the economic success of the enterprise.

More successful enterprises practice what can be conventionally defined as a market strategy. Among those enterprises are shipyards and R&D institutes which managed to redirect their production in accordance with the demands of the market in conditions of crisis, to assimilate into international markets, to escape their dependence on the state military order and to reorient themselves to the needs of civil shipbuilding. As a rule, such enterprises were leaders of shipbuilding in Soviet times, they had a potent technological base and, accordingly, well-equipped centers for professional training. In crisis times, they maintained state support, though a pruned one. Professional training centers created at such enterprises may afterwards develop into economically independent market structures engaged in professional training of workers not only for their own organizations, but also for other shipbuilding enterprises. A characteristic example of such an enterprise is the 'Admiralteyskie Verfi' industrial association [Admiralty Shipyards] which is the leader of shipbuilding in St Petersburg. This association has developed a functioning corporate system of continually raising the level of professional skill. This system has involved up to 75–80 per cent of the personnel and is intended for all categories of employees - from highly qualified workers to top managers of the enterprise. The educational centre at 'Admiralteyskie Verfi', created in 1995, has developed from the subdivision of the enterprise into an independent structure. Now it provides training for 4,000 persons in demanding working professions, instructs hundreds of specialists, and supervises the practical training of more than 500 students. Thirty teachers work at the centre, which has equipment for videoconferencing, four computer classes and its own fiber-optic network for Internet access.

Another type of industrial enterprise are those plants perched on the edge of economic survival. In situations where salary is the primary factor in attracting and/or retaining workers at the enterprise, less successful enterprises become losers. They try to solve the deficiency in qualified personnel primarily by reanimating their organizational structure of training and by raising the level of workers' professional skill, which was characteristic for Soviet times. The practice of tutorship (coaching – in western terminology) and systems aimed at staff adaptation have reappeared, with the work of qualifying commissions being reactivated. At the same time, the absence of workers' interest in raising their professional skill is a specific problem. Since the earnings of workers at less successful enterprises are, to a considerable extent, being formed at the expense of shadow prerequisites, workers are not interested in wasting time and energy on training and obtaining higher qualifications.

The aforementioned types of enterprise obviously do not cover the full spectrum of strategies aimed at providing the enterprise with qualified personnel; however, they do give a general notion about the intensifying economic differentiation between enterprises which has, in turn, resulting in the 'deepening' of differentiation of opportunities in the sphere of training and raising the level of the staff's professional skill.

The change in the general approach to personnel management, including in education and retraining, has become, in our opinion, an important new trend. It should be noted that the term 'personnel' (characteristic for an organizational-oriented approach) has ejected the term 'cadres' (usual for the Soviet period and typical for the state-oriented approach) from industrial discourse. This in itself can be treated as a symptomatic fact reflecting certain changes in management mentality. The work with personnel began to be regarded as a priority; in addition to traditional staff departments, enterprises started to establish services for personnel management, entrusting them with extensive tasks (for example the system of staff selection, certification, motivation; expert estimations; the evaluation of the state of health; the estimation of personnel's competence, and so on.). According to the heads of various divisions at several enterprises, there has been a steady growth in spending on training and raising the level of personnel's professional skill. Of vital importance is the fact that the sources of financing the work aimed at the development of the staff have changed: now it is not budgetary funds, but rather the means of the enterprise (that is, its profits, or a fixed-percentage allocation from the wages fund).

Another new tendency is *the appearance of new players* in the field of professional education. Enterprises are not always able to cope with problems independently. The developed consulting network is an innovation in the external infrastructure of the Russia's business. Nevertheless, dealing with consulting services is a practice which has only just begun to develop.

A number of new intersectoral training organizations engaged in training specialists, including educational centers (six educational centers have been established at shipbuilding enterprises in the Northwest region – 57 enterprises) and non-commercial partnerships (new organizational forms of cooperation between educational institutions and enterprises), can also be referred to as recently appeared 'players'.

One example of a noncommercial partnership is the 'Protei' research and educational centre for supplementary education. Since 1999, it has been a member of the Association of European Research Educational Centers for Network Internet Technologies and renders services to both the partners and the founders (Marine Technical University and 'Admiralteyskie Verfi'), and also to customers from Russia and countries in the region and beyond. Another example of noncommercial partnership is the Intersectoral Training Centre for training and retraining managers and top managers of enterprises of shipbuilding industry of the Northwest federal district, created on the base of Central Scientific Research Institute of the Technologies of Shipbuilding.

Successful R&D organizations establish their own educational centers and create programs of supplementary education for students of different higher schools. Students-trainees are provided with additional stipends, and are guaranteed a place of employment to be given after graduating from the institute. In the course of additional training, students work at enterprises and receive the themes for their term papers and degree theses ibidem.

Cooperation with foreign partners in the sphere of training and raising the level of personnel's professional skills is another of the new tendencies. In recent years, the participation of Russian enterprises in international projects with introduction of European and Scandinavian experience (that of Germany and Finland, in particular) has become more active.

Network information and intellectual technologies for continued professional training are becoming increasingly required. In two years a team of experts (ten specialists in total, including researchers, teachers, experts and programmers) developed original software, a network intellectual information environment. It has become an information constituent for supporting professional development, and planning and managing personnel at 'Admiralteyskie Verfi'.

In summary, we describe the situation that has been developed in the sphere of professional training for shipbuilding during the recent years as dual. In conditions of improving economic situation in the shipbuilding industry and increasing demand for training qualified personnel, one can identify new tendencies connected with an orientation towards integrating the intellectual potential of science, industry and education. New forms of cooperation (in comparison with the Soviet period) between educational institutions and enterprises have appeared, international experience has been introduced and new training technologies have been tested. It should be noted that the abovementioned processes of integration concerned, first of all, technical specialists, and their training and retraining. This is explained by the fact that for such high-tech industry as shipbuilding, the maintenance of innovative potential is extremely important. As regards working professions, there are also the examples of successfully solving the problem of personnel in which large-scale enterprises create well-equipped training centers where workers are trained, mastering key professions and raising the level of their qualification.

However, for all benefits and significance of the abovementioned tendencies, they cannot essentially change the general situation with professional training in the shipbuilding industry of St Petersburg and of the Northwest region, in particular. The process of 'washing-out' high-qualified specialists during the period of crisis impacted not only enterprises, but also higher educational institutions. The technical base of educational establishments has become obsolete to a considerable degree. As a result, the general professional level of graduates from institutes who come to work to R&D institutions has proven to be extremely low. In some scientific research institutes graduates have to be re-examined in profile subjects if they want to work there. Specialized technical schools with their out-of-date technical base and unsatisfactory level of training, still remain the basic source of personnel replenishment. On leaving technical schools, the majority of graduates do not go to enterprises to work in the profession for which they received training.

The situation is aggravated by the problem of the out-of-date unified educational standards that are the norm in state educational institutions. Many of these norms have remained since Soviet times and no longer correspond to the contemporary technological level of the shipbuilding industry development. In this sense, the creation of intersectoral and branch educational centers, though being important and necessary, has thus far not noticeably influenced the current situation with regard professional training in the region. A cardinal change of the situation must consist of a complex reform of the entire system of professional education and personnel training for the enterprises of the shipbuilding industry.

About the Program of Personnel's Professional Training for the Shipbuilding Industry

The 2004–08 Program of Professional Training For Shipbuilding Industry approved by the City Government in 10 October 2004, is one such attempt at large-scale reform (see above). The Shipbuilding enterprises and the territorial organization of shipbuilding trade unions (TOT) acted as its initiators. The program provides a complex of measures which should fundamentally change the scheme of interaction between educational establishments and shipbuilding enterprises. For realization of these measures, it is supposed to create the Coordination Centre of Training and Retraining Personnel for the Shipbuilding Industry of St Petersburg. It is expected that it will be a noncommercial partnership involving educational establishments of different levels and enterprises of the shipbuilding industry. The program of professional training proposes the creation of a modern 'thorough system' of training personnel which would cover all stages: 'secondary school, specialized technical school, college, institute, enterprise/ organization.'

The realization of the program envisages the allocation of 249.3 million rubles from the federal budget and the budget of St Petersburg, and 300 million rubles from funds of enterprises. Thus, training will be organized on a shareholding principle. At the same time, the city budget will be responsible for general education, and enterprises for professional education of specialists. The program is intended to realize the interests of all participating parties: the city administration will receive taxes; employers will hire qualitatively trained personnel; workers will obtain workplaces and worthy wages; and trade unions will get an opportunity to control and regulate the process of training and raising the level of professional skill of workers at enterprises.

This was called a 'pilot' program in the sense that the case of shipbuilding will show whether the state and business are able to join efforts in solving the problem of personnel. The control over realization of the Program is specified in a separate item in the Tripartite regional agreement signed by the trade unions, the government, and the Union of Employers of the City. According to the Program, it is supposed to train and graduate not less than 11,000 specialists for professional elementary education, 2,200 technicians and 2,717 engineers, and also to raise the level of qualification of 60,000 persons.

One of the primary goals to be achieved by the Coordination Centre is the forecast of the shipbuilding industry's need for specialists of different professional levels. The state order for professional training of personnel for shipbuilding enterprises will be formed on the basis of the Center's general prognosis. This is another important innovation in the city system of professional education. Within the frame of the state order, the city administration will determine the main directions of educational sphere development which would be most required in the nearest years, and will create the basic budgetary positions according to these directions. Moreover, based on main specialties, the city authorities are going to initiate changes of educational standards proceeding from the offers of enterprises (at a number of enterprises, some standards have already been developed; for example, 'Baltiyskiy zavod' [Baltic Plant] has already elaborated its own standards).

In order to attach graduates of educational establishments to shipbuilding enterprises, there are plans to introduce the system of target training on a contractual basis. It is assumed that a (budgetary) student will sign an agreement under which he/she will be obliged to work at the enterprise for a certain term during the study and after graduation. The student would have to choose the appropriate enterprise which corresponds to his/her specialty. The practice of concluding student's contracts already exists and is used by organizations which participate in financing partner specialized schools or educational institutions within their structure. The program is not limited by these measures. Enterprises have to allocate an essential part of the means for the scheduled development of the material base of educational institutions. In addition, it is planned to promote international cooperation (organization of training abroad, grant programs and so on). Hence, realization of the program is intended to restore the coordination of professional personnel training for the shipbuilding industry, though now on a different organizational and financial basis. In the opinion of representatives of trade unions, it is nothing but a 'return' to better-left-forgotten, 'old' form, which is in reference to the 'Soviet' centralized system of professional education. The necessity of a centralized approach and cooperation between enterprises and educational institutions for solving the problem of personnel is dictated, on the one hand, by the peculiarities of the shipbuilding industry (such as the high-tech, large-scale, synchronization of production), and on the other, by the growing problem of deficiency in qualified personnel. The majority of enterprises can hardly solve this problem on their own.

It is obvious, that a lot of complexities are encountered in the course of realizing the program. Some of them are of an organizational character – for example, the composition of the Council as governing body of the Program has not yet been confirmed. Consequently, the financing of the program to be executed by enterprises of the city is not implemented in full because the size of entrance fee has not yet been authorized.

However, deeper problems are concealed in the legal regulations of the labour sphere. For example, the head of personnel department at 'Severnaya Verf" remarked in an interview that the new Russian Labour Code practically does not take into account the concern of the employer organization which has financed employee's education. In the case of a student's refusal of his obligations, he should provide complete reimbursement of his training; however, in the existing practice there are no precedents of positive court decisions in favour of enterprises.

It is clear that by offering a salary that is lower than the specialist's market-value (adjusted to the costs of his training, for example, at technical college), the enterprise has no guarantee that the worker will not be enticed away by another company which has invested nothing in his education. Even if the enterprise provides for all training expenses and includes them in the contract, the student will always find a way not to pay, having appealed to the Labour Code. Hence, an effective realization of the program demands a reconsideration of the positions of the contract system in the context of the Labour Code. This question, however, is within the competence of the federal centre.

The Employment Service has not been involved in the program. Swedish or German models provide for obligatory participation of national employment service in the system of professional education. Such service is one of shareholders of technical schools (enterprise being another). Moreover, it composes its own annual request for admission of entrants.

As a result of recent re-structuring, the employment service has been placed under federal authority. If previously it dealt with local executive power (labour market forecasting, financial support, training, and retraining referred to the activity of local authorities), this service has now completely been deprived of financial and organizational independence, and hence is not able to respond flexibly and quickly to changing situations and market demands.

Concluding Remarks

Summarizing some findings of the analysis of changes, one can ascertain the destruction of the institutional and financial bases of the Soviet system of professional training in shipbuilding. this resulted from the liquidation of the planned economy, changes of forms of property, and pruned state financing during the period of reforms. The situation has been aggravated by a general economic crisis which hit the shipbuilding industry in the early 90s. The main task of that period was to preserve highly qualified personnel, rather than to develop it.

It is quite clear that the disengagement from the crisis and the further development of shipbuilding industry is impossible without solving the task of training and retraining qualified personnel. The main problem at the moment is the lack of any coherent system of professional training in shipbuilding industry. The 'old' system of professional training that was effective under the economic conditions of centralized planning does not exist any more while no new one has been created to replace it in recent years. It is notable that any attempts to solve the problem at institutional level (we witness them at present) are made with the participation of the state. The program of reforming the system of professional education in shipbuilding industry is based upon the state order. This program pursues, in the first turn, strategic aims, that is to help the whole of professional education out of the system crisis.

As regards the enterprises themselves, they actually have agreed with new 'rules of play' in the sphere of professional education, having become initiators and financial guarantors of the program. Meanwhile, while the program continues to be unrealized, the enterprises have been training and retraining personnel proceeding from their economic potentialities. One can argue that there is a further differentiation gap between shipbuilding enterprises. This is reflected in level differentiation in training personnel.

References

Ejova, L. (1996), 'Metodika Otsenki Socialnoj Napryazhennosti Strategii Adaptatsii Socialnyh Grupp k Novym Uslovijam', *Vestnic Sankt-Peterburgskoy Technicheskoy Akademii.*

Dakhin, V. (1999), 'Evolyutsija I revolyutsija v Russijskom krizise', *Pro et Contra* 4: 3, 134–54.

Gaidar, E. (2003), 'Ekonomicheskiy Rost i Chelovecheskiy Factor, Rossia na distantsii dvukh vekov', *Vestnik Evropy*, volume IX.

Goskomstat (1996), *Socialnaya sfera Rossii*, Statisticheskiy Sbornik, Moscow

Guriev S., Lazareva O., Rachinskij A. and Tsukhlo S. (2003), *Korporativnoe Upravlenie v Rossiiskoy Promyshlennosti* (Moscow: MONF, No. 149).

Kabalina, V. (ed.) (1997), *Predpriyatie i Rynok. Dinamika Upravleniya i Trudovykh Otnosheniya v Perekhodny Period (Opyt monograficheskikh issledovaniy 1989–1995)* (Moscow: ROSSPEN)

Kabalina, V. and Sidorina, T. (1999), 'Munitsipalizatsiya social'noy sfery v period reform', *Obschestvo i Ekonomika* 9, 64–92.

Olimpieva, I. and Ejova, L. (2002), 'Changing Personnel Management System in a Transitional Economy', in Lang, R. (ed.): *Personalmanagement im Transformationsprozess* (Munchen und Mering: Rainer Hampp), pp. 339–44.

Patrushev V.D. and Temnitskij, A.L. (1995), *Real'noe Povedenie Rabochikh Promyshlennosti v Sfere Truda v Period Perekhoda k Rynochnym Otnosheniyam* (Moscow: IS RAN).

—— (2000), *Trudovye otnoshenija na novom chastnom predpriyatii (sotsiologicheskiy analiz dannykh tryokh issledovaniy)* (Moscow: IS RAN).

Tukumtsev, B.G. (1999), 'Sotsial'no-trudovye Otnosheniya v Kontekste Gosudarstvennykh Interesov', *Sotsial'no-trudovye Otnosheniya: Sostoyanie i Tendentsii v Rossii*, (Samara), pp. 6–20.

Vasiliev, S.A. (ed.) (2001), *Desyatiletie Ekonomicheskikh Reform v Sankt-Peterburge* (St Petersburg: GP MCSEI 'Leontiefskiy Centr')

Veber A.V., Shifrin S.I. (2002), 'Etapy Sozdaniya Informatsionnogo Kompleksa Podderzhki Professional'nogo razvitiya I upravleniya personalom', *Spravochnik po Upravleniyu Personalom* 4.

Internet-based references

Zhuravslaya E., Lazareva O., Pirtilla J., Solanko A., Khaaparanta P. and Jurikkala T. 'Infrastruktura I sotsial'naya sfera rossiiskih predpriyatii', Working paper, [website] (2003), <http://www.cefir.org/Papers/firm&pubservice_report_rus.pdf>

Chapter 11

Pay in Russia

Graham Hollinshead

Introduction

In a volume devoted to HRM in Russia, it is instructive firstly to reflect upon pay as a feature of HRM in the Western context. In an original formulation of the HRM concept (Beer et al.1984), reward systems occupy a pivotal position as an 'HRM policy choice'. According to the authors, an HRM perspective on reward was concerned not only with traditional concerns with pay, but also with the symbolic significance of reward systems and their role in nurturing desirable attitudes and behaviour amongst employees. In formulating reward policies, the main issues to be confronted by management were:

- The balance between intrinsic rewards such as feelings of competence, achievement, responsibility, significance, influence, personal growth and meaningful contribution, and extrinsic rewards such as promotions, salary, fringe benefits, bonuses and so on
- The application of systems which are most effective for maintaining employee perceptions of equity, both in terms of internal corporate relativities and external comparisons outside the organization
- Whether there were benefits in introducing performance related pay systems, either at the individual or group/organization level.

In drawing distinctions with 'traditional' concerns with pay, new pay became a powerful strategic tool to be utilized by management in order to engender higher levels of employee performance and commitment to the achievement of corporate goals. In essence, whilst pay still needed to be equitable in its implementation, taking into account internal and external relativities, the instrument of pay could should be applied in a more discriminating fashion by management, allocating pay resources where individuals or groups were 'adding value' to corporate activities. In the West, the new discourses of HRM correlated with broader structural changes in pay systems. Firstly, albeit on a differential basis, European countries have witnessed a decentralization in the level of pay determination towards the level of the establishment, or even the workplace. Determination of pay by the individual employer has also been the norm in the US (Brewster and Hegewisch 1994). Secondly, there has been a discernible, yet internationally differentiated move away from collectively determined and standardized rates, towards more flexible and individually or team orientated, forms of payment (ibid).Thus, the notion of HRM is inextricably bound up with the modernization of reward, yet in post Communist Russia, the forces of economic liberalization have impacted upon pay in an uneven and contradictory fashion.

Pay Determination in Socialist Structures

In the former communist bloc, state ownership of industry had been associated with a low but stable standard of living as the state kept unemployment, wages and pensions under control (Blasi et al. 1997). Indeed, the socialist model of pay had been centred upon notions of egalitarianism, the state as provider of pay and other social benefits, the critical role of women in the labour market, and trade unions as a passive force, acting as a transmission belt for both state and enterprise management in the disbursement of welfare. This was consistent with official theory in the USSR under which there could be no private ownership of productive resources leading to a minority of owners and a majority of wage labourers (White 2000). Equally, private ownership of factories was not permitted and it was illegal to live off the labour of others, whilst it was also compulsory to work (ibid). A general mandatory wage scale applied to all workers. According to Prokopenko (1994) various traditional tendencies were apparent in payment systems. Firstly, the prevailing egalitarian philosophy resulted in compensation levelling between highly skilled and unskilled workers regardless of individual performance and in the subsequent loss of motivation for top level performance. Second, the Soviet idea of an incentive scheme was that everybody earned more (Wynd and Reitsch 1991) with social peace in an organization being felt to be more important than income differentials. Third, workers possessed a strong bargaining position with employers due to the virtual impossibility, in a centrally planned economy, that they could be made redundant. Thus a managerial conundrum was how to stimulate workers to improve performance in the transition period whilst avoiding inflationary wage levels. A common problem across Central and Eastern Europe was that 'workers get their salaries for just showing up, if the supervisor wants them to do any work he must "pay for it" (Pearce 1991). Fourth, fringe benefits were a critical element in compensation where shortages of consumer goods and services prevailed. For example, in CIS countries, a large 'soft' rouble salary was a weak motivator where there were too many roubles in circulation and almost no consumer goods. A wide variety of bonuses and premiums were awarded from holidays and year end bonuses to tax-free clothing allowances amounting to 20 to 30 per cent of basic salary. These were accompanied with important 'social benefits' including housing, holiday accommodation and even schooling for children. Another unique policy instrument was 'management by special favours' (ibid) by which employees were tacitly permitted to break rules relating to use of organizational resources for their own purposes, or absenteeism.

Macro Level Reform – The Effects of Privatization on the Distribution of Pay

Gradual moves towards economic pluralism had occurred through the Gorbachev and Yeltsin eras, so that by 1990 around 80 per cent of the working population was employed in the state sector, with the remainder being engaged in trading co-operatives, commercial farming, or joint enterprises, and with the first onset of unemployment affecting around two million people (*Finansy i Statistika* 1991). However, the rapid programme of privatization incepted in 1991 was associated with a radical overhaul of the national system of incomes distribution in Russia. Mirroring 'shock therapy' in the privatization of industry, the liberalization of pay played out in an extreme fashion in Russia, creating an elite cadre of 'winners', but also sizeable proportion of economic 'losers', including the emergence of a new underclass.

According to statistics published by the International Labour Organization and the World Bank (2004) approximately 27 per cent of the Russian population live below the subsistence level, which has been calculated at standing at 2500 roubles a month (70 Euro) (Tyuryukanova 2005). Furthermore, it has been estimated that approximately one third of the poor live in 'extreme poverty' with an average income of less than half the subsistence minimum. (*Financial Times* 1999). As White (2000) points out, the 'new poor' includes large families disadvantaged by the rising cost of bringing up children, inhabitants of towns where the factory providing a single source of employment had closed, or the new ranks of the unemployed. Although many in this category are close to starvation, their quality of life exceeds that of a destitute ten per cent of the population, including beggars, the homeless, orphans, alcoholics, drug addicts and prostitutes. The position of the new poor in Russia has been exacerbated in 2004 by an array of governmental measures serving to liquidate state provided social benefits that were a prominent feature of the Soviet era. Most affected groups include pensioners, war veterans and Chernobyl clean up workers. As Volkov and Peters (2004) report, established social benefits, including the free use of public transportation, discounts on residential utilities, a free local telephone service, free medication, free annual treatment at sanatoriums and health resorts, free artificial limbs and wheelchairs for invalids and guaranteed employment for the disabled have been 'monetarized', now being replaced by a monthly compensation ranging from 300 (8 Euro) to 1,550 roubles (42 Euro). The measures also include cuts in the monthly subsidies for students and people with dependent children, as well the elimination of a 25 per cent premium in wage compensation for rural teachers and doctors. (ibid). Pensioners have also experienced real declining living standards over the past decade. As from August 2002, the average pension rate was 1900 roubles (55 Euro) a month, which is close to subsistence levels. Many male workers do not survive long enough to receive pensions, with an average life expectancy of 59 years. Even so, survivors have experienced late payment of pensions due to the dwindling base of taxpayers (*The Economist* 2003).

By way of stark contrast, a recent article in T*he New York Times* (2005) reveals that Russia now has 27 billionaires, exceeded only by 57 in Germany and 341 in the

USA (Arvedlund 2005). The majority of the Russian 'super rich' cadre control raw materials and associated industries, whilst others represent new business fields such as telecommunications, construction, food production and retail. Indeed the greatest part of shareholdings in the largest Russian enterprises is in the hands of this small social grouping, the 23 largest business groups accounting for approximately 57 per cent of all Russia's industrial production (World Bank 2003). In terms of personal income, the President of Lukoil receives $1.5 million per annum, with the possibility of a $2.2 million bonus. In large scale enterprises, such as the United Mechanical Engineering Works and the Tyumen oil company, basis executive salaries amount to approximately $500,000 per annum (Volkov and Debenberg 2005). According to the World Socialist Web, the President of Basis Element Aluminium, Oleg Deripaska, paid taxes of $294 million on his income in the Siberian Republic of Khakassia, this constituting 105 of total annual revenue for the Republic. Subsequent World Development Reports published by the World Bank (2004) have suggested that a fifteen fold income gap has emerged between the richest and poorest ten per cent of earners. Such polarization is unprecedented in the Western experience and equates only with Latin American and African countries. Senior state officials may also be counted amongst the more modest beneficiaries of radical economic reform. On April tenth 2004, a new wage scale was introduced raining their salaries by several thousand Euro a month. President Putin's own salary was doubled to over 150,000 roubles (4,100 Euro) a month, whilst the deputy head of his administration now receives more than 90,000 roubles (2,500 Euro) a month (Volkov and Peters, 2004). State officials are also eligible to receive a wide array of bonuses, including country homes, transportation and medical services (*Izvestiya*, 2004a).

Following privatization, the social differentiation of income has also occurred according to region and industrial sector. Recent statistics produced by the State Statistical Committee of Russia and CE Research, reporting Average Monthly Gross Earnings for 2002, reveal that in Moscow City, and the Ural Federal District, this figure is approximately 6,500 roubles a month, or 220 Euro, compared with an equivalent of around 4,300 roubles in Siberia (140 Euro) or 3,400 roubles (110 Euro) in Privolzhsky. Of course, as Blasi, Kroumova and Kruse (1997), point out, figures on average earnings need to be treated with some care as they do not take account of earnings in the substantial informal economy, estimated to constitute around one quarter of total economic activity, or the under-reporting of wages by employers in order to escape taxes. As Kim (1997) has revealed, the same occupation could attract quite different benefits Moscow, St Petersburg and Vladivostok. So, for example, a secretary with good English, PC experience, good typing in Russian and English and some prior work experience could expect to earn 11,427–17,113 roubles (330–495 Euro) a month in Moscow, 5,713–11,427 roubles (165–330 Euro) in St Petersburg and 11,427–22,854 roubles (330–660 Euro) in Vladivostok. Disparities in pay on the basis of region are well illustrated by a recent hunger strike undertaken by air traffic controllers in Rostov-na-Donu in southern Russia. The controllers are employed by Aeronavigatsiya Yugo, which is the subsidiary of a larger state corporation and are responsible for an area comparable to some of the larger states in Europe. The grievance of staff relates to average monthly earnings of approximately 2,000 roubles a month (55 Euro), which controllers claim is only half comparable rates for the same job and employer in Moscow. Due to its state owned status, however, company managers are unable to resolve the dispute at local level and need to refer the issue to a higher authority (BBC Monitoring 2005).

Liberalization of pay has also been associated with the emergence of a 'topsy turvy' hierarchy of occupations from a Western perspective. According to Blasi et al. (1997) in late 1995, workers in industry earned 111 per cent of the average wage, workers in construction earned 131 per cent, and workers in transportation earned 152 per cent. Those employed in the State controlled education and health sectors earned 80 per cent of the average, whilst agricultural workers earnings fell below 50 per cent of the average. Underlying these statistics is the question of how changing ownership structures have affected earnings in the wake of privatization. Recent statistics produced by State Statistical Committee of Russia and CE Research (2004) reveal that, as at 2002, average earnings in foreign owned enterprises, at 9,348 roubles (or 315 Euro a month) are approximately twice those paid by State owned or local private enterprises. Whilst those working in foreign owned enterprises have benefited in a relative sense from recent economic reforms, public sector workers have experienced real decline in their standard of living, including teachers, physicians, nurses and low ranking civil servants (Volkov and Denenberg 2005). Even more adversely affected have been those in rural communities, which has been a focal point of Russian national life and folklore. Villages have suffered through the migration of more highly skilled workers (for example machinery specialists) to urban locations, and through the dismantling of former state benefits such as medical care, job training and entertainment.

Thus, over the past ten to fifteen years the emergence of income differentiation across the economic face of Russia, has, from a Western perspective, occurred in an irrational and unsystematic fashion. It is only in recent years that very modest signs of mitigating the income gulf between rich and poor have emerged, with the rate of statutory minimum pay being hitched in successive years since 2000 to its current level at around 1,700 roubles, or 50 Euro a month. In June 2005, the Minister of Economic Development and Trade was predicting a rise in real disposable incomes by 39 per cent between 2005 and 2008 and wage rises of 44 per cent over the same period in real terms. (BBC Monitoring International Reports 2005). A critical factor in separating status between occupation groupings has been the economic might of enterprise ownership in a volatile and immature market environment. Although the extreme gap between rich and poor in the new Russia undoubtedly represents a threat to social stability, it has been argued, on the more positive side (Blasi et al. 1997), that differences in wages are actually an indication that the free market is beginning to work, as the wages of employees begin to follow what people are willing to pay for the goods they produce.

Deregulation of Pay and Gender

According to the Soviet constitution, women possessed equal rights in training and remuneration, they were expected to take an equal part in social and political life, and were allowed to combine these duties with the responsibilities of motherhood through paid maternity leave and a reduction in working hours (White 2000). As White (2000) points out, nearly all women had a job in the late Soviet era, and they represented just over half the workforce. Although women tended to be concentrated in traditionally 'female occupations', for example teaching, translating, book-keeping and librarianship, they also constituted 60 per cent of engineers, economists and officials in management and administration, and around two thirds of all doctors (*Vestnik statistiki* 1992a). However, despite official rhetoric, women's earnings were only equivalent to two thirds of male income by the early 1990s. (*Vestnik statistiki*, 1992b, 53). Furthermore, the Soviet era was characterized by the overloading of female duties, demanding the fulfilment of maternity and household chores, combined with official employment and social activities (International Labour Organization 2000) Following the programme of privatization in the early 1990s, there has been a re-ordering of occupational status in Russia, effectively downgrading professions in education, health, culture and social welfare in which female employment is concentrated, and bolstering new 'masculine' strongholds in trade, finance and commerce. Consequently, in the post-Soviet era, female earnings have declined to represent only 45 per cent to 50 per cent of income of male counterparts (*Izvestiya* 1998). Reportedly, many women accept jobs at lower levels of skill and remuneration in exchange for non-monetary benefits, such minimum overtime hours, and access to child care. Women are over-represented amongst the unemployed, and are increasingly obliged to take up positions in the burgeoning shadow, or informal, economy, which is completely unregulated. The International Labour Organization (2000) report also finds that much female employment is hazardous in nature as women are induced to engage in unsafe productive activity attracting compensatory high rates of pay and promising early retirement. Such developments have occurred against a back cloth of the 'feminization of poverty' (White 2000). Thus, families with two, three or more children have found themselves to be in acute financial difficulty, particularly if headed by a single mother. Such families are blighted by declining female incomes, and reduced child benefits, which are estimated to cover just three per cent of necessary expenditure for a child (Volkov and Denenberg 2005).

Enterprise Level Pay

In the Soviet era, the climate for industrial relations was highly legalistic, with labour codes prescribing the rights and duties of the parties within a broader framework of labour law. At enterprise level, tightly regulated collective contracts served to implement central instructions from the party state in the workplace. Thus, the function of enterprise management in the field of pay was primarily administrative, servicing the implementation of contractual arrangements concerning pay. New ownership structures in Russia have been associated, however, with the ceding of primary responsibility for pay determination to enterprise managers within the context of a new labour code enacted in 2002, which stipulates that employers should adhere to minimum pay provisions and that basic conditions of employment (for example hours of work, holiday time, payment terms and social insurance) should be covered in signed and written employment agreements relating to each individual's employment.

An important question in the wake of privatization has been the extent to which workers, and their trade union representatives, would be actively involved in pay determination. In this respect, it is important to note that in other Central and East European transitional societies, for example, Poland and Hungary, trade unions participated in the reconstruction of autonomous industrial relations through tripartite dealings with employer and government counterparts which assisted in the development of institutions and procedures for the deregulation and decentralization of pay determination and collective bargaining (Hollinshead 2000). In Russia, however, trade unions have largely been marginalized in the course of privatization and precluded from active involvement in wage determination. According to Blasi et al., the weakness of trade unions during economic reform was predestined by their past (107). During the Soviet era, trade unions were closely involved in the administration of welfare benefits at workplace level, and in the distribution of social benefits (for example apartments, consumer goods and foodstuffs). Although labour-management agreements existed in many enterprises, trade unions were pre-occupied with formulating working conditions, resolving disputes between workers and managers, and assisting managers rather than defending workers rights (Blasi et al. 1997). Currently, the Russian labour movement is dominated by the Federation of Independent Trade Unions if Russia (FNPR), which is a direct successor to Soviet era unions, and many of whose officials enjoy close relationships with enterprise managers. Thus, despite Russian trade unions formally representing the interests of some 60 per cent of the labour force, employees have yet to achieve a truly independent voice at enterprise level. Failure to properly call management to account has been associated with the massive violation of labour law, prompting the International Labour Organization (ILO) to call for 'the promotion and realization of international labour standards, fundamental principles and rights at work' and the 'strengthening of tripartism and of social dialogue' (International Labour Organization 2001). The disenfranchising of workers through privatization also occurred through the diminution of their status as stockholders, which had previously allowed them to elect general directors. Despite retaining the technical right of representation at board level following corporatization, in practice workers have been denied representational rights as shareholders through the common practice of their being obliged to sign proxies transferring their voting rights to managers (Blasi et al. 1997). More assertive trade union action on their behalf might have consolidated the position of workers as owners through the establishment of trusts, but there is no evidence that this has occurred (ibid). Nevertheless, some financial gain has accrued to employees and former employees following the selling of their enterprise through the realization of the value of their shares.

Blasi et al. (ibid) interviewed several hundred general directors in the mid 1990s to ascertain their view of the role of trade unions within enterprises, and to investigate modes of decision making affecting employment, including wage determination. The managers generally took the view that trade unions were not equal partners in the negotiating process, and that they not sufficiently robust to represent workers' interests in an independent fashion. Indeed a number of the managers had taken action to abolish union presence in their enterprises, one replacing the traditional union with a company based alternative, and another directly providing social benefits to workers as opposed to using the union transmission belt for disbursement purposes. In the latter enterprise, food and consumer goods were being sold at a discount, hospitals, schools and housing were being financed, and even holidays in the Crimea were being provided. The survey also provided useful insights into the actual process of pay determination. Defining the compensation system as 'systemless' one manager explained how her enterprise raised wages two or three times a month to offset inflation. In another enterprise, the General Director took unilateral action to increase wages each month to prevent workers being lost to a neighbouring plant. At a building materials plant Krasnoyarsk, the manager explained that pay was increased four times in the year to respond to government increases in the minimum wage, and also price rises.

In a study of forms of employment and compensation in a sample of 44 Russian enterprises in 1996, Russell and Callanan (2001) investigated how changes in ownership and increased exposure to market forces had affected employment practices in the early post-reform era. A critical question for the researchers was the extent to which new private, privatized, and state owned enterprises departed from traditions of the late Soviet enterprise. The survey covered enterprises with varied ownership across five industries: manufacturing, construction, retail, personal services, science and scientific services in the cities of Moscow, Orenberg and Syzran. The results of the study demonstrated important patterns of continuity and change in the immediate post privatization era, suggesting a level of adjustment on the part of all enterprises to contextual forces of the market. Perhaps surprisingly, former state owned enterprises had abandoned bonus systems with the greatest alacrity, no longer being able to afford them, whilst these had been adopted by new private enterprises. Resonating previous traditions in the newly privatized environment, smaller private concerns were inclined to pay bonuses in order to recruit and retain scarce staff. At the specific industrial level, payment of bonuses was most frequent in science and scientific services whilst payment by the hour was most common in manufacturing and least common in retail. Payment by the piece was most common in construction and manufacturing and least common in retail. For both state and privately owned enterprises, larger concerns were most likely to use both payment by results and payment by the hour, this being in keeping with the expectation that size promotes differentiation.

Non-Payment of Wages

In both state and privately owned sectors of the economy, a chronic problem experienced in post-communist Russia has been the non payment of wages. This has not only caused distress to workers, fuelling a number of strikes and protests in the mid 1990s, but has also stifled the flow of funds through financial institutions via taxation, this contributing towards general economic slowdown and serious under funding of public services, culture and science. The problem is well illustrated by article appearing in *The Moscow Tribune* (2002) in which the Prime Minister is reported as announcing that teachers, doctors and other employees working in the financed sectors should not count on previously promised incomes for approximately a year. According to the Prime Minister, the government still owed some 1.5 billion roubles to employees working in the state run sector. Current evidence from trade unions in Russia would suggest that there around 35,000 enterprises owing workers wages, amounting to 2000 billion roubles (or 59 billion Euro). Survey evidence produced in the late 1990s (World Development Report 1998/99) revealed that only 18 per cent of Russians were paid regularly, 25 per cent were being paid irregularly, and 57 per cent were not being paid at all, but feared losing their job. White (2000) identifies a number of poignant organizational and personal examples of the effects of non payment. Workers in a Krasnoyask factory, where payments had not been made for year, erected a gravestone in the form of a 500 rouble note to commemorate their last payday (*Investiya* 1997). One individual, after a year without pay, committed suicide by jumping from the factory roof of his enterprise, leaving a message that the factory director should pay for his funeral (*Investiya* 1996). White also reports upon the common practice of offering payment in kind rather than cash. Workers in a clock factory in Penza received rolls of toilet paper instead of bonuses (Transition 1997). Other examples included payment in the form of tins of pineapple, pickled cucumber or vodka (ibid).

The Emergence of a New Salaried Class

As the Russian labour market has become more differentiated, there is evidence of a growing demand for qualified specialists. The Russian newspaper *Izvestiya* (2004b) reported that in construction and trade sectors, professionals are highly sought after, not just in Moscow, but in the regions where rapid business expansion in occurring. The article reveals that the salaries of financial specialist surged by 29 per cent from 2003 to 2004. Specialists in taxation enjoyed a 38 per cent increase over the same period, whilst finance analysts benefited from the highest increase of 45 per cent. It was reported also that the wages of logistics and procurement specialists had also grown significantly, with leaders in this sector being procurement managers and customs brokers. Human Resource and Training and Development Managers were also in demand, with Heads of Personnel in large companies having gained from 35 per cent wage increases since 2003. Camiah and Hollinshead (2003), in a study of 'new' Russian managers and Western expatriates, found a cadre of highly mobile young

Russian managers, many of whom were female, operating in newly established joint ventures in the Moscow region. These 'market-orientated' managers were fluent in English, highly educated, and had accumulated considerable experience of 'Western' style management practices (Puffer 1996). As well as being highly opportunistic and ambitious, the new Russian managers had acquired the 'trappings' of their Western equivalents, driving expensive cars, using mobile phones, being IT proficient and dressing smartly. Although studies of this nature remain sporadic, they point towards an emerging 'bubble' of managerial, professional and knowledge workers in the new Russia, whose career expectations and conditions of employment increasingly resemble those of their Western counterparts.

When East Meets West – Pay and Motivational Issues in Mew Joint Ventures

Following the liberalizing of the Russian economy, there has been a slow, but relatively sure flow of foreign direct investment into the country. Accompanying finance from Western corporations has been the arrival of expatriates into uncharted, and culturally distant, territory. A recent study by Camiah and Hollinshead (2003) recognizes the role of expatriates in defining a new normative order in embryonic joint ventures. According to the study, which is based upon parallel interviews of 'new' Russian managers and their Western counterparts in the Moscow region, a climate of mutual mistrust pervades the interaction between these groupings

On one hand Russian managers, who, despite their apparent market orientation, still exhibited some traditional Soviet values and found the pay gap dividing themselves and their Western counterparts to be unacceptable. One Russian manager in the survey referred to it as 'a type of apartheid' that still resonated badly in the aftermath of communist egalitarianism. The observation may well have been rooted in underlying misgivings about the profit motive which has been seen by Russians to epitomize individualistic, materialistic and competitive Western style capitalism (Puffer and McCarthy 1995). This was well captured by one Russian manager who stated:

> There is a feeling that Russians are being treated as second class citizens. They are paid much less than the expatriates, who, in addition, have large living allowances, live in better accommodation than Russians and frequently have a chauffeur.

On the other hand, expatriates in the survey expressed concern about the heavily pragmatic and opportunistic orientation of their Russian counterparts towards the new organization. One stated:

> A Russian will change jobs for a difference of 50 dollars a month… Russian employees are purely money driven, there is such a contrast as to how other nationalities make their choice about the place of work. It's incredible, it's all about money.

The survey therefore revealed the interplay of negative perceptions between the emerging cadre of Russian managers and their Western counterparts. From the

Russian perspective, the expatriates represented the personification of capitalist forces on Russian territory, and the appearance of managerial 'prospectors' from the West seemed to prompt mirrored motivational responses on the part of the indigenous management group. In a climate of considerable economic insecurity, including doubt about the sustainability of foreign direct investment, it was perhaps understandable that the Russians were 'making hay while the sun shone' and acting in a highly opportunistic fashion.

The study concluded that primary responsibility rested with Western corporations investing in Russia to 'uncross the wires' and to enhance levels of trust in West/East joint ventures. Accordingly it was incumbent upon such enterprises to assist in the fuller integration of expatriates into the realities of Russian life and work in order to mitigate the effects of status differentials, it was necessary to re-engineer organizational relationships between expatriates and local managers to remove in-organization 'glass ceilings', and it was necessary to review the interface between the organization and its environment, with Western enterprises accepting responsibility for matters such as urban regeneration, environmental protection, training and job creation.

Reforming and Modernizing Pay

This chapter has charted emergent features of pay in Russia which are strongly associated with immature and volatile market structures. Most notably, we have identified profound inequities in national income distribution, absolute poverty across much of the working population, and a 'systemless' approach to the determination of pay, which rests virtually unilaterally in the hands of management. Undoubtedly the crisis in pay needs to be urgently addressed by policy makers and industrial stakeholders in Russia and beyond. The agenda for reform may be divided into two main categories as follows.

The Application of International Standards

If Russia is to move forward as a trading nation, it is clear that chronic, and seemingly intractable, problems in the field of pay need to be addressed. The non payment of wages violates established notions of fairness, as does the existence of a statutory minimum rate which constitutes a tiny fraction of average wages and remains below subsistence levels (International Labour Organization 2004). Action to increase the minimum wage level is important as proportional enhancements will be stimulated at levels above the minimum in order to maintain established relativities. The issue of discrimination and 'equal' pay is becoming pressing as deregulation of pay has clearly disadvantaged certain groups, particularly women and older workers. As a recent conference in Moscow organized by the ILO-CEET and the Russian Ministry of Labour there was broad consensus amongst participants that progress in addressing such problems could feasibly be made through the formulation of a negotiated incomes policy, and the removal of the current government's tax-based approach to income regulation, which has led to new income distortions, penalized productivity improvements, encouraged a shift into non monetary forms of remuneration and contributed to the non declaration of incomes by the better paid (International Labour Organization 2005). An institutional prerequisite to the implementation of effective incomes policy will be the strengthening of the fledgling Russian Tripartite Commission, which included representatives of government, trade unions and employers organizations. Following the example of a number of its East and Central European counterpart countries, the transition from planned to market economic structures may be consolidated through the building of independent and pluralist institutions able to formulate policies on income and other matters in a consensual fashion, thus maintaining broader social coherence (Hollinshead 2000). Moves towards the strengthening of tripartism and independent collective bargaining are currently underway, a recent top level meeting having been convened between the ILO Director General, Juan Somavia, the Russian Minister of Labour and Social Development, the Russian Vice Premier and Senior Trade Union and Employers Organization representatives on the subject of Social Partnership. Foreign owned ventures will also need to recognize the significance of international labour standards in the Russian context, and formulate employment strategies in keeping with the emerging institutional and pluralistic climate. This has been well illustrated by the case of US owned fast food chain McDonalds which initially resisted trade union organization at its food processing plant McComplex, but was forced to recognize the Commerce and Catering Workers' Union for collective bargaining purposes in October 2000 following protests and demonstrations by the union.

Human Resource Management

A prerequisite for the reform of pay in Russia is clearly the generation of funds at enterprise, and at national, level upon which to base pay enhancements. To date, a double bind has confronted many Russian enterprises, where lack of productivity has been associated with impoverished human resources, poor profitability in turn precluding the possibility of pay enhancement. The relationship between wages and salaries and economic performance and productivity has been obscure in the Russian context. (International Labour Organization 2005). In this respect, the aforementioned Western concept of Human Resource Management may be useful in guiding developments, despite the acknowledged epistemological constraints associated with seeking to apply this concept in a 'universalistic' fashion across national boundaries (Brewster 2001). Following the guiding principles of HRM, Russian enterprise managers could benefit from shifting the primary focus of their attention from *external* factors conditioning the level and type of pay (for example minimum wages and inflation), towards the *internalization* of policies for pay determination. Such a shift in focus would also imply a move from reactivity and lack of systematization in formulating pay towards greater levels of proactivity and sophistication at enterprise level. If enterprise managers were to assume greater responsibility for managing their own internal labour markets, with recourse to the instrument of pay, various strategic dividends could accrue. Firstly, it would be possible to relate pay specifically to local conditions in order to attract and retain staff. Secondly, and perhaps more importantly, pay could be applied in a more discriminating fashion in order to promote higher levels of corporate productivity, possibly by differentiating reward within the organization to reflect varying levels of performance and contribution. Thirdly, the HR 'lever' of pay could be connected more assiduously with other areas of employment activity (for example training and development) in order to upgrade human capital within the organization. Following Prokopenko (1994), the refashioning of pay as a mechanism to drive corporate performance implies profound organizational culture change in the post communist environment. Important, and potentially contested, 'mindset' shifts would the abrogation of equity in favour of personal financial gain and the dilution of notions of collective solidarity in favour of principles of individual motivation (ibid). Of course, the re-engineering of pay demands a heightening of sophistication in respect of the management function itself and the acquisition of greater strategic awareness on the part of enterprise managers. Market orientated thinking on the part of post-communist managers is notoriously difficult to achieve (Child 1993), although possibly the joint ventures that have already experimented with modern employment practices Russian soil will provide a useful source of learning.

Conclusion

Pay in Russia has constituted a material embodiment of dominant political, economic and social structures and values. Low but standardized pay during the communist era, combined with social benefits and full employment epitomized the socialist values of paternalism, collectivism and anti-materialism. The explosive approach taken to economic transformation in the early 1990s was accompanied by a rupturing of monolithic payment systems, creating an elite of super rich 'winners' whilst condemning a sizeable proportion of the working population to live at or below subsistence levels. As Russia seeks to enter into a new stage of market maturity, and to become integrated into global trading structures, there is a pressing need to regenerate business performance across the breadth of the Russian economy. Greater managerial sophistication in the formulation of pay policies at enterprise level, together with the alleviation of major inequities to meet international standards, may be instrumental in facilitating a more benign correlation between pay, enterprise profitability through higher quality output, and national economic performance.

References

BBC Monitoring International Reports (2005), 'Russian Minister Forecasts Sharp Rise in Disposable Incomes', 16 June.

BBC Monitoring International Reports, (2005), 'Air Traffic Controllers Hunger Strike Widens in Southern Russia', Russian HTV, 10 June.

Beer, M., Spector, B., Lawrence, P.R., Quinn Mills, D. and Walton, R.E. (1984), *Managing Human Assets* (New York: Free Free).

Blasi, J.R., Kroumova, M. and Kruse, D. (1997), *Kremlin Capitalism, Privatizing the Russian Economy* (Ithaca and London: Cornell University Press).

Brewster, C. (2001), 'HRM: The Comparative Dimension', in Storey, J. (ed.) *Human Resource Management; A Critical Text,* 2nd edition (London, Thomson Learning).

Brewster, C. and Hegewisch, A. (eds) (1994), 'Policy and Practice in European Human Resource Management', The Price Waterhouse/Cranfield Survey, (London and New York, Routledge).

Child, J. (1993), *Society and Enterprise between Hierarchy and Market, Societal Change between market and organization* (Avebury: Aldershot).

Camiah, N. and Hollinshead, G. (2003), 'Assessing the Potential for Effective Cross-cultural Working between "new" Russian Managers and Western Expatriates', *Journal of World Business* 38: 3, 245–61.

Financial Times, 30 April 1999, Russia.

Finansy i Statistika (1991), 'Narodnoe Khozyaistvo SSSR v 1990g' (Moscow).

Hollinshead, G. (2000), 'ACAS in Poland and Hungary, Helping to Build Institutions for Dealing with Industrial Conflict', ACAS Occasional Paper no. 57, London.

International Labour Organization (2000), *Russia and other CIS Countries; A Break with the Past*, (Geneva).

International Labour Organization (2001), *Program of Cooperation Between the International Labour Organization and the Russian Federation for the Period 2000–2001*, (Geneva).

International Labour Organization (2004), The ILO SRO-Budapest Bulletin, Newsletter, 2–94.

International Labour Organization (2005), 'What Wage Policy for Russia?' Budapest Bulletin Newsletter, 2–94.

Izvestiya, 9 October 1996.

Izvestiya, 4 November 1997.

Izvestiya, 19 April 1998.

Izvestiya, 17 April 2004a.

Izvestiya, 15 November 2004b.

Kim, A. (1997), *Employment Practices in Russia* (St Petersburg: Bisnis).

Moscow Tribune, 'Kasyanov Announces Salary Freeze Year End in Budget-Financed Sector', 29 January 2002.

New York Times, (2005), 'In Russia's boom, riches and rags', 15 April.

Pearce, J. (1991), 'From Socialism to Capitalism: The Effect of Hungarian Human Resource Practices', *Academy of Management Executive* 5: 4, 76–82.

Prokopenko, J. (1994), 'The Transition to a Market Economy and its Implications for HRM in Eastern Europe', in Kirkbride, P.S. (ed.), *Human Resource Management.*

Puffer, S.M. (1996), 'Understanding the Bear: A Portrait of Russian Business Leaders', Puffer, S.M. (ed.), *Management across Cultures: Insights from Fiction and Practice* (Oxford: Blackwell).

Puffer, S.M. and McCarthy, D.J. (1995), 'Finding the Common Ground in Russian and American Business Ethics', *California Management Review* 37: 2, 29–46.

Russell, R. and Callanan, V. (2001), 'Firm-Level Influences on Forms of Employment and Pay in Russia', *Industrial Relations* 40: 4, 627–34.

State Statistical Committee of Russia and CE Research, 'Labour Costs Russia', 2004.

The Economist (2003), 'Pensions in Russia', 31 July.

Transition (1997), 4 April, 6, 40.

Tyuryukanova, E. (2005), 'Forced Labour in the Russian Federation Today', International Labour Organisation, (Geneva).

Vestnik statistiki, (1992b), 1, 53.

Vestnik statistiki, (1992a), 1, 65.

Volkov, V. and Denenberg, J. (2005), 'Wealth and Poverty in Modern Russia', *World Socialist Web*.

Volkov and Peters (2004), 'Russia: Putin Lays Siege to Social Benefits', *World Socialist Web*.

White, S. (2000), *Russia's New Politics; The Management of a Postcommunist Society*, (Cambridge: Cambridge University Press).

World Development Report (1998/99), *Knowledge for Development* (New York: Oxford University Press for the World Bank).

World Bank (2003), World Development Indicators, Washington DC.

World Bank (2004), World Development Indicators, Washington DC.

Wynd, W. and Reitch, H. (1991), 'Soviet and American business students: similarities and differences', *Journal of Education for Business* July/August, 339–40.

PART III
HRM PRACTICES IN MULTINATIONAL COMPANIES

Chapter 12

Western-Russian Acquisition Negotiations and Post-Acquisition Integration: A Case Study

Kenneth Husted and Snejina Michailova

Introduction

Russia has changed its position as the second largest economy in the world during Soviet times to the twelfth largest at present. Throughout the 1990s, the country's GDP growth rates have been among the lowest and the country risk the highest in the world. With an immature institutional environment, insufficient infrastructure, and important cultural and institutional differences with the West, Russia is a challenging host country for Western investments. And yet, Russia remains an attractive destination for many Western companies. In spite of numerous difficulties, a number of firms have been forging ahead with long-term commitments and investments (Shama 1997; Puffer et al. 1998). One of these firms is the Danish multinational Rockwool, the world's largest manufacturer of stone wool and one of the four largest producers of mineral wool in the world. Rockwool Group has more than 7,500 employees and a turnover of nearly EUR one billion. With more than 20 factories in Europe, North America and East Asia, and a global network of sales companies, trade offices, and commercial partners, the Rockwool Group covers most parts of the globe. Rockwool's biggest market is Germany (23 per cent) followed by the Benelux countries (20 per cent), France (12 per cent), and UK and Denmark (8 per cent each).

Rockwool's growth originates both from organic growth and acquisitions. Since the market for its products has remained relatively steady over the past decade, investment levels have been kept high. Rockwool has expanded heavily internationally over the years. The first expansion wave was in the mid-1960s. Existing companies were acquired and new factories where built in most West European countries. Originally the main focus was Scandinavia and the rest of Western Europe, but since the 1980s and continuing to the present, heavy investments have been made in Northern America, Asia and Eastern Europe. The large size of the markets and the relatively cheap labour in Eastern Europe offered great potential for Rockwool to expand their activities. Rockwool opened factories in the former GDR, in Poland, and in Hungary. Russia was present on Rockwool's international activities map for more than 30 years through export and selling activities. In 1995 the company established a representative office in Moscow. When the sales increased, Rockwool started considering seriously the option of starting a production in Russia. The company decided to select and acquire an existing Russian manufacturer instead of starting a green field investment. Rockwool identified a number of Russian factories and investigated a few, which it selected as potential target firms. The final choice was Mostermosteklo, a Russian manufacturer situated in Zheleznodorozhny, a town with around 120,000 inhabitants. 35 km east of Moscow, Zheleznodorozhny is not considered part of the Moscow municipality, though it is a part of the Moscow administrative region [*oblast*].

Negotiating with the selected potential partner and the initial steps towards establishing and managing the new relationship are, among others, two critical factors for the success of an investment. An acquisition negotiation is a challenging process both in terms of its very nature, but also because it affects the subsequent relationship between the two parties. The negotiations may affect the willingness and ability of the management teams to work together in the new business combination (Walsh 1989). When negotiations cross borders, they become inherently challenging. Another country's politics, culture, and corporate governance policies can erect nearly insurmountable obstacles (Sebenius 1998). A number of studies have focused on the integration process following the acquisition and in particular on integration barriers (Haspeslagh and Jemison 1991). The emphasis has primarily been on cultural clashes (Buono et al. 1985; Nahavandi and Malekzadeh 1988), communication difficulties (Schweiger and DeNisi 1991), employees' perceptions and reactions (Risberg 2001), and conflict resolution (Blake and Mouton 1985). The present chapter presents the key challenges Rockwool met in the process of negotiating with the Russian partner and in the first year after the acquisition and how Rockwool dealt with these challenges.

The Pre-Acquisition Background

After serious investigations Rockwool decided to acquire the Russian company Mostermosteklo (MTS). MTS was founded by the state in 1956 and functioned as a big conglomerate [*kombinat*]. It produced stone wool fireproof insulation materials, fibreglass and other construction components. The diversification of its products was very high. The enterprise was the primary supplier to Moscow and the Moscow region construction industry and has been the strategic Moscow factory for producing insulation material for the building industry. MTS's business has been the primary business in the local town along with a wood processing plant and two industrial ceramic factories.

MTS was privatized in 1994. The majority of the shares went to Rosprom, a large Russian industrial holding company. The company's managers, workers and pensioners acquired a minor part of the shares. Almost all of the factory's clients were local, the only product sold abroad was fibreglass. Most clients concluded separate purchase agreements on a transaction by transaction basis and only very few had long-term (one year) contracts. MTS had no marketing department and no sales representatives working in the field. The company never had client files nor any sales material. Its distribution strategy was not clearly defined. It had an order entry department, which dealt with customers mainly over the telephone and on a day-to-day basis. In 1996, approximately 28 per cent of the sales were conducted on the basis of barter trade. The company had a few one-year non-binding supplier contracts and a large number of short-term agreements.

MTS employed more than 1,300 employees with an average age of 44, most of whom lived in the local town Zheleznodorozhny. In periods when production was slow, many workers were kept at a partial pay in order to preserve the core group of skilled labour. The employees were promoted to management positions mainly from within the company and often started from positions in the production. The number of managers was unrealistically large and did not really imply that all who were called managers had management functions. The appraisal system was very rigid and inflexible so in order to reward employees financially, they were simply promoted to management positions. MTS was paying officially the highest salaries in Zheleznodorozhny.

MTS's general director was about 60 years old when Rockwool started the acquisition negotiations. He has been working in MTS since 1967 climbing the latter from foreman through head of workshop and deputy general director on commerce. He had a strong technical background and was increasingly market oriented. He was the main decision maker in the company and the majority of the employees strongly associated the company's achievements with his personal abilities and skills.

The Acquisition Negotiations between Rockwool and Mostermosteklo

Rockwool did not want to acquire MTS as a whole; it was interested in taking over only the unit producing stone wool. This meant that the big conglomerate had to be split into two parts. The splitting process turned out to be more difficult than expected. The take-over negotiations started in the beginning of 1997 with a due diligence procedure by an international auditing company.

The due diligence report confirmed that the stone wool producing unit was significantly more profitable than the rest of the company and accounted for approximately 43 per cent of MTS's total revenues. MTS had recently bought two modern productions lines for stone wool production from Finland. Only one of them was operating due to lack of funds for installing the other line: that caused a great deal of non-exploited production capacity. The management claimed that due to the imported production lines MTS's products were of best quality in Russia.

In July 1998 the terms of taking over MTS's stone wool producing unit were outlined and agreed upon, and the final take-over was almost completely ready to take place. However, the point of signing the contract could still not be reached and the acquisition negotiations had to continue. In this situation, the headquarters in

Denmark decided to establish a Task Force Group (TFG) to work in Russia for six months and execute part of the pre-work before the eventual takeover. The aim was to prepare the necessary planning basis and to work out the strategies and plans for the future. In an environment characterized by strong differences in terms of national culture, language, attitudes and practices between Russians and Danes of how to run an enterprise, it was meaningful to invest in establishing such a group.

18 August 1998 (the day after the collapse of the rouble!) the TFG consisting of five Danes from Rockwool Denmark arrived in Russia. Within a few days the value of the rouble plummeted from DKK 1.2 per rouble to DKK 0.4 per rouble. The serious rouble crisis had both serious positive and negative impact on preparing the business plan and negotiating the acquisition. A positive factor was that the local production became much more competitive *vis-a-vis* foreign production. However, in order to exploit this opportunity efficiently, it was important that the quality of the local products could match the quality of foreign products. At that time, MTS's products were of a better quality than other locally manufactured products, but still behind the quality of foreign products. The TFG believed that the quality gap could be reduced and later closed by introducing components and ingredients of better quality and through focused development efforts.

The takeover was complicated by the need for involving a high number of stakeholders which all had claims to be included in the negotiations. A number of various factors needed to be considered, such as Rockwool's uncertainty about the political consequences of the economic crisis in Russia, the changes introduced by the Russian authorities regarding the payment rules (which became much stricter as a consequence of the crisis). A broad range of practical details needed to be negotiated as well. An example was the construction of a new road to this part of the conglomerate, which Rockwool did not consider to acquire – Rockwool bought the main entrance to the factory and did not want this road to be used by others. Patience turned out to be one of the most important qualifications in the negotiation period.

The TFG was staffed with mature, robust and open-minded people with a solid Rockwool background in marketing and sales, production, finance, and personnel policy. They were sent to Russia after a four-day course concerning the nature of doing business in Russia. Language training did not precede the expatriation. The first six months were considered a kind of due diligence and only upon the completion of this period did the expatriates decide whether they wanted to stay. Their ability to live not just in another country but also in a system, which differs vastly from the Danish one in many important aspects, was seriously challenged. The Westerners occupied all main managerial positions (CEO, director of business relations, production director, commercial director, director of economics, and HR director). The expectations were high and so was the uncertainty about the work to be done during the following months – partly because of the very nature of the project work, but more in relation to the fact that the team should work and live in Russia. The Danish expatriates had to adjust to a 'New World' both at the factory and in the flats they rented in Moscow. An Englishman who had been living in Russia for several years and had previously been working as manager of the Rockwool representation in Moscow and speaks fluent Russian joined the Danish team.

Two of the members of the TFG decided to return to Denmark after the group's assignment was accomplished. They did not prolong their stay in Russia: one was not able to adapt and did not like the assignment from the very beginning, the other one left because his family was not willing to move to Moscow. At that time, it became clear to the members of the Danish team that expert knowledge was of secondary importance. They realized that a serious effort should be invested in selecting the right expatriates in terms of their ability to adapt to a different environment and in preparing them prior to their assignment abroad.

MTS's managers and employees did not speak any other language but Russian, and the Danes did not speak Russian. The Danes hired five English speaking Russians in order to be able to communicate with the Russian staff. Translators became a natural and important part of the every-day organizational life. Although the interpreters were good, the work could have gone wrong if a good cooperation with the management and the key employees in MTS was not established. There were periods with high uncertainty due to the fact that the TFG was often not given the information they needed to perform their work. The Russian managers were very careful in terms of what and how much information they should provide to the TFG. This made the information exchange very effort-demanding and time-consuming and the communication not very straightforward. Although MTS could see a number of benefits by being acquired by Rockwool, MTS's people did not always provide the information required and did not always cooperate wholeheartedly. Good conversations, patience, retaining the initiative in getting closer to the deal and working towards getting a green light from MTS's CEO were the tactics that made it possible for the TFG to get the needed insights into the factory.

Another difficult issue during the acquisition negotiations was caused by the fact that MTS's CEO wanted to keep secret the names of the managers and employees selected to work in the new company up to the last moment. His argument was that the secrecy would preserve the needed discipline among the employees. To Rockwool this situation was far from optimal because it prevented the Danish investor from training the staff they were going to take over – for example accounting staff who preferably had to be able to keep the books according to the Generally Agreed Accounting Principles from day one.

The conclusion of the TFG was that although the challenges related to the weak rouble were enormous, although there was a strong need for organizational restructuring and development and although the Russian authorities were highly bureaucratic, there was a basis for doing business in Russia. The market size was attractive, Rockwool knew how to produce and sell high quality products, the production facilities could be upgraded and the administrative processes could be substantially improved within one year. An important factor was the motivation of the management team to make the acquisition a success. Three of the five Danes in the TFG expressed their readiness to work in Russia after an eventual takeover and the whole group shared the opinion that the plans could be fulfilled. On the basis of these and other considerations, the TFG recommended the takeover. One of the important lessons learned over this two-year period was that negotiations in Russia can take a very long time. It was uncertain until the day of signing the contract whether the takeover would really take place or the negotiations would collapse:

> We believed that we could do it faster, but there were a lot of barriers not only in terms of language, but in a cultural and social sense. Many of the people here thought that we were the big bad Westerners who came here to cheat and exploit. This was an image that took a long time to change. Well, we went at it and we finally got our negotiation partners to smile. (CEO, quoted in Export, 1999, November, p. 28)

The acquisition contract was signed 11 February 1999 and Rockwool finally took over a part of the MTS conglomerate, the one producing stone wool. A new company with the name ZAO 'Mineralnaya Vata' (MV) was born.

> Signing the contract was a very formal procedure. We had to sit without moving for three nights and negotiate – the first two nights without a result. Only the third time we succeeded and on the February 11, 1999 the factory was ours. (Danish CEO, quoted in Export, 1999, November, 28)

Table 12.1 Calendar of events 1996–1999

Date	Event
in 1996	Rockwool investigates the opportunities for taking over a local production in Russia
Spring 1997	First contact to Mostermosteklo
Spring 1997	Due diligence
Fall 1997	Negotiations start
Summer 1998	Take-over almost ready to be realized
August 1998	Collapse of the rouble and establishment of a Danish task group at Mostermosteklo
Fall 1998	Negotiations re-opened
February 1999	Signing the contract and take-over

Despite all difficulties during the acquisition negotiations, Rockwool and MMS have established certain communication patterns as well as a certain level of trust, which made the entire post-acquisition processes less troublesome.

Post-Acquisition Integration Challenges

Once the contract was signed, the acquisition was effectuated already the following day. After signing the contract, not only did physical facilities have to be 'divided', between the two companies, but also people. 541 Russians and five Danes started officially working together. 541 was negotiated as a number between Rockwool and the Russian shareholders of MTS. As of 1 May 1999 all people who had been working in Rockwool's representative office in Moscow became part of MV. The 12 employees in Moscow and in four other Russian cities were, as of that date, included in MV's reporting. They are now selling for a Russian company, MV, and no longer for Rockwool Denmark. The number of 541 was rather an outcome of the negotiations than based on a careful analysis of what was needed to carry the workload. The number was much higher than what is required in the West for running a production facility of the size of the one that Rockwool took over. There were several reasons for this: each employee in the Russian factory was responsible for only one function, there was an extremely high number of maintenance staff due to aging facilities, there was no tradition for outsourcing of selected maintenance functions, the level of computerization was very low, and the access to spare parts was problematic.

Several activities, meetings, announcements, seminars and presentations were conducted immediately after the takeover in order to introduce Rockwool to clients, authorities, sellers and the local town's population.

The Acquirer's Main Goals

Rockwool's overall objective was to transform MV from a typical Russian enterprise (large number of employees, high degree of bureaucracy, very limited market orientation, restrained focus on revenue and profit) into a Western-style company operating in Russia with Russian employees.

The short-term objectives were defined in the following way:

- To initiate improvements in 1999 in order to bring the products at least to the quality level of the main foreign competitor in Russia; to enlarge the range of products
- To become known on the market as the new Rockwool local producer who is producing and selling high quality brand products; to build up MV's distribution network
- To price MV's products like other Western suppliers but reflecting the willingness of the market to substitute a foreign produced product with a domestic
- To train the respective groups of managers and employees:
    - in Western fundamental accounting techniques in English (the Russian managers and employees) and in Russian (the Danish managers) in marketing and sales

- in IT
- in management including the clarification of notions, such as responsibility and obligations
- in security (bearing in mind that Rockwool's security principles are very strict).

The long term objectives were:

- To become known and respected as market leader on the Russian market
- To expand the production capacity, alternatively establish new production in other locations in Russia.

Changing the Guality and Price Strategy

MV's main customers became mainly Western constructing companies, which demanded isolation material of Western quality. Lately, also local Russian constructing companies have started to demand high quality products, and MV has noticed an increased demand for its products from this segment. In the beginning Rockwool concentrated on catching up on product quality. One year after the takeover, MV was able to manufacture products almost on level with products from other Rockwool production facilities around the world. Consequently, MV has been able to increase its prices to a level closer to the level of foreign made products. In one year of operation MV has also doubled the production volume.

Changing the Organizational Structure

Many information meetings were conducted in the beginning:

> I was holding a lot of speeches in the beginning. It was necessary to tell about Rockwool, about the company's history and ideas in order to improve the working climate here. However, I was talking to deaf people in the beginning – the employees were simply standing and looking down. (Danish CEO, quoted in Export, 1999, November, 28)

A serious effort has been made to study the previous organizational structure and identify who is where in the seven-level hierarchy. In the summer of 1999, there were 65 managers in MV, but the HR director and the other Danish managers knew only around ten of them. Additionally, they did not really know what their exact functions, obligations and responsibilities were:

> We don't know whether they are bell-boys or managers. (HR director)

Compared to MTS's structure, a number of changes were introduced in MV's organizational configuration. Already on the first day the Production Department was merged with the position of the Chief Engineer under one production director. The roles and responsibilities of the different departments and the links between

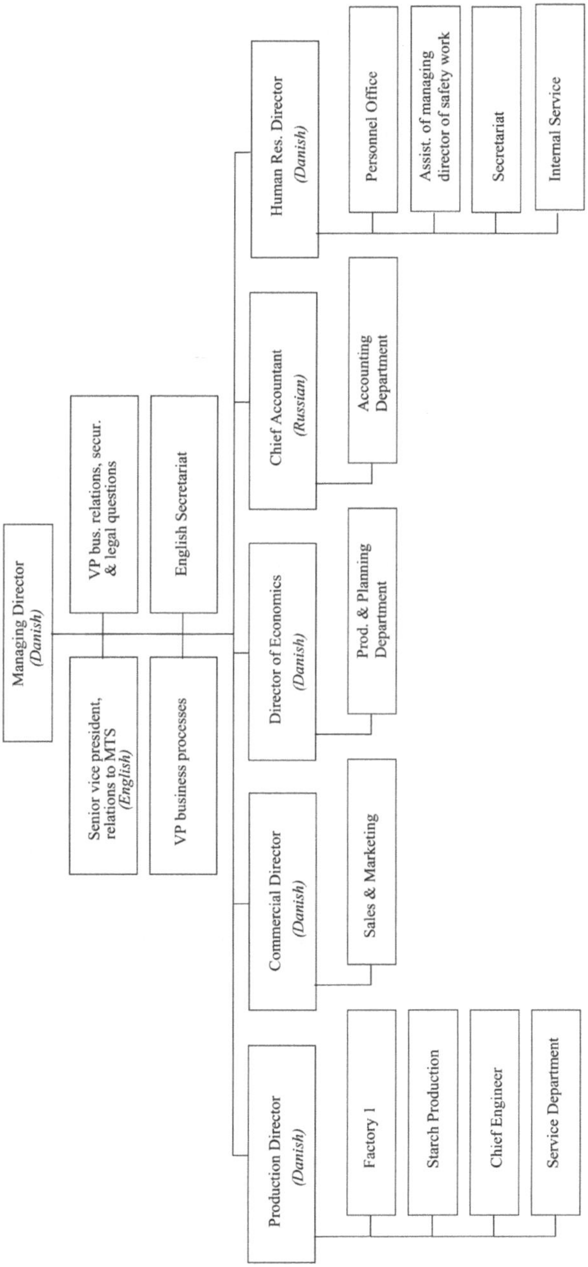

Figure 12.1 Organizational structure of MV

them were clearly defined. Sales and Marketing (under the commercial director) and HR were established as new departments. Sales engineers have been appointed to work in the field. The Danes occupied the key management positions of managing director, commercial director, production director, finance and IT director and HR director.

Besides these immediate actions, it was clear for the Danish management team that the work on optimizing the structure would be continuous. The idea behind not undertaking more drastic changes than the ones described was that MV should be able to function from day one after the takeover before other fundamental changes were undertaken.

Additionally, the HR director conducted a 'closed' personnel evaluation regarding managers and key employees in terms of whether and to what extent they were able and willing to change. One of the problems he faced was that if some of the managers or employees got fired, it would be difficult to find appropriate people to replace them: qualified people were in Moscow and typically, they were not interested in working outside the capital.

> Mostermosteklo is only 37 km from the Red Square in Moscow but the mental distance between the local city here and Moscow is 3–4,000 kilometres. (HR director)

At the same time, an effort was invested in identifying whether the respective person and the functions she/he was fulfilling fitted each other. The aim was to keep people who were not good in the management positions they occupied but were well qualified to execute other functions in the organization.

Staff reduction

When Rockwool signed the contract with the Russians, the Danes shut down one old production line and fired 40 employees paying them nine months of severance pay, an amount that secured very good living conditions for a longer period in Zheleznodorozhny. The Danes were put under pressure by MTS's general director to pay this amount. He claimed that if Rockwool dismissed these employees without substantial payments, he would feel obliged to employ them in his factory.

In the period February–November 1999, the number of employees was reduced from 541 to 460. 100 were fired and new were employed in the Sales, Logistics and IT departments. During the first two weeks eight employees were dismissed because of consumption of alcohol on the job. Regarding potential newcomers, the Danish CEO commented:

> We are looking for people not older than 25. They were 14–15 years old when the communist system collapsed – an age when a person still can be re-programmed.

Training and Education

Ambitious training programs have been started, the participation in the Yeltsin program being one example. The Danish managers have identified those Russian managers and employees who they believed should receive English language training. The Danes started taking Russian language lessons immediately after they began working in MV. For both purposes a teacher has been hired to give English lessons to the Russian managers and employees and Russian lessons to the Danish managers. Initially, the teacher worked part-time but later she became employed on a full-time basis.

The existing IT equipment – both hardware and software – have been modernized and IT teaching and training was initiated. A room for teaching equipped with all necessary appliances has been arranged and the teaching took place in groups of seven to eight people.

Additionally, four Russians from the production department were sent for a week to Denmark and two others to France to visit Rockwool's laboratories in these countries. The visits proved most valuable in terms of learning and knowledge transfer. During the visit in Denmark for example, the Russians discovered that they had been measuring some of the technical parameters in the wrong way for long time.

The Danish managers also identified the need for training the sales staff. As a part of developing the products' image, a new packaging was developed with the product name MIN VATA as logo in the recognizable Rockwool red and white colours thereby making the products visible from a distance of 200–300 meters. Rockwool's efforts have been recognized by the Royal Danish Embassy in Moscow, which conferred to the company the business prize for 1999 for its 'long-term oriented investments on the Russian market.'

Rockwool's Lessons after the First Year of the Acquisition

One of the facts the Danish management team was confronted with from the very beginning was that many of the functions in MTS were repeated, which meant different people were responsible for exactly the same tasks. The Danish managers also found out that the company they acquired had in fact a very flat organizational structure in the sense that all decisions were made by the General Director. The decision-making was extremely slow:

> One hour in Denmark is equal to at least four hours here. (Vice CEO)

The Danes realized very quickly that the Russians' planning horizon did not exceed 24 hours:

> Before we came here, the Russian managers were meeting every single morning at 10.30 in order to decide what will happen during the day. That was their time perspective. (Vice CEO)

> Whenever I put a deadline that is beyond the next day, the Russians become extremely confused. (Production Director)

Other specificities identified by the Danish staff in MV were:

> Russians often came with explanations, such as 'According to Russian law, this and that could not be done or changed'. However, we have never seen these laws. (CEO)

> The Russian managers and employees answer questions only when they are put under pressure to do so. (Vice CEO)

> The Russians here never say what they think and what they want. This often makes me feel that what they do is a big black box. Additionally, they formulate things in a very general and theoretical way. (HR director)

The Danish managers in MV also found the Russians to be incredibly authoritarian and enormously bureaucratic. They also found them being extremely proud of being Russians and disliking being corrected, especially by foreigners. Moreover, Russians hated admitting mistakes.

During the course of the first year, the Danish team successfully encountered many challenges and achieved most things that could reasonably be expected. The most important lessons learned during the first post-acquisition year can be summarized as following:

- Preparation in vital before starting working in Russia
- Identify and send the right expatriates
- Heavy bureaucracy is part of the daily life
- Language is a problematic issue
- The cultural barriers are very big and should not be underestimated
- Patience, patience, patience
- The practice of setting specific goals for the employees and rewarding them accordingly works well.

Some of the Danish managers' concerns during the first year of the integration process were:

- whether it is possible to change the company culture bearing in mind that the Russian employees spend only 1/3 of their time in the company and the rest in a world that is very different
- what tools for motivation and leadership might be appropriate in the Russian context in order to make them integrative elements of the personnel policy in MV.

Conclusion

One way to reveal post-acquisition synergy is to utilize the differences in efficiency between the two firms and improve the 'weak' firm through transfers of resources from the acquiring firm to the acquired firm in the form of managers, management systems, knowledge, capital, and so on. The purpose is to replace or renew the consolidated practices of the target firm (Weston et al. 1990; Nooteboom 1999), which sometimes requires the replacement of management (Manne 1965) or heavy rationalizations in the non-efficient target firm. This differential efficiency approach is well illustrated by the case of Rockwool's acquisition of Mostermoseklo.

Rockwool's case is also an illustrative example of the fact that strategic fit between the acquirer and the acquired company needs to be combined with organizational and cultural fits before synergy can be achieved (Larsson and Finkelstein 1999). In Rockwool's case, the acquisition decision was primarily based on identified existing dimensions related to strategic fit between the two companies, for example the fact that the resources of the two firms were complementary. The primary challenges that appeared during the first year of the partnership were related to organizational and cultural fits. Utilizing a strategic fit opportunity requires a simultaneous integration of operational procedures and people (Birkinshaw et al. 2000). Rockwool has succeeded both during the acquisition negotiations and in establishing a well-functioning cooperation with the Russian partner in the post-acquisition integration process because it was oriented towards the human side of the acquisition as much as towards the production and technology side.

The case presented in this chapter is different from many others described in the literature in respect to the fact that Rockwool acquired not merely an existing Russian company, but only a part of it. The process of splitting the target company in terms of both physical facilities and people, was difficult and consumed much of the acquisition negotiation time. It took almost two years to negotiate Rockwool's acquisition of part of MTS. The negotiations had broken down once during this period and were close to a second breakdown shortly before signing the contract. At the same time, because they turned out to be lengthy and difficult, they also created a very good opportunity for the two parts to get to know each other, each other's work styles, preferences and values. The Danish and the Russian counterparts gradually learned how to communicate and solve problems together. This has facilitated to a great extent the cooperation during the initial stage of the post-acquisition integration.

Acknowledgement

The authors gratefully acknowledge the financial support provided by Rockwool International A/S for conducting the research presented in this chapter.

References

Birkinshaw, J., Bresman, H. and Håkanson, L. (2000), 'Managing the Post-Acquisition Integration Process: How the Human Integration and Task Integration Processes Interact to Foster Value Creation', *Journal of Management Studies,* 37: 3, 395–425.

Blake, R. and Mouton, J. (1985), 'How to Achieve Integration on the Human Side of the Merger', *Organizational Dynamics,* 13: 3, 41–56.

Buono, A., Bowditch, J. and Lewis, J. (1985), 'When Cultures Collide: The Anatomy of a Merger', *Human Relations,* 38: 5, 477–500.

Export (1999), November.

Haspeslagh, P. and Jemison, D. (1991), *Managing Acquisitions: Creating Value through Corporate Renewal*, (Oxford: The Free Press).

Larsson, R. and Finkelstein, S. (1999), 'Integrating Strategic, Organizational, and Human Resource Perspectives on Mergers and Acquisitions: A Case Survey of Synergy Realization', *Organization Science,* 10:1, 1–26.

Manne, H.G. (1965), 'Mergers and the Market for Corporate Control', *Journal of Political Economy,* 73: 2, 110–120.

Nahavandi, A. and Malekzadeh, A. (1988), 'Acculturation in Mergers and Acquisitions', *Academy of Management Review,* 13: 1, 79–90.

Nooteboom, B. (1999), 'Innovation, Learning and Industrial Organisation', *Cambridge Journal of Economics*, 23, 127–150.

Puffer, S.M., McCarthy, D.J. and Zhuplev, A.V. (1998), 'Doing Business in Russia: Lessons from Early Entrants', *Thunderbird International Business Review*, 40: 5, 461–84.

Risberg, A. (2001), 'Executives Perceptions in Foreign and Domestic Acquisitions: An Analysis of Foreign Ownership and Its Effect on Executive Fate', *Journal of World Business,* 36: 1, 58–84.

Schweiger, D. and Denisi, A. (1991), 'Communication with Employees Following a Merger: A Longitudinal Field Experiment', *Academy of Management Journal,* 34, 1, 110–135.

Shama, A. (1997), 'From Exploiting to Investing: A Survey of US Firms Doing Business in Russia', *The International Executive*, 39: 4, 497–518.

Sebenius, J.K. (1998), 'Negotiating Cross-Border Acquisitions', *Sloan management Review*, 39: 2, 27–41.

Walsh, J.P. (1989), 'Doing a Deal: Merger and Acquisition Negotiations and Their Impact upon Target Company Top Management Turnover', *Strategic Management Journal*, 10: 4, 307–22.

Weston J.F., Chung, K. and Hoag, S. (1990), *Mergers, Restructuring, and Corporate Control*, (New Jersey: Prentice-Hall).

Chapter 13

Hospitable or Hostile? Knowledge Transfer into the Russian Host Environment[1]

Adam Smale and Vesa Suutari

Introduction

Attracting higher levels of FDI is argued to represent one crucial step Russia must take in order to facilitate its transition from a transforming economy to one that is competitive on the world stage (Denison 2001). Based on the consistently increasing inflows of FDI into Russia over the past five years, it would appear that much progress has already been made. Not discounting the often poorly acknowledged wealth of skill and talent that already exists throughout Russia (Jankowicz 2001), this foreign investment trend almost inevitably implies that Russia's economic success will depend on its ability to assimilate and internalize certain key aspects of western know-how and, moreover, necessitates Russian business partners to form effective relationships with their western counterparts. For Russian and western businesses alike, however, this has typically proven to be a fraught process with cultural differences typically cited as the root cause (for example, Elenkov 1997; Michailova 2000; May et al. 2005).

In the same way that cross-border transfers of know-how are critical to the future growth potential of the Russian economy, they are also highly significant at the organizational level in contributing to the performance of MNCs (Kogut and Zander 1993). Once more, however, their inherent difficulty and high failure rate often means that the expected benefits fail to materialize (Gupta and Govindarajan 2000; Jensen and Szulanski 2004). Of the extant research on knowledge transfers within MNCs, Russia has been portrayed as a 'knowledge sharing hostile' environment in which knowledge sources and recipients tend to exercise behaviours contrary to effective knowledge dissemination (Hutchings and Michailova 2004). Western expatriates have subsequently faced significant challenges not only in conveying new knowledge, but also in stimulating an information-sharing culture amongst Russian workers and managers (May et al. 1998). Indeed, multiple barriers to

1 The authors would like to thank Research Assistants Eero-Pekka Oja and Riitta Niemelä for their assistance in data collection.

organizational learning have been shown to exist in subsidiaries of MNCs in Russia which continues to stimulate the need for further empirical research on the mutual learning processes inherent in knowledge transfers between western expatriates and Russian employees, especially in the context of economic, socio-cultural and political transformation (Engelhard and Nägele 2003). However, whilst these avenues of research have produced revealing insights into knowledge-related impediments at the individual and organizational levels, there has been comparatively less emphasis on integrating these with those impediments manifested in the national institutional composition of the Russian host country.

Accordingly, the principal aims of this study are firstly, to investigate the type of knowledge that is being transferred via expatriates to the Russian host context. This not only allows for a clearer understanding about the currently perceived knowledge requirements of Russian affiliates, but also demonstrates the type of roles that western expatriates are expected to perform in the host organization. Indeed, the second aim of the study is to provide a more in-depth account of precisely what kind of roles the expatriates have to play in the transfer process in order to ensure effective implementation. The third and final aim is to identify which of the impediments to knowledge transfers are considered by expatriates to be significant obstacles in the Russian host environment.

The following sections begin by discussing the increasing strategic significance of knowledge and its effective transfer within a multinational network. The theoretical foundations of the knowledge stickiness framework to be applied in this study are then introduced as well as the theoretical developments which have come to conceptualize expatriates as key organizational mechanisms of knowledge transfer. After presenting the results of the study, the study draws some tentative conclusions and points towards implications for HRM.

Knowledge Transfers and the Russian Host Context

The Strategic Significance of Knowledge and its Cross-Border Transfer

In addition to the complex balancing of global and local forces, the international management of multinational firms has also been conceptualized as the effective development and diffusion of knowledge within a network of subsidiaries (Bartlett and Ghoshal 1991). Likewise, the knowledge-based view of the firm promotes knowledge as the most strategically significant resource and accordingly emphasizes the capacity of a firm to effectively integrate and transfer knowledge (Conner and Prahalad 1996; Grant 1996). Accordingly, 'knowledge transfer capacity' is seemingly emerging as one of the most significant explanatory factors in the performance of multinational corporations (Martin and Salomon 2003).

In the context of knowledge transfer, MNCs essentially seek to gain competitive advantage through the leverage of knowledge by implementing similar organizational practices and technology throughout their network of subsidiaries in multiple locations (see for example Kogut and Zander 1993). This is particularly critical in those host subsidiary locations where there are significant perceived discrepancies between the levels of knowledge required and those that exist. The research in knowledge transfers has thus focused on the facilitators and inhibitors associated with MNCs from developed countries upgrading and maintaining the knowledge repositories of their counterparts in developing or transforming country contexts (see for example Gamble 2003; Wang et al. 2004; Riusala and Suutari 2004).

A Knowledge Transfer Perspective on Expatriation

In view of the often tacit and context-specific nature of the knowledge needed to be transferred, organizations have been forced to develop and utilize increasingly sophisticated mechanisms of knowledge transfer. Due to their capacity to store and teach the subtle human elements of knowledge, expatriates have become one such means of facilitating a smooth and unproblematic transfer process (Bonache and Brewster 2001). The international HRM literature describes expatriates as fulfilling a variety of organizational roles ranging from the more functional purpose of filling staff vacancies to the more strategically-oriented roles of personal, managerial and organizational development (see for example Edström and Galbraith 1977; Ondrack 1985). Alternatively, expatriate staffing choices made by MNCs have been described as emerging from organizational responses to perceived strategic needs for control, coordination, and the transfer of know-how amongst foreign affiliates (Torbiorn 1994). The focus of this study, however, is based on the subsequently developed notion of expatriates as a mechanism of knowledge transfer (see for example Downes and Thomas 2000; Hocking et al. 2004; Riusala and Suutari 2004).

A knowledge transfer perspective on expatriation is not intended to imply an entirely distinctive and independent role for expatriates, rather it is argued that the transfer of knowledge is one generic intent of *all* strategic expatriate assignments, whereby only the type of knowledge and the means of transfer differ from one assignment to another (Hocking et al. 2004). In this way, and whilst acknowledging the other potential and no less important purposes of international assignments, the knowledge transfer perspective allows for a more in-depth analysis about what is transferred and which factors help or hinder expatriates in this role (Riusala and Suutari 2004). Moreover, this approach is instructive for international HRM insofar as it highlights the adjustment needs and skill sets of expatriates as well as the knowledge-based development needs of local host employees.

Impediments to Knowledge Transfers – A Framework

It would appear that the key strategic role apportioned to international knowledge transfers within MNCs has been responsible for explorative studies into the causes of their reported difficulties and disappointing success rates (see for example Ghoshal and Bartlett 1988; Zander and Kogut 1995). One notable classification of these impediments has been referred to as internal stickiness factors (von Hippel 1994; Szulanski 1996). Indeed, amidst several theoretical frameworks that attempt to explain the nature and manifestation of impediments to knowledge transfers, it is argued that these have been accompanied by only few rigorous and systematic attempts at empirical investigation (see for example Gupta and Govindarajan 2000; Bhagat et al. 2002; Foss and Pedersen 2002).

The theoretical framework applied in this study is principally based on two academic contributions. Firstly, Szulanski's (1996; 2003) in-depth empirical analysis of internal stickiness factors is adopted insofar as its general approach, interpretation of stickiness and some of its stickiness factors are shared in this study. The second theoretical foundation of the model is Kostova's (1999) development of a cross-disciplinary approach to analyzing the transfer of strategic organizational practices, in which institutional theory is elected to depict how transfer processes are embedded in different host contexts. Supplemented by a thorough review of the relevant extant literature, the subsequent knowledge stickiness framework has been developed and applied in both qualitative (Riusala and Suutari 2004) and quantitative

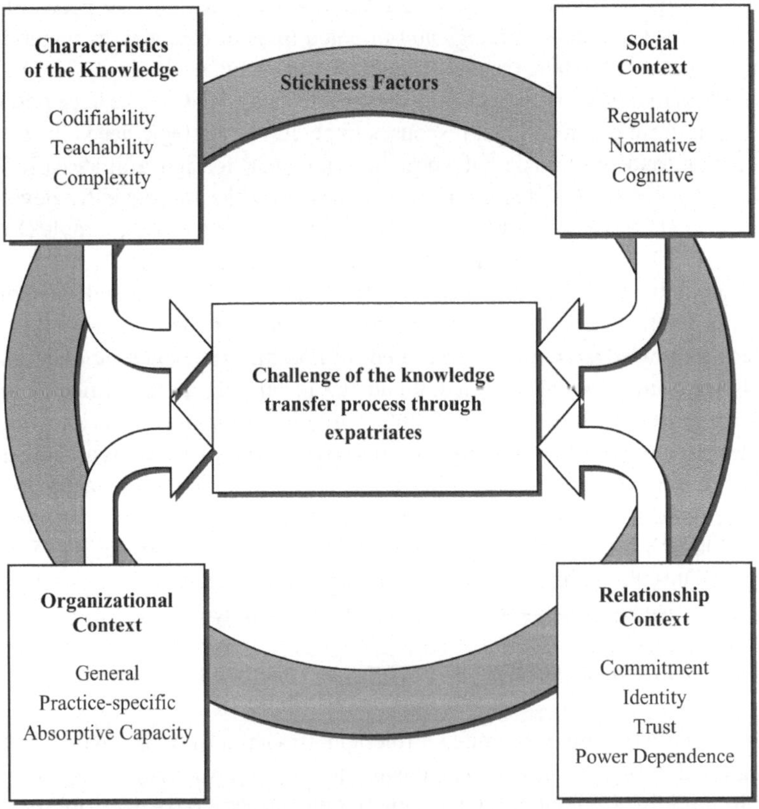

Figure 13.1 Stickiness factors in international knowledge transfers through expatriates

Source: Adapted from Riusala and Suutari (2004)

(Riusala and Smale, forthcoming) studies. The knowledge stickiness framework is now briefly presented and is represented diagrammatically in Figure 13.1.

Within the framework, the notion of 'stickiness' is intended to represent a process-based measure as opposed to one that is outcome-based. In this way, it refers to how challenging the knowledge transfer is perceived to be according to the personal experiences of key actors in the process, in our case the expatriate. This interpretation is essentially the same as Szulanski's (1996) definition of the degree of '*difficulty*' or '*perceived eventfulness*' (1996, 30) and avoids the fraught process of objectively trying to define the meaning of success in knowledge transfers which often possess multiple aims.

Characteristics of knowledge As can be seen from Figure 13.1, the first classification of stickiness factors encompasses those challenges associated with the degree of tacitness manifest in the knowledge being transferred. Whilst the concepts of explicit and tacit knowledge (Polyani 1962) are well established, they are particularly relevant from an intra- and inter-organizational knowledge transfer perspective since 'explicit' refers to knowledge that can be documented, structured and is thus easily transferable, whereas 'tacit' refers to knowledge that resides in the human mind, manifests itself in behaviour and perception and is subsequently hard to transfer (Nonaka and Takeuchi 1995). Accordingly, empirical studies have typically found that the more tacit forms of knowledge negatively impact the speed and ease of transfers (Zander and Kogut 1995; Szulanski 1996) and, moreover, can even represent the most significant determinant of knowledge transferability (Simonin 1999), dominating other host-country related impediments (Jensen and Szulanski 2004).

An alternative and more detailed approach to addressing the degree of knowledge tacitness is proposed by Kogut and Zander (1993). In their study, perceived 'codifiability' measures the extent to which the knowledge in question can be explicitly articulated in document form. Perceived 'teachability,' on the other hand, refers to how difficult it is to teach the knowledge to a new audience, in particular within a classroom-type setting. Lastly, 'complexity' refers to the manifestation of critical and interacting elements within the knowledge which thus render it difficult to separate and measure.

Social Context The knowledge stickiness framework acknowledges that the transfer process does not simply take place within an isolated organizational setting, but must also confront impediments manifested at the national level. With regards to the social context, the culturalist school asserts that a clash in values and norms which support certain features of the host-country environment will affect the smoothness and success of a cross-cultural transfer, in which the magnitude of challenges is positively related to the 'cultural distance' between source and recipient (see for example Hofstede 1980; Bhagat et al. 2002). Kostova (1999), however, elects for institutional theory and the corresponding country institutional profile (CIP) to conceptualise the relevant features of a country's social context. In this way, the CIP and the subsequent degree of 'institutional distance,' distinguishes between 'regulatory' (such as laws and regulations), 'normative' (such as values and norms), and 'cognitive' (such as interpretations and frames of thought) dimensions in explaining potential differences in host-country institutional environments.

Organizational Context In addition to the national level, unfavourable conditions for knowledge transfers can also manifest themselves at the organizational level, in particular with regard to the incompatibility of corporate cultures (Bhagat et al. 2002). Kostova (1999) classifies two such types of organizational culture incompatibility, namely 'general' and 'practice-specific'. 'General' level effects are essentially the strength of orientations towards learning, innovation and change, whereas 'practice-specific' compatibility refers to the fit between values implicit in the particular practice being transferred compared to the underlying cultural values of the host firm. The third potential organizationally based impediment that may prove decisive in knowledge transfers reflects the recipient's understanding and application of new knowledge. Defined broadly as the ability and motivation of the organization to acquire, assimilate and exploit outside knowledge (Cohen and Levinthal 1990), 'absorptive capacity' is expected to directly influence the overall level of difficulty in the transfer process (Minbaeva et al. 2003).

Relational Context Since the transfer of tacit knowledge often requires numerous individual exchanges (Nonaka 1994), the state of parent-subsidiary relations is therefore highly significant. Empirical evidence also leads us to expect that the relational context will have a notable impact of transfers of knowledge. Indeed, the relational variable in Szulanski's (1996) study (described as an 'arduous relationship') proved to be a very significant predictor of internal stickiness. Kostova (1999) breaks down the relational context into the two measures of 'attitudinal' and 'power/dependence,' in which attitudinal relationships are characterized by recipient levels of 'commitment', 'identity' and 'trust' towards the parent company. Subsidiary dependence, or lack of autonomy, is grounded in resource dependence and institutional theory, and refers to the extent that subsidiaries are either reliant on the parent or motivated by legitimacy.

Having outlined the framework of the study, attention is now turned to the host context in which it will be applied – Russia. In particular, the justifications for studying the Russian host destination are discussed with a specific emphasis on why, from a knowledge transfer perspective, the much maligned business and wider socio-economic environment warrants further empirical investigation.

Destination Russia

The developments which have transformed Russia and its social, political and economic infrastructure have occurred in such a dramatic and turbulent fashion that one could forgive potential investors and business partners for being skeptical not only about the current state of the Russian business environment but also about its likely future direction. Indeed, when one then factors in the recentness and the relatively short period of time in which these significant changes have taken place, investing in Russia might still appear to many as an unjustifiable risk. Although Russia represents a potentially attractive market for foreign investors, there still exists a multitude of reasons why businesses might not be able to capitalize on it. As summarized by Michailova (2000),

> … with a weak legal system, an unpredictable economy, and short-lived governments, Russia has the reputation as a country with paradoxical realities and shocking experiences, a country that is in a systematic collapse and general chaos, and is one of the most difficult markets to enter (2000, 99).

In comparison to the performance of other post-communist economies such as Poland and China, Russia is viewed as continually falling short of its full economic potential and has, albeit somewhat reluctantly and sporadically, been turning towards western market principles to shape reform. Of particular relevance to this study, the past ten years have seen expatriates consistently rate Russia to be one of the most challenging host environments in which to do business, although expatriate presence in Russia still remains high (GMAC 2004). There would appear to be a need, therefore, for more support and guidance both for the international HRM activities of organizations and for the international assignees themselves.

Despite the poor track record that Russia has accumulated, recent successful attempts at reform as well as the positive experiences of international investors would together appear to provide some hope and certainly justifies revisiting the Russian host context in more depth. Indeed, as the largest territory in the world, with one of the largest populations and a very healthy GDP, there still exists a very keen interest, both inside and outside of Russia, to re-establish an effective infrastructure conducive to economic growth and the liberalization of Russian markets. For instance, Russia's greater stability and tighter integration into the wider international community under Putin's leadership has been much welcomed due to both Russia's large market potential and, furthermore, its need to attract the kind of FDI that can assist the transition from its current transforming economy status to one that is competitive on a world scale (Denison 2001). This, together with other signs, might suggest that the Russian market is warming to foreign investors and no longer should be regarded as the hostile and unpredictable environment that has typically been publicized. For example, a recent report published by SITRA (2005) – the Finnish National Fund for Research and Development – highlights an overall perception amongst Finnish companies of large 'physic distance' between Finland and Russia, but argues that in overstating the risks of doing business in Russia many companies are missing out on realizable opportunities for success. The report goes on to describe the largely positive experiences from those Finnish organizations who took the risk and persisted in the Russian market. Indeed, confidence in the recent institutional and societal developments as well as patience with the inevitable teething problems are considered to be an appropriate and rewarding approach amongst potential investors (McCarthy et al. 2000).

A further cause for optimism is the emerging new generation of Russian managers who are described as more willing to embrace western values and market-oriented management practices and whose values are a lot closer to those of western managers than the previous generation (Elenkov 1997). However, whilst there is increasing evidence of convergence in managerial values between Russian and western managers, the heterogeneous nature in which these values are acted out through managerial behaviour still requires circumspection on the part of western counterparts (Alexashin and Blenkinsopp 2005).

Methodology

In order to mitigate the traditional weaknesses of the structuralist and hence implicitly ethnocentric approach to knowledge transfers from developed countries into CEE host contexts (Lang and Steger 2002), the study adopted a qualitative

Table 13.1 Biographical data of Finnish expatriate sample

Interviewee no.	Age	Position	Sector	Experience in Russia (years)
1	47	Head of Division	Finance/Banking	6
2	31	Country Manager	Manufacturing	7
3	43	Country Manager	Food	5
4	39	CEO	Manufacturing	5
5	54	CEO	Construction	27
6	48	CEO	Telecommunications	2
7	48	CEO	Paper	3
8	42	Area Manager	Retail	15
9	51	Area Manager	Construction	24
10	49	Sales Manager	Transport	11
11	56	Country Manager	Construction	7
12	47	Country Vice President	Consulting	11
13	54	Project Manager	Finance	11
14	50	Head of Division	Public sector	6
15	44	Area Manager	Real Estate	5
16	50	Project Manager	Construction	4
17	45	Country Manager	Banking	8
18	49	Country Manager	Healthcare	6

methodology. In this way, although the study assumes a largely one-way transfer of knowledge, the use of interviews facilitates the collection of deeper insights into the critical human and social processes inherent in the cross-cultural interactions between western expatriates and Russian host employees (Camiah and Hollinshead 2003). In particular, the qualitative approach facilitates a clearer identification and reporting of resistance, conflict and heterogeneity surrounding transfers, which have been argued to be more appropriate conceptualizations in the post-socialist context (Clark and Geppert 2002).

The data for the study was collected via semi-structured telephone interviews among Finnish expatriates operating in Russia at that time. A total of 18 expatriate managers were interviewed over a two-month period in the Spring of 2005. Contact information for the expatriates was provided by Suomen Ekonomiliitto – SEFE (the Finnish union for qualified economic graduates) and was supplemented via the 'snowballing' method. Biographical data of the expatriate sample is shown in Table 13.1.

The interview structure followed closely the aims of the study and the corresponding 'stickiness' framework. Questions therefore focused on the types of knowledge transferred, the expatriate's role within the transfer process and the types of impediments faced. All interviews were recorded and fully transcribed. The 18 interviews were then reorganized thematically and content analyzed in order to isolate common issues arising from the data. These key themes served to form the basic classification of the data, which in the results are highlighted through the use of direct quotations. The validity of the study's methodology and findings was observed in a number of ways. For example, all interviewees were given a chance to read over the questions prior to being interviewed. Furthermore, a similar version of the adopted interview structure had been successfully applied in a recent study amongst Finnish expatriates in Poland (Riusala and Suutari 2004), which provided additional support as to its clarity and relevance. Validity was also increased through the application of established theories and measures to the subject under study.

Limitations

It is pertinent to mention that this study should of course be interpreted in light of its limitations. Firstly, the study only expresses the views of Finnish expatriates. Whilst they are employed by different kinds of organizations in various functional capacities, it is entirely feasible that different experiences would be found amongst expatriates of different nationalities. Secondly, only the perspectives of expatriates are represented. In this way, the study excludes the views of local employees and therefore also does not seek to acknowledge the possibility that expatriates themselves may in fact represent an impediment to the knowledge transfer process. This is especially relevant in an extremely challenging Russian host context which requires a heightened level of cross-cultural awareness (Fey et al. 1999). Thirdly, Russia represents the largest territory in the world including a large variety of regions, religions, cultures and languages. It is therefore important to note that our sample only represented views from the larger industrialized city contexts, predominantly Moscow and St

Petersburg. Caution is therefore required in any subsequent generalizations drawn from this study.

Results and Discussion

The results are presented in line with the objectives of the study, namely the type of knowledge transferred, the role of the expatriate in these processes followed by the identification of stickiness factors which manifested themselves in the Russian host context during the transfer.

Type of Knowledge Transferred to Russian Affiliates

On analyzing the responses, the Finnish expatriates stressed that there are essentially two dominating logics which explain why certain types of knowledge are transferred to Russia. Firstly, MNCs have made conscious efforts to increasingly integrate and even standardize their policies, processes and practices in areas of core competency. Behind these developments is the continued globalization of business, the drive towards increased efficiencies and related pressures for greater consistency amongst foreign affiliates. This was pointed out by several interviewees:

> I would say that all the basic ways of operating come from the parent company. We aim to do everything here in a similar manner as we do it in Finland. This is for the reason that you do not have to use extra resources and energy to think about how to manage a retail business. This means, for example, accounting, marketing, human resource management …. When new employees are recruited we tell them about our business idea, basic values and so on. From that perspective our concepts are pretty clear.

> I have experience of working in Russia, Germany and Sweden. I would say that Russia does not differ from other locations where Finns have subsidiaries. The knowledge transfer needs are about the same no matter whether the country is Russia or somewhere else. The knowledge transfer needs are not necessarily related to the development level of the country. It is one perspective, but not the only one. We often think that when the development level of the country is low, we have to transfer everything. And when development level is not low, we don't have to transfer anything. In both cases the expectations are wrong.

Secondly, there are context-related development needs which also determine the type and extent of international knowledge transfers. As indicated by an earlier survey among Finnish expatriates, such context-related transfer needs appeared to be highest in the context of transition economies in Central and Eastern Europe (Smale et al. 2005). The interviewees described the context-related transfer needs in Russia in the following manner:

> I would say that knowledge transfer needs are extensive in Russia. They have lived here as if in a different world until 1990 compared to what we have been used to in Western

> societies. Many issues starting from the basics have been strange and new to locals. If we talk at a general level, one reason why Russians want foreign investment is that through such investments it is possible to get access to the transfer of latest knowledge.
>
> With regard to knowledge transfer needs we can say that everything is very new in the bank sector in this country. From this starting point it has been clear from the beginning that there was a need to transfer Western knowledge here.

One additional factor that explained the identification of current knowledge transfer needs was the length of time that the business operation had been established in Russia. As one respondent stated:

> The knowledge transfer needs were extensive at the initial stages. We have been here already for such a long time that the biggest boom of knowledge transfers is already over. Such issues have already been pretty much transferred and it is now much more about fine tuning.

When analyzing the types of knowledge in more detail, it appeared that the cross-border transfer of *management knowledge* took place in all organizations. It was therefore clearly the most common type of knowledge that was deemed necessary to transfer to Russia. As highlighted in a previous expatriate study by Engelhard and Nägele (2003), this type of knowledge transfer is necessary since Russian managers are often seen to be lacking certain management skills, in particular, in the areas of strategic planning, effective decision-making and problem-solving. From a business education perspective, it has also been argued that Russian managerial development needs to focus not only on the transfer and teaching of management knowledge, but also on the change of attitudes and behaviour (Czinkota 1997). The transitional nature of business values and the existence of cultural differences, however, are argued to require specific consideration when transferring management knowledge to Russian managers (May et al. 2005). In the study's sample, the respondents stated, for example, that

> We transfer quite a lot. It can be sliced into two major parts. First is strategic management at the board level … and then management principles within these strategic frameworks.
>
> I would say that the major [transfer] needs are in the area of handling the complex 'organizational whole'. People have a really fragmented view … so they don't understand systematic thinking, that is, what impacts on what … . This kind of systematic understanding about the functioning of a whole organization is missing … and then understanding the consequences of one's actions, and goal-oriented thinking …, there we have had a lot of dialogue. … and also that kind of future-oriented planning. That is probably the most difficult area. Everything is taking place 'ad hoc' … . I am transferring knowledge in these kinds of areas.

One strong justification for the transfer of certain types of knowledge from the West into Russia is the suggestion that the Communist era rendered many organizations lacking in knowledge about how to carry out business functions since the strategy, finance, sales and marketing functions were primarily managed by the state (Fey and Denison 2003). It might therefore not be surprising to find that behind the dominant role of managerial knowledge transfers came a range of other more functional types of knowledge. Of the wide range of functionally related knowledge transferred, *technological knowledge* was fairly commonplace, and to a large extent depended on the nature of the business. The respondents stated, for example, that:

> You will need to transfer some technological knowledge. But actually the situation with technological knowledge is pretty good in Russia.

> At first, there were transfers of the latest technology and methods.

Empirical research has revealed that the HRM practices between Finland and Russia vary significantly (Fey et al. 2004) and that the idiosyncrasies of the Russian business environment have given rise to many barriers to HRM effectiveness (May et al. 1998). However, there are also potentially positive effects from investing in certain Western-oriented HRM practices for the improvement of Russian subsidiary performance (Fey and Björkman 2001). The data from the present study reveals that this transfer of *human resource management knowledge* (policies and practices for example) was also found to be common in different kinds of organizations. One of the most commonly cited areas was that of compensation.

> We are adjusting personnel policy, rewarding and so on to parent company principles.

The ethnocentric and culturally dominant approach inherent in transferring cultural knowledge from the West into CEE countries has been much criticized and deemed inappropriate, particularly in view of the recent progress that has been made together with the valuable knowledge and expertise that already exists in this region (Lang and Steger 2002; Jankowicz 2001). Also referred to as 'culture transfer/socialization,' some of the expatriates interviewed commented that they have been involved in the socialisation of subsidiary staff through company cultural knowledge transfer (Hocking et al. 2004). The expatriates stated, for example, that:

> My role is to transfer our culture and values here.

> The corporate vision and values always have to be transferred. If these differ across units, we cannot even operate.

Lastly, the transfer of *marketing* knowledge also appeared though not as commonly as, for example, the transfer of managerial and technological knowledge. The respondents that were involved in these transfers commented, for example, that:

> One of the knowledge areas where transfers are necessary is of course sales and marketing.

> One of the [transfer] areas is customer relationship management and those kinds of practical issues.

Expatriate Involvement in Knowledge Transfers

It is argued that the existing knowledge gap between Russian employees and their western counterparts refers more to tacit forms of knowledge and intuition than explicit and more technical forms of knowledge, and accordingly it should be addressed through knowledge transfer mechanisms that rely on '... *close interaction, context-related communication and socialization* ...' (Engelhard and Nägele 2003, 275). Furthermore, it has been found that cultural distance is positively related to expatriate presence (Harzing 2001). This would seem to lend support to the strong presence of expatriates in Russian subsidiaries.

The expatriates' experiences in this study largely support the view that a successful international transfer of complex and tacit types of knowledge is rendered almost impossible without staff transfers across borders (see for example Torbiorn 1994). It was also stressed that in Russia this is the case even with less complex knowledge:

> If you transfer a document from one location to another and think that things will start to operate in the way that you want, then in 99 per cent of cases it will not work that way. This mistake Finns make too often. You have to start from the assumption that the knowledge is very complex and difficult, even though it might be pretty simple.

> When we talk about this kind of tacit and explicit knowledge, it cannot be processed through technical transfer mechanisms. That is one clear reason for me to be here. Some issues are difficult to get through technical channels – it requires a person to talk about issues 'between the lines' – to present it in a more explicit form. If you talk about business models and business concepts, they usually require this kind of explanation and description. It is pretty much the expatriate's role to transfer this kind of tacit knowledge to an organization. Through daily interaction, you process it into a more understandable and explicit form.

The expatriates also stated that their transfer to Russia is particularly important given the significance of personal relationships in development processes, which typically involve the transfer of new knowledge. Expatriates stressed this as follows:

> I would say that in Russia personnel transfers and the interaction between two persons has a more central role than in other locations. Russia is not that kind of country like Finland in which we aim to use videoconferences and other such kinds of technology. Here, it is much more important to stand face-to-face, discuss in person, be together and meet regularly.

> In Finland we use a lot of technology, short text messages and e-mails, whereas in Russia these are rare practices. Russians like to call and interact. For them, speaking is very natural whilst Finns will send a message if that is enough.

In line with extant research (see for example Downes and Thomas 2000), it was also pointed out that since knowledge transfer needs are most extensive in the initial stages of international operations, the demand for expatriates is also greatest at that crucial phase. It was commented that:

> In the beginning of the project we had a lot of experts from Finland and also from Poland - part on long-term and part on short-term assignments. In that way, there were those kind of personal-level knowledge transfers. Now it has moved on to a larger extent to 'electronic' channels of transfer … . When you make extensive changes the role of personnel transfers increases.

In general, the findings appeared to reflect earlier research which has highlighted the autonomous nature of expatriate involvement (see for example Riusala and Suutari 2004) and the emergent rather than deliberate nature of expatriate roles (Hocking et al. 2004). Indeed, many expatriates reported that they had a lot of autonomy to decide what kind of knowledge transfer needs there existed and thus what kind of development programs should be created in order to fill the knowledge gaps. For example, the expatriates observed:

> I have a high level of autonomy except with regard to reporting guidelines to headquarters since there we have very strict guidelines as in every company … . Everything else is pretty much in my own hands.

> I have a lot of freedom to use the know-how which we have in the company. I am a sort of coordinator or ambassador here, and my role is to acquire the necessary knowledge … .

The role of expatriates in the face of greater efforts at global integration were still seen as pivotal insofar as they continued to act as important intermediaries between the headquarters and the local unit. This serves to remind us of the other key strategic roles often assigned to expatriates, namely those traditional functions of control and coordination (see for example Edström and Galbraith 1977; Ondrack 1985).

Impediments to Knowledge Transfer in the Russian Host Context

Characteristics of Knowledge The extant literature highlights the complex nature of knowledge to be integrated into the Russian context from a number of perspectives. One dominant theme is how the Western characteristics of knowledge being transferred to Russian organizations render the process as particularly problematic. For example, it is suggested as being often too easy to underestimate the complexity involved in teaching and applying free-market principles as well as conveying their implications in an environment still showing signs of its communist past (May et al. 1998). Subsequently, there has been a call for research on the 'travel of ideas' (as opposed to knowledge) and the inherent problems involved in translating western business concepts in Central and Eastern Europe (Camiah and Hollinshead 2003).

Codifiability and Complexity In reference to the data, the low degree of knowledge codifiability in transfers to Russia was observed by most of the respondents, in that they were often said to comprise elements that could not be expressed in written form. This is arguably a logical finding in the sense that other more cost effective transfer mechanisms than expatriates (corporate intranet bulletins or policy manuals for example) would have been used to transfer more explicit forms of knowledge (Bonache and Brewster 2001). This, together with acknowledgements of high knowledge complexity, is confirmed by statements such as:

> The knowledge we [expatriates] are transferring is typically very complex. Where possible, all the more simple types of knowledge, which can be put into more strict, quantitative type of formats, will be transferred through IT systems.

> The knowledge we are transferring is such that it requires transfers of staff who have experience in how to do that task. You cannot arrange it, let's say, through documents and training only. It is clear that it is not easy to transfer this kind of knowledge.

Teachability The teachability of the knowledge that is transferred varied from case to case. In many situations the expatriates did not perceive the knowledge to be too difficult to teach to local Russian employees. This of course might be related to the fact that in all cases, the expatriate was used as a knowledge transferor and thus the more tacit forms of knowledge could be taught through personal interaction. Comments that reflected these mixed opinions included:

> It is not so difficult to teach locals this kind of knowledge. If you can motivate them they are pretty quick to learn.

> The teaching of this kind of knowledge is a very complicated process. To teach them so that they can use the knowledge and the technology is not easy at all.

Within discussions of knowledge characteristics and the challenges related to complexity, it is pertinent to acknowledge the significant role of language. Indeed, language is argued to be potentially the single biggest obstacle to a successful cross-border knowledge transfer (Simonin 1999). In the Russian context, greater language proficiency amongst Western managers has specifically been encouraged in view of the complexities involved in the Russian contextualization of Western terms (Camiah and Hollinshead 2003). It was therefore interesting to note that over half of the expatriate respondents considered themselves to be proficient in the Russian language. Once more, this might explain the general feeling amongst respondents that the characteristics of knowledge render transfers problematic, but far from impossible.

Social Context

Regulatory The first of the institutionally based impediments is the regulatory context into which the new knowledge must be integrated. The current Russian business environment has been characterized as a cumbersome network of rules and regulations left over from the centrally planned economic system, underpinned by a 'bureaupathological' attitude that angst and uncertainty can be avoided through excessive bureaucracy (Kets de Vries 2001). From an institutional and, more specifically, regulatory perspective, this continues to render Russia quite a unique business environment in which to operate.

Evidence of this bureaucracy and confusing body of legislation was observed by many of the respondents:

> Legislation causes challenges and problems; it is very different. For example, financial accounting issues are handled in a certain way in Finland, but here those issues have to be carried out in a much more complex way … the bureaucracy is incredible. I would say that we need two or three times more accountants here than in a similar organization in Finland. There are still very contradictory instructions and guidelines are very unclear, and difficult to make sense of. You need to acquire permission for everything. It is really difficult to understand how the application procedures go and what the schedules are. Sometimes you think that you cannot do anything in this country without specific permission.

> The legislation is very unpredictable, in particular the interpretation of this legislation. Sometimes a law is drawn up which will then apply to the last 15 years.

However, some of the more experienced respondents indicated that the situation regarding legislation in many areas has improved significantly in recent years. As one respondent states:

> Businessmen always claim that the Russian law system doesn't work well and that laws and interpretations of these laws change all the time, and they are pretty much right about this. However, with regard to the problems that Finns have with legislation, and in particular with customs officials, are 90 per cent caused by themselves since they do not know local laws and expect the laws to be written out like legislation is in Finland. They have not done their homework. Russian legislation has improved a lot during the last five years and you just have to know that legislation, in particular the taxation laws. That will remove around 80 per cent of the problems.

In discussions on the Russian regulatory environment, the prevalence of corruption and unethical behaviour was raised. Whilst many respondents acknowledged the existence of corruption, the responses demonstrated the differentiated nature of how organizations and expatriates define corruption and how they have approached it.

> Everyone is talking about corruption and I would like to expand on this concept a bit. You have to understand that here personal interests are often intertwined with 'promoting' the progress of procedures. If you have not taken care of those interests, the issues will not progress well. It does not mean that you have to use bribes, although at the extreme it may take the form of the corruption. On the other side of the continuum, it even takes such forms that if you are not considerate or polite enough the issues will not progress well … . Corruption is unacceptable, but we do not always handle such issues of politeness very well.

> Competition is tough here and the competitors can harm each other in many ways. You can buy a tax inspection here. You can also buy a lot of other kind of 'teasing' here – you can buy negative articles from journals. A few years ago [a consultancy firm] published a price list of how much these kinds of teasing methods cost here. It is pretty common.

Normative The extent to which national cultural values and norms clash with the knowledge being transferred is captured in the normative stickiness factor. Crucially, from the normative perspective, it is argued that a lack of historical contact between Russia and the West and their vastly different ideological, religious and social backgrounds are both reasons for the sizeable cultural distance and context differentiation that face western expatriates (Husted and Michailova 2002). In turn, this is argued to affect the capabilities of both transferors and receivers of knowledge to engage in effective knowledge transfer (May et al. 2005).

Russian culture has been described as placing strong values on hierarchy, formal status and anti-individualism (Michailova 2002). Indeed, initiative and ambition have historically been discouraged and even punished (Puffer 1994). Features of the communist system such as strong centralization, the dominance of formal rules and the lack of tolerance for pluralism and diversity have also shown to be barriers to the sharing of ideas (Michailova 2002). Furthermore, the longstanding acceptance of and desire for strong leadership in Russian organizational settings is argued to have bred a 'learned helplessness' amongst Russian employees, who instead of taking the initiative, exhibit signs of passive dependence and wait for further instructions to come from the top (Kets de Vries 2000).

Collectively, these cultural characteristics were still found to undermine the ability for Russian employees to innovate and use their self-initiative. As observed by several interviewees:

> The Russians are really obedient. This is quite a contrast to what many Western people expect. One aspect of such obedience is that they do not try to find solutions or initiate ideas but will just happily do what has been told. That kills creativity and the initiation of new practices in work organizations.

> There are such problems where people ask too much and expect military-style orders. There is a lack of self-initiative … . You have to say everything in a more detailed and strict manner.

> Here the organizational system is very vertical and high. The CEO is almost like a God and then there is a lot of empty space below. This historical way of operating limits the possibilities of those at lower levels to innovate and initiate new ideas.

One significant normative barrier closely related to the lack of self-initiative is the noted Russian apprehension and negative attitude towards failure and making mistakes. This attitude can also manifest itself in the hiding of bad news in an attempt to avoid harsh realities as well as to avoid being the unpopular messenger (Kets de Vries 2001). The expatriates confirmed the current relevance of such issues in the following manner:

> If someone at the middle level makes an independent decision, and even though the decision was right from the company point of view, the manager who hears that he has been bypassed in decision-making will hand out strong negative feedback ... even if there is an emergency situation and he really has to make the decision or otherwise things get worse – and even if he makes a good decision and things get better – even then he can get strong criticism from his boss.

> The system is so management oriented and there is a fear of mistakes. They don't read the instructions or guidelines and try to understand something on their own, but instead they want to get the interpretation from the boss. Then responsibility for it is shifted to the boss.

The Russian organizational context has been characterized as a knowledge sharing hostile environment (Michailova and Husted 2003) whereby the behaviours of organizational members would appear to implicitly contradict attempts at facilitating knowledge transfers. This type of behaviour was generally attributed to an overall lack of open communication within Russian organizations. It was commented, for example, that:

> Here the general rule is 'do not tell to anyone'. In Russian organizations the horizontal flow of information has always been a problem. When you keep your own information without sharing it, it has traditionally been beneficial to you. That is the starting point in Russian culture.

> If you had to stress one developmental aspect which should be focused on, then it would be communication skills … . In this respect there are lots of areas for improvement in Russian affiliates so that local supervisors inform their subordinates about issues ... . It [knowledge] is easily blocked and is used as a tool of personal power.

The tendency to formulate and to adhere to strict work descriptions was also pointed out as an outcome of traditions associated with communism. The inflexibility that this creates was described by one of the Finnish managers:

> When certain specific tasks are described in your job description, then the interpretation is that you don't have to do – or you are not even allowed to do – any tasks outside that description. This means that the flexibility to assume any new tasks, even temporarily, is very low. If water is running from the tap all over the place, and if fixing it is not in anybody's job description, then it is just allowed to keep on running.

Cognitive Comprising individual interpretations and frames of thought, there was some evidence to suggest that cognitive stickiness factors have affected knowledge transfers into Russia. Although Russia still finds itself amidst far-reaching societal transformations, there is argued to be a certain stability to the essential nature of Russian character which has remained consistent over time (Kets de Vries 2001). Such consistency, however, is potentially problematic when western and correspondingly free-market principles require cognitive shifts on the part of Russian employees.

For instance, Engelhard and Nägele (2003) comment that, *'as Russian employees' individual experiences of working in a market economy are most often relatively limited, they frequently lack cognitive frames of reference which help absorb [implicit] knowledge schemes'* (2003, 268). This could also be interpreted from certain expatriate responses:

> Russians are highly educated, most even overeducated for their jobs, but the logic of that knowledge has disappeared … . Our way of thinking and the frameworks that we bring from Western societies, it is very unfamiliar to Russians … . It is difficult for them to understand the context from which we are talking … and then they try to connect the recent knowledge to the environment that there used to be.

> The people are smart here, that is not the problem. It is more a question about whether we are really talking about the same issue, that is, when we use our terminology, frameworks and concepts, do those really mean the same for both parties.

A further cognitive impediment was found to manifest itself in Russian tendencies towards pride (Czinkota 1997) and 'chauvinism' (Camiah and Hollinshead 2003). As described by several expatriates, these types of attitudes often led to an overall resistance to learn from others and adopt new practices, for example:

> In Russia they have this kind chauvinism and 'world power' mentality that they know things a little bit better than anyone else.

> I came here to integrate two units after a merger. With the Russian attitude that would have been an impossible task since both were so convinced about their excellence, of being better than the other, leaving no room for compromise.

These perceived feelings of superiority amongst Russians have also contributed to Western solutions being met with simple rejections based on rather vague arguments that 'this will not work in Russia' (Camiah and Hollinshead 2003). Furthermore, strong group affiliation and suspicion towards outsiders has been argued to perpetuate the 'not-invented-here' syndrome (Michailova and Husted 2003). Russian mindsets such as these were also evident according to some of the interviewed expatriates:

> They have reserved attitudes toward foreigners. The Russian mentality is such that it is commented 'this does not fit here' and then just afterwards it might be asked 'what was the question actually about'.

> The general doctrine is that Russia is a very developed country, actually the most developed in the world and thus no external help or knowledge is required. They have it all here. It is a sort of self-sufficiency, and they really believe in that. It is really difficult to make the point that the transfer of this knowledge is really beneficial to them.

Lastly, cognitive differences also surfaced between Russian employees and Finnish expatriates in their conceptions of time. Engelhard and Nägele (2003) found that expatriates perceive Russian workers to be disproportionately oriented towards the present and the past resulting in an inability to make strategic plans for the future. Similar observations were made by some of the respondents:

> One negative issue that comes to my mind is the attitude of living day-by-day, and living with the attitude of 'let's just see what happens'.

> There is a clear difference to Finland with regard to time concepts. People here are not really worried about the more long-term future. They have been used to thinking that everything might be totally differently again tomorrow.

Organizational Context

General Western attempts to plan and implement ambitious organizational change programmes in Russia often experience serious difficulties and are forced to confront a number of barriers to the change process (Michailova 2000). In addition to the observed avoidance of mistakes and the lack of self-initiative cited previously as normative stickiness factors, there were mixed perceptions amongst respondents about the more general Russian organizational context regarding change, learning and the adoption of new ideas. For example:

> At the employee level there is a general resistance against anything new. On the clerical side there is a basic resistance towards all the instructions and guidelines which come from abroad.

> It is not very easy to get new ideas through. People like to remain content with the workload they have. The idea is that every time they have to take on some new task, they ask what they can get rid of, that is, do I leave out this part of the job or that one … people are pretty satisfied with the current situation and with the security associated with it.

In fact, the issue of organizational resistance to change seemed to divide the expatriates' opinions. Those with more positive experiences commented, for example:

> … our guys even make direct contact to Finland if they need some knowledge. They are really interested in learning new things, starting new initiatives and so on.

> We have very young and enthusiastic staff. I would say that they would like to have more training than we are able to offer them.

Practice-specific Referring to the compatibility between the values implied by a particular practice and the values underlying the culture of an organization, the practice-specific stickiness factors were difficult to identify from the data. In the present study this was because the focus of discussion was on all kinds of knowledge which were transferred. Thus, the practice-specific knowledge transfer challenges were neither widely discussed nor in any detail. It was nevertheless apparent from the interviews that the amount of impediments did seem to be related to the type of knowledge that is transferred. However, the problems which were highlighted often related to the general societal context rather than organization-specific issues. For example, different conceptions of time typically created more problems in transferring certain strategic management principles to Russian units, despite the general environment regarding learning and change being adequate.

Absorptive capacity In terms of the ability to learn and understanding new knowledge, Russia has traditionally always placed a high value on education. Subsequently, Russia boasts a very high literacy rate together with a highly skilled and well-educated workforce (Kets de Vries 2001). Indeed, the Western interviewees in a recent study by Camiah and Hollinshead (2003) attest to the high intellectual calibre, technical ability and language proficiency of their Russian co-workers.

Similarly, the Finnish expatriates' views on the absorptive capacity of Russian locals were fairly positive, acknowledging the high level of general education and their capability to think on a more abstract level. It was commented, for example, that:

> People are very competent and efficient when they understand what they are doing and what is expected out of them. You have to explain the goals very clearly, after that, things normally go well.

> Learning capacity is not a problem. All Russian clerical staff are very highly educated and the theoretical education is pretty good … .

Some of the respondents clarified further that absorptive capacity is dependent on the knowledge being transferred. In this sense, whilst the high basic level of education establishes a solid foundation, some other types of knowledge are still fairly unknown.

> Their education is often in a different field [than the one in which they work], but it gives you a basis to start from … . Many of them do not have an education in the business field, but have, through societal transitions, ended up working in areas very far from their own field of education … . We have made an agreement that besides their work they will study an MBA or something else similar.

Relational Context

Commitment The first of the relational stickiness factors that could affect cross-border knowledge transfers is the low level of commitment from the host subsidiary towards the goals of the parent. It is regarded as somewhat ironic that in a collectivist culture such as Russia, employees have in fact been shown to demonstrate questionable organizational commitment, focusing instead on self-preservation (May et al. 1998). Indeed, Western expatriates have voiced concerns about Russian colleagues who tend to exercise little organizational commitment and who are predominantly motivated by short-term, material goals (Camiah and Hollinshead 2003).

In the present study, the expatriate managers' experiences of Russian organizational commitment were very diverse.

> In our company, as at others in which I have worked, commitment is a great challenge. If another company pays a little bit more, 80 per cent of employees are ready to leave.

> I would say that at the managerial level most of the people have stayed for a long time and thus they appear to be committed to the organization. It is another matter at lower levels. There seems to be a general rule in the retail sector that half of the sales people 'change' on a yearly basis … when you know this you can prepare for it. But it causes horrific costs.

In several cases the respondents talked about the short time period after which employees can leave the company. This sometimes creates difficulties, especially when those leaving are not interested in the consequences of their actions for the employer. For example, as one expatriate explains:

> The notice period is only two weeks in Russia. It is normal that when employees find a new job they will leave in two weeks … . Western companies have to think hard about how to keep the knowledge within the company so that it does not leave with those who leave for vacation and do not come back. They will inform you today and you won't see them again as of tomorrow … . It is a common idea that it is alright to leave in that way. It is even not uncommon that employees press the delete button on their computer when they leave so that all the information is lost.

However, there were also clearly more positive experiences with regard to commitment. For instance, it was widely observed that international organizations in fact possess high status as employers in Russia.

> Whenever the people understand what is expected out of them, then they try to do their best in line with that. In our company the people have stayed for a long time and the best ones have been here since we started [in 1988] …. We have informed them that we will not take in any external managers and that people can, through their own work, get more responsibility. Results-based compensation is another issue which has had an effect.

Several respondents were even surprised at the industrious nature of Russian employees.

> Employees are very committed and stay longer if required – without any pre-warning people can sit here until 10 or 11 [pm] or come to work during the night if needed. I have just called our lawyer about an issue that needs be sorted out this week – he cancelled his vacation and came back to work.

Identity It might be assumed that Russian employees will not all identify closely with a Western organization in view of Russia's well-documented aversion to the West and its corresponding values. Michailova and Anisimova's (1999) case study of Russians working in a Danish multinational in Russia demonstrated that Russians fell into two groups. Whilst one group of Russian employees were perceived to be 'insiders' and generally felt proud to work for the organization, exhibiting self-motivation and fostering close relationships with foreign colleagues, the 'outsiders', however, did not identify with the organization and made clear distinctions between Russians and non-Russians. Particularly relevant in the Russian collectivist culture, if Western organizations and their expatriates are part of the out-group then they can expect paranoia, heightened levels of suspicion and relationships marred by distrust (Kets de Vries 2001).

The Finnish expatriate views on local perceptions of identity with the parent were very mixed. For example:

> The employees identify themselves with the large international organization.

> In our case, 80 per cent of the staff identify themselves with the local, Russian affiliate.

Russian employees have been described to be often caught up in 'double-bind' situations insofar as they have to respond to two substantially different sets of leadership styles and expectations represented through their local Russian manager versus the Western expatriate (Michailova 2002). Accordingly, it is uncertain whether Russian employees will identify more with the Russian subsidiary or with the wider international organization. One respondent elaborates on this:

> In a categorization between identity towards the parent company or the host unit, there is a third class – the work collective. Russians use this term work collective when they mean the informal working group in which you work. It is extremely important to Russians. In the first level, the commitment is toward this work collective, then to the host unit and only then towards the parent company … . The meaning of the group is very high.

Trust Trust issues lie at the heart of many barriers to effective knowledge sharing within Russian organizational settings (see for example Husted and Machailova 2002; Hutchings and Michailova 2004). As knowledge transmitters, a lack of trust might logically result in knowledge hoarding behaviours amongst Russian employees, particularly if the intended receivers are regarded as 'outsiders'. These feelings were also partly reflected in the data, for example:

> I think employees trust that we are, to our best ability, trying to do good business here and in that way the employees also feel fine … . On the other hand this is a country in which people always think that someone is trying to con them. Wherever there is a foreigner involved, the Russians think that there is a conspiracy against them. In that way the Russians are very sceptical.

> There is no trust automatically. You have to build it and it is definitely a very long process. You do not earn trust for free. The trust toward the employer or any official authority does not exist naturally … . In Finland we have a general trust toward authorities, but in Russia there is

> a huge mistrust toward official authorities. The parent company is easily viewed as one of those official authorities.

The issue of building trust through closer networks of relationships was a common theme in many of the interviews and led to discussions about the informal nature of such relationships. Indeed, many authors have stressed the significant role of personal networking (or '*blat*') and interpersonal relationships when conducting business in Russia (see for example Michailova and Worm 2003; Hutchings and Michailova 2004). Similarly, the study by Engelhard and Nägele (2003) highlights the frustrations of expatriate managers over the existence of informal communication networks, which served to disrupt communication and the transfer of knowledge.

The continued importance and use of informal, personal networks was described in the following ways:

> They have this kind of informal culture and networks. You should always acknowledge these beforehand. Formal structures are only half the truth ... also in relationships with pubic authorities, it is much better to go there and deal with the issues with the 'right' contacts and partners.

> In Russia the networks will often create solutions for everything, that is, whom you know. In Russia it is a sort of 'must' that you have your own networks. Elsewhere, you promote the issues through official routes. Here, it is much more efficient if you can first call someone and ask who you should contact and what this issue actually means.

Power dependence Insofar as it is clear to Russian businesses that they can greatly benefit from the inflow of Western capital, know-how and technology, it is equally apparent to Russians that the Russian market represents a potentially very profitable opportunity. Russians are also aware, therefore, that foreign investors require their support and guidance in order to conduct business in a challenging and fairly unique environment. In turn, this intriguing balance of power and dependency is likely to affect attitudes towards the transfer of knowledge and its subsequent acceptance.

However, the role of power dependence was not stressed as a key factor in explaining the difficulties of knowledge transfers to Russia. Whilst the expatriate managers typically described the affiliates to be fairly dependent on parent company resources, they generally did not believe this to be the most significant relational factor. As one of the respondents states:

> If I were to put these [relational factors] into an order of importance when thinking about knowledge transfers, it would be commitment, trust and then finally identity and power dependence neck and neck.

In contrast, one expatriate stressed the importance of power dependence as a strategic organizational resource and necessary in pursuing the tight integration of activities:

> I would say that there is pretty strong power dependence, but so it should be too … . I think that is an advantage. Actually, I think that the only way to succeed in Russia is to have a strong dependence relationship … .

A note on generational differences Before drawing any conclusions from the study's results, it is particularly pertinent here to qualify the findings in view of the distinct differences found between the generations of Russian employees and managers. It has been argued elsewhere that this is necessary since the older generation have a tendency to view neo-communist ideology in a favourable light, whereas the younger generation appear keen to embrace a more liberal brand of western market principles (Camiah and Hollinshead 2003). Furthermore, although Russia's old school of managers have been characterized by dogmatism through their pre-occupation with the past (Kets de Vries 2001) and their lack of openness to new ideas, there is evidence to suggest that new Russian managers are now as accommodating as their Western counterparts (Elenkov 1997).

Indeed, it is interesting to note that the Finnish companies in this study typically recruit young employees, often intentionally. Some of the differences between older and younger generations of Russian employees were described in the following manner:

> We don't have many representatives from the older generation. Around 80 per cent of our employees are around their 30s. 95 per cent are under 35. Clearly this new generation is different to the one before 1995. The companies with young management are in many areas already more developed than Western companies, for example in the use of AV-technology … . There has been a dramatic change. Russia is no longer a traditional socialist country when you consider commercial organizations. In public organizations [however] there are more representatives from this older generation and thus this old thinking can still be clearly seen.

> The older generation is fearful of 'masters' and there are a lot of questions on the smallest details as to whether they can do this or that. They often ask what they should do … . In the younger generation the bad side is that they run after money so much. If someone offers 100 Euros per month more, that can be a reason to leave. They also put more value on the quality of life and are not willing work long days.

Summary and Conclusion

The present study's aims were to identify (1) the type of knowledge transferred via Finnish expatriates to the Russian host subsidiary environment, (2) the role expatriates played in these transfer processes, and (3) the impediments that were encountered.

With regard to the types of knowledge, both context and non-context related reasons were cited. The non-context related factors mainly referred to the noticeably increasing focus by MNCs on the tighter global integration of practices and processes. Within the Russian context-specific reasons, transfers of management knowledge were clearly a dominant feature, followed by transfers of cultural and functionally-oriented knowledge. Whilst the type of knowledge transferred highlights continued development needs on the part of Russian management, more specifically in the area of strategic management, there was also evidence to suggest that Russian employees are becoming more adept at the internalization of western concepts and frameworks. Interestingly, however, there were no reported instances of 'reverse' knowledge transfers back to the Finnish 'home' country.

The role that expatriates play in knowledge transfers was regarded as relatively autonomous and critical in view of the complex nature of knowledge to be relayed. Even in cases where the knowledge was not perceived to be complicated, expatriates stressed the importance of face-to-face contact in conveying new ideas.

Several significant impediments ('stickiness factors') to knowledge transfers were identified by the expatriates, however they were by no means universal. The general perception was that although the knowledge is often uncodifiable, complex and difficult to teach, the characteristics of knowledge were rarely the most significant impediments to a successful transfer. In this regard, the country-level, *social* stickiness factors were more problematic. In particular, confusing legislation, low levels of self-initiative, lack of open communication and misalignments in cognitive mindsets concerning western principles were identified as key obstacles. Despite some underlying scepticism about doing business with 'outsiders', the Russian *organizational* context was generally considered to be conducive to learning and change. On an individual level, whilst the general education level and work ethic were perceived to be very high, the lack of education and training in career-relevant disciplines was cited as a key constraint on Russian employees' absorptive capacity. With regard to *relational* impediments, the findings were very mixed insofar as expatriates' opinions on organization commitment identity, trust and power dependence were often divided. Nevertheless, one common theme which arose was the continued importance attached to informal, personal contact networks and the nurturing of these relationships with parties both within and outside of the organization.

It should be stressed that although this study has focused on impediments and therefore on the 'negative' attributes of the Russian host environment, the respondents, especially those with most experience, were also quick to acknowledge those areas which have witnessed significant improvements, even to the extent that they were perceived as more favourable than in Finland. This was identified as being most evident in the extensive differences that exist between older and younger generations of Russians and between commercial and public sector organizations.

Implications for HRM

The findings of the present study speak to the international activities of the HR function in two main ways. Firstly, the identification of challenges that western expatriates currently face in the Russian business environment can better inform subsequent efforts in expatriate pre-departure training, both in terms of anticipating adjustment challenges and in developing appropriate knowledge-based skill sets. Indeed, the pivotal role of expatriates and their support from HRM in facilitating transfers of knowledge to Russia, whilst diminishing, is likely to continue to be the most effective organizational mechanism in the near future. Secondly, the study draws on current insights into some potential development needs of Russian employees. In this regard, particular attention needs to be paid to the speed and direction of transitions in Russia which will determine the appropriateness of HRM interventions. Accordingly, the reported energy and thirst for knowledge amongst younger generations of Russians needs to be addressed by HRM strategies that support their development in career-relevant disciplines whilst simultaneously responding to their increased mobility.

References

Alexashin, Y. and Blenkinsopp, J. (2005), 'Changes in Russian Managerial Values: A Test of the Convergence Hypotheses?' *International Journal of Human Resource Management* 16: 3, 427–44.

Bartlett, C.A. and Ghoshal, S. (1991), *Managing Across Borders: The Transnational Solution* (London: London Business School).

Bhagat, R.S., Kedia, B.L., Harveston, P.D. and Triandis, H.C. (2002), 'Cultural Variations in the Cross-Border Transfer of Organizational Knowledge: An Integrative Framework', *Academy of Management Review* 27:2, 204–21.

Bonache, J. and Brewster, C. (2001), 'Knowledge Transfer and the Management of Expatriation', *Thunderbird International Review* 43: 1, 145–68.

Camiah, N. and Hollinshead, G. (2003), 'Assessing the Potential for Effective Cross-Cultural Working between "New" Russian Managers and Western Expatriates', *Journal of World Business* 38: 3, 245–61.

Clark, E. and Geppert, M. (2002), 'Management Learning and Knowledge Transfer in Transforming Societies: Approaches, Issues and Future Directions', *Human Resource Development International* 5: 3, 263–77.

Cohen, W.M. and Levinthal, D. (1990), 'Absorptive Capacity: A New Perspective on Learning and Innovation', *Administrative Science Quarterly* 35: 1, 128–152.

Conner, K. and Prahalad, C.K. (1996), 'A Resource-Based Theory of the Firm: Knowledge versus Opportunism', *Organization Science* 7: 5, 477–501.

Czinkota, M.R. (1997), 'Russia's Transition to a Market Economy: Learning about Business', *Journal of International Marketing* 5: 4, 73–93.

Denison, D.R. (2001). *Managing Organizational Change in Transitional Economies. Lawrence Erlbaum Associates* (New Jersey, Mahway).

Downes, M. and Thomas, A.S. (2000), 'Knowledge Transfer through Expatriation: The U-Curve approach to Overseas Staffing', *Journal of Managerial Issues* 12: 2, 131–49.

Edström, A. and Galbraith, J. (1977), 'Transfer of Managers as a Coordination and Control Strategy in Multinational Organizations', *Administrative Science Quarterly* 22: 2, 249–63.

Elenkov, D. (1998), 'Can American Management Concepts Work in Russia? A Cross-Cultural Comparative Study', *California Management Review*, 40: 4, 133–156.

Elenkov, D.S. (1997), 'Differences and Similarities in Managerial Values between US and Russian Managers', *International Studies of Management and Organization* 27: 1, 85–106.

Engelhard, J. and Nägele, J. (2003), 'Organizational Learning in Subsidiaries of Multinational Companies in Russia', *Journal of World Business* 38: 3, 262–77.

Fey, C.F., Pavlovskaya, A. and Tang, N. (2004), 'Does One Shoe fit Everyone? A Comparison of Human Resource Management in Russia, China, and Finland', *Organizational Dynamics* 33: 1, 79–97.

Fey, C.F. and Denison, D.R. (2003), 'Organizational Culture and Effectiveness: Can American Theory be applied in Russia?', *Organization Science* 14: 6, 686–706.

Fey, C.F. and Björkman, I. (2001), 'The Effect of Human Resource Management Practices on MNC Subsidiary Performance in Russia', *Journal of International Business Studies* 32: 1, 59–75.

Fey, C.F., Nordahl, C. and Zätterström, H. (1999), 'Organizational Culture in Russia: The Secret to Success', *Business Horizons* 42: 6, 47–55.

Foss, N. and Pedersen, T. (2002), 'Transferring Knowledge in MNCs: the Role of Sources of Subsidiary Knowledge and Organizational Context', *Journal of International Management* 8, 1–19.

Gamble, J. (2003), 'Transferring Human Resource Practices from the United Kingdom to China: the Limits and Potential for Convergence', *International Journal of Human Resource Management* 14: 3, 369–87.

Ghoshal, S. and Bartlett, C.A. (1988), 'Creation, Adoption and Diffusion of Innovations by Subsidiaries of Multinational Corporations', *Journal of International Business Studies* Fall, 365–88.

GMAC Global Relocation Services (2004), Ten Years of Global Relocation Trends: 1993–2004, GMAC Global Relocation Services.

Grant, R.M. (1996), 'Prospering in Dynamically Competitive Environments: Organizational Capability as Knowledge Integration', *Organization Science* 7: 4, 375–87.

Gupta, A.K. and Govindarajan, V. (2000), 'Knowledge flows within Multinational Corporations', *Strategic Management Journal* **21**, 473–96.

Harzing, A.-W. (2001), 'An Analysis of the Functions of International Transfer of Managers in MNCs', *Employee Relations* 23: 6, 581–98.

Hocking, J.B., Brown, M. and Harzing, A-W. (2004), 'A Knowledge Transfer Perspective of Strategic Assignment purposes and their Path-Dependent Outcomes', *International Journal of Human Resource Management* 15: 3, 565–86.

Hofstede, G. (1980), *Culture's Consequences: International Differences in Work-Related Values* (Beverly Hills: Sage).
Husted, K. and Michailova, S. (2002), 'Knowledge sharing in Russian Companies with Western Participation', *International Management* 6: 2, 17–28.
Hutchings, K. and Michailova, S. (2004), 'Facilitating Knowledge sharing in Russian and Chinese Subsidiaries: The Role of Personal Networks and Group Membership', *Journal of Knowledge Management* 8: 2, 84–94.
Jankowicz, A.D. (2001), 'Limits to Knowledge Transfer: What they already know in the Post-Command Economies', *Journal of East-West Business* 7: 2, 37–59.
Jensen, R. and Szulanski, G. (2004), 'Stickiness and the Adaptation of Organizational Practices in Cross-Border Knowledge Transfers', *Journal of International Business Studies* 35: 6, 508–23.
Kets de Vries, M. (2001), 'The Anarchist within: Clinical Reflections on Russian Character and Leadership Style', *Human Relations* 54: 5, 585–627.
Kets de Vries, M. (2000), 'A Journey into the "Wild East": Leadership Style and Organizational Practices in Russia', *Organizational Dynamics* 28: 4, 67–81.
Kogut, B. and Zander, U. (1993), 'Knowledge of the Firm and the Evolutionary Theory of the multinational corporation', *Journal of International Business Studies* 24: 4, 625–45.
Kostova, T. (1999), 'Transnational Transfer of Strategic Organizational Practices: A Contextual Perspective', *Academy of Management Review* 24: 2, 308–24.
Lang, R. and Steger, T. (2002), 'The Odyssey of Management Knowledge to Transforming Societies: A Critical Review of a Theoretical Alternative', *Human Resource Development International* 5: 3, 279–94.
Martin, X. and Salomon, R. (2003), 'Knowledge Transfer Capacity and its Implications for the Theory of the Multinational Corporation', *Journal of International Business Studies* 34: 4, 356–73.
May, R.C., Puffer, S.M. and McCarthy, D.J. (2005), 'Transferring Management Knowledge to Russia: A Culturally Based Approach', *Academy of Management Executive* 19: 2, 24–35.
May, R., Young, C.B. and Ledgerwood, D. (1998), 'Lessons from Russian Human Resource Management Experience', *European Management Journal* 16: 4, 447–59.
McCarthy, D.J., Puffer, S.M. and Naumov, A.I. (2000), 'Russia's Retreat to Statization and the Implications for Business', *Journal of World Business* 35: 3, 256–74.
Michailova, S. (2002), 'When Common Sense becomes Uncommon: Participation and Empowerment in Russian Companies with Western Participation', *Journal of World Business* 37: 3, 180–187.
Michailova, S. (2000), 'Contrasts in Culture: Russian and Western Perspectives on Organizational Change', *The Academy of Management Executive*, 14: 4, 99–112.
Michailova, S. and Husted, K. (2003), 'Knowledge-Sharing Hostility in Russian Firms', *California Management Review* 45: 3, 59–77.
Michailova, S. and Worm, V. (2003), 'Personal Networking in Russia and China: Blat and Guanxi', *European Management Journal* 21: 4, 509–19.

Michailova, S. and Anisimova, A. (1999), 'Russian Voices from a Danish Company', *Business Strategy Review* 10: 4, 65–78.

Minbaeva, D., Pedersen, T., Björkman, I., Fey, C.F. and Park, H.J. (2003), 'MNC Knowledge Transfer, Subsidiary absorptive Capacity, and HRM', *Journal of International Business Studies* 34: 6, 586–99.

Nonaka, I. and Takeuchi, H. (1995), *The Knowledge-Creating Company* (New York: Oxford University Press).

Nonaka, I. (1994), 'A Dynamic Theory of Organizational Knowledge Creation', *Organization Science* 5: 1, 14–37.

Ondrack, D. (1985), 'International Transfers of Managers in North American and European MNCs', *Journal of International Business Studies* 16: 3, 1–19.

Polanyi, M. (1962), *Personal knowledge: Towards a Post-Critical Philosophy* (Chicago: Chicago University Press).

Puffer, S.M. (1994), 'Understanding the Bear: A portrait of Russian Business Leaders', *The Academy of Management Executive* 8: 1, 41–54.

Riusala, K. and Smale, A. (forthcoming), 'Predicting Stickiness Factors in the International Transfer of Knowledge through Expatriates', *International Studies of Management and Organization.*

Riusala, K. and Suutari, V. (2004), 'International Knowledge Transfers through Expatriates: A Qualitative Analysis of Internal Stickiness Factors', *Thunderbird International Business Review* 46: 6, 743–70.

Simonin, B.L. (1999), 'Transfer of Marketing Know-How in International Strategic Alliances: An empirical Investigation of the Role and Antecedents of Knowledge Ambiguity', *Journal of International Business Studies* 30: 3, 463–90.

SITRA (2005). Suuri maa, pitkä kvartaali. Suomalaisyritysten kokemuksia Venäjän kehittyvästä kapitalismista [*Large Country, Long Quarterly. Experiences of Finnish Companies on the developing Capitalism of Russia*], Tapani Mäkinen (ed.) Sitra Reports 48, (Helsinki: Edita Prima Oy).

Smale, A., Suutari, V. and Riusala, K. (2005), 'Host-Country Effects on Knowledge Transfers through Expatriates', *proceedings of the 8th Conference on International Human Resource Management*, (Australia).

Szulanski, G. (1996), 'Exploring Internal Stickiness: Impediments to the Transfer of Best Practice within the Firm', *Strategic Management Journal* 17: 27–43.

Szulanski, G. (2003). *Sticky Knowledge: Barriers to Knowing in the Firm* (London: Sage).

Torbiorn, I. (1994), 'Operative and Strategic Use of Expatriates in New Organizations and market structures', *International Studies of Management and Organization* 24: 3, 5–17.

von Hippel, E. (1994), '"Sticky Information" and the Locus of Problem Solving: Implications for Innovation', *Management Science* 40: 4, 429–39.

Wang, P.; Tong, T.W. and Koh, C.P. (2004), 'An Integrated Model of Knowledge Tansfer from MNC parent to China Subsidiary', *Journal of World Business* 39: 168–82.

Zander, U. and Kogut, B. (1995), 'Knowledge and the Speed of the Transfer and Imitation of Organisational Capabilities: An Empirical Test', *Organizational Science* 6: 1, 76–92.

Chapter 14

Human Resource Management Practices in Russia and Canada: Convergence or Divergence?

Sudhir K. Saha

Introduction

An important aspect of international human resource management (IHRM), according to Dennis Briscoe (1995), concerns the need of IHR managers to understand HR practices in the countries in which their companies operate. IHRM scholars such as Roberts, Kossek and Ozeki (1998), and Adler and Bartholomew (1992) stressed the importance of finding a way of developing 'globally competent people' who would be able to function well in a global business environment. How do we develop globally competent managers who are able to function well in this global business environment? We believe that it is primarily a matter of education and training led by sound research. We need to have a sound basis of information about international human resource management before we can train and educate such expatriate managers. This article presents findings from a survey of Russian and Canadian managers about their managerial values and human resource decisions. One of the prime objectives in the research was to generate information and interest concerning HRM practices in both Canada and Russia.

Literature Review

Interest in how Russian managers behave as compared to the Western managers had grown unabated since the early 1990s as Russia undertook initiatives to make a transition from a communist system to a Western style socio-economic and political system. For example, Fey and Björkman (2001) studied the effect of human resource management practices on MNC subsidiary performance in Russia. The results from their study found that investments in HRM practices in Russia substantially assisted firms in improving their performance. The study by Fey and Björkman underscored the need to further study the kind of HR practices they have in Russia and find how Western companies could align their HR practices with those from Russia.

Many Western organizations, both in the public and private sectors, have now established inter-organizational relationships (through Foreign Direct Investment,

Joint Ventures and other types of business arrangements) with Russian organizations in all socio-political, economic, cultural and business sectors. Thelan and Zhuplev (2001) estimated that Western organizations have had a very significant influence on Russian economy with respect to exports, imports and foreign investments in Russia. They estimated that there were over ten thousand foreign businesses operating in Russia (BISNIS).

A number of scholars, both Russian and Western, have made observations to the effect that the transition of the Russian economy to a market economy had been less than satisfactory. For example, a report (BISNIS) estimated that total foreign direct investment in Russia amounted to $61 per capita, as compared with 389 dollars for Poland, and 967 dollars for the Czech Republic. These scholars found many reasons for the lack of success in transition efforts. For example, Vlachoutsicos (1998) of the Center for East European Studies (CEES), Copenhagen Business School, suggested that Russian transition to a market economy had not been successful because the Western managers have misunderstood 'Russian managerial practices and decisionmaking methods.' He argued that it was essential for the Russian Communitarian value system to be reconciled with market economy values and management practices of the West. Snejina Michailova (1997, 2000) found many reasons for failure in transition that included 'managerial attitudes and behaviour of Russian managers, a contrast in managerial perspectives between the Western and Russian managers engaged in the process of organizational change.' Thelan and Zhuplev (2001) have presented one of the best descriptions of difficulties faced by foreigners wanting to do business in Russia. They said, 'Foreign investors face a number of challenges and deterrents in Russia; some of the most commonly cited problems include taxes, corruption, an ever changing regulatory environment that lacks transparency, a labyrinth of government bureaucracies, weak shareholders' rights, and weak contract law.'

Reasons for slow progress in transition efforts could be many and varied. Social scientists (Afanassieva 1999; Ardichvili and Kuchinke 2002; Bigoness 1996; Hickson and Pugh 1995; King, Barnowe and Pauna 2000; Thelen and Zhuplev 2001, and Vlachoutsicos and Lawrence 1996), however, generally agreed that the success of any change effort including economic and socio-political transitions was dependent on the existence of an appropriate national culture, managerial values, and human resource practices. A growing literature on Russia suggest that Russian managerial values and practices, specially the part that clashes with fundamental values of a market economy, are systemic causes to success/failure of transition of the Russian economy. The study reported here made an effort to understand Russian HR practices and managerial values and how those compared with managerial values and HR practices of Canadian managers.

If one accepts the hypothesis that arises out of the current literature on Russian managerial practices and their outcomes, it becomes imperative to dig deeper and find answer to the following questions: What do Russian managers think about the importance of human resource management practices (HRM)? How are the Russian HRM practices similar and/or different from Western HRM practices? Will Russian

HR practices converge in or diverge from practices of other countries like Canada? What are the beliefs and values of Russian managers that may move forward or slow down the pace of transition to a market economy? How do values of Russian managers compare and contrast with those of managers from the Western countries? The current study is an attempt to find answers to the above questions taking Canada and Russia as the two target countries. The author believes that answers to the questions will enable Russian and Western managers to work cooperatively and successfully in businesses that have been established in Russia today. It should be noted that Canada and Russia were chosen as targets of the current investigation because of the growing economic and social ties between the two countries. Another reason for the choice was that Canada could reasonably be considered a country that represents a model of Western Managerial values and Western HRM practices. This research, however, acknowledges the fact that all Western managers do not behave the same way, and that there is both convergence and divergence found in international HRM practices (Sparrow, Schuler and Jackson 1994) among some of these countries.

The study was guided by previous work on international HRM by a number of scholars (Morgan 1986; Saha 1989, 2002, and 2003; Sparrow, Schuler and Jackson 1994; Kanter 1998; Dowling 1999). According to Morgan (1986), international HRM should be viewed as interacting cubic relationships among three classes of variables such as human resource activities (such as procurement, allocation, and utilization), countries (such as host, home and other), and type of employees (such as host-country, parent-country, and third-country). He suggested that a fit among the three classes of variables should determine specific IHRM practices.

Saha (1989) presented a model of IHRM that hypothesized that HRM practices in a given country would be influenced by managerial values and attitudes, organizational structure, and many other environmental and organizational factors (such as culture, economy and political factors). For example, inn a Western country like Canada, corporations feel compelled both legally and socially to do everything that they can to avoid accidents and injuries; while in some of the developing nations in Asia and Eastern Europe health and safety issues draw headlines only when employees are killed or sustain serious injuries (Saha 1989; Saha et al. 1999). The author espoused a contemporary view that suggests that IHRM practices in any organization is a product of many micro and macro variables that interact with each other in many ways.

Dowling and Welch (2004) provided a theoretical framework that suggested that five classes of variables such as the cultural environment, the industry, complexity of operations, size of domestic market, and attitude of senior management influenced international HRM activities. Sparrow, Schuler and Jackson (1994) suggested that for competitive advantage there is both convergence and divergence in the way a firm utilizes the HRM policies practices. In the context of human resource management practices, the hypothesis of convergence means universality of HRM principles and practices regardless of national environments, while divergence hypothesis assumes the influence of culture, people and organizations in each nation determining their HRM principles and practices.

The study is part of a series of studies conducted by the author and his associates from a number of different countries to determine similarities and differences of HRM practices in the world. Earlier studies have established that human resource practices in countries like Canada, Czech Republic, Bangladesh, Hong Kong, India, and Pakistan had certain similarities and differences. For example, Canadian managers attached significantly greater importance to health and safety, and training and development as compared to managers from Bangladesh, Czech Republic, Hong Kong and Pakistan. Some similarities among these countries were that managers from all six countries favoured a performance-based compensation system. They also favoured participative management. These studies provided support to the hypothesis that managerial value differences make a difference in HR decision-making involving health and safety, employee training, performance evaluation, and pay for performance. These studies also showed and convergence and divergence of HR practices in those countries despite the economic, political, social and cultural differences.

A question that could be raised by critics concerns the kind of hypotheses that underlay this research. At the time of this study there were not sufficient literature available on the subject of this study so that some definite hypotheses could have been formulated and tested. The investigation was considered truly exploratory and thus avoided formulating any hypothesis. Having said that, it was also true that we had some speculation based upon our own research in the past as to how some of the findings would turn out. Rather than stating these conjectures in terms of hypotheses in this section, they would be discussed as the article presents the findings below.

Method

Data were collected from Russia and Canada by mailing questionnaires to the respondents. This questionnaire was developed by the author in 1991 to conduct international studies of human resource management practices. This questionnaire had been used in a number of studies including the current one. The questionnaire was translated into Russian language for data collection. The questionnaire was entitled, 'Critical Incidents for Managerial Decisions' and contained several items relating to human resource decisionmaking. These critical incidents described hypothetical decision situations with respect to human resource management issues such as health and safety, training, employment equity, compensation and performance evaluation. Using the critical incident methodology, it was possible to make the HR issues very clear and specific as opposed to being a theoretical construct or concept.

Once the respondents read the case incidents, they were to record their decisions and explain the reasons behind their decisions. For example, the incident on health and safety described a specific safety situation and asked a respondent as to how he/she was going to deal with it (that is, would they allocate funds for improving health and safety?). Managers from both countries were asked to rate the importance of each of the above mentioned HR issues on a seven point Likert-type rating scales, seven being extremely important to one being not important at all. Two hundred respondents were contacted in Canada. All respondents were practicing managers. They were contacted through a management development center, in-company management development programs, and a business school. Participation in the research was voluntary.

Part 2 of the questionnaire was entitled, 'Managerial Values' comprising of 25 five-point Likert-type scales on family, spirituality, work ethics, fatalism, religion, equity, teamwork, and some other workplace beliefs and values. The reliability of the value scales was tested and was found to be acceptable. Reliability scores (for example Cronbach's Alpha) ranged from 0.71 to 0.87. The final part of the questionnaire elicited demographic information concerning age, education, sex, marital status, and nature of employment of the respondents. The questionnaire was scrutinized and passed by a Committee for Ethics in Research in one of the universities involved in this project.

Data collection from Russia involved several steps: First, a Professor who teaches Russian language translated the questionnaire into Russian. Once the translation process was complete, a research assistant originating from Russia checked the questionnaire for meaning and adequacy. The research assistant also assisted in data collection, and translation of opinions of Russian managers into English. Russian managers were chosen on a convenience basis from a cross-section of private and public sector organizations from Moscow, Tomsk, Omsk, Novosibirsk, Barnaul, Biysk and Novokuznetsk. Data were collected from managers who were knowledgeable about HR practices of their organizations. The respondents held managerial jobs ranging from first level to the executive level; they were chosen based upon their knowledge of human resource practices in their respective organization.

Complete responses were received from 93 Russian and 150 Canadian managers. Data were collected from the two countries utilizing similar data collection procedures. Statistical analysis of data involved mainly descriptive statistics (computation of Means, SDs, and also testing for statistical differences between the two samples). Since the data on HR practices are based upon fairly objective information, statistical testing for reliability of data was not considered essential.

Findings

Perceived importance of HR issues: Managers from both countries were asked to rate the importance of some basic human resource management issues such as health and safety, training and development, employee performance, employee attitude, employment equity, especially equity between males and females. A manager, whether Russian or Canadian is usually required to deal with these fundamental human resource management issues. It is expected that a similar view held by both Russian and Canadian managers would lead to cooperation. Table

14.1 reveals the importance attached by managers from Canada and Russia on some HR issues. Managers from Russia indicated a significantly greater concern for pay for performance, and employee attitude as HRM issues as compared to Canadian managers. In the current economic situation of Russia, it was expected that pay as a managerial issue would be influencing Russian managers more than Canadian managers. Similarly, importance given to employee attitude (deference to managers' authority) by Russian managers as compared to Canadian managers was also expected. Previous studies had revealed that Managers from the Soviet block countries attached a significantly higher importance to employee attitude than Western managers.

Other differences observed (statistically insignificant but directionally true) between the two samples included the following: Canadian managers showed more concern for health and safety and employment equity. Russian managers, in their part, were higher in their concern for training and development. Legislations for health and safety and employment equity are very strong in Canada. Naturally the Canadian concerns for the two shown in this study by Canadian managers appeared to be justified. Similarly, Russian managers have been operating in an environment in which training and development are extremely important for Russian organizations to be successful. Naturally, Russian managers were found to have expressed the higher concerns for training and development in the current investigation. No statistical difference was observed in the opinion of managers from both countries on the importance of employee performance.

Table 14.1 Perceived importance of HR issues by Canadian and Russian managers

HR Issues	**Canada** (N=150)		**Russia** (N=93)		T test
	Mean	SD	Mean	SD	
Health & Safety	5.9	1.8	5.6	1.4	NS
Pay for Performance	4.5	1.7	4.9	1.5	S
Training & Development	5.3	1.8	5.6	1.4	NS
Employee Performance	5.9	1.8	5.9	1.2	NS
Employee Attitude	5.7	1.8	6.5	0.8	S
Employment Equity	4.5	2.1	4.1	2.2	NS

The scales range from 1=Low to 7=High

The readers should also note that a very different interpretation of the results reported in Table 14.1 was also conceivable. Mean scores from both samples were so high and so close that one could argue that the views of Russian and Canadian managers were very similar. On a practical day-to-day operation, managers from the two countries were not likely to disagree with one another as to the *importance* of the HR issues investigated in the study.

Human Resource Decisionmaking

While the rating of perceived importance of HR issues certainly provided an interesting comparison between Russian and Canadian managers, what would these managers actually decide when they were confronted with a specific human resource problem? This was thought to be a more significant aspect of this study between Russian and Canadian managers. Rating the importance of an HR issue may simply indicate the desirability of a manager's choice: however, an actual decision on a specific HR problem reveals much more about the behaviour of managers in a given situation. Utilizing the Critical Incident Methodology as described in the Method section of this paper, managers were placed in a situation in which they had to validate their opinion on a specific HR issue. That is, they were to make funding decision to solve HR problems described in the critical incidents for them. Results derived from analysis of data on HR decisions made by both Canadian and Russian managers appear in Table 14.2 of the paper.

It appeared that a significantly fewer number of Russian managers were willing to provide funding for improvement of *health and safety* in workplaces despite the fact the case incident showed safety problem that required more investment to prevent accidents and injuries. Canadian managers, on their part, did approve full/partial funding in much greater number. This finding can be interpreted in a number of ways. Health and safety laws in Canada are so strong that employee can refuse to work if they think that the work environment poses threat to their health and safety; the same cannot be said for Russian legislations. Also, the economic disparity between the two countries may also be a reason for reluctance to spend money for health and safety. The difference in spending can also be explained in terms of differences in managerial values and beliefs.

Previous studies (Shenkar 1995; Tung 1981) showed that monetary *compensation* was a preferred method of motivation in Western countries like Canada while a communist country like China depended on other ideological and non-monetary methods of motivation. Many reports about Russian economy suggested that non-monetary method of compensation is prevalent widely in Russian organizations. There are other socio-economic and political differences between Canada and Russia. Based upon the above, the study hypothesized that Canadian managers would show a greater support for pay for performance based compensation policy as compared to the Russian managers This hypothesis was, however, not supported in the findings reported in Table 14.2. Russians value incentive systems, bonuses, and benefits packages. 'It is often the combination of bonuses and benefits packages that are the determining factors when Russian employees will choose to join or leave a firm' (Fey et al. 1999).

Findings reported in Table 14.2 on the HR issues of *Pay for Performance* and *Merit Pay* were very interesting despite the fact that the study found no statistically significant difference between the two samples concerning the two aspects of employee compensation policy. A significant majority of both samples appeared to be saying that they were in favour of Pay for Performance Policy (which means that an increase in performance should be followed by an increase in compensation). However, when they were asked to grant a pay increase to a subordinate who showed superior performance, only a half of both samples agreed to grant the pay increase. Desirability of having a performance-based pay system, and not giving a pay raise when a subordinate actually shows superior performance demonstrated a management dilemma that was evident in this study.

On the issue of employee *training and development*, the study found that both Russian and Canadian managers were overwhelmingly in favour of investment in

Table 14.2 Human resource decisions by Canadian and Russian managers

Human resource management decisions	**Canada** (N=150) in %	**Russia** (N=93) in %	**T test**
Funding for Health & Safety			
No funding	0.7	4.3	S
Full funding	66.6	60.2	
Partial funding	24.0	35.5	
Pay based upon performance			
Affirmative	77.7	76.3	NS
Negative	22.3	23.7	
Recommend pay increase for performance			
Yes	50.4	45.2	NS
No	49.6	54.8	
Funding for Training & Development			
Yes	96.3	93.5	NS
No	3.7	6.5	
Dismiss for poor performance			
Yes	1.4	11.8	S
No	98.6	88.2	
Dismiss for poor attitude			
Yes	11.2	32.2	S
No	88.8	67.8	
Dismiss for both poor performance and attitude			
Yes	72.8	94.6	S
No	27.2	5.4	
Employment equity decision			
Hire female over male	35.0	79.6	S
Hire male over female	65.0	20.4	

training. It is interesting to note that a significant majority of Russian managers, despite resource shortages, were in favour of a decision to invest money in training and development. The wide publicity given in Russia to the idea that investment in training would be one of the most important factors for economic progress appears to have spread well amongst the Russian managers. Thus this study provided some evidence that Russian managers had bought the idea of investing in training and development as a method of improving the operation of the Russian economy. Similarly, years of Canadian publicity on the virtues of training and development have also influenced Canadian managers well.

In previous studies (Saha 1989, 1999), it was found that *performance evaluation criteria* varied from country to country depending upon managerial values and local culture. This was true especially for the boss-subordinate relationship and job performance. The emphasis put on 'soft' criteria like loyalty and deference to the boss varied between Eastern and Western cultures. For example, in India, Pakistan, Hong Kong, and China, the managers thought that attitude was more important than performance whereas Western managers put more emphasis on performance as compared to attitude. This study, therefore, included two criteria, subordinate attitude, and subordinate performance for consideration of managers for evaluating performance of their subordinates. In Table 14.1, it has been already reported that Russian managers rated subordinate attitude significantly more important than Canadian managers. The study, however, found no difference between Canadian and Russian managers their rating of the importance of performance as one of the criteria for performance evaluation.

To study what managers would actually decide when confronted with attitude and/or performance deficiency, managers were given performance record of three different subordinates called X, Y and Z regarding subordinates' attitude and performance. The subordinate X had good attitude but poor performance. The subordinate Y had good performance but poor attitude toward superiors and co-workers. The record of subordinate Z revealed both poor performance and poor attitude. Russian and Canadian managers were given the choice of firing these subordinates. Table 14.2 shows the result of data gathered on what these managers actually decided. For performance deficiency, 1.4 per cent of Canadian sample fired the subordinate X, while only 11.8 per cent of Russian managers did the same. For poor attitude 32.2 per cent of Russian managers fired the subordinate Y, while only 11.2 per cent of Canadian managers did the same supporting our hypothesis. For having both poor attitude and poor performance, 94.6 per cent of Russian managers decided to fire the subordinate Z, while only 72.8 per cent of Canadian managers made a similar decision. A point worth noting about the behaviour of managers from the two countries was that Russian managers were less forgiving of their subordinates who showed performance and/or attitude problems.

Employment equity for men and women is a significant issue in human resource management. There is EE legislation in Canada on this issue. There is also a lot of publicity given in Canada on the desirability of hiring women when their ratio in the workplace was not adequate. Russian and Canadian managers were asked to decide what they would do about employment equity. If there was a choice given whether to hire a man or a woman when the employment of women is a hot button issue, what would be their choices? Results shown in Table 14.2 indicated that a overwhelming majority (79.6 per cent) of Russian managers decided to hire a female over male to deal with a hiring gap between men and women. The Russian sample had 45 females and 48 males; thus the result cannot be due to the composition of the Russian sample. Only 35 per cent of Canadian managers decided to hire a female over a male to bridge the employment gap. 69 per cent of Canadian respondents were males and 31 per cent were females. The lower percentage of females chosen by managers in the Canadian sample could be partly due to the composition of the sample. However, the composition of Canadian sample could not explain away the huge difference observed between the choices made by Canadian and Russian managers. Russian managers said that they were more likely to choose a female candidate over a male candidate to reach employment equity goal. A content analysis of the responses provided by Russian managers in an open-ended section of the questionnaire revealed a number of explanation for the choice of majority of Russian managers: that they were concerned with the situation where female to male ratio was low; that females deserved a better treatment in employment. Majority of the Canadian sample of managers disagreed with the above views. This finding is further discussed below.

Managerial beliefs and values: The primary objective of this research investigation was to find similarities and differences in human resource management practices between Russian and Canadian managers. It was, however, deemed necessary to find an explanation as to why these differences exist between Russian and Canadian HRM practices. In IHRM literature, many reasons have been cited for cross-national differences in HR practices including economic, political, social, industrial, organizational and cultural factors (Mendenhall and Oddou 2000; Dowling, Welch and Schuler 1999). Over the last several decades, an impressive amount of literature has been gathered to show that beliefs and value differences exist among managers in different countries causing differences in managerial behaviour (Haire, Ghiselli and Porter 1966; Cummings and Schmidt 1972; England 1978; Hofstede 1980; Shenkar 1995, and Adler 1997).

Based upon the previous research evidence, a decision was made to investigate value differences as possible explanation for differences in human resource practices. It should be noted that the investigation did not assume that a managerial value is *the only factor* that cause a manager to act differently; many other factors influence managerial decision-making such as laws, industrial customs and practices, as noted earlier in this paper. Because so few empirical studies have been conducted so far on comparing Russian and Canadian managers, we did not have the benefit of an established conceptual framework. The study, therefore, used value items that were used in similar international studies by the author and his associates (Saha et al. 1995, 1997, 1998, 1999). Another important point of this research was that the study was guided by the idea that those value items should be chosen that relate to contemporary workplace issues like workplace equity, manager-subordinate relationships, teamwork, morality, spirituality and so on. There are many excellent instruments and measures of managerial values such as those developed by Allport et al., England, Kluckhom, Hofstede, and Rokeach. However, a decision was made to develop items that would explain HR practices.

Table 14.3 Managerial beliefs and values

Beliefs and values	**Canada** (N=150)		**Russia** (N=93)		**T test**
	Mean	SD	Mean	SD	
Family is most important	4.1	1.4	1.4	0.8	S
Poor work ethics in people	3.6	1.3	3.3	1.2	NS
Internal control I	3.7	1.3	2.4	0.9	S
Moral attitude	3.8	1.3	1.4	0.8	S
Employment equity is unfair	2.4	1.2	2.7	1.2	NS
External control	2.4	1.2	3.1	1.2	S
Affirmative action	3.5	1.3	2.2	1.1	S
Internal control II	3.4	1.2	1.9	0.9	S
Participative leadership	3.2	1.4	1.8	1.0	S
Belief in astrology	1.6	0.9	3.3	1.2	S
Respect for ancestors	4.3	1.3	1.3	0.7	S
Trust in people	3.5	1.4	2.5	1.2	S
Family more important than individual	3.0	1.4	2.0	1.0	S
Internal control III	3.3	1.3	2.0	0.9	S
Enjoy being part of a group	3.7	1.3	1.6	0.8	S
Spiritual over material	3.5	1.3	2.3	1.0	S
Faith in supervisors	3.7	1.5	2.3	1.1	S
Giving priority to needs of others	2.6	1.2	2.8	1.3	NS
Faith in God	2.8	1.5	2.9	1.3	NS
Equality in a small group	3.2	1.3	2.2	1.1	S
Unions are unimportant	3.5	1.4	2.1	1.2	S
Pleasing the boss	2.5	1.3	3.2	1.0	S
Socializing at work	2.5	1.3	3.6	1.0	S
Being ambitious	3.8	1.3	2.5	1.1	S
Hire employees based on selection scores only	1.8	2.2	3.1	1.1	S

The scales range from 1=Low to 7=High

Table 14.3 shows 25 items that were formulated and utilized to measure the similarities and differences in the beliefs and values of Russian and Canadian managers. Importance of family, work-ethics, trustworthiness of people, moral and spiritual attitude, belief in one's own ability to control work and family situations, employment equity and affirmative action, equality, participation, teamwork, attitude toward supervisors and socializing at work were some of the important items that were included in the survey of some managerial predispositions toward HR practices. As expected, Russian and Canadian managers were found to be significantly different in 21 out of 25 value items shown in Table 14.3.

Canadian managers, as compared to Russian managers, attached less importance to family as an institution, and were also less sure of their ability to control situations in their workplaces and personal life. On workplace issues like 'enjoy being part of a group', 'equality in a group', and 'participative leadership', Canadian managers were less favourably predisposed to these ideas as compared to the Russian managers. Canadian managers also showed less trust in people and in the work ethics of their workers.

Russian managers, on the other hand, cared less about pleasing the boss and socializing at work. They also considered themselves ambitious. They believed less in the idea of selecting employees on the basis of their performance in selection tests and were more agreeable to the idea of affirmative action. Russian managers put more value in union membership as compared to Canadian managers. They were also stronger believers on spirituality over material possessions.

Both samples, however, were similar in their 'faith in God' (that is low faith). On the subject of employment equity both samples agreed that they were unfair. Both samples also thought there were 'poor work ethics in people'. Canadian and Russian managers were both neutral about the idea of 'giving priority to the needs of others'.

Discussion

This paper has presented a report of an investigation designed to compare human resource management practices and managerial values between Canada and Russia. This was a very modest attempt. The research was very exploratory in nature as it embarked on a study of Russian managers in which very few publications are available in the Western media. The investigation, notwithstanding being exploratory in nature, produced some valuable information that could lead to future enquiries on the subject of Russian human resource management practices. Highlights of the findings from the study included the following:

Russian managers, as compared to the Canadian managers, showed more importance for training and development of employees, pay for performance compensation policy, and employee attitude. Canadian managers, on their part, attached more importance to health and safety issues, and employment equity. Prevailing legislations in Canada, in addition to other factors, may be responsible for the concern shown by Canadian managers. In Russia, there is a strong campaign for training and development that might have shaped the Russian managers' opinions. Economic conditions surrounding payment of wages to employees in Russia may have also shaped the opinion of managers in that country regarding pay for performance compensation policy.

The investigation also looked at what managers in the two countries would decide when they were confronted with specific case incidents involving health and safety, training and development, pay increase, firing subordinates for a cause, and hiring women for affirmative action. A larger proportion of Canadian managers, as compared to Russian managers, decided to fund health and safety projects. Managers in both countries decided overwhelmingly in favour of funding training and development projects. Similarly, managers in both countries showed a decision dilemma regarding compensation policy: while a significant majority in both countries decided in favour of pay for performance, only a half of the two samples actually came up with a decision to grant pay increase for a subordinate who has shown superior performance. This was an interesting finding because the investigation provided evidence that there was a discrepancy in what managers said they would do and what they actually did. Russian managers were more likely to fire a subordinate for poor attitude; they were also more likely to fire a subordinate for deficiency in performance and/or attitude. Canadians appeared to be more forgiving of shortcomings of their subordinates.

On affirmative action for women, a significantly larger percentage of Russian managers decided to hire females over males. A discrepancy was evident in the behaviour of Canadian managers: while they expressed a more favourable opinion on employment equity, many of them were not willing to hire a female over a male when a situation needed that. This discrepancy could be explained in a number of ways. The Canadian EE legislation is considered to be voluntary in terms of compliance, and this fact may have influenced the behaviour of Canadian managers. Also, it is possible that Canadian managers support EE goals on paper as a politically correct thing to do, but they would not really hire women unless they were forced to by government hiring quotas. Why did the vast majority (virtually 80 per cent) of Russian managers in the Russian sample were willing to hire females over males? We do not have any reliable data that could provide a definite answer to the question, but we did ask managers to provide their reason(s) behind their decision. Majority of respondents left the blank space provided to them unused. Some of them however, used the space, to suggest that they did choose females over males because the females deserve equality (the case incident showed that the number of females was less than males in their organization). Even though this study did not compare new Russian values with old Soviet value system, findings reported in Table 14.3 provided evidence that Russian managers attached a lot of importance to family, enjoyed group work, and valued the concept of equality in a group. Russian managers were also trusting of employees and believing in their work ethics.

The purpose the study was to gather information about Russian and Canadian managers so that managers from both countries who were engaged in international projects could work with full cooperation and understanding. As in other similar investigations, the author did not assume any superiority of any national HR practices. The goal was to generate a profile of management practices in both Canada and

Russia so that managers would be able to appreciate each other's opinions and values, and integrate their views and find solution to business problems that are mutually beneficial. Managers from both countries should be advised to work cooperatively and to respect the views of managers from the other country by coming to a joint decision that would benefit their businesses. The study showed that both Russian and Canadian managers thought that HRM practices were important for effective performance of their organizations even though they did diverge somewhat in their decisions concerning human resource matters. Thus, the study found, following earlier investigation by Sparrow, Schuler and Jackson (1994) that there is both convergence and divergence between Russian and Canadian HRM practices.

References

Adler, N.J. (1997), *International Dimensions of Organisational Behaviour, 3rd Edition* (Cincinnati, Ohio: South-Western College Publishing).

Adler, N. and Bartholomew, S. (1992), 'Managing Globally Competent People', *Academy of Management Executive* 6: 3, 52–65.

Afanassieva, M. (1999), 'Managerial Responses to Transition in the Russian Defense Industry', Work in Progress (Business School, The University of Hull).

Ardichvili, A. and Kuchinke, K.P. (2002), 'Leadership Styles and Cultural Values among Managers and Subordinates: A Comparative Study of Four Countries of The Former Soviet Union, Germany, and US', *Human Resource Development International* 5: 1, 99–117.

Bigoness, W.J. and Blakely, G.L. (1996), 'A Cross-national Study of Managerial Values', *Journal of International Business Studies* 7: 4, 739–52.

Briscoe, D. (1995), *International Human Resource Management*, Englewood Cliffs (N.J.: Prentice-Hall).

Cummings, L.L. and Schmidt, S.M. (1972), 'Managerial Attitudes of Greeks: The Roles of Culture and Industrialization', *Administrative Sciences Quarterly* 17: 2, 265–72.

Dowling, P.J., Welch, D.E. and Schuler, R.S. (1999), *International Human Resource Management, 3rd Edition* (South-West College Publishing).

Dowling, P.J. and Welch, D.E. (2004), *International Human Resource Management, 4th Edition* (Thompson).

England, G.W. (1978), 'Managers and Their Value Systems: A Five-Country Comparison', *Columbia Journal of World Business* 35–44.

Fey, C.F., Engstrom, P. and Björkman, I. (1999), 'Doing Business in Russia: Effective Human Resource Management Practices for Foreign Firms in Russia', *Organizational Dynamics* 28, 2.

Fey, C.F. and Björkman, I. (2001), 'The Effect of Human Resource management Practices on MNC Subsidiary Performance in Russia', *Journal of International Business Studies* 32: 1, 59–75.

Haire, M., Ghiselli, E.G. and Porter, L.W. (1966) *Managerial Thinking: An International Study* (New York: Wiley).

Hofstede, G. (1980), *Culture's Consequences: International Differences in Work Related Values* (Beverly Hills, CA: Sage Publication).

Hofstede, G. (1993), 'Cultural Dimensions in Management Theories', *Academy of Management Executive* 7: 1, 81–93

Kanter, R.M. and Dretler, T.D. (1998), 'Global Strategy and its Impact on Local Operations: Lessons from Gillette Singapore', *Academy of Management Executive* 12, 4.

King, G.J., Barnowe, J.T. and Pauna, D. (2000), 'Values of Baltic Management Students', *Lithuanian Quarterly Journal of Arts and Sciences* 46, 3.

Mendenhall, M. and Gary, O. (2000), *Readings and Cases in International Human Resource Management, 3rd Edition*, (South-West College Publishing).

Michailova, S. (1997), 'Interface between Western and Russian Management Attitudes: Implications for Organizational Change', Working Paper, No. 8, (Copenhagen Business School).

Michailova, S. (2000), 'Contrasts in Culture: Russian and Western Perspectives on Organizational Change', *The Academy of Management Executive* 14: 4, 99–112.

Morgan, P. (1986), 'International Human Resource Management: Fact or Fiction', *Personnel Administrator* 31: 9, 43–7.

Negandhi, A.R. (1979), 'Convergence in Organisational Practice: An Empirical Study of Industrial Enterprises in Developing Countries', in Lammers, C.J. and Hickson, D.J. (eds) *Organizations Alike and Unlike* (London: Routledge and Kegan Paul).

Roberts, K., Kossek, E. and Ozeki, C. (1998), 'Managing the Global Workforce: Challenges and Strategies', *The Academy of Management Executive* 12: 4, 93–106

Saha, S.K. (1989), 'Managing Human Resources: An International Comparison. Administrative Sciences Association of Canada', *Personnel and Human Resources Division Proceedings* 10, 9.

Saha, S.K. (1995), 'Differences in Managerial Values: Do they Influence HRM in Different Countries? Managing in a Global Economy', *Proceedings of the Sixth International Conference*, EAM, June 11–15, Singapore, 66–70.

Saha, S.K. (1997), 'A Comparative Study of Human Resource Decisions and Managerial Values: How Different are some Pakistani and Canadian Managers? Managing in a Global Economy', *Proceedings of the Seventh International Conference*, EAM, June 15–19, Dublin, Ireland, 26–30.

Saha, S.K. and Fiesta, I. (1999), 'Managerial Values and Human Resource Decisions: A Comparative Study of Some Czech and Canadian Managers', *Proceedings of the Eighth International Conference*, Eastern Academy of Management, Prague, Czech Republic.

Shenkar, O. (1995), *Global Perspectives of Human Resources Management*, Englewood Cliffs (NJ: Prentice-Hall).

Sparrow, P., Schuler, R.S. and Jackson, S. (1994), 'Convergence or Divergence: Human Resource Practices and Policies for Competitive Advantage Worldwide', *International Journal of Human Resource Management* 5: 2, 267–99.

Thelen, S. and Zhuplev, A. (2001), 'Comparing Russian and American Attitudes on Ethical Issues in Managing Small Firms in Russia', Submitted to *USASBE/SBIDA* 2001 Annual Conference, (Orlando, Florida).

Tung, R.L. (1981), 'Patterns of Motivation in Chinese Industrial Enterprises', *Academy of Management Review* 6, 481–9.

Tung, R.L. and Miller, E.L. (1990), 'Managing in the Twenty-first Century: The Need For Global Orientation', *Management International Review* 30: 1, 5–18.

Vlachoutsicos, C. (1998), *Russian Management: Value Systems and Inner Logic*, Working Paper no.14, Center for East European Studies, (Copenhagen Business School).

Zeira, Y. and Banai, M. (1984), 'Present and Desired Methods of Selecting Expatriate Managers for International Assignments', *Personnel Review* 13: 3, 29–35.

Internet-based reference

Vlachoutsicos, C., The Dangers of Ignoring Russian Communitarianism', (1998), [website] <http://www.worldbank.org/transitionnewsletter/oct98/wdi.htm>

Chapter 15

The Effect of Human Resource Management Practices on MNC Subsidiary Performance in Russia

Carl F. Fey and Ingmar Björkman

It is now commonly accepted that employees create an important source of competitive advantage for firms (Barney 1991; Pfeffer 1994). As a result, it is important for a firm to adopt human resource management (HRM) practices that make the best use of its employees. The above trend has led to increased interest in the impact of HRM on organizational performance, and a number of studies have found a positive relationship between so called 'high performance work practices' (Huselid 1995) and different measures of company performance. Furthermore, some empirical evidence supports the hypothesis that firms that align their HRM practices with their business strategy will achieve superior outcomes (for recent reviews, see Becker and Gerhart 1996; Becker and Huselid 1998; Dyer and Reeves 1995; Guest 1997).

The implications of these findings for multinational corporations, however, remain to be investigated. Most studies of the relationship between HRM and organizational performance have been conducted on the domestic operations of US firms, with a smaller number of studies carried out in Europe (for example, Guest and Hoque 1994) and Asia (Ngo et al. 1998). Scholars of international business have so far focused on the extent to which HRM practices within multinational corporations are globally standardized and/or locally adapted (Rosenzweig and Nohria 1994; Taylor et al. 1996) and largely ignored the relationship between HRM and firm performance (for an exception, see Ngo et al. 1998). Our review of the literature indicates a serious lack of large-sample empirical studies designed to investigate whether extensive use of 'high performance' HRM practices and a good alignment between HRM and firm strategy have positive effects on the performance of foreign subsidiaries located in transition economies like China or Russia. To fill some of the above mentioned voids, this study will examine the relationship between HRM and foreign subsidiary performance in Russia.

The choice of Russia enables us to investigate whether the same positive performance effects of HRM practices observed in previous research also hold for Western subsidiaries located in an economy in transition. While business performance of foreign companies in Russia to a large extent depends on external macro factors like general legislation and its frequent change, individual firms can do little to affect the external environment. This study aims to investigate an important issue which firms can influence, their HRM practices. Several authors have pointed to the importance of HRM and provided anecdotal discussions about HRM or discussed one dimension in depth (for example, Juplev et al. 1998; Laurence and Vlachoutsicos, 1990; Longenecker and Popovski 1994; May et al. 1998; Magura 1998; Puffer 1997; Radko and Afansieva 1999; Shekshnia 1994, 1998; Vikhanski and Puffer 1993; Welsh et al. 1993). However, little systematic Russian-language research exists on HRM issues and the Western literature investigating Russian management is also very limited. Recent studies such as Elenkov (1997, 1998), Holt et al. (1994), and Ralston et al. (1997) have shown that significant differences exist in the national cultures of Russia and the United States (and Western European countries). It has also been suggested that different HRM practices may be appropriate for Russia than for Western countries (Elenkov 1998; Juplev et al. 1998). This hypotheses, however, has yet to be tested. To the best of our knowledge, ours is the first large-sample study of the relationship between a variety of HRM practices and HRM strategy alignment and firm performance in the Russian context.

In addition to contributing to our understanding of the effects of HRM on foreign subsidiary performance in Russia, the current research project may also begin to address the wider question of how to effectively manage human resources in subsidiaries located in different environments. This study will also advance the literature by differentiating between HRM practices used for managerial and non-managerial employees. Despite the fact that most firms have different policies for these two groups of employees and a largely European tradition of studying different employee groups, earlier studies on HRM firm performance have either lumped together different groups of employees or studied only a certain employee category. Including both groups of employees in the same study allows us to investigate whether or not same or different HRM practices for managers and non-managerial employees are associated with superior firm performance.

To set a context for the study, the following section reviews research on the relationship between HRM and firm performance and HRM in Russia and then develops the present study's hypotheses. Subsequent sections describe the methodology of the research, report the results, and finally provide a discussion of the implications of the study.

Theoretical Background and Hypothesis

Recent theoretical work on the resource-based view of the firm (Barney 1991) supports the notion that HRM may be an important source of competitive advantage. Barney (1991) argues that resources lead to sustainable competitive advantages when they are valuable, rare, inimitable, and non-substitutable. While technology, natural resources, and economies of scale can create value, resource-based theory argues that these sources of value are increasingly available to almost anyone anywhere and they are easy to copy, especially when compared to complex social systems like human resource systems (Ulrich and Lake 1990). As a result, several authors (for example, Pfeffer 1994; Snell et al. 1996; Wright and McMahan 1992) have contended that human resource systems may be a better source of core competencies that can lead to sustainable competitive advantage. This interpretation is consistent with Hamel and Prahalad (1994, 232) who suggest that core competencies are normally people-embodied skills.

As noted by Wright and McMahan (1992), since human performance is normally distributed, human resources meet the first two of Barney's (1991) criteria of being valuable and rare. HRM systems that successfully develop and engage employees to participate in company activities are likely to enhance the value and rareness of a company's human assets (Arthur 1994; Snell et al. 1996). Further, unlike capital investments or patents, a well-developed HRM system is an 'invisible asset' (Itami 1987). Human resource strategies are difficult to imitate because of path dependency and causal ambiguity (Barney 1991; Collis and Montgomery 1995), thus meeting Barney's (1991) third condition. HRM systems are path dependent since they consist of policies that have evolved over time. A competitor may understand that a particular HRM system is valuable. However, because such systems are unlikely to work the same way if they were removed from the context where they are operating, a competitor cannot simply buy HRM systems in a market. In addition, to copy a HRM system successfully, it is necessary to understand how all relationships inside the system work. Because HRM systems are 'invisible assets', they are difficult to understand. Finally, it is difficult to think of a good substitute for a well-developed HRM system; thus HRM systems also meet Barney's (1991) fourth and final requirement for a resource to be a source of sustainable competitive advantage.

The bulk of previous work on the effect of HRM on firm performance has focused on the domestic operations of US firms. Human assets, however, may be an even more important determinant of the performance of foreign subsidiaries of multinational corporations in countries in transition like Russia since foreign firms often want local employees to change their behavioural patterns and carefully thought-out HRM policies are likely to be needed to accomplish this task. As a result, several authors have suggested that human resource management policies are especially critical to a firm's success in Russia (Fey et al. 1999; Longenecker and Popovski 1994; May et al. 1998; Puffer 1993; Radko and Afanasieva 1999; Welsh et al. 1993). Further, compared to Western countries, relatively few employees in Russia are trained in modern market-oriented work practices (Shekshnia, 1994). Recent surveys have indicated that foreign executives view investments in the development of local employees as important sources of competitive advantage (Shekshnia 1998; Kravchenko 1999). Hence, these employees may become an important resource which, due to the scarcity of such human assets, is even harder to duplicate in Russia than in Western countries.

A considerable literature exists on the relationship between individual HRM practices and organizational performance. However, during the last decade, the personnel/HRM field has shifted from a micro focus on individual HRM practices to a debate on how HRM as a more holistic management approach may contribute to the competitive advantage of the organization. The shift from examining single HRM practices to systems of practices entails focusing on the interrelationship between the various elements of the HRM system.

Dimensions of the HRM System

Becker and Huselid (1998) noted that researchers may either examine the total HRM system or develop and empirically verify key dimensions of the HRM system through methods such as factor analysis. The latter approach assumes that HRM practices group most accurately into several HRM sub-systems and 'that to arbitrarily combine multiple (HRM sub-)dimensions into one measure creates unnecessary reliability problems' (Becker and Huselid 1998, 63). This latter approach was followed in this study. Unfortunately, only limited theory specifies precisely how HRM practices should be bundled together (Ngo et al. 1998). Furthermore, most existing work attempting at identifying dimensions of HRM practices has been conducted in studies of domestic firms. Therefore, our approach was first to identify some key HRM dimensions and then to perform an exploratory factor analysis to determine precisely which factors exist in data from Russian subsidiaries of Western parent companies.

We took as our starting point the factor structure reported by Ngo et al. (1998) in their study of the relationship between HRM and foreign subsidiary performance in Hong Kong. Based on a principal component factor analysis with varimax rotation, Ngo. et al. (1998) obtained two factors with reliability scores of at least 0.64: (1) 'structural training and development', and (2) 'retention-oriented compensation'. HRM policies related to training and development and employee compensation are central in the HRM literature, and similar factors have been reported by several other researchers such as Becker and Huselid (1998, 74). An important earlier study by Huselid (1995), however, obtained a slightly different factor structure: one factor that contained items on compensation and promotion (closely related with Ngo et al.'s (1998) compensation factor) and another containing items on employee feedback and skill development. Finally, Delaney and Huselid (1996) divided HRM practices into those that enhance employee skills, motivate employees, and structure the workplace. Hence at least the following four HRM dimensions can be identified in previous work: training and development, employee pay system, employee feedback, and workplace organization.

Our exploratory factor analysis on the HRM practices for managerial employees revealed three HRM dimensions: employee development; feedback systems, and pay/organization (reported in Table 15.1 later in the chapter). A separate factor analysis for HRM practices for non-managerial employees led to the same items loading strongest on the same factors, but resulted in somewhat less clean results (higher cross-loadings). These three factors resemble those obtained in previous empirical research and discussed in the theoretical HRM literature. Therefore, the relationship between these three HRM dimensions and their relationship with firm performance was examined in the present study to facilitate comparison between managerial and non-managerial employees. Additionally, as will be discussed below, we hypothesized that efforts at aligning HRM with business strategy would have a positive impact on performance.

Employee Development

Employee development can be expected to be an important determinant of company performance. A variety of HRM practices are related to the development of the human resources of the firm. First, company investments in both technical and non-technical training are likely to have a positive impact on the extent to which the firm actually succeeds in developing the skills/knowledge of its employees. Training was suggested to be a high performance HRM practice in research by, among others, Delaney and Huselid (1996), Huselid (1995), Koch and McGrath (1996), and MacDuffie (1995). Generally, a positive relationship has been established between employee training and organizational performance (for example, Delaney and Huselid 1996; Koch and McGrath 1996). Delery and Doty (1996) offer an exception.

Employment security is seen by several authors (for example, Pfeffer 1995) as an important part of high performance HRM practices. Companies that provide their employees with job security signal a long-standing commitment to their workforce, whom in turn are more motivated to develop special skills and competencies that are valued by their company, but perhaps not to the same extent on the external labour market. Employees who perceive that their jobs are secure are also more likely to suggest productivity improvements and to take a more comprehensive and long-term view of their jobs and the company's performance. Conversely, companies are more inclined to take a long-term view on how to develop their employees. In their study on employees in the US banking sector, Delery and Doty (1996) showed a positive relationship between employment security and firm performance.

Companies may use career management programs to assist their employees in career planning. When the company provides this service, one important aim is to identify sequences of job assignments that help employees gain the skills and knowledge viewed as important in the company. A well-functioning company career planning system may also encourage employees to take more responsibility for their own development, including the development of skills viewed as significant in the company (Doyle 1997). It should be noted that a career planning system not only helps ensure that employees have the skills they need to advance in the company, but also may help ensure that employees possess the mix of skills that the firm believes is important for its future success. In other words, the provision of career planning assistance may have a positive effect on the level and type of skills and knowledge in the company (Doyle 1997).

Finally companies which promote employees from within the firm are likely to perform well since this feature provides a strong motivation for employees to work hard in order to be promoted (Lepak and Snell 1999; Pfeffer 1994). In addition, a philosophy of internal promotion means that a firm has decided to invest in its employees and is thus committed to them. All of the HRM practices listed above can be considered mutually related investments in developing the competencies of the employees. There is no a priori reason to believe that employee development practices would not have a significant positive effect on managerial as well as non-managerial employees.

Employee Development in Russia

Employee development may be of even greater importance in Russia than in Western countries (Radko and Afanasieva 1999; May et al. 1998). Many Russians lack basic business skills because of the historical absence of capitalist-style businesses in Russia, and research on Russia management has revealed that managers view training as an important source of competitive advantage (Jukov and Korotov 1998; Shekshnia 1998). An interview-based study of 18 Western firms conducted in 1997–98 also pointed to the importance of competence development in general and training in particular (Fey et al. 1999). This study also reported that '... the most important factor in retaining managerial employees was showing them that the company was committed to Russia and there was room for them to advance in the organization' (Fey et al. 1999, pp. 78). Retaining valuable and scarce personnel is a challenging issue that firms in Russia must wrestle with. Thus, commitment to investments in development-oriented HRM practices is likely to improve a firm's ability to retain key human resources. This conclusion indicates that both internal promotions and career management programs should be important in the Russian context. Finally, in a study by Holt et al. (1994), Russian managers, as compared with US managers, placed a higher value on security, and Elenkov (1998) found that Russian managers scored significantly higher on measures of uncertainty avoidance than did US managers. In an economy riddled by high levels of unemployment, it is also likely that non-managerial employees place high value on job security.

In conclusion, HRM practices contributing to development of both Russian managers and other employees can be expected to be positively related to firm performance. As a result of the discussion above, our first hypotheses are:

> Hypothesis 1a: A positive relationship exists between the extent a firm develops its managerial employees and firm performance.

> Hypothesis 1b: A positive relationship exists between the extent a firm develops its non-managerial employees and firm performance.

Pay/Organization

Several studies have identified extensive use of teamwork and decentralized decision making as important high-performance HRM practices (Arthur 1994;

MacDuffie 1995; Pfeffer 1995). Non-hierarchical organizations have a number of potential advantages. Lower-level employees often have more detailed knowledge about organizational issues than do the top executive(s) and can more rapidly and intelligently respond to operational problems. Team-based organizations encourage employees to pool their ideas to come up with creative solutions to problems. Additionally, this organizational form may enhance employee commitment to the organization. This approach is consistent with research that suggests that employee participation can have a statistically significant positive effect on satisfaction and performance at work (Wagner 1994). Communication across organizational sub-units can be seen as an important ingredient in the functioning of a decentralized organization, because extensive information is needed to integrate operations across sub-units. In the absence of a strong central leadership, this horizontal information flow becomes even more important.

Most studies have included performance-based compensation as one of the high performance HRM practices (for example, Arthur 1994; Delery and Doty 1996; Huselid 1995; MacDuffie 1995), and in their study Delery and Doty (1996) identified performance-based compensation as even the single strongest predictor of firm performance. In addition, several different theoretical perspectives have been used to show the effectiveness of performance-based compensation systems, including transaction cost theory (Jones and Wright 1992), control theory (Snell 1991), and agency theory (Eisenhardt 1988). Empirical studies on the relationship between performance-related pay and company performance have found a positive relationship.[1] Studies on the market reaction to the adoption of incentive plans have also reported positive stock market reactions (see Rajagopalan 1997). Based on expectancy theory (Vroom 1964), it can be expected that, if a company provides rewards desired by the employee in question, this employee is more likely to perform in a way that will bring him/her the reward. However, of crucial importance is that the performance-based compensation system is aligned with other parts of the HRM bundle. To the extent that the company extensively uses teamwork and that decision-making is de-centralized, there is a need to reward organizational employees who contribute to a successful implementation of this organizational form. Thus, rewards should not be distributed based on a narrow definition of the output of each individual but also based on appraisals of how well the individual contributes to the performance of the team, the unit, or the company as a whole depending on the company's structure. These objectives might, for instance, be included in the person's performance appraisal.

---

1 Mabey and Salaman (1995) point out that firms should base performance-related compensation systems on meaningful goals, robust performance measures, significant rewards, and well-established links between performance and rewards in order to obtain positive performance effects. In the present study we will not investigate the details of the compensation system. It should also be noted that some scholars are more skeptical of the effects of performance-related pay).

Pay/Organization in Russia

While few local Russian companies use pay for performance for their employees (May et al. 1998), Fey et al. (1999) reported that approximately 80 per cent of the Western firms in their study used some kind of performance-based compensation system, most typically with bonuses being linked to the performance of the firm. The firms' experiences with bonus systems were positive, and other scholars have reached the same conclusion (Juplev et al. 1998; Puffer 1997; Puffer and Shekshnia 1994). Puffer and Shekshnia (1994) note that bonus systems are especially helpful in Russia since they contribute to employees' motivation to work towards the company's objectives which are often quite different from objectives to which local employees previously have been exposed to. Furthermore, field experiment research carried out by Welsh et al. (1993) has shown a strong positive effect of group-based extrinsic rewards on the performance of groups of Russian factory workers.

Research on Russian firms has generally found the relationships between Russian workers and managers to be strained. Russian managers tend to view workers with disdain, and May et al. (1998) report that this attitude towards lower-level employees has not changed a great deal during the 1990s. Puffer et al. (1997) found that Russian managers tend to attach low value to workers' participation in decision making. Elenkov (1997) also found that the Russians in his sample scored much higher on Hofstede's (1980) power-distance dimension than did US respondents. In conclusion, the traditional image of Russian leaders as authoritarian holders of unquestioned power and who exert micro-controls appears still to hold some validity (Puffer 1994). Western-owned firms that manage to overcome this tendency towards a top-down work organization may have a valuable competitive advantage in Russia. The peer-based control that goes with a bundle of HRM practices centered around performance-based compensation tied to group/company performance, appraisals, team work, decentralization, and horizontal communication may also fit well with Russia's collective orientation (Bollinger 1994; Elenkov 1997, 1998). Thus, peer-based control can partially replace an extensive management control structure. Teamwork has also been suggested (but not empirically tested) to be a high performance HRM practice in Russia (Magura 1998). We find the arguments for a proposed relationship between this bundle of HRM practices to be particularly strong for non-managerial employees, but the same line of reasoning can also be used for analyzing the relationship between top executives and middle and junior managers.

Consistent with these arguments, we hypothesize that:

Hypothesis 2a: A positive relationship exists between managerial HRM practices affecting the design of work and a corresponding reward system, and firm performance

Hypothesis 2b: A positive relationship exists between non-managerial HRM practices affecting the design of work and a corresponding reward system, and firm performance.

Feedback Systems

Previous research has shown that employees are more motivated when they know what is going on in the firm. Sharing of information on, for example, strategy and company performance conveys to the employees that they are trusted. Further, it is important that employees know what is going on in a firm so that they can use the knowledge that resides in the firm to its fullest potential (Pfeffer 1998). As a result, it is important that firms use information-sharing programs.

The existence of a well-functioning complaint resolution system may help alleviate situations of perceived injustice or conflicts in the company. Both the process of handling the complaint and the outcome of the process may influence employee perceptions of how firms deal with the situation (Morrison and Robinson 1997). To the extent that a complaint is properly handled, the employees are more likely to maintain a high level of commitment to the organization. The administration of attitude surveys among the employees may have a similar effect. The use of attitude surveys has also been found beneficial since using such surveys helps top management to understand the desires and ideas of employees. Often employees have good ideas that can help the firm if implemented. In addition, top management may learn of small changes in the design of work that can be made and will make many employees much happier and thus more motivated.

Feedback Systems in Russia

Russian managers have been found to be reluctant to share information, and May et al. (1998, pp. 455) report that they have 'observed a virtual "obsession" among some Russian managers to manipulate and control employees'. Conversely, Russian employees appear to mistrust their superiors deeply (May et al. 1998; Puffer and McCarthy 1995). This distrust, however, does not necessarily mean that superior feedback and communication are without importance in Russia. In their research on Russian factory workers, Welsh et al. (1993) found that feedback by superiors on employee functional behaviours and personal praise had positive effects on productivity. Research by Shekshnia (1998) also suggested that a positive correlation existed between the level of employee understanding of organizational strategy and acceptance of organizational culture on the one hand and business results on the other. By sharing information with the employees, top management may help alleviate the feeling of mistrust and suspicion between employees and top managers that has characterized Russian organizations (May et al. 1998). Jukova and Korotov (1998) also suggest (but do not empirically test) that facilitating information sharing inside firms is important in Russia. Together, these studies indicate that bundles of HRM practices that facilitate employee feedback and company information sharing may help foreign-owned firms obtain competitive advantages in Russia. Such practices are likely to be important for middle and junior managers as well as for other employees. Hence, we arrive at the following hypotheses:

Hypothesis 3a: A positive relationship exists between managerial HRM practices facilitating feedback and firm performance

Hypothesis 3b: A positive relationship exists between non-managerial HRM practices facilitating feedback and firm performance.

HRM Strategy Alignment

Scholars have suggested that a good fit between HRM strategies and the business strategy of the firm tends to lead to superior outcomes (for example, Delery and Doty 1996). In other words, when the company's HRM practices support firm strategy, superior performance is expected. Empirically, the Miles and Snow (1978) or Porter (1980) strategic types have been used to classify firm strategies. Research has provided some support, albeit limited, for a positive HRM strategy alignment effect.

The relatively weak support for the effects of HRM strategy alignment on organizational outcomes should come as no surprise as it is difficult to specify what constitutes good alignment in research across firms and industries (Becker and Gerhart 1996). In fact, the resource-based view (Barney 1991) suggests that the appropriate configuration and strategic alignment of HRM practices may be idiosyncratic and complex. Furthermore, the whole idea of 'fit' with a certain strategy 'seems inappropriate for a world in which there are high levels of dynamic and unpredictable change' (Hiltrop 1996, 630). Therefore, instead of examining the statistical relationship between HRM practices and measures of firm generic strategies as typically done in previous research, it may be more appropriate to analyze the degree to which companies actively pursue the alignment of strategy and HRM practices (Becker and Huselid 1998). This approach enables researchers to collect data on the process of alignment, that is, the extent to which there is an on-going configurational strategic alignment of HRM in an area which is constantly changing (Mabey and Salaman 1995).

HRM Strategy Alignment in Russia

We have not been able to find any previous research set in Russia which has investigated the relationship between HRM strategy alignment and firm performance. However, we see no theoretical reason why efforts at aligning HRM with strategy would not have a positive impact on performance in Russia as has often been suggested to be the case in other countries (see previous section). Therefore, the following hypothesis will be tested:

Hypothesis 4: The more efforts undertaken to align HRM practices with firm strategy, the better the firm performance.

Methodology

A list of 395 foreign firms operating in Russia was constructed based on lists of Finnish, Swedish, US, German, and British firms operating in Russia. To be part of the list, firms had to be active in January–March 1998 when data collection was conducted, have at least 15 employees, have been operating in Russia for at least three years, and be located in Moscow or St Petersburg. Joint ventures with at least 80 per cent foreign ownership were treated as foreign firms for this study since in practice it has been found that they tend to be managed as wholly foreign-owned subsidiaries (Makino 1995). Of the 395 firms, only 361 firms could be contacted. Thus, 34 firms had either moved to another part of Russia or gone out of business since the list was created.

Contact was made with a human resource manager, general manager, or deputy general manager in each of the remaining 361 firms and the project was explained. Because of considerable fear of anonymous researchers in Russia (likely a result of a desire for secrecy following communism), in most cases a personal meeting was arranged with the manager to further explain the project, learn more about the respondent's firm and HRM practices, and have the questionnaire completed. In some cases questionnaires were simply left at the firm in person for the manager to complete. Non-respondents were reminded three times to complete the questionnaire via telephone. In cases where the questionnaire had not been received after three telephone calls, additional copies of the questionnaire and a reminder letter were faxed to the respondent, followed by a final follow-up telephone call. This process resulted in 101 responses, representing a 28 per cent response rate (of the actual number of firms at the point of data collection), which is good for a challenging environment like Russia.

Among the respondents were 38 HRM managers and 63 general managers or deputy general managers. T-tests were used to investigate the difference between means for the sub-samples of HRM managers and senior managers for the HRM practices and firm performance. Because no significant differences were uncovered, the two subgroups were combined in the analysis that follows. The participating firms were from a variety of foreign countries: 33 from USA, 29 from Sweden, 21 from Finland, nine from Germany, and nine from Britain. The participating firms also varied in size with 40 having 15–49 employees, 17 having 50–99 employees, 12 having 100–199 employees, 22 having 200–999 employees, and ten having 1000 or more employees.

The questionnaire was pre-tested on a sample of five managers in Russia, and slight adjustments were made as a result of their comments. The questionnaire was then translated into Russian using a thorough translation-back translation procedure.

Independent Variables

Drawing on, among others, the questions in the research instrument used by Huselid (1995), the respondents in the present study were asked the following: 'To what extent are each of the following HRM practices used for managers in your firm. Please choose a number between one and five, where one = "to a little extent" and five = "to a great extent".' Similar perceptual scales have been commonly used in studies of HRM practices and organizational performance (for example, Delery and Doty 1996; Ngo et al. 1998; Snell and Dean 1992; Wright et al. 1999). The questionnaire covered HRM practices (see Table 15.1) related to employee development, pay/organization, and feedback systems commonly included in previous studies of HRM conducted in the United States, Europe, and elsewhere. Following Becker and Huselid (1998), HRM strategy alignment was measured through subjective assessment of the degree to which the company analyzes alignment of HRM with business strategy. Specifically, HRM strategy alignment was measured by asking respondents to what extent they agreed (measured from strongly agree to strongly disagree) with the following statement: 'Our firm conducts formal analyses to determine how best to adjust human resource management practices to fit with firm strategy.'

Dependent Variables

This study used a performance measure comprised of four five-point subjective managerial assessment questions. Respondents were asked how their firm was performing regarding market share, sales growth, profitability, and quality of products/services (where one = poor and five = outstanding). This measure is desirable since Russian accounting standards are still emerging and firms use different accounting standards which makes it virtually impossible to obtain comparable financial information. While perceptual data may introduce limitations through increased measurement error and the potential for common method bias, the benefits outweigh the risks in this case. Further, precedence exists for using perceptual measures of performance in similar research (for example, Delaney and Huselid 1996; Youndt et al. 1996). Additionally, prior research has shown that subjective measures of firm performance correlate well with objective measures of firm performance (Geringer and Hebert 1991; Powell 1992). Following Roth and O'Donnell (1996), managers at headquarters of 20 of the Russian subsidiaries were also asked to evaluate independently their subsidiaries' performance using the same scale as described above to check how their perceptions correlated with those of the respondents. The estimates made by headquarters and subsidiary managers were significantly correlated at D=.82, providing support for asking only subsidiary managers to evaluate performance.

Control Variables

Data were analyzed using correlation analysis and regression analysis. In the regression analysis, several control variables were also included. The number of years that a foreign corporation has operated in Russia might influence HRM outcomes and firm performance. Companies with more experience in Russia have gone through a learning process concerning how to operate in the Russian context, and a positive relationship may exist between firm experience and HRM outcomes as well as firm performance. Therefore, the age of the subsidiary was included as a control variable. Firm size was also controlled for since larger firms might have more resources to devote to the business. The log of the number of employees in the subsidiary was taken so that a few large firms would not affect the results disproportionately. The home base of the foreign multinational corporation was included as a control variable as several studies have shown that US companies tend to differ from multinational corporations from other Western countries in terms of the HRM practices implemented in overseas settings (for a review, see Ferner 1997). This variable was measured as a dummy variable (US/non-US parent firm).

Finally, to further control for the potential impact of other factors, we ran separate regression analyses with industry (represented using dummy variables for two-digit SIC codes) and the national cultural distance between Russia and the subsidiary's parent's home country (using the index developed by Kogut and Singh (1988), Russian values were taken from Elenkov (1997)). None of these variables were significant, and thus they were dropped from the regression analyses reported in this article to preserve degrees of freedom.

Results

The first step in our analysis was to conduct a principal component factor analysis with varimax rotation on the individual HRM management practice items (see Table 15.1). The HRM managerial employee practice items factored into three factors with low cross loadings.

The first factor (bundle of HRM practices) which we label 'development' is comprised of technical training, non-technical training, non-entry level jobs filled from within the firm, assistance provided for career planning, and job security. The second factor 'feedback' is comprised of information sharing programs, complaint resolution system, and attitude surveys. The final factor 'pay/organization' is made up of performance appraisals, group/company performance in pay, teamwork, decentralized decision making, and interdepartmental communication. The indexes all had Cronbach's Alphas above .675, close to the suggested reliability level of .70 (Nunnally 1978). A separate factor analysis for HRM practices for non-managerial employees led to the same items loading strongest on the same factors, but resulted in somewhat less clean results (higher cross-loadings). Cronbach's Alphas for the employee HRM factors were all over .650.

Table 15.1 Rotated component matrix*

Variable	**Factor 1** Development	**Factor 2** Feedback	**Factor 3** Pay/ Organization
Technical training	**.561**	.339	.008
Non-technical training	**.607**	.287	.287
Non-entry jobs filled from within firm	**.601**	.104	.297
Assisting in career planning	**.634**	.331	.008
Job security	**.748**	-.222	.140
Information sharing programs	-.007	**.636**	.230
Complaint resolution system	.236	**.621**	.002
Attitude surveys	.180	**.790**	.125
Performance appraisals	.252	.116	**.531**
Group/company performance in pay	.006	-.009	**.872**
Teamwork	.335	.364	**.565**
Decentralized decision making	.274	.197	**.456**
Interdepartmental communication	.149	.354	**.616**
Eigenvalue	2.53	2.22	2.15
% variance explained	19.44	17.08	16.50
Alpha	.737	.677	.718

*Bold type indicates the factor HRM practices best factored to.

Table 15.2 provides the means, standard deviations, and bivariate Pearson correlations for the main variables used in the regression equations. Consistent with much prior research on the relationship between HRM practices and firm performance, all six correlations between firm performance and the bundles of HRM practices for managers and non-managerial employees were positive and statistically significant. Also, HRM-strategy alignment was positively correlated with firm performance (at $p<.05$). This result provides preliminary support for all of our hypotheses. A more refined analysis to test these hypotheses, however, will follow. Particularly high correlations (.72 and higher) existed between each of the bundles of HRM practices for managers and their corresponding HRM practice bundles for non-managerial employees. Therefore, we addressed this potential problem in our analysis by running separate analyses for the two employee groups.[2] It is also encouraging that the order

2 Correlations between the three HRM dimensions (for either managers or non-managers) indicate that they are unlikely to be totally independent. Therefore, if entered simultaneously into a regression equation, multicolinearity could be a problem. However, as results were consistent when running the full models (including control variables, HRM bundles for either managers or non-managers, and HRM strategy alignment) as compared with running separate models for each of the HRM bundles, we report only the full models containing either all three managerial HRM bundles or all three non-managerial HRM bundles.

Table 15.2 Correlations[1,2]

Variables	**1**	**2**	**3**	**4**	**5**	**6**	**7**	**8**	**9**	**10**
1. PERFORMANCE										
2. Manager Development	.476**	–	–	–	–	–	–	–	–	–
3. Man. Pay/Organization	.289**	.450**	–	–	–	–	–	–	–	–
4. Manager Feedback	.403**	.581**	.421**	–	–	–	–	–	–	–
5. Employee Development	.443**	.775*	.525**	.519**	–	–	–	–	–	–
6. Employee Pay/Organization	.535**	.420**	.723**	.503**	.480**	–	–	–	–	–
7. Employee Feedback	.321**	.494**	.511**	.725**	.682**	.518**	–	–	–	–
8. HRM-Strategy Fit	.269*	.204*	.220*	.071	.265**	.328**	.138**	–	–	–
9. Years Firm in Russia	.166	.175	.331**	.205*	.157	.232*	.115*	.030	–	–
10. Log of Employees	.330**	.360**	.332**	.147	.260*	.303**	.109	.068	-.025	–
11. US Parent	.187	.077	-.042	-.041	.062	.121	.064	.050	-.071	.042
Mean	**2.62**	**3.26**	**2.77**	**3.92**	**3.15**	**2.1**	**3.17**	**2.63**	**12.20**	**1.33**
SD	**0.78**	**0.95**	**1.07**	**1.10**	**0.92**	**1.01**	**0.90**	**1.30**	**9.23**	**0.47**

1 *p<.05, **p<.01, ***p<.005, ****p<.001
2 Sample size = 101 firms

(in terms of size) in which the HRM bundles are correlated with firm performance is consistent with the order (in terms of size) of the betas in the regression equations.

Regression analysis was used to test our specific hypotheses. Model 1 in Table 15.3 shows the results of the regression analysis for the HRM practices for subsidiary managers. The model was highly significant, with an R^2 of .339 and an adjusted R^2 of .287. Management development and managerial feedback systems as well as HRM strategy alignment were significantly related with firm performance, providing further support for hypotheses 1A, 3A, and 4. However, there was no significant relationship between pay/organization and organizational performance. Of the control variables, firm size was significantly related with firm performance indicating that larger firms slightly outperformed smaller firms in our sample.

Table 15.3 Regressions on firm performance[1,2,3]

Independent Variables	**Model 1** Managers	**Model 2** Employees
Log of number of employees	.222*	.163*
Age of firm in years	.113	.064
US/Non-US	.144	.124
HRM-Strategy fit	.192*	.069
Employee development	-	.245*
Employee pay/organization	-	.352****
Feedback to employees	-	.073
Manager development	.221*	-
Manager pay/organization	-.040	-
Feedback to managers	.201*	-
R^2	.339	.379
Adjusted R^2	.287	.330
F	6.519****	7.768****
N	101	101

[1] Dependent variable = firm performance
[2] Standardized regression coefficients are shown.
[3] *p<.05 , **p<.01, ***p<.005, ****p<.001

Model 2 shown in Table 15.3 reports the analysis of the data on non-managerial employees. Also this model was highly significant, R^2 being .379 and adjusted R^2 .330. Whereas the results support hypotheses 1B (employee development) and 2B (pay/organization), no statistically significant relationship was found between employee feedback or HRM strategy alignment and firm performance. Firm size was again significantly related with firm performance. Employee Pay/Organization had by far the largest beta (standardized regression coefficient) indicating that it had the largest effect on firm performance.

In conclusion, consistent support was obtained for hypotheses 1A (management development), 1B (employee development), 2B (pay/organization for non-managerial employees), and 3A (feedback to managerial employees). Like much previous research, our results provide mixed support for the importance of alignment of HRM with strategy. Thus, only partial support is provided for hypothesis 4.

Discussion and Conclusion

The results of this study provide relatively strong support for the existence of a positive relationship between HRM practices and the performance of Russian subsidiaries of Western corporations. At a general level, this result is largely consistent with results obtained in studies of HRM firm performance conduced in other geographical settings (Becker and Gerhart 1996; Guest 1997; Becker and Huselid 1998). A contribution of the present study is corroborating these results in the context of foreign subsidiaries of Western multinational companies located in a country in transition.

The relationship between the use of HRM practices and firm performance, however, did not hold across the three bundles of HRM practices (employee development; feedback systems, and pay/organization) for managers and non-managerial employees studied in the present study. While a strong positive relationship was found between both management development and employee development, and firm performance, a decentralized and team-based organization with corresponding pay systems was positively related with firm performance only for non-managerial employees; the opposite was found for the relationship between feedback and firm performance. It is well known that firms tend to use different HRM practices for these two groups of employees, yet surprisingly most previous studies on HRM-firm performance have asked questions about HRM practices for the firm as a whole or only focused on one particular employee group. This study suggests that, at least in the Russian context, firms should focus on different bundles of HRM practices for managerial and non-managerial employees. One of the conclusions of our study is that future studies should follow our lead and collect separate data for different employee groups despite the additional challenges this causes.

Both management and employee development were significantly related with firm performance. Because of Russia's transformation from a communist to a capitalist society, most Russian managers have limited traditional management training and little experience in many areas of business. At the same time, Russian managers tend to be highly educated in some other area – often with a Ph.D. in science/engineering due to the Soviet Era's focus on these disciplines. In fact, Soviet society highly valued education and this tradition remains an important value for most Russian people today. Given the educational/experience gaps and interest in business education that most Russians have (Shekshnia 1998; Fey et al. 1999), it is not surprising that Russian managers and hence their firms benefit from various training initiatives. Also non-managerial employee development was important for firm performance. Again, this can be expected. A focus on employee development, including employment security, is likely to be reciprocated by employees in terms of high levels of organizational commitment. Investments in employee training may also be important for Western firms striving to achieve a competitive advantage through high-quality products and services, features that were not paid much attention to during the earlier planned economy. Future comparative research on other economies in transition is needed in order to establish the generalizability of these findings.

Several studies have identified extensive use of teamwork and decentralized decision making as important high performance HRM practices, especially in combination with reward systems linked with group performance (Arthur 1994; MacDuffie 1995; Pfeffer 1995). In our study we found a positive relationship between this HRM dimension and firm performance only for non-managerial employees. We can only speculate why there was no positive relationship between this HRM factor for managers and firm performance. During the communist regime personal initiatives were not only discouraged, but were even punished (Puffer 1993). The hierarchical nature of the Russian society may also discourage individual responsibility taking and initiatives on the part of middle managers (Elenkov 1998), something that Western expatriates have viewed as a common problem in Russia (May et al. 1998). It could be that while a focus on collective responsibility and group-based bonuses works well for non-managerial employees, firms need to focus more on individual responsibility taking and rewards based on individual performance for managers. More research is obviously needed on this point, both in Russia and on the operations of Western subsidiaries located in other transition economies.

While we found that implementing HRM practices that facilitate Russian managers in providing feedback to top management and in obtaining more information about activities in the firm was highly significantly related to firm performance, having such HRM practices for non-managerial employees had little effect on firm performance. One possible explanation is related to the high power distance found among Russians (Elenkov 1997). Many Russian top managers share little information with their colleagues (May et al. 1998), and middle and junior managers may not have the information they need to do their jobs efficiently. Conversely, the opinions of lower-level managers may not be encouraged and known by Russian top managers. Firms with extensive flows of information between top management and managerial employees may thus have a competitive advantage in Russia. In contrast, non-managerial employees may neither expect an extensive information flow between them and the leadership of the firm, nor may top-down information be as important for their jobs as for the middle and junior managers. More research on this issue is needed to unravel factors to explain these results. Of interest would also be to collect longitudinal data on the impact of feedback for non-managerial employees on firm performance. A plausible hypothesis would be that over time feedback's importance as a determinant of firm performance will decrease for managerial employees. This will occur because foreign firms are increasing the information flow between top management and middle management (leading to a loss of competitive advantage for firms already doing it). However, feedback will likely become more important for non-managerial employees. Moreover, research in other geographical settings is also clearly warranted to determine how generalizeable/divergent results are. For instance, it would be of interest to do comparative analyses of the relationship between employee feedback and firm performance in other high power distance countries as well as in low power distance countries.

Several implications for managers follow from our results. First, Western firms should realize that their performance in Russia is influenced by different HRM practices for managerial and non-managerial employees. Second, not all HRM practices are equally important. Specifically, management and employee development, feedback and information systems for managers, and extensive use of teamwork and decentralized decision making combined with reward systems based on group performance for non-managerial employees have positive effects on firm performance. As a result, the above HRM practices are the most important HRM bundles on which foreign firms in Russia should focus their efforts.

The HRM literature includes considerable debate about the importance of aligning HRM practices with firm strategy. Our results are in line with most previous research (Becker and Huselid 1998) in that they provide only limited support for the hypothesized positive relationship between efforts at aligning HRM practices with firm strategy and firm performance. Future work would benefit from analyzing both the efforts at aligning HRM practices and strategy (investigated in this study) and the outcome of these efforts. Case studies would probably be the best methodological choice for investigating the interaction between HRM systems and firm strategy and how this relationship impacts on performance.

Like all research, the present study has several limitations. Our paper begins to explore the question of causality. However, causality can actually be tested only with data collected at different points in time. For instance, while we in this chapter have argued that HRM tends to be a driver of firm performance, previous research has also shown that increasing profits tend to lead to higher investments in training (Hendry et al. 1989). Thus, the field would greatly benefit from more time-series studies that can better address causality (Becker and Huselid 1998). Future research would also benefit from developing more sophisticated measures of firm strategy to assist in investigating the importance of the alignment of HRM practices with firm strategy in order to achieve maximum performance. Similar to many previous studies in this field, data on HRM practices were collected through perceptual scales. Another possibility would be to use more specific behavioural scales (Becker and Huselid 1998). Generating responses with these scales might be more difficult, but the responses would be more accurate. It would also be useful in future studies to collect performance data from other respondents to minimize the risk of common method bias. While this study makes important contributions to our understanding of the relationship between HRM and foreign subsidiary performance in general and in Russia in particular, this study is clearly only a first step and additional research is needed on this issue both in Russia and in other geographical settings.

References

Arthur, Jeffrey B. (1994), 'Effects of Human Resource Systems on Manufacturing Performance and Turnover', *Academy of Management Journal* 37, 670–87.

Barney, J.B. (1991), 'Firm Resources and Sustained Competitive Advantage', *Journal of Management* 17, 99–120.

Becker, B. and Barry, G. (1996), 'The Impact of Human Resource Management on Organizational Performance: Progress and Prospects', *Academy of Management Journal* 39, 779–801.

Becker, B. and Huselid, M.A. (1998), 'High Performance Work Systems and Firm Performance: A Synthesis of Research and Managerial Implications', *Research in Personnel and Human Resource Management* 16, 53–101.

Bollinger, D. (1994), 'The Four Cornerstones and Three Pillars in the House of Russia Management System', *Journal of Management Development* 13: 2, 49–54.

Collins, D.J. and Montgomery, C.A. (1995), 'Competing on Resources: Strategy for the 1990s', *Harvard Business Review* 73:4,: 118–128.

Delaney, J.T. and Huselid, M.A. (1996), 'The Impact of Human Resource Management on Perceptions of Organizational Performance', *Academy of Management Journal* 39, 949–69.

Delery, J.E. and Doty, H. (1996), 'Models of Theorizing in Strategic Human Resource Management: Tests of Universalistic, Contingency, and Configurational Performance Predictions', *Academy of Management Journal* 39, 802–35.

Doyle, M. (1997), 'Management Development', in Ian Beardwell and Len Holden (eds), *Human Resource Management – A Contemporary Perspective* (London: Pitman).

Dyer, L. and Reves, T. (1995), 'Human Resource Strategies and Firm Performance: What do we know and where do we need to go?', *The International Journal of Human Resource Management* 6: 3, 656–70.

Eisenhardt, K. (1988), 'Agency and Institutional theory Explanations: The Case of Retail Sales Compensation', *Academy of Management Journal* 31, 488–511.

Elenkov, D.S. (1998), 'Can American Management Concepts Work in Russia: A Cross-Cultural Comparative Study', *California Management Review* 40: 4, 133–56.

Elenkov, D.S. (1997), 'Differences and Similarities in Managerial Values between US and Russian Managers',*International Studies of Management and Organization* 28:1, 85–106.

Ferner, A. (1997), 'Country of Origin Effects and HRM in Multinational Companies', *Human Resource Management Journal* 7, 19–37.

Fey, C.F., Engström, P. and Björkman, I. (1999), 'Effective Human Resource Management Practices for Foreign Firms in Russia', *Organizational Dynamics* Autumn, 69–80.

Geringer, M.J. and Hebert, L. (1991), 'Measuring Performance of International Joint Ventures', *Journal of International Business Studies* 28, 249–63.

Guest, D.E. (1997), 'Human Resource Management and Performance: A Review and Research Agenda', *International Journal of Human Resource Management* 8, 263–76.

Guest, D.E. and Hoque, K. (1994), 'The Good, the Bad, and the Ugly: Employment Relations in New Non-Union Workplaces', *Human Resource Management Journal* 5, 1–14.

Hamel, G. and Prahalad, C.K. (1994), 'Competing for the Future', *Harvard Business Review* 72, 122–28.

Hendry, C., Pettigrew, A. and Sparrow, P. (1989), 'Linking Strategic Change, Competitive Performance, and Human Resource Management: Results of a UK Empirical Study', in R. Mansfield (ed.), *Frontiers of management* (London: Routledge).

Hofstede, G. (1980), *Culture's Consequences: International Differences in Work-related Values* (Newbury Park, CA: Sage).

Holt, D.H., Ralston, D.A. and Terpstra, R.H. (1994), 'Constraints on Capitalism in Russia: The Managerial Psyche', *California Management Review* 36: 3, 124–36.

Huselid, M.A. (1995), 'The Impact of Human Resource Management Practices on Turnover, Productivity, and Corporate Financial Performance', *Academy of Management Journal* 38, 635–72.

Itami, H. (1997), *Mobilizing Invisible Assets* (Boston: Harvard University Press).

Jones, G. and Wright, P. (1992), 'An Economic Approach to Conceptualizing the Utility of Human Resource Management Practices', in K. Rowland and G. Ferris (eds), *Research in Personnel and Human Resource Management* 10, 271–300, (Greenwich, CT: JAI).

Jukova, M. and Korotov, K. (1998), 'From a Personnel Department in Soviet Union to a Human Resource Department in Russia', *People and Labor* 8, 88–91, (in Russian).

Juplev, A.V., Konkov, A.G. and Kisner, V.F. (1998), 'Motivation and Problems of Small Enterprise: The Experience of Russia and USA', *Human Resource Management* 8, 44–53. (in Russian).

Koch, M.J. and McGrath, R.G. (1996), 'Improving Labor Productivity: Human Resource Management Policies do Matter', *Strategic Management Journal* 17, 335–54.

Kogut, B. and Singh, H. (1988), 'The Effect of National Culture on Choice of Entry Mode', *Journal of International Business Studies* 19: 3, 411–32.

Laurence, P.R. and Vlachoutsicos, C.A. (1990), *Behind Factory Walls: Decision Making in Soviet and US Enterprises* (Boston, MA: Harvard Business School Press).

Lepak, D.P. and Snell, S.A. (1999), 'The Human Resource Architecture: Towards a Theory of Human Capital Allocation and Development', *Academy of Management Review* 24:1, 31–48.

Longenecker, C.O. and Popovski, S. (1994), 'Managerial Trials of Privatization: Retooling Russian Managers', *Business Horizons* 37:6, 35–43.

Mabey, C. and Salaman, G. (1995), *Strategic Human Resource Management* (Oxford: Basil Blackwell).

MacDuffie, J.P. (1995), 'Human Resource Bundles and Manufacturing Performance: Flexible Production Systems in the World Auto Industry', *Industrial Relations & Labor Review* 48, 197–221.

Magura, M.I. (1998), 'Patriotism of Personnel and their Relation to the Organization – A Firm's Major Competitive Advantage', *Human Resource Management* 11, 20–28, (In Russian).

Makino, S. (1995), *Joint Venture Structure and Performance: Japanese Joint Ventures in Asia', Unpublished Ph.D. Dissertation* (Canada: University of Western Ontario).

May, R; Young, C.B. and Ledgerwood, D. (1998), 'Lessons from Russian Human Resource Management Experience', *European Management Journal* 16:4, 447–59.

Miles, R.E. and Snow, C.C. (1978), *Organizational Strategy, Structure, and Process* (New York: McGraw Hill).

Morrison, E.W. and Robinson, S.L. (1997), 'When Employees Feel Betrayed: A Model of how Psychological Contract Violations Develop', *Academy of Management Review* 22, 226–56.

Ngo, H.-Y., Turban, D., Lau, C.-M. and Lui, S.-Y. (1998), 'Human Resource Practices and Firm Performance of Multinational Corporations: Influences of Country of Origin', *Journal of International Human Resource Management* 9, 632–52.

Nunnally, J. (1978), *Psychometric Theory* (New York: McGraw Hill).

Pfeffer, J. (1994), *Competitive Advantage through People: Unleashing the Power of the Work Force* (Boston: Harvard Business Press).

Pfeffer, J. (1995), 'Producing Sustainable Competitive Advantage through the Effective Management of People', *Academy of Management Executive* 9, 55–69.

Pfeffer, J. (1998), *The Human Equation. Building Profits by Putting People First* (Boston: Harvard Business Press).

Porter, M.E. (1980), *Competitive Strategy* (New York: The Free Press).

Powell, T.C. (1992), 'Organizational Alignment as a Competitive Advantage', *Strategic Management Journal* 13, 551–8.

Puffer, S.M. (1993), 'A Riddle Wrapped in an Enigma: Demystifying Russian Managerial Motivation', *European Management Journal* 11, 473–80.

Puffer, S. M. (1997), 'Soviet and American Managers' Reward Allocations: A Dependency Approach', *International Business Review* 6, 453–76.

Puffer, S.M. and McCarthy, D.J. (1995), Finding the Common Ground in Russian and American Business Ethics. *California Management Review* Winter, 29–46.

Puffer, S.M., McCarthy, D.J. and Naumov, A.I. (1997), 'Russian Managers' Beliefs about Work: Beyond the Stereotypes', *Journal of World Business* 32, 258–76.

Puffer, S.M. and Shekshnia, S.V. (1994), 'Compensating Local Employees in Post-Communist Russia: In Search of Talent or Just Looking for a Bargain?', *Compensation and Benefits Review* September-October, 1–9.

Radko, S. and Afanasieva, A. (1999), 'Conservation of Labor Potential and Maximization of Income', *People and Labor* 7, 81–85, (in Russian).

Rajagopalan, N. (1997), 'Strategic Orientations, Incentive Plan Adoptions, and Firm Performance: Evidence from Electric Utility Firms', *Strategic Management Journal* 18, 761–85.

Ralston, D.A., Holt, D.H., Terpstra, R.H. and Kai-Cheng, Y. (1997), 'The Impact of National Culture and Economic Ideology on Managerial Work Values: A Study of the United States, Russia, Japan, and China', *Journal of International Business Studies* 28, 177–207.

Rosenzweig, P.M. and Nohria, N. (1994), 'Influences of Human Resource Management Practices in Multinational Corporation', *Journal of International Business Studies* 25, 229–51.

Roth, K. and O'Donnell, S. (1996), 'Foreign Subsidiary Compensation Strategy: An Agency Theory Perspective', *Academy of Management Journal* 39, 678–703.

Shekshnia, S. (1994), 'Managing People in Russia: Challenges for Foreign Investors', *European Management Journal* 12, 298–305.

Shekshnia, S. (1998), 'Western Multinationals' Human Resource Practices in Russia', *European Management Journal* 16, 460–65.

Snell, S.A. (1991), 'Executive use of Human Resource Management Controls to Improve Firm Performance: Modeling Effect of Administrative Information', *Academy of Management Best Papers Proceedings* 277–81.

Snell, S.A. and Dean, J. (1992), 'Integrated Manufacturing and Human Resource Management: A Human Capital Perspective', *Academy of Management Journal* 35, 467–504.

Snell, S.A., Youndt, M.A. and Wright, P.M. (1996), 'Establishing a Framework for Research in Strategic Human Resource Management: Merging Resource Theory and Organizational Learning', *Research in Personnel and Human Resource Management* 14, 61–90.

Taylor, S., Beechler, S. and Napier, N. (1996), 'Towards a Model of Strategic International Human Resource Management', *Academy of Management Review* 21, 959–86.

Ulrich, D. and Lake, D. (1990), *Organizational Capability: Competing from the Inside Out* (New York: Wiley).

Vikhanski, O. and Puffer, S.M. (1993), 'Management Education and Employee Training at Moscow McDonalds', *European Management Journal* 11, 102–107.

Vroom, V. (1964), *Work and Motivation* (New York: Wiley).

Wagner, J.A. (1994), 'Participation's Effect on Performance and Satisfaction: A Reconsideration of Research Evidence', *Academy of Management Review* 19, 312–31.

Welsh, D.H.B., Luthans, F. and Sommer, S.M. (1993), 'Managing Russian Factory Workers: The Impact of US-based Behavioural and Participative Techniques', *Academy of Management Journal* 36, 58–79.

Wright, P.M. and McMahan, G.C. (1992), 'Theoretical Perspectives for Strategic Human Resource Management', *Journal of Management* 18, 295–320.

Wright, P.M., McCormick, B., Sherman, S. and McMahan, G.C. (1999), 'The Role of Human Resource Practices in Petro-Chemical Refinery Performance', *International Journal of Human Resource Management* 10, 551–71.

Youndt, M.A., Snell, S.A., Dean, J.W. and Lepak, D.P. (1996), 'Human Resource Management, Manufacturing Strategy, and Firm Performance', *Academy of Management Journal* 39, 836–66.

Index

The Contributors

Tatiana Andreeva is a Senior Lecturer in Organizational Behaviour and Organizational Change at the St Petersburg State University School of Management. Since 2000 she has been involved in management consulting (including different forms of training) for Russian companies from various industries, ranging from aircraft construction and engineering to meat processing and fashion. She received her PhD in Economics from the St Petersburg State University School of Management.

Moshe Banai is a Professor of Management at the Zicklin School of Business, Baruch College, The City University of New York. Professor Banai has published over 80 refereed articles, book chapters and conference proceeding on the subjects of international human resource management and organizational behaviour in transitional economies. His current research interests include control and alienation in transitional economies, career management of expatriate managers, cross-cultural negotiation and the relationships between culture and national and organizational performance measures.

Ingmar Björkman is a Professor of Management and Organization at the Swedish School of Economics in Helsinki, Finland. He is also affiliated with the INSEAD Euro-Asia and Comparative Research Center. He received his PhD at the Swedish School of Economics. Ingmar Björkman's research interests focus on international human resource management, knowledge creation and transfer in multinational corporations and integration of international mergers and acquisitions. His latest book is *The Handbook of Research in International Resource Management* (Edward Elgar Publishing, 2006), co-edited with Günter Stahl. He is a regular contributor to international academic journals.

Michel E. Domsch is a Professor of Management and Head of the Institute for Human Resource Management and International Management at HSU, Helmut Schmidt University in Hamburg. Since 2004 he has also been the Director of the MDC Management Development Centre at HSU. His academic credentials include work as a research fellow at Harvard Business School. He received his Ph.D. and his postdoctoral degree (lecture qualification) in Business Administration from the Ruhr University in Bochum, Germany. Michel Domsch spent 10 years working for British Petroleum in Germany and Great Britain and has been a management consultant for more than 20 years. His consulting work includes projects on employee satisfaction, gender diversity and family-friendly policies, work-life balance and leadership development. His clients are from the industrial and public sectors. His research focuses on International HRM, gender and diversity, auditing and work time flexibility.

Lubov Ejova is a research fellow at the Center for Independent Social Research in St Petersburg, Russia. She works as a coordinator of research projects in industrial sociology and marketing. She received her MA in sociology from St Petersburg State University of Economics and Finance. From 1995 to 1998 she worked as a sociologist at the biggest submarine shipyard in Europe and this experience played an important role in determining her further research interests, which are mainly focused on labour relations and post-Soviet transformation processes in the sphere of industrial production. Alongside with the above-mentioned research topics she is also interested in studying a wide range of social and economic problems in contemporary Russia. Lubov Ejova also works as a lecturer at the High Economic School at St Petersburg State University of Economics and Finance where she teaches the course 'Social Partnership'.

Carl F. Fey is an Associate Professor at the Institute of International Business at the Stockholm School of Economics (SSE) in Sweden. Carl Fey, who is American, has been helping SSE for the past six years to develop a branch campus (Stockholm School of Economics in St Petersburg) for executive development work and research in St Petersburg, Russia, where he serves as Associate Dean of Research. Carl Fey has been a Visiting Professor of International Business at China Europe International Business School in Shanghai, China. Carl Fey's teaching, consulting and research focus on the extent to which management theories developed in the West need to be modified to work well in transition economies like Russia or China. In particular, his work has focused on organizational culture, human resource management, joint ventures, knowledge management and leadership. Carl Fey has spent considerable time living in both Russia and China and has published many journal articles in leading academic journals like *Organization Science* and *the Journal of International Business Studies* as well as practitioner journals like *European Management Journal* and *Organization Dynamics*. Currently, all of Carl Fey's teaching is on various executive programmes primarily in the areas of international business, organizational behaviour and strategy. In addition to teaching, Carl Fey has considerable experience running executive programmes. Carl Fey has served as a consultant for many firms, especially multinational corporations in Russia (for example, Carl Fey was a consultant for Russia's largest foreign direct investment deal).

Graham Hollinshead is a Reader in International Resource Management at the University of Hertfordshire, and is also a member of the International Faculty at Copenhagen Business School. He has published extensively in the field of organizational transformation in post-socialist societies, including articles in *Management Learning, The Journal of World Business* and *The European Journal of Education*. He has also been engaged as a consultant by the Deutsche Gesellschaft für Technische Zusammenarbeit (GTZ) and the European Center for Peace and Development (ECPD) to upgrade capacities in HRM amongst Serbian managers and academics.

Kenneth Husted is Professor in Innovation and Research Management and is Head of Department for the University of Auckland, Business School (Tamaki) in New Zealand. Born in Denmark, Kenneth Husted previously worked for the Copenhagen Business School as Research Director, Management of Innovation and Knowledge (MINK) until his appointment in New Zealand in early 2005. Kenneth Husted worked at CBS from 1996 and completed his PhD in 1998 (*Industrial Research: Control and Autonomy*). Kenneth Husted's main research interests are in the fields of management of R&D, research management, corporate entrepreneurship and knowledge management. He has had work published in over 40 international business publications.

Sofia V. Kosheleva is a Professor of Human Resource Management, Doctor of Psychology and Chair of the Personnel Management Department at the St Petersburg State University School of Management. She is a member of the Russian Psychological Society and a corresponding member of the International Academy of Ecology and Life Protection Sciences. Since 1989 she has been engaged in research projects and training programmes for top and middle managers working for Russian companies from different spheres, including virtual companies. Her research interests focus on comparative research of organizational and psychological problems in the context of HRM practices, psychological problems of personality development, top managers' professional awareness as well as psychological mechanisms of decision-making processes. She has published articles in academic and business journals in Russia, monographs and textbooks about organizational psychology and management. The list contains 70 publications.

Tatiana Kovaleva is an Assistant Professor at the St Petersburg International Management Institute. She attended Schulich Business School in Canada (Corporate Governance), Manchester Business School in England (Small Business Management), and served an internship at the Michigan Business School. She has successfully managed international projects sponsored by USAID, EuroAsia and IREX. She has been involved in training programmes in HR management, change management, organizational behaviour and corporate governance and has worked on more than 30 successful consulting projects with small and medium-sized businesses (restructuring, business process optimization, HR strategy and procedures, planning and key performance indicators, simulation systems). Tatiana Kovaleva is a member of the Exchange Program Association in St Petersburg and of the International Simulation and Gaming Association.

Irina Kozina is a Lead Researcher at the Institute of Management of Social Processes at the Moscow Higher School of Economics. Since 1991, she has been conducting research on the labour market and the transformation of labour relations in Russian enterprises, which has resulted in more than fifty publications in journals and edited volumes, including *International Sociology*, *Voprosy Economiki* [Economic Issues], and *Sotsiologicheskie Issledovaniya* [Sociological Research]. She received her PhD from the Institute of Sociology of the Russian Academy of Sciences.

Donna E. Ledgerwood is a senior professional in Human Resource Management and an Associate Professor of Human Resources Management at the University of North Texas. Active professionally, Donna is a former president of the Southern Management Association and former president of the Southwest Academy of Management. She has four degrees from the University of Oklahoma and has published in *the Labor Law Journal, the Monthly Labor Review, HR Magazine, the Journal of Business Ethics* and *the Journal of European Management.* Donna Ledgerwood also has authored the sections involving Health, Safety and Environmental Risk Management for the Blackwell Dictionary of Human Resource Management, the Blackwell Encyclopedia of Human Resource Management and published a case in Cases and Exercises in Human Resources Management. Donna lived in Europe for four years and founded her own HR consulting company in 1980. She has worked with over 60 organizations within the United States, Great Britain and Russia. Her major professional interests are increasing productivity, preventing litigation actions and decreasing workers compensation via organizational surveys and training.

Marina G. Libo has been General Director of Adventure Races, a consultancy specializing in team building, since 2004. She graduated from the Economic Department of St Petersburg State University in 2000. She worked as a Research Assistant at the Stockholm School of Economics in St Petersburg from 1997 to 2004 and defended her Ph.D. at the St Petersburg State University in 2003. The title of her Ph.D. project is "The Telework Concept as a new HR form in virtual organizations in Russia". She now works as a teambuilding experience trainer and does local research and publications on teambuilding, team work, leadership and HR.

Tatjana Lidokhover is a Research Assistant at the Institute for Human Resource and International Management at HSU, Helmut-Schmidt-University in Hamburg. Her research focuses on German-Russian joint venture management, which is also the central subject of her PhD project. Tatjana Lidokhover studied Sociology and Business Administration at the University of Hamburg. In 2004 she also participated in the European Human Resource Management Master Programme, studying and doing project work in Lyon, Bordeaux and Ghent.

Henrik Loos is recruitment manager at PriceWaterhouseCoopers Russia in Moscow. After earning a bachelor degree from the University of Essex and a masters degree from the St Petersburg State University, he worked in marketing and HR in Germany as well as in Russia. He has also taught as a DAAD-lecturer at the Academy of

National Economics in Moscow. His current interests include recruitment strategy, processes and instruments as well as intercultural management.

Daniel J. McCarthy is the Alan S. McKim and Richard A. D'Amore Distinguished Professor of Global Management and Innovation at the College of Business Administration, Northeastern University, Boston, USA. He is co-founder and co-director of Northeastern's highly ranked High-Technology MBA programme. He has been a member of the editorial board of The Academy of Management Executive, and has more than 80 publications, including four editions of Business Policy and Strategy, as well as Business and Management in Russia, The Russian Capitalist Experiment, and the recently published Corporate Governance in Russia. He is the lead director of Clean Harbors, Inc., and has consulted in the US and Europe for more than 40 companies. Early in his career, he was president and co-founder of Computer Environments Corporation and served as a director on its board, as well as the board of its sister company, Time Share Corporation, and other private company and non-profit boards. Daniel McCarthy holds AB and MBA degrees from Dartmouth College and a DBA from Harvard University. He is a Fellow at the Davis Center for Russian Studies at Harvard University, and is one of the top three scholars internationally in business and management in Russia and Central and Eastern Europe, based on a *Journal of International Business Studies* article analyzing publications in 13 leading journals from 1986–2003.

Ruth C. May is an Associate Professor of Global Business at the University of Dallas, College of Business, Graduate School of Management. She has been involved since 1993 in the design and execution of management training programs for Russian organizations. She has published papers on Soviet/Russian management in *the Academy of Management Journal*, *Academy of Management Executive*, *European Management Journal*, *International Journal of Entrepreneurship*, *Journal of Emerging Markets*, *Multinational Business Review* and *Socialist Labor Journal* (Russia). Her academic credentials include training at the London School of Economics and the Leningrad Education Center in St Petersburg, Russia. She received her PhD in Strategic Management from the University of North Texas.

Snejina Michailova is a Professor of International Business at the Department of International Business at The University of Auckland Business School, New Zealand. She holds a PhD degree from Copenhagen Business School, Denmark. Her main areas of research are knowledge management (with a focus on knowledge sharing) and cross-cultural management (with a focus on Western businesses in Russia). Her work has appeared in *Academy of Management Executive*, *California Management Review*, *Employee Relations*, *European Management Journal*, *International Management*, *Journal of World Business*, *Journal of East-West Business*, *Journal of Knowledge Management*, *Management Learning* and *Organizational Dynamics*, among others. Snejina Michailova is the European Editor of Journal of World

Business. She has been involved in a number of international projects aiming at knowledge transfer from Western to Eastern Europe

Irina Olimpieva is a research fellow at the Center for Independent Social Research in St Petersburg, Russia, and coordinator of the research division 'Social Studies of Economy'. She is also a project manager for projects in Economic Sociology. She received her Candidate of Science (PhD) degree at St Petersburg State University of Economics and Finance. Her professional interests encompass a wide spectrum of social problems particularly relating to post-socialist economic and social transformation, including post-Soviet industrial and labour relations, transformation of the scientific sphere and post-socialist changes in the rural world. Recent research projects and interests have focused on transformation of social partnership systems in Russia as well as on informal mechanisms of economic functioning and development. Irina Olimpieva also works as a lecturer for the the MA programme, 'Studies in European Societies' developed by the Centre for German and European Studies (Bielefeld University) and St Petersburg State University where she teaches the course 'Industrial Relations: Legal Framework, Collective Bargaining and Deregulation.'

Sheila M. Puffer is a Professor of International Business at Northeastern University, Boston, USA. She is also a fellow at the Davis Center for Russian Studies at Harvard University and recently served as Program Director of the Gorbachev Foundation of North America. She has been recognized as the #1 scholar internationally in business and management in Russia, the former Soviet Union, and Eastern Europe based on a Journal of International Business Studies analyzing publications in 13 leading academic journals from 1986–2003. Sheila Puffer has more than 100 publications, including over 50 refereed articles and eleven books including *Behind the Factory Walls: Decision Making in Soviet and US Enterprises*, *The Russian Management Revolution*, *Managerial Insights from Literature*, *Management International*, *Business and Management in Russia*, *The Russian Capitalist Experiment*, *International Management*: *Insights from Fiction and Practice, and Corporate Governance in Russia.* She served as the editor of *The Academy of Management Executive* and as a member of the Academy's Board of Governors from 1999–2002. She worked for six years as an administrator for the Government of Canada and has consulted for a number of private and non-profit organizations. Sheila Puffer earned a degree from the executive management programme at the Plekhanov Institute of the National Economy in Moscow, and holds BA (Slavic Studies) and MBA degrees from the University of Ottawa, Canada, and a PhD in business administration from the University of California, Berkeley.

William D. Reisel is an Associate Professor of Management at the Tobin College of Business, St John's University, Department of Management. William Reisel has published more than 40 refereed articles, book chapters, and conference proceedings on the subjects of attitudes in international business, ethics, and organizational behaviour.

His current research interests include employee job insecurity, worker alienation, and the application of integrated social contracts theory (ISCT) to the distribution of life-saving HIV medicines.

Sudhir Saha is a Professor of Organizational Behaviour and Human Resource Management at the faculty of Business Administration at the Memorial University of Newfoundland. He has teaching experiences with many other universities including the University of British Columbia in Canada, the Chinese University of Hong Kong in Hong Kong, Rajshahi University in Bangladesh, the Lahore University of Management Sciences in Pakistan, the Indian Institute of Foreign Trade in India, and the Czech Management Centre in the Czech Republic. Sudhir Saha has also worked with the Federal Government of Canada for a brief period in the Canada Employment division. Funded by the Canadian International Development Agency, Sudhir Saha has provided enrichment workshops for professors in Bangladesh and Nepal. Sudhir Saha has published more than fifty research papers on organizational behaviour topics such as leadership, motivation, job satisfaction, managerial attitude and managerial stress. Much of his research work also concerns comparative and international management issues concerning human resource management practices. He has conducted research investigations on people and organizations in Australia, Bangladesh, Canada, China, the Czech Republic, Hong Kong, India, Ireland, Nepal, Pakistan, and Russia. Sudhir Saha is a member of the Academy of Management and the Administrative Sciences Association of Canada.

Stanislav Shekshnia has been an Adjunct Professor of Entrepreneurship at INSEAD since 2003. He has taught graduate and executive courses in entrepreneurship, leadership, international management and people management and lectured at ESCP-EAP, HEC, Northeastern University, California State University at Hayworth, Stockholm School of Economics, Moscow State University and International Management Institute in St Petersburg. Stanislav Shekshnia has over 15 years of graduate level teaching experience. His specific areas of interest are leadership, entrepreneurship, leadership development and succession, cross-cultural management, organizational culture and change management. Stanislav Shekshnia combines the perspecitves of a business executive and an academic. Between 1991 and 2002 Stanislav Shekshnia held the position of CEO of Alfa-Telecom, served as President and CEO at Millicom International Cellular, Russia, was Chief Operating Officer of VimpelCom, and Director of Human Resources, Central and Eastern Europe of Otis Elevator. He served as Chairman of Vimpelcom-R and as a board member of a number of Russian companies. In 2005 he became Chairman of the board of directors of SUEK, the largest Russian energy and coal company. Stanislav Shekshnia is the author, co-author, or editor of five books, including *The New Russian Business Leaders* (2004; with Kets de Vries, Korotov, Florent-Treacy), *Corporate Governance in Russia* (2004; edit. with Puffer and McCarthy), Russian Management bestseller *Managing People in Contemporary Organization* (seven editions since

1995). Stanislav Shekshnia lives in Paris, but frequently travels to his motherland for business and hunting expeditions.

Adam Smale is a Researcher and Lecturer in the Faculty of Business Studies at the University of Vaasa, Finland. He is writing his PhD thesis on the global integration of HRM and knowledge transfer and is involved in research projects relating to knowledge transfer in developing countries, global diversity management and cultural integration in multinational companies.

Tatyana A. Soltitskaya is an Associate Professor of Organizational Behaviour at the St Petersburg State University School of Management. Since 1995, she has been involved in the design and execution of management training programmes for Russian organizations. She has been a director of Executive Education at the School of Management since 2004. She received her PhD in social psychology from St Petersburg State University. Her academic credentials include training at the Stockholm Institute of Management (Sweden), at the Haas School of Business and at Pittsburgh University (USA) as well as with the Manchester Careers Service, and Manchester Polytechnic University (England).

Vesa Suutari is a Professor of Management and the Vice Dean of the Faculty of Business Studies at the University of Vaasa, Finland. His major research projects have been related to cross-cultural management, expatriation, global careers, and other areas related to international HRM. He has published papers in edited books and in journals such as *International Journal of Human Resource Management*, *Journal of World Business*, *Journal of Managerial Psychology*, *Thunderbird International Business Review*, *Scandinavian Journal of Management and Personnel Review*, and has also guest edited special issues on international HRM in journals such as *Personnel Review*, *Thunderbird International Business Review* and *International Studies of Management and Organization*. He is actively involved in adult education and training in his areas of expertise.

Vera Trappmann, M.A. and Dipl.Soz., is a Fellow at the Cultural Sciences Faculty at the European University Viadrina at Frankfurt (Oder). She studied sociology at the University of Bielefeld as well as Russian and East European studies at Stanford University. She has worked on several comparative European projects on labour studies. Currently she is writing her PhD thesis on institutional and cognitive patterns of structural change in Russia and Poland. Her main research interests are: the European Union, Russia, transformation theory, social policy and qualitative research methods. Together with A. Kutter, she is the editor of *The Legacy of Accession: Europeanization in Central and Eastern Europe* published by Nomos Verlag, 2006.

Valery Yakubovich is an Assistant Professor of Organizations and Strategy at the University of Chicago Graduate School of Business. His articles on job search and recruitment in the Russian labour market appeared in *American Sociological Review*, *European Sociological Review*, *Work and Occupations*, *International Sociology* and edited volumes. His current research explores interdependencies between social networks and economic behaviour of individuals and firms in the context of modern telecommunication technologies. Ongoing projects include a study of advantages and disadvantages of personal referrals in Internet-based recruitment and the role of social interactions in a virtual workplace. He received his PhD in Sociology from Stanford University.